On British Islam

PRINCETON STUDIES IN MUSLIM POLITICS

DALE F. EICKELMAN AND AUGUSTUS RICHARD NORTON, SERIES EDITORS

A list of titles in this series can be found at the back of the book.

On British Islam

RELIGION, LAW, AND EVERYDAY PRACTICE IN SHARIʿA COUNCILS

John R. Bowen

PRINCETON UNIVERSITY PRESS

Princeton and Oxford

Published by Princeton University Press, 41 William Street, Princeton, New Jersey 08540
In the United Kingdom: Princeton University Press, 6 Oxford Street, Woodstock, Oxfordshire OX20 1TR

press.princeton.edu

Library of Congress Cataloging-in-Publication Data

Bowen, John R.
On British Islam : religion, law, and everyday practice in shariʿa councils / John R. Bowen.
pages cm — (Princeton studies in Muslim politics)
Includes bibliographical references and index.
ISBN 978-0-691-15854-9 (hardcover : alk. paper) 1. Islam—Great Britain—History—21st century. 2. Islam and politics—Great Britain. 3. Muslims—Political activity—Great Britain. 4. Islamic law—Great Britain. 5. Religion and law—Great Britain. 6. Muslims—Legal status, laws, etc.—Great Britain. 7. Islamic sects—Great Britain—History—21st century. 8. Great Britain—Politics and government. I. Title.
BP65.G7B696 2016
297.1′40941—dc23 2015025099

British Library Cataloging-in-Publication Data is available

This book has been composed in Linux Libertine

Printed on acid-free paper. ∞

Printed in the United States of America

10 9 8 7 6 5 4 3 2 1

To my father

Contents

Acknowledgments

I carried out the work that led to this book during the period 2007–13. Over that time I met many new colleagues, made many new friends, and accumulated more than a few intellectual debts.

Let me start with the invitation to spend time in the Anthropology Department at the London School of Economics in 2010 thanks to a Leverhulme scholarship. This stay and subsequent shorter visits made possible a long period of fieldwork and introduced me to a number of new friends and colleagues. I would like to thank the entire department staff but would single out, for their help and companionship, Mukulika Banerjee, Maurice Bloch, Fenella Cannell, Matthew Engelke, Yan Hinrichsen, and Deborah James.

I especially thank the many British Muslim scholars of Islam who welcomed me into their working worlds to learn more about what they do. I single out Khurram Bashir, Amra Bone, Haitham al-Haddad, Khola Hasan, Suhaib Hasan, Usama Hasan, Atif Matin, Ibrahim Mogra, Abu Sayeed, and Faiz ul-Aqtab Siddiqi for their patience and openness. Among the many other British colleagues who have contributed to my thinking on these issues are Qamar Bhatti, Robin Griffith-Jones, Stephen Hockman, Aina Khan, Maleiha Malik, Werner Menski, and Prakash Shah. Portions of chapter 10 appeared in John R. Bowen, "How Could English Courts Recognize Shariah?", *St. Thomas Law Review* 7 (3): 411–35, 2011.

At Princeton University Press, once again I am delighted to thank Fred Appel for his ideas and support, and for this volume I am grateful to Natalie Baan and Cathy Slovensky for their careful editorial work. At Washington University I remain grateful for the support of Georgia Dunbar Van Cleve and her late husband Bill, as well as for all the day-to-day support that all of us fortunate to work here derive from the university as a whole. I also received valuable support from the National Science Foundation (#0961272, 2010).

My parents and my wife and children continue to offer love and encouragement. My father, a lawyer and judge, has taken special interest in this project, and to him I dedicate this book.

PART 1

Pathways

CHAPTER 1

Why Shariʿa in Britain?

IN OCTOBER 2013, BRITISH PRIME MINISTER DAVID CAMERON ANNOUNCED THE launch of an Islamic bond (a *sukuk*) and celebrated his government's commitment to make London one of the world's great centers for shariʿa financing. But a few months later, a moral panic swept Britain over claims that state-aided schools in Birmingham were promoting shariʿa and Islamic extremism. BBC programs, the home secretary, and several prominent members of the House of Lords warned of shariʿa councils endangering the rule of law and gender equality throughout Britain.

This study of British Islam highlights issues and practices surrounding shariʿa. Shariʿa is both lauded and denounced more loudly and more often in Britain than anywhere else in the West. Both Prince Charles and then archbishop of Canterbury Rowan Williams have called for drawing on Islamic principles to, respectively, save the environment and resolve conflicts among Muslims. But Britain also has some of the most vehement Islam bashing anywhere, with the *Daily Mail*, the *Sun*, and on occasion the *Telegraph* warning of threats to Britain posed by Islam and particularly by shariʿa. Already in 1997, the chilly climate toward Islam led the Runnymede Trust to issue an influential report denouncing "Islamophobia."[1]

"Shariʿa" (*sharīʿa*) can mean both the broad path God set out for Muslims and a particular set of normative teachings.[2] In both senses it has a particularly high profile in Britain. Why? I try to account for this particularity by looking at British Islam through two lenses. The first is historical: How and why did Muslims create distinctive religious institutions in Britain? How did the pathways they followed shape what sort of Islam they built? The argument is implicitly contrastive: What features of the British experience with Islam differentiate it from the experiences of other European countries?

The second lens is ethnographic and focuses on everyday practices in Britain's shariʿa councils, tribunals that answer Muslims' questions and give Islamic divorces. (These divorces have no effect in English law.) I trace the ways the Muslim scholars who sit on these councils apply the resources of Islam to resolve immediate practical issues. I also mention schooling, mosques, finance, and halal certification, but I concentrate on the shariʿa councils for three reasons. First, they represent a prolonged and unique experiment in meeting Islamic needs in a Western country. Second, they highlight and illuminate Britain's specific relation to Islam. Finally, they have become a flashpoint in British public debates, drawing the ire and fire of many commentators even as they adapt to the English legal environment.

How *can* this work? How can such a well-developed set of quasi-legal shariʿa-based institutions function relatively smoothly in a secular society? And how *does* this work? How do clients approach councils, and how do Islamic scholars from diverse origins make judgments? Do their judgments show up in court? And what does and should the broader public think about how they judge?

COMMUNITIES

The first question—how can this work?—leads us toward the notion, more widely accepted in Britain than most anywhere else in Europe, that values come from communities, mainly religious ones, whether Christian, Jewish, Muslim, or other. Such was the force of then archbishop of Canterbury Rowan Williams's 2008 defense of Muslims who wished to draw on shariʿa to run their own affairs. The idea of distinct communities avoids posing difficult and often uncomfortable questions about "British values" or Englishness. It gives (and draws on) an imperial tone: we share the fact that we don't have to share. It also allows one to defend an Anglican, public-school elitism as constituting just another "community."[3]

But how broadly accepted is this notion of multiple, diverse communities? In 2014, half of the people living in Britain thought that to be "truly British" you had to have British ancestry. One-quarter said you needed to be Christian. No doubt had the question been about "Englishness," the numbers would have been much higher. These responses remind us that many Britons remain suspicious of a Britishness that wanders too far from a shared cultural core of pubs and churches.[4]

Indeed, extending the national welcome to new religious communities has always been problematic. It has involved "tolerating" dissenting Protestants, and then Catholics and Jews, and now Muslims.[5] The effort is always resisted and always shaky, and gives rise to particular anxieties and challenges, once about Catholics and now about Muslims. Even well-informed commentators draw lines between "conservative" Islam and its "liberal" counterparts, considering the former as dangerously close to the Taliban, and only the latter as truly integrated, particularly when these liberal Muslims dance at nightclubs, offer red wine to guests, and profess their love for the queen.[6] These cultural preferences are understandable, but they may keep us from attending to the ways even conservative British Muslims can adapt to conditions of life in Britain, including how they have construed and applied shariʿa: without the red wine but within the law.

What of Muslims' ideas about Britain? A Gallup poll taken in 2009 in Britain showed that when compared with the population as a whole, Muslims identified more strongly with Britain (77 percent versus 50 percent) and had more confidence in the judiciary (76 percent versus 55 percent). British Muslims also more strongly identified with both their country and their religion than did French or German Muslims. A 2011 poll of two thousand people taken by the think-tank Demos revealed that Britons differed little by religion in how likely they were to say that they were "proud to be a British citizen": 88 percent of self-declared Anglicans and Jews, 83 percent of Muslims, and 79 percent of the population as a whole agreed with this statement.[7]

And yet things are not all rosy. A few years earlier, a Pew survey showed that British Muslims were more likely than Muslims in other European countries to see relations between "Muslims" and "Westerners" as generally poor, and more likely to say that there is a conflict between "being a devout Muslim" and "living in a modern society"—indeed, more likely to say both things than were people in Jordan or Pakistan.[8] So, perhaps British Muslims find British institutions to be fine but modern British society to present problems.

In the popular British press, Muslims appear as self-isolating. In recent years this portrayal has focused on Islamic institutions, including schools and shariʿa councils; critics claim that these institutions oppress women, violate human rights, and aim at setting up a parallel society, with its own legal system. "One Law for All" is the slogan of some who rail against this supposed separatism. These criticisms of Muslims could be set aside as instances of "Islamophobia." Some commentators do so. But those who criticize the direction of British Islam can point to the growth of private Islamic schools that have resisted outside inquiry. They can point to conservative positions on issues of gender and politics taken by some Islamic public actors in Britain. How readily can *these* Muslims be considered as simply one more community within the loosely structured British state?

Approach

In what follows, I examine how and why Islamic institutions developed as they did in Britain. I argue that the particular contours of Islam in Britain have much to do with British imperial history and what we may call British applied political philosophy. If French republicanism, applied at home and to some extent abroad, helps explain the shape of Islam in that country, as I have argued in earlier works,[9] the corresponding case can be made for Britain.

So goes part of this book. But the empirical difference between the two countries means that we must examine different objects in the two cases. If, in earlier works on France, I traced how French Islamic leaders taught and debated Islamic norms in rather unexceptional, even anodyne settings—schools, mosques, and large assemblies—it was because French Muslim public figures were adapting their institutions to the tight legal and cultural constraints of French public life. France does not see itself as multiple communities in one state but as a collection of citizens ideally subjecting themselves to the dictates of their shared ideas and habits through the medium of the state. French Muslims built institutions that either mirrored their non-Islamic French counterparts (Islamic schools and institutes look like other schools and institutes) or mirrored their already-legitimate Muslim-world equivalents (mosques that resembled those in Fez were fine). Ways of preparing halal foods followed a pattern already made legitimate by Jewish dietary and abattoir practices. French Muslims have made very little institutional innovation, in part because there is low tolerance for such innovation in France, and in part because the relatively low level of doctrinal differences among them meant that there was little impulse for institutional specialization.

In Britain, by contrast, Islam is fractured, divergent, and institutionally creative. The legal pluralism of the Indies administration, the fractious character of North Indian Islam, and the British idea that religious communities nurture social life have, together, contributed to the emergence of a British Islam with multiple institutional forms. Some British schools or councils have sought to highlight continuities with their Asian sources, and often that choice has meant erecting boundaries in their new homeland. Others have emphasized new roots in a British urban neighborhood and have drawn on Asian ties for that new purpose. Still others have constructed new internal pluralisms that play out old divisions in new places.

This varied British topography of Islam has engendered open disagreements and debates. It has also nurtured the continued existence of conservative Islamic traditions that are easy to present in the press as exhibiting insufficient integration into British life—and that contrast sharply with the progressive direction of Islamic thought found in US mosques.[10] The visibility of Asian modes of dress, the continued high rates of transcontinental marriage, and, my focus here, the very public flourishing of shariʿa-oriented bodies all signal to many in Britain a problem with the integration, modernity, or gender relations associated with Islam. But the take-home message of this book is that British Muslims, most of them anyway, are in the long and messy process of creating institutions that make sense in Islamic terms and also in British ones. British Muslims are adapting to British ways of life, as are French and German Muslims to ways of life in those countries.[11] This message is rarely heard in Britain—or elsewhere—but it is urgent that we hear it if we are to build new ways of living together.

Understanding the shape of British Islam today demands both history and ethnography: how things developed and how they work. I begin by sketching out the sources and broad contours of British Islamic institutions before focusing on the shariʿa councils. I argue that British Islamic life is not the simple transposition to Britain of Asian practices; it is filtered through new institutions that are both British and Islamic. To understand them, we must look at their specific historical trajectories and their everyday practices.[12]

Studying these shariʿa-based institutions requires studying how they adapt to their environment and how their diverse participants adjust to each other. Institutional analysis, as I see it, requires both a genealogy of specific institutional forms and an ethnography of the processes and debates that shape everyday working life—and that may recursively reshape those forms. This last component of the study will lead us to ask how conditions for "performativity" are debated and provisionally realized, and how actors propose multiple and context-specific justifications for their judgments. This dimension of the project brings it into the domain of what I have been calling the anthropology of public reasoning, extended in this work to take on a more thoroughgoing analysis of institutional workings and changes.[13]

Studying reasoning and justification also highlights the ways in which British Muslims draw on pan-Islamic as well as British ways of judging—transnational continuity as well as local fit. British Islamic scholars sitting on shariʿa councils see themselves as following in a long lineage of Islamic scholars and judges. In fourteenth-century Morocco or in twenty-first-century Britain, Indonesia, or Egypt, scholars and judges arrive at judgments only after considering the texts and traditions of Islam, the way their society works, the personal situation of a client or litigant, and the many legal and political constraints they face. They do not so much "apply" the law as seek to render a judgment that will be fair, acceptable, and workable. Of course, this is also what British civil court judges do, working from different texts and traditions.[14]

Exposition

The book proceeds in four parts. In part 1, "Pathways" (chapters 1 to 3), I examine how Muslims came to Britain, settled, and developed Islamic spaces and boundaries. Chapter 2 traces physical movement. Muslims came to Britain mainly (though not only) from South Asia, and they settled in certain cities and neighborhoods. They encouraged others to join them. Many of these new residents of Britain have sought to maintain their ties to the homeland through marriage and through forms of economic cooperation. These practices befuddle the logic of generations: Can you be of the third generation when your mum was born in Pakistan? They also reinforce ties of shared ethnic and religious community within certain British neighborhoods. Transnational connections and local concentrations reinforce each other.

Chapter 3 follows a second kind of pathway, one concerning ideas and practices of religion and politics. In India, British rule both validated religious governance of family affairs and drove Islamic leaders to carve out their own spaces for teaching, learning, and the administration of Islamic law. In postcolonial Britain, the same logics of religious governance and autonomy facilitate efforts to transpose Islamic institutions to London or Birmingham. We travel to London, the Midlands, and the North to see how these politico-religious pathways inscribe certain spatial patterns of boundaries and networks on Britain. These patterns inject religious meaning into the demographic processes examined in chapter 2.

In part 2, "Practices" (chapters 4–7), I examine the workings of Britain's most extensive shariʿa council, headquartered in eastern London but with branches across England. Chapter 4 provides the background on women's divorce and the emergence of the councils and attempts to explain why Islamic divorce has become the focus of shariʿa council practices. In chapter 5 I examine the social life of the London council, shaped as it is by the temporalities of moving along files and receiving clients. Chapters 6 and 7 concern two overriding and perennial worries of this and other councils—and, indeed, of state Islamic bodies in the Muslim-majority world. The anxiety of *performativity* asks about the capacity of scholars (or judges) to divorce a couple: Whence that authority? What justifies dissolving marriages at all? On a theoretical plane, this case recalls Jacques Derrida's critique of J. L. Austin on performativity: namely, that "felicity conditions" are never assumed; they can always be challenged. No foundations exist for the shariʿa councils—but do they exist for courts in Muslim countries? The anxiety of *justification* asks about the selection among competing types of argumentation. Is it more important to let a woman get on with her life by accepting her petition for divorce or to uphold Islamic moral principles by refusing to reward improper behavior on her part? Or is there a textual admonition in the Qurʾan or hadith that would outweigh either of these two bases for judgments? There is no clear metarule for deciding among these alternative types of justification, hence, a never-ending debate among scholars.

In part 3, "Variants" (chapters 8 and 9), I ask how practices differ when quite different institutions turn to the field of shariʿa. Some of the most trenchant criticisms of shariʿa councils in Britain (and elsewhere) concern male scholars' attitudes toward women. Do things differ when women play a major role? We consider the Birmingham Central Mosque's council, where women take the lead. Chapter 9 asks the corresponding question of a Sufi institution. In previous chapters we are inside a roughly "Deoband/Salafi" world; how can one construct a shariʿa-oriented set of institutions within an explicitly and visibly Sufi world? How does it change procedures and outcomes, or does it? These two contrasting cases show that each of the major shariʿa councils in Britain is strongly shaped by its local origins and pathways of development—and therefore they should be seen as instances of institutional adaptation.

Finally, in part 4, "Boundaries" (chapters 10–13), I move back out to Britain-wide debates about the proper role of religion in law, schools, and public life. Fears and accusations circulating in England about Islam and shariʿa councils focus on two contentions. The first, examined in chapter 10, is that English law has "recognized" shariʿa, a worry given credence by the 2008 remarks of Rowan Williams, then archbishop of Canterbury. Are these fears well founded? Do shariʿa councils find their judgments enforced by civil courts? Are there arguments on which shariʿa and English law do or can converge? The second accusation, the topic of chapter 11, is that Islamic institutions—shariʿa councils but increasingly Islamic schools as well—are keeping Muslims from fully integrating into English, or British, society. Why do some invocations of shariʿa—such as David Cameron on shariʿa financing—invite applause and others invite moral panic? The issue seems to be not shariʿa per se but worries about conservative social and moral forms of religiosity. Chapter 12 explores the broader normative questions raised by these examples. Can conservative Muslims be accepted as "British"? Who gets to set the terms of convergence for people whose starting points are firmly held and strikingly different? I propose that rather than setting up conditions for "translation" (Habermas) from religious to universalistic language, we should explore ways that members of different traditions are able to preserve their starting points and work toward points of practical convergence. I offer examples of successful and failed attempts to do so, and urge that normative political theory attend as much to everyday practices as to highly public statements. In chapter 13 I offer some concluding observations about the specificity of the British context.

A note on terminology: I generally situate the study in "Britain" but sometimes I mention "England." The relationship between these two entities is not always clear, as the vacuity of recent calls for firming up "British values" suggests. But in general, I distinguish between the British political framework and the laws of England and Wales, for which I use (despite my own Welsh heritage) "England" as a short term of reference. Laws are different in Scotland and, to a lesser extent, Northern Ireland, and here I follow common legal usage. In addition, sometimes I use "English" to stress the perceived ethnic contrast between "Asians" and "English." Many people refer to themselves or others as "British Asian"; I have never heard anyone say "English Asian."

CHAPTER 2

Transplanting Ties

THE SHAPE OF BRITISH SHARIʿA HAS A LOT TO DO WITH WHERE BRITISH Muslims came from and where they now live. We start our story not with Islam but with Muslim men and women as they journey to and settle in Britain.

Migrating to Britain

Although Muslims living in Britain today trace their origins to many parts of the world, the majority have roots in former British India, and mainly in today's Pakistan and Bangladesh. Furthermore, within those two countries, a small number of districts have contributed in strikingly disproportionate numbers to the Muslim population of Britain. The concentrations began with historical accident but, once in place, reproduced themselves through practices of "chain migration," whereby one generation of immigrants pulled another after it. The results are concentrations of closely related people in certain British neighborhoods.

Muslims began coming to Britain in the nineteenth century. Many settled in port cities: Liverpool, Cardiff, and London. They came from South Asia and, with the 1869 opening of the Suez Canal, from Yemen. Prominent South Asian Muslims began to build an Islamic landscape in Britain. For example, in 1899, Shah Jahan, the female sultan of Bhopal, funded construction of the first purpose-built British mosque, located in the London-area town of Woking. In the early twentieth century, the mosque became a center for British Muslims under the leadership of Lord Headley, who had converted to Islam while working in India, and of a prominent Lahore barrister, Khwaja Kamaluddin.

Muslims came in larger numbers after the Second World War, when Britain welcomed workers to rebuild its cities and factories. The 1948 Nationality Act gave citizens of former British colonies the right of free movement to and from Britain, and West Indians and South Asians dominated this immigrant stream. Freedom of movement facilitated chain migration: a man would come to Britain, work for a period in Birmingham or Manchester (where he lived in crowded conditions with other men from the same village), and then return home and let a cousin take his turn at the work opportunities.[1]

As more Commonwealth citizens came to Britain, racist reactions grew stronger. The 1958 antiblack riots in Notting Hill marked a new rise in open hostility.[2] Resentment at immigrants grew still further as jobs became scarcer, creating political pressures to limit immigration—even as bills were passed to prevent racial discrimination. The 1962 Commonwealth Immigrants Act restricted entry to those with job vouchers obtained through the Ministry of Labour. Anticipating the law's passage, many rushed to Britain, including wives and children of men who already had residence rights. The entry screw was turned further in 1971, when the new Immigration Act required work vouchers with fixed expiration. But few vouchers were given out, and in practice, the only people able to come were dependents of people who were already legally resident in Britain. Workers now brought family members as "anchors." Racism grew as well: by 1974, the British National Party, created in 1967, urged the repatriation of all nonwhite immigrants.

Although some thought that reducing labor immigration would mean fewer immigrants, in fact more people arrived than ever before, now under the banner of family reunification. New efforts were made to reduce the flow by scrutinizing claims to marriage. The 1981 British Nationality Act ordered immigration authorities to distinguish between marriages conducted merely for purposes of immigration and those arranged legitimately. Of course, this was difficult to do, and in 1983 the government mandated the "primary purpose rule": a married couple now had to prove that they had known each other before the wedding and that the primary purpose of the marriage was not to secure entry to the UK. In a culture where marriage is often arranged, these new rules meant that thousands of spouses were denied entry. Finally, the 1988 Immigration Act withdrew entry guarantees from dependants of people already legally resident. Tony Blair's government abolished the primary purpose rule soon after coming to office in 1997, but both Labour and Tories from time to time propose new efforts to restrict immigration.[3]

Specific events abroad have prompted bursts of immigration. Indian Muslims living in East Africa, many of them originally from Gujarat, arrived in the 1960s from Kenya, and in the early 1970s from Uganda after their expulsion by Idi Amin. They included thousands of Ismailis, members of the branch of Shiism led by the Aga Khan. Turkish Cypriots came during the 1950s and 1960s to escape chronic conflict in their homeland; many Kurds (and Turks) came from Turkey to flee persecution. Iraqi immigration grew during the Gulf War in 1990–91 and then after the US invasion in 2003. Iranians settled in the years immediately after the 1979 Iranian Revolution. Britain has the largest Somali community in Europe, most of them arriving during the Somali civil war in the 1980s and 1990s.[4] The multiple Muslim communities in Britain today are mainly Sunni, but include thousands of Shiites from Iran, Lebanon, Iraq, South Asia, and East Africa. Britain also has the headquarters of the Ahmadiyya movement, followers of the nineteenth-century leader Mirza Ghulam Ahmad, who regard themselves as Muslims but who are not considered as such by most Sunnis and Shiites.[5]

The successive waves of new Muslim immigration, coupled with a continuing stream of new spouses and family members, have meant a steady rise in the number of foreign-born Muslims, even though a growing number of Muslims were born in Britain.[6] From 2001 to 2011 the number of Muslims living in Britain but born overseas nearly doubled, from 828,000 in 2001 to 1.4 million in 2011. In areas where most Muslims live, the percentage of British residents who are foreign-born, regardless of religion, continues to increase. In the West Midlands, this figure went from 7.6 percent in 2001 to 11.2 percent in 2011; for London the increase was from 27.1 percent to 36.7 percent. Muslims are much more likely than other British residents to be born abroad: In 2011, 47 percent of British Muslims were born in Britain, in contrast to 89 percent of Christians and 93 percent of those claiming no religion. Muslims as a whole are also increasing in numbers relative to Christians, and Britain as a whole became more "Asian" between 2001 and 2011. The percentage of residents self-identifying as Asian or as a subcategory of Asian rose from 4.4 percent to 6.8 percent while "whites" declined from 91 percent to 86 percent. Muslims are becoming an increasingly visible part of the British landscape, *and* more of them are foreign-born.

Pakistanis in the North and the Midlands

Although British Muslims come from many different countries and live throughout Britain, many live close to those of similar background. These concentrations contribute to the particular features of British Islam. By and large, Pakistanis have tended to settle in the North or in the West Midlands, and many Bangladeshis have gathered in East London; these two countries have contributed the vast majority of British Muslims.

The origins of these Muslim immigrants are even more specific than this. Most of the Pakistanis came from a small set of places: Mirpur district in Azad Kashmir, parts of Peshawar, certain villages and towns in northern Punjab, especially Gujrat and Jhelum, and Attock district. Most Bangladeshis came from one district, Sylhet.

Why this concentration of origin points? Recruitment mechanisms and historical accidents both played roles. In the nineteenth century, the army and navy drew recruits from Punjab, and Mirpuris worked in steamship companies; many ended up in Britain. Recruitment, like migration, often worked through networks of kin and neighbors. A second wave of Mirpuris arrived in 1961 when the British government gave entry visas to thousands of villagers whose homes were threatened by a dam project; the dam eventually submerged the lands of about 250 villages. One estimate has the Mirpuris at

70 percent of the British Pakistani population, living mainly in former mill towns in the North.[7] Many Mirpuris see themselves as Kashmiris first and foremost, and they closely follow the continuing military struggle between Pakistan and India for control of that territory.

An ethnographic account of Pakistanis living in Oxford found that nearly everyone came in definable migration chains, usually sponsored by homeland kin.[8] The chain pattern meant that people ended up living with relatives, and that social control over the lives of the British-resident women and men could be exercised by relatives in Britain and in Pakistan, following multiple pathways of letters, visits, and telephone calls. This structure of communication and control remains critical to the arrangement and management of transcontinental marriages. A bride who traveled "back" to Pakistan to marry would quickly return to England, leaving the new husband to begin the long process of obtaining an entry visa. The families concerned might assume (rightly or wrongly) that the dense transnational ties would make it possible to keep the marriage going until the husband could join his wife. Sometimes this did not work, and some of the resulting requests for religious divorces ended up in the shariʿa councils.

The same desire to maintain moral control also fueled family migration. Many wives of those Pakistani men who left for work in England decided to join their husbands, sometimes to ensure that no immoral behavior took place. Their numbers increased during the 1960s and 1970s, as it became more and more difficult to move back and forth for work purposes and, consequently, more men stayed on in Britain. Wives could still come as family members of British residents and then apply to become British citizens. Many did. The number of people from Pakistan living in the UK went from 25,000 in 1961 to 119,000 in 1971. By 2001 the census reported that 706,539 residents of England and Wales identified themselves as Pakistani, and by 2011 the number had grown to about 1,125,000.[9] The relative contribution of Pakistanis to the immigration stream also rose during this period. They first appeared in the top ten origin countries in 1971, when they were fifth in numbers of immigrants. They moved to third place in 1981, where they remained, behind India and Poland, in 2011.[10]

People moving from Pakistan to Britain settled either in the North (West Yorkshire and the Lancashire cities of Bradford, Leeds, and smaller towns) or in the West Midlands (in and around Birmingham). But many Pakistanis also live in Glasgow, Bristol, Luton, and, of course, London, particularly toward the northeast part of the city. They came to work: in the textile mills in Lancashire, in the steel mills of West Yorkshire, and in manufacturing in the Midlands. Today, the cities of Bradford and Birmingham have the largest settlements of people from Pakistan, along with their children and grandchildren.[11] They make up the large majority of Muslim residents of these cities and districts. In 2011, Birmingham was 22 percent Muslim;

Waltham Forest, in northeast London, was also at 22 percent; and Bradford was at 25 percent.

In two respects the spatial concentration of Pakistanis in Britain is even greater than this account would imply. First, people coming from the same town in Pakistan often live in the same city or neighborhood in Britain: for instance, people from Jhelum concentrate in Waltham Forest, and people from Attock tend to live in Bradford or Birmingham. Pakistanis in Birmingham are overwhelmingly of Mirpuri origin.[12] Second, some urban neighborhoods are peopled heavily by families who belong to one lineage grouping (*biraderi*) or who came from one village.[13] The result is large residential areas where families live their lives speaking in Punjabi or in Urdu (or in other languages and dialects), with English as a second language, often first learned at school. Their neighbors are people with whom they have ties stretching back to the homeland. As children from the great wave of immigration reached marriageable age in the 1980s, their extended kin networks steered many of them to seek spouses from among their relatives living either nearby or in Pakistan, thereby reproducing these local hyperconcentrations.

Bangladeshis in East London

Bangladeshis came largely from one district, Sylhet, for reasons having to do with local land regimes. Sylhetis were much more likely than other Bangladeshis to be small landholders. They were therefore more likely to enjoy the economic security necessary to sponsor an emigrant, because when someone leaves, the family loses a laborer.[14] By the mid-nineteenth century, many Sylheti men were leaving for Calcutta to work in shipping as lascars (sailors), as men from Gujarat and Mirpur left to work on ships in Bombay; all three groups are heavily represented in Britain today. Some men jumped ship once they arrived in London, establishing communities that then became the destinations for later arrivals.

In the 1960s, Sylhetis settled in northern cities, such as Oldham, Birmingham, Bradford, and Manchester, hoping to work in factories. They, too, engaged in chain migration. But more went to London, and, in particular, to the East London borough of Tower Hamlets near the Docklands. According to 2011 census data, 54 percent of British Bangladeshis live in London, 33 percent of them in Tower Hamlets. They make up about one-third of Tower Hamlets residents.[15] Bangladeshis are thus much more concentrated in one place than are Pakistanis. By 2011, 95 percent of Bangladeshis living in Britain originated from Sylhet, and most of these came from just a few subdistricts, making their settlement highly concentrated both in origin and in destination.

Bangladeshis began to bring over wives and children in the 1970s, a decade later than the Pakistanis.[16] Bangladeshis living in Britain numbered 6,000 in

1961, rose to 162,835 in 1991, 275,395 in 2001, and 447,000 in 2011. Of the 2001 population of British Bangladeshis, just over half had been born in Bangladesh.[17] In relative terms, Bangladeshis only made it into the top ten of immigrant populations in 1991, rose to fifth place in 2001, and then dropped to sixth place in 2011.[18]

Thus, if Pakistanis live in a number of centers across Britain, Bangladeshis are concentrated in East London, and, more specifically, in Tower Hamlets. This concentration has facilitated the rise in social and political importance of one institution, the East London Mosque, which we discuss in chapter 3. No single place, and no single organization, has the same importance for Pakistanis.

Spatial Dynamics

How concentrated are these populations? What are the effects of concentrations? We can mean different things by "concentration." Consider three British cities and the predominant images they project.

In Bradford, 15 percent of the total population identify themselves as of Pakistani origin, most coming from Mirpur. Bradford also has a high index of ethnic segregation, meaning people are highly likely to live near people like themselves, and pupils are even more segregated in schools than in neighborhoods; they have been called "semi-lingual in three languages" when they enter school. Worries about segregation, triggered by the 2001 riots in Bradford and other northern cities, led to a series of studies about immigration and religious geography in Bradford (see below), and eventually to a much-discussed 2012 Channel 4 television series called *Make Bradford British*, a title implying that Bradford had not yet quite moved into the category of Britishness. Even though whites are now moving into minority districts, for many Britons a mention of Bradford calls up images of Pakistani-Muslim neighborhoods that have little contact with largely white areas: a segregated city.[19]

Birmingham presents a different story. It has a large concentration of Muslims in another sense, that of sheer numbers. Birmingham is the UK local authority with the largest number of Pakistanis, and they are concentrated in particular neighborhoods (Sparkbrook, Small Heath). Often these concentrations are structured around kin groups. This type of concentration has given these communities a high level of local political representation. Their large numbers across the city have also supported a number of spacious mosques of diverse orientations, from Sufi to Salafi, including several quite visible mosques in the central part of the city. Birmingham also has large communities of South Asian Sikhs and Hindus who live in the same or adjoining neighborhoods. The city has had its own signature Muslim television show, the BBC's *Citizen Khan* series, which features Pakistani family life and the importance of the mosque, but not a Pakistani-only social life. Pakistani Muslims may be hugely present in Birmingham but they live near other minorities (as well as whites) and are not seen as segregated to the same degree as are their Bradford counterparts.[20]

London offers a third sense of Muslim concentration. Greater London has the largest Pakistani population, and by far the largest Muslim population, of all British cities. But London Pakistanis are spread across multiple local authorities, even if they are quite numerous in Waltham Forest, toward the northeast. Of course, London does have the highly concentrated Bangladeshi population in Tower Hamlets (especially in Spitalfields ward), but even Tower Hamlets has a cosmopolitan feel: the City is nearby, Brick Lane attracts tourists, and Mile End has high-ranking Queen Mary University. London has many major Islamic organizations, including the Islamic Shariʿa Council (ISC) (which we will examine in part 2), the East London Mosque, and a number of Islamic social or university-based associations. Muslim London's television presence tends to come through exposé-style one-offs about the dangers of shariʿa and radicalism; the cosmopolitanism of the city makes claims about Muslims living in isolated fashion more difficult to sustain.[21]

If many immigrants chose to live with their kin, their choice was often also highly constrained. Poor immigrants were disproportionally unable to afford anything other than poor-quality housing, and they faced rental discrimination. We would expect that if people lived in a concentrated area because they could only afford housing there, as their economic situation improved, they would move away, lowering concentration. This seems to be the case in Manchester, for example.[22] Bangladeshis arrived poorer and later than others, and generally had only rentals available to them. In the Tower Hamlets borough, they remain renters in flats, in part as the legacy of past council housing policies that discriminated against new arrivals. Those who have remained are much poorer than those who moved out: in the early 2000s, Bangladeshis living in Tower Hamlets had an unemployment rate four times as high as did Bangladeshis living in the more prosperous northwest London borough of Brent.[23]

Despite concentration, we should not think of immigrants as immobile. In Birmingham, for example, most South Asians, whether Muslim, Hindu, or Sikh, live in the portion of the central city that lies south of the difficult-to-cross highway interchange. Many of these families do change homes, but usually in a nearby, more prosperous neighborhood. As sociologist Khursheed Wadi explained to me in May 2013, people move to better-off areas as their fortunes improve, "but Pakistanis still end up living next to other Pakistanis, for example, moving from Sparkhill just southward to Moseley; they stay in that part of South Birmingham." One can have both ethnic concentration and residential mobility.

For an example of how this secondary migration works, consider Leicester, which, like other former mill towns in the Midlands, has large numbers of South Asians. Leicester's textile mills and the local factories of the once-worldwide-distributed Imperial Typewriters attracted many immigrants. Indeed, some of the mosques and the Sikh and Hindu temples of today are located in former factory buildings. The city also has a very large concentration of Indians, both Muslims and Hindus, and many of them had quite specific trajectories. The city attracted a large percentage of families who, originally from India's northwestern coastal area of Gujarat, had settled in East Africa and then were forced to leave in the 1960s and 1970s.[24] These relatively well-off families initially settled in several different parts of Leicester, but many then moved within the city so as to live near families with the same language, religion, and memories.

I first visited Leicester in 2008 to see Muslim leader Ibrahim Mogra at his house in the Evington ward of the city. He described to me how it came to be that *everyone* on his street was an African Asian who originated from Gujarat. "Once a mosque had been built here, run by Gujaratis, then others sought to move here, and they would pay a premium for houses; people were happy to sell to them."[25] These moves also increased the percentage of African Asians in certain Leicester state schools.

Possibly, these secondary moves within such cities as Birmingham and Leicester neither increase nor decrease overall levels of ethnic concentration. If the migration taking place largely in the 1960s and 1970s led to ethnic segregation in certain neighborhoods, thereafter people have moved in smaller numbers and for a variety of reasons. Some of these secondary moves spread people out slightly; others may have added to ethnic concentration. At the same time, population growth in the areas of initial concentration has probably balanced out-migration, meaning that neighborhoods look as if they were preserving a set rate of segregation.[26] Nonetheless, some observers argue that by the 1990s, British Muslims had less contact with non-Muslims than they had in the 1970s.[27]

As we saw above, by the 1970s more of the migratory stream consisted of families moving to settle in Britain. This shift from mainly labor migration to mainly family migration led to two changes in the institutional landscape of Islamic Britain. First, families made new demands to local British institutions regarding family matters. They asked for the inclusion of Islamic materials in religious curricula, for halal food, and for cemetery space. Muslims formed local organizations to address these needs, largely following ethnic or regional lines in accord with the British government funding policies at the time.

Second, as the number of Muslim migrants grew, so did religious and ethnic specialization. People could look for others "like them" in a more fine-grained way. Concentration became more narrowbanded. Neighborhoods that once included Muslims from several parts of the world now became majority Mirpuri, or East Asian, or Yemeni (or, as in Leicester, Gujarati East African). At the same time, people of similar origins began to construct dense

FIGURE 1. Birmingham Central Mosque after Friday Prayers, 2010

networks spanning several neighborhoods and often centering on mosques.[28] Mosques specialized and increasingly reflected the religious divisions of the homelands. Communities imported religious teachers and preachers from their origin regions, and these officials interpreted community issues through sectarian religious lenses. The result has been characterized as a "patchwork of communities" defined ethnically, within which religious organizations play increasingly important roles.[29] This is the setting for the development of Islamic institutions that will occupy us for the remainder of this book.

It is nonetheless important not to see South Asians as simply transporting religious affiliations with them to Britain. These affiliations have developed out of rivalries among Islamic groups in Britain as they seek to establish control over mosques, as well as in the trajectories of thousands of individual Muslims who have passed through different kinds of Islamic groups as they sought their own pathways to spirituality, or identity, or camaraderie. These mechanisms will become apparent in the discussions that follow.[30]

MARRYING AND RECONNECTING

Along with residential choice, marriage provides a second mechanism for maintaining (or reducing) concentration and cohesion among British

Muslims. One of the real surprises to come out of recent research on British Muslims from Pakistan is that trends in marriage contradict one of the basic tenets of migration studies. Most immigrant populations adapt to host country demographic patterns. For example, birth rates for immigrants from Muslim societies have declined in Europe for immigrants, but even more so for the second and third generations.[31] But for there to be clear "generations," there must be a process of settlement and local marriage. Immigrants marry others who have also settled in the host country, and when the children of all those "first-generation" immigrants marry, they marry either each other or native women and men who are not of the same immigration origin, which creates a "second generation."

Such has not been the case for British Pakistanis. On three dimensions, British Pakistanis continue to marry both in the family and across continents. First, British Muslims generally have been overwhelmingly marrying their co-ethnics, people from the same origin. Surveys taken in 1997–2002 found that 98 percent of Bangladeshi women, 94 percent of Pakistani women, and 92 percent of Indian women married co-ethnics.[32] Second, British Pakistani Muslims prefer to marry "close" in two senses: more than one-half marry first cousins, and most Mirpuri Muslims (the majority of British Pakistanis) marry someone from the same village. The medical consequences of continued patterns of close-cousin marriage have been a matter for increasing concern in Britain.[33] Finally, observers place the rate of transcontinental marriage at 57–69 percent, and they find that these percentages have remained stable in recent decades.[34]

Now, as is the case for many societies in the belt stretching from North Africa across South Asia, many Pakistanis practice close-family marriage. It is not surprising that some of those emigrating from Pakistan to Britain would carry that preference with them. But what *is* surprising is that, rather than declining with length of settlement in the UK, rates of close-cousin marriage appear to be rising. Why?

Marriage patterns develop as adaptations to specific socioeconomic situations. A study of British-born Pakistanis in Oxford, most with ancestry from Punjab, found that 59 percent of marriages were between first cousins and only 13 percent were between unrelated people. Even the small numbers of unrelated marriages may be done to preserve caste status among high-ranking people. These marriages were all arranged by parents or other guardians. A study in Yorkshire found a rate of 55 percent for, again, people whose parents came from Mirpur.[35]

These figures concern British-born descendants of Mirpuris. How do they compare with their counterparts born in Pakistan? In the Oxford sample, among couples born in Pakistan, only 37 percent had married first cousins. Comparable data from elsewhere in Britain show remarkably similar rates for "pioneer-generation" marriages, between 33 percent and 35 percent between first cousins. Data from Pakistan taken as a whole indicate a range of 36 percent to 49 percent.[36] Pakistanis become more likely to marry their cousins when they move to Britain.

Why might close-cousin marriages *increase* with residence in Britain? Some British Pakistanis see themselves as obliged to propose a marriage between their children and those of their siblings. A desire to maintain caste status and to preserve shared economic interests partially explains this sense of obligation, as it does the tendency to bring a husband or wife to Britain from Pakistan. Indeed, 71 percent of the marriages in the Oxford Pakistani sample were between a British resident and a Pakistani resident (with men and women in equal proportions in both categories), and were overwhelmingly close-kin marriages. Women tended to have weaker bargaining positions in these marriages than did men, and the British women were more likely to divorce than were the British men.[37]

But emotional ties between siblings also weigh in the balance, and indeed a transnational marriage, by creating spatial and emotional distance between the spouse who travels and her or his parents, may create the impetus for contracting a second such marriage in order to bring the parties closer together. British Pakistanis may also prefer a spouse from the subcontinent to preserve culture and religion. At the same time, these close-kin marriages also carry risks, including the far greater social and emotional consequences of divorce. You divorce not just your spouse but your aunt's or uncle's child.[38]

Alison Shaw and Katharine Charsley's fieldwork projects in Pakistan and in several UK sites (Bristol, Oxford, Leeds, and High Wycombe) give us important insight into the range of reasons and emotions surrounding transcontinental marriages—and also prevent us from taking material on divorce, such as that presented later on in this book, as indicative of how well such marriages fare. Both anthropologists stress the meanings of the term *rishta* as both "match" and "connection," in the dual sense of social and emotional connection. In the transcontinental context, maintaining existing connections becomes even more emotionally important and creates demand for a higher frequency of close-kin marriages. Finding a spouse "back home" from among a beloved sibling's children is not the continuation of a backward custom but a way to negotiate the social, emotional, and sometimes economic strains of holding an extended family together across a very long distance. It is worth repeating that spouses who travel to Britain to marry close kin are as likely to be women as men, and such marriages are, therefore, not to be seen as a way to reproduce the older pattern of male out-migration under the guise of marriage—a notion that underlies claims that such marriages are made for illegitimate reasons.[39]

Potential spouses also weigh the probable emotional consequences of marrying a particular cousin in terms of their personal like or dislike of the potential spouse, the preferences of their own parents, and the character of their future in-laws. In this sense there is no easy dichotomy between "love" and "arranged" marriages, even though Pakistanis do use these terms. Pakistani relatives have a clear interest in sending dependents to Britain by way of marriage—and that is virtually the only way they can send them. The British-resident relatives may also have reasons for keeping up family ties, economic as well as social and emotional, in cases where relatives have joint interests in enterprises and in land. But they also experience moral pressure from their Pakistan-based siblings to help out a niece or nephew. Helping them out is a way to show their own willingness to live up to their obligations and, for those who have not achieved high status, honoring these obligations as an alternative route to high status.[40]

In subsequent chapters we will read about problems that such marriages may cause, but we should note that many British Pakistanis (and others as well) find satisfaction in their own arranged marriages. The ambivalence many feel is reflected in a web forum exchange in 2013.[41] A young woman distinguishes her feelings about the process and her feelings toward the chosen cousin.

> I am going to Pakistan in a few months' time with my parents to get married to my first cousin. . . . That thought alone makes me sick to my stomach. But, I wouldn't mind too much if the guy wasn't an arrogant and selfish guy who has at least 3 girlfriends as I'm writing this. . . . I know you guys will advise me to not marry him if I don't like him, but I have a problem, my parents would be okay about it if I said no to marrying him, but they want me to be married by 22, and cannot find a guy in the UK as most of our relatives are in Pakistan or completely out of my age range, and my parents aren't keen on marrying me to someone they don't know properly, and I don't want to stereotype, as I know from this site that there are decent Pakistani guys, but judging from my brothers-in-law and most Pakistani relatives that I have, I don't think I can ever marry a Pakistani.

One responder says, "Yeah, story of a lot of British Pakistani girls . . . but in your case, you're lucky that your parents aren't forcing you." Others ask her if there are sisters or aunties in whom she can confide; she says yes, "but the problem in my life is that there is no villain; it's the circumstances that are wrong."[42] The writer seems to accept the situation as beyond her control, and perhaps beyond anyone's control—"there is no villain."

Generations

But will these practices of close marriage not die out? The mechanisms that reproduce close-kin marriages and transcontinental marriages do not come with a date of expiration, and, indeed, these marriage strategies appear to derive from the very social facts, settlement in a new country, that were once assumed to signal their demise. Evidence of change is unclear.[43]

For more highly educated Muslims, a break in these patterns may come from new patterns of travel. Although young British Muslims are mostly of a South Asian background, it seems that few travel to that part of the world to study Islam. They now have access to traditional Islamic schools in Britain, notably the Dar al-ʿUlum schools found in many cities and Barelvi Sufi versions of the same. Going to Pakistan would not seem to bring a clear advantage. To be sure, some do this. But more choose to go to the Arabic-speaking world, in particular, to schools in Cairo or in Saudi Arabia. Changes in British laws can also make it more difficult for British men or women to sponsor a spouse for settlement. In 2012, for example, new rules required proof of a higher income and a firm job by the party living in Britain.

And yet, ties between British Muslims of Pakistani background and Pakistan continue to be reinforced by frequent family visits, even if the imagination of the homeland has changed. On such visits, children are given expensive presents to hand out to relatives in Pakistan; their high value documents the success of the extended kinship unit. Girls, and especially boys, return from these visits proud of their Pakistani connections. But whereas the Pakistani men who arrived in Britain in the 1950s and 1960s planned to return home with money to be used for the benefit of their homeland kin, these plans rarely worked out: men who did return to Pakistan faced social and bureaucratic obstacles to starting up businesses. Marta Bolognani found that younger Bradford men and women now imagine Pakistan as a refuge in the face of British racism, each thinking with different images—the green fields of Mirpur, or the hills of the North-West Frontier. Some families will send young girls or troubled boys "home" to Pakistan to repair or to guarantee their good character, a kind of inoculation against English vices.[44]

Transposing the Kin Group

Another factor tending to keep in place these transcontinental marriage patterns is the practical importance of the extended kin group, the *biraderi.* The biraderi maintains transcontinental ties because they benefit group members both in Britain and in Pakistan. Kin living in Britain send remittances back home, and see their own social status raised through this act.

One of the major biraderis is the Bhatti group in Birmingham. In May 2013, I spoke with Qamar Bhatti, who had become the leader of the biraderi, "the network of cousins," as he put it, at his father's death in 2011. Many of these "cousins" come to see him at the family house, sometimes with business questions and often with personal problems. He estimates that about thirty thousand people, spread over Britain and in some parts of Europe, belong to the biraderi. His is one of perhaps half a dozen large Pakistani biraderi in Birmingham; others include the Raja, the Chaudhry, and the Khan groups. In the past, some of them have entered politics and several Labour councillors in Birmingham were elected due to support from their own biraderis.

His father tried to counter the tendency to settle together in Birmingham: "Why come here; we are already here," he would say, so at his behest their families settled all across Britain. His father was a property developer and participated in building several of Birmingham's mosques, including the (Barelvi Sufi) Ghamkol Sharif Mosque and the Birmingham Central Mosque. When he was eighteen years old, Qamar began to serve as a translator; he accompanied men to offices and would know which forms to give to whom, and the officials would talk with him because he spoke English well and would take care of the matter. He eventually took over his father's role of mediating between the city planning offices and Islamic groups seeking to build mosques or schools. Although he (and the members of his biraderi) are Sufis, he worked with Deobandis and Salafis as well.

Sometimes mosques divide along biraderi lines. Earlier in 2013, two biraderis competed for control of a mosque located in the Birmingham neighborhood of Aston. Qamar said, "The two groups are related to each other but something came between them, perhaps a problem with a marriage—often it is a marriage issue—and one group wanted to take over the microphone from the leadership. I was called in, and I said to the leadership, 'we need to call in the police because there could be a fight if this happens.'"

Qamar collects *zakat* (the obligatory annual payment used for charitable and religious purposes) and initiates projects with his biraderi. After his father died they formed a foundation, and now they have an office in Rawalpindi, where his father was born. "It is just a desk," Qamar explained, "and we are not charged for it, but that way we can call people in to meet there with us via Skype." Their major project involves two medical clinics in rural areas that are staffed by the government, "but they have to find their own medicines so we arrange to provide those. It is much cheaper to buy them there; they come from Singapore or somewhere else in Asia; we work with a doctor who practices in Lahore, and she buys them in bulk. We call her and send the money. Some people here give their zakat to the foundation. We plan to add two more clinics."

He spoke of developing kin-focused projects in Birmingham:

> We meet once a year on the anniversary of my father's death and discuss what to do; it is a formal meeting. We take care of property that people here inherit in Pakistan. For example, a guy comes by and says he has four buildings in Islamabad. I say I will sort it but am busy and fail to do so. He leaves off the keys to the buildings for me with a note saying that he wanted to donate them to the foundation, and I call up someone I know

> there and he checks it out and says they are worth billions of pounds in value. The local guy turns out tenants who won't pay and arranges to collect rents from the others. I call the owner and ask for his account, but he said he had donated them, so I call his mother, and she gives me their account details and I arrange to have rents put into that account. It turned out to be enough for their two daughters' lavish weddings in Pakistan years later!

He also arranges to pay brokers in Pakistan to get clients' property through court quickly, to get the title after a death, and has them charge a reasonable rate.

The Bhatti biraderi facilitates economic transactions across the transcontinental divide, offers social support to immigrants and their descendants, and carves out a social space in which trust can operate to make marriage and mutual assistance possible. It can also be the basis for mobilizing kin against a rival group, as in the case of the Aston mosque dispute. It is both localized, with a heavy concentration in and around Birmingham, and worldwide. This sort of network has nothing to do with "segregation"; it has everything to do with creating worldwide social capital.[45]

I have highlighted features of British Muslims' pathways that shaped a sense of localized communities. South Asian Muslims came from a small set of places and settled in concentrated neighborhoods. Many, especially those from Pakistan, have reproduced ties to the homeland through close-kin marriages and transcontinental kin groups. These practices have strengthened allegiances to their homeland region and their ethnic identity. In chapter 3, we trace the development of boundaries and networks that emerge from a different source: the religious differences developed in South Asia and reproduced in Britain.

CHAPTER 3

Islamic Topographies

NOW WE MOVE FROM DEMOGRAPHIC PATHWAYS TO ISLAMIC ONES. PATTERNS OF movement and settlement set the stage for religious actors to create new Islamic institutional spaces. British Islamic actors have employed three distinct processes to create these spaces: they reproduce South Asian religious differences in Britain, they adapt Islam to the opportunity structures found in Britain, and they maintain transnational ties to religious or political movements elsewhere. To some degree, these three processes—reinforcing boundaries, adapting locally, maintaining transnational ties—figure in all Islamic actors' practical schemas for shaping British Islam.[1]

Let me start with an example of the British spatial and religious realities for which we need to account. I mentioned Ibrahim Mogra in chapter 2. I chose him as a guide to the politics of space and religion in Leicester, mainly because of his informed perspective: he is active locally as the head of a Leicester Islamic school but also nationally as a leader in the Muslim Council of Britain. Ibrahim came to Britain as part of the wave of South Asians fleeing persecution in East Africa. Born in Malawi, he was educated in the Dar al-'Ulum school in Bury, one of many British schools associated with South Asia's Deobandi tradition of religious education, which I discuss below. After further education at Cairo's Al-Azhar, he settled in Leicester.

One day in April 2013, Ibrahim, wearing a stocking cap and nursing a cold, met me at Leicester train station. With a dark beard and shaved mustache, and wearing a long white gown, he looked every bit the Deobandi scholar that he is. And yet, when we reached the main Deobandi mosque in town, the Omar Mosque, he stopped the car some distance away and told me that he was no longer welcome there. At issue were some of the radio broadcasts he regularly delivers during the month of Ramadan, which urge Muslims to move beyond the nineteenth-century teachings of South Asian scholars and grapple with the modern world. "But the Deobandis here, they take everything that was ever said by their elders in the subcontinent as if it had been cast in stone," he said.

Close to the mosque we found the state-supported Madani High School, which is run by Deobandis. At first the school officials had tried to allow only pupils from Deobandi families to attend, or at least to keep out children whose parents were part of the main competing religious orientation, the Barelvi Sufis. But such a policy would have been in violation of English law, and eventually they abandoned it. Nonetheless, the vast majority of the pupils are children of Deobandi-affiliated families, and most of them share the East African roots of Ibrahim and the Omar Mosque's directors.[2]

We continued our tour of Muslim Leicester and arrived at the Barelvi Sufi mosque, physically the largest mosque in town but with not quite as many worshippers as its Deobandi counterpart. Located near the train station, it is the best-known Leicester mosque. "They welcome me with open arms, and I bring visitors here now," said Ibrahim. But they do so exceptionally for him; in general, Barelvi Sufis consider the Deobandis to be on the wrong path because they show insufficient respect for the prophet Muhammad.

Across Muslim Britain, disputes over the control of mosques often concern attempts by either Deobandis or Barelvis to keep the other group out of leadership positions. From where did these efforts to bound off and restrict access to institutions come? In chapter 2, we saw how residential histories have produced spatial concentration for many British Muslims, and we saw such concentration for this group of Gujarati Deobandis in Leicester. However, these processes do not explain the *religious* divisions and hostilities signaled by Ibrahim. To understand these, we must return to developments in the British Indies during the late nineteenth century.

The North Indian "Islamic Triangle"

We can perhaps best understand the contours of South Asian Islam by beginning with Sufism. Members of Sufi orders follow a spiritual guide, a *sheikh* or *pir*, and many other Muslims also recognize the powers associated with shrines dedicated to past sheikhs. By the sixteenth century, the beginning of the Mughal period, a number of Sufi orders were localized in lodges.[3] Each order was structured around a spiritual lineage or *silsilah*, along which the follower (*murīd*) could trace a line of spiritual ascent through his sheikh to the founder of the order and (usually) on upward to a companion of the prophet Muhammad. The orders differed according to the recitations used in devotional sessions, whether music was used, and in their stances toward political power and toward particular elements of Islamic law. Ordinary South Asian Muslims made pilgrimages to these shrines.

The shrine was allied to the mosque. Often the two existed next to each other. One of the most important shrines (*dargah*) is in Ajmer, a city in India's northwestern province of Rajasthan. Ajmer's thirteenth-century Dargah Sharif shrine is the holy tomb of the saint Muʿin al-din Chishti, the apical saint of the Chishtiyyah order's spiritual genealogy. The site is visited by Hindus as well as Muslims. This shrine also illustrates the imbrications of Sufi shrines with temporal rule. Dargah Sharif first became important in the sixteenth century when the Mughal emperor Akbar began to visit the tomb.

It continues to carry legitimating power today. When anthropologist Peter van der Veer visited the shrine in 1986, by then located in independent India, he discovered that Pakistani president Muhammad Zia-ul-Haq had recently paid the saint a visit. Zia was seeking to symbolically buttress his own rule back home by linking himself to the dynasty of the Mughals by way of the saint.[4] Sufi legitimation overcame geopolitical frictions.

During the eighteenth century, the Mughal Empire waned and polities fragmented.[5] Successor states assumed independent power, new kingdoms were carved out of imperial lands, and the British began to control parts of the subcontinent. As political authority weakened, autonomous religious authority grew. This authority could be that of a Sufi sheikh with his spiritual lineage or that of a scholar (*ʿālim*, pl. *ʿulamāʾ*) with his learning. Shrines and their mosques combined the two types of authority. In their efforts to build new centers of authoritative learning, Sufi sheikhs enjoyed one major advantage, in that they already had regional power bases linked to sacred shrines, particularly in the northwestern regions of Sind and Punjab.

By contrast, the scholars (or ʿulamaʾ) had fewer preexisting centers of power and influence. They set out to build new ones, often in the form of religious schools. At the Farangi Mahal school in Lucknow, they developed an Islamic studies curriculum called the Dars-i Nizami, which, in modified forms, is still used in Islamic schools in South Asia and Britain.[6] They also set a lasting pattern of embracing Sufi teachings, as well as linguistic, historical, and legal learning, thus merging the roles of scholar and sheikh in a school setting. Foremost among these scholars was Shah Wali Allah of Delhi (d. 1762), who responded to political decline by seeking a revival of Islamic knowledge that highlighted the importance of studying the reports of Muhammad's statements and deeds, the hadith.

By the nineteenth century some scholars worked in regional courts as judges and advisers. But as the British expanded their spheres of control, they devised their own law codes as a basis for any official ruling according to Muslim, or Hindu, or other laws, effectively bypassing the Islamic judge. Some scholars responded by issuing religious advice directly to Muslims as written legal opinions or fatwas. Fatwas could be printed and distributed widely, and in some cases were given the stamp of a particular school rather than only that of an individual scholar. Issuing fatwas directly to an Urdu-reading public linked Muslims across northern India, where by the middle of the nineteenth century a separate religious sphere began to emerge.[7] This sphere relied on diverse symbols of community, such as public observances of religious festivals, the continued activity of Islamic intermediaries between ordinary Muslims and British rulers, or a heightened emphasis on reforming personal religious practice.[8] This emphasis increased the importance of the ʿulamaʾ.

But Islamic scholars nonetheless perceived a crisis in religious authority. Some argued, for example, that religious scholars or judges no longer had the right to dissolve a marriage at a wife's request, a process called *faskh,* which we will encounter throughout this book.[9] This sense of crisis was accentuated by the uprisings and repressions that occurred in 1857, referred to variously as the Indian Rebellion, the Uprising, or the Mutiny. The harsh British response included killing many of those accused of rebellion, and occupying or razing schools and mosques, and led to the replacement of rule by the British East India Company with rule by the queen, now empress of India.

Muslim scholars reacted by turning still more sharply away from the British state. Many left Delhi and other large cities to rebuild centers of learning in smaller towns farther away from British power. These scholars developed social spaces for living in accord with Islamic social norms and spirituality rather than entering into governmental service or engaging in political activity. These efforts to create nonstate Islamic spaces would later inspire the rise of Islamic legal bodies in both independent India and Britain.

Eventually, the most influential of these new social spaces was the Dar al-ʿUlum school founded in 1867 in the north-central Indian town of Deoband.[10] Students came to the Deoband school already proficient in Arabic and in studies of the Qurʾan. At Deoband, teachers used the older Dars-i Nizami curriculum but now gave greater weight to the study of hadith and law, a development that reflected the influence of Shah Wali Allah's teachings. The school's language of instruction was Urdu rather than the court language of Persian or the many vernaculars. The school thus reinforced Urdu's emergence as the shared language of Muslims in northern India (and eventually among those who migrated to Britain). Some of the early students went on to found new schools in which the same or similar curricula were taught. The new Deobandi schools depended on public contributions. Thus was born the international networks of financial support and schools that currently continue to underwrite much Islamic educational activity in the subcontinent and abroad.[11]

The Deobandi schools spawned new Islamic social movements, differing among themselves in the emphases they gave to jurisprudential debate, teaching, or missionary work. The major teachers in the Deoband schools combined the two Islamic roles of the scholar and the sheikh: the person so knowledgeable in Islamic legal sciences that he could dispense a legal opinion, and the person so adept in the pursuit of mystical knowledge through a Sufi path that he may lead a local Sufi lodge. They thus followed the path of the scholar Abu Hamid al-Ghazali (d. 1111) in uniting the pursuit of shariʿa (norms or law) and *tariqa* (the Sufi path). Senior scholars of the Deobandi tradition continue to advocate the proper pursuit of pathways to God through the Sufi practices of meditation and remembrance called *tasawwuf,* even though they may criticize certain practices that suggest idolatry. In this respect they can be seen as reformist Sufis as well as legal scholars.[12] But some of today's followers of the Deobandi tradition are hostile to all forms of tasawwuf; this hostility was aggravated by the common cause made with Arab Salafis in the jihads fought in Afghanistan.

Deobandi scholars follow the Hanafi legal school, one of the four major Sunni schools or traditions (sing., *madhhab*). Each such school draws on the Qur'an, the reports (hadith) of the Prophet's acts and statements, reasoning by analogy (*qiyās*) to new situations, and the consensus of scholars (*ijmāʿ*). Deobandi scholars urged Muslims to follow a single scholar or set of scholars rather than drawing their own conclusions from scripture or from a variety of opinions. They argued that Muslims needed to find certainty in a time of social disorder (*fitnah*), such as that which bedeviled late nineteenth-century British India. This position meant that Deobandi teachers were less likely than some other scholars to quote the scriptural sources from which they drew, lest people begin to debate among themselves over the choice of source.

From the Deobandi schools and teaching developed the Tablighi Jamaʿat, founded by Maulana Muhammad Ilyas (1885–1944), whose members were devoted to traveling and teaching about Islam. Tablighi followers are expected to spend a certain number of days each year engaged in door-to-door visiting, to remind Muslims of their religious duties.[13]

Their approach to learning set the Deobandis apart from the Ahl al-Hadith (Urdu: Ahl-e-Hadith), the "people of the hadith," who urged Muslims to base their decisions on scripture and not limit their interpretations to the four major legal schools. They count among their predecessors the scholar Ibn Taymiyyah (1263–1328). Deobandis and Ahl al-Hadith share a number of concerns. They exercise *ijtihād* (or independent legal reasoning), to arrive at new solutions to problems. They agree that Muslims should base their religious practices on a proper sense of *tawhīd* (God's unity), and for that reason oppose the observance of saints' birthdays and making pilgrimages to the graves of holy men, on grounds that such practices are tantamount to polytheism.

This position places both movements in their opposition to a third, that of Barelvi Sufis, a name that derives from the scholar Ahmad Riza Khan Barelvi (1856–1921), from the town of Bareilly in Uttar Pradesh. The Barelvis stress the importance of venerating saints and of seeking intercession from saints for the benefit of the living. A majority of South Asian Muslims living in Britain today probably would agree with the Barelvi position on these issues, although far fewer of them are active members of Sufi orders. Although all three approaches (*maslak*s) are part of the Sunni family in Islam, and thus can call themselves Ahl al-Sunnah wal-Jamaah (People of the Path and of the Community), Barelvis appropriate this latter phrase to refer to themselves in distinction to other Sunni orientations. Like the Deobandis, they follow the Hanafi legal school.

By the early twentieth century, these three religious pathways—Deobandi, Ahl al-Hadith, and Barelvi—had established themselves in north-central India as distinctive, alternative ways of living a life as a Sunni Muslim. Each possessed its own institutional bases outside the political parties and the British-backed legal institutions. The idea of Islamic nonstate institutions, competent to rule on matters involving Muslims, grew out of these sociopolitical conditions.[14] It would lead prominent scholars to argue for the creation of Muslim courts, or at least for Muslim councils that could fill the role of a *qadi* (a Muslim judge who rules according to the shariʿa) but without state involvement. This argument was to be revived years later in Britain by those setting up the first shariʿa councils.[15]

Of course, there are many Sunni Muslims living in South Asia who do not identify themselves with any of these traditions. There are also educational and political movements, including the political movement and party Jamaat-e-Islami, founded in 1941 by Abu Aʿla Maududi (1903–79), which had an urban base in Pakistan and developed branches in Britain. There are also Shiʿi and Ahmadi forms of Islam in South Asia and in Britain.

Nonetheless, the three-way opposition among these references, especially the opposition Deobandi/Barelvi, has been foundational for the development of Islamic institutions in Britain. Social movements and political parties influenced by these traditions also emerged in colonial South Asia, and later became active in India, Pakistan, and Bangladesh; these will be mentioned when relevant. These South Asian pathways have become the institutional armature of Sunni Islam in Britain today, and their lines have hardened.

In sum, the legacies of the South Asian background are, first, the "Islamic triangle" (Deobandi/Barelvi/Ahl al-Hadith) that yields both transnational networks and cleavages in Britain; second, the idea that in minority situations, whether in India or in Britain, Muslims should create the necessary local institutions; and, third, the hope for eventual state recognition of their institutions. We will see these three legacies in detail in what follows.

Reinforcing Boundaries in Leicester

But how did these legacies transpose onto the British landscape? Let us return to Leicester for a moment, and to Ibrahim Mogra. Much of his energy is devoted to reducing boundaries among Muslims, and between Muslims and others. By 2014 he had occupied a number of leadership roles within the nationwide Muslim Council of Britain, an umbrella organization initially created to maintain dialogue with the government, including on interfaith relations. When he took me on a tour of Leicester in 2013, we began by visiting the chaplaincy service at the University of Leicester. "It is easier to work on interfaith dialogue than intrafaith dialogue," he remarked.

When I asked him to explain, he said that the Deobandi and Barelvi mosques continually criticized each other: "The preacher at the Omar Mosque sometimes will speak against Barelvis, usually because word got around that a Barelvi preacher had spoken against the Deobandis—because word always gets around. Usually it concerns the prophet Muhammad: Deobandis will charge Barelvis with holding up Muhammad to be holy, while the Barelvis will criticize the Deobandis for failing to respect him." The Omar mosque is located in Evington, the ward where most Indian Muslims in Leicester live—and indeed, the place with the highest concentration of Indian Muslims in England. Most families living near the mosque are African Asian Muslims, like himself.

Ibrahim continued his account of the hostilities he has encountered: "For example, I said that I would never teach the Bahishti Zewar to my daughter, because it does not fit with life here. I would never say, as it does, that the wife should walk three paces behind the husband; to the contrary, you should hold her hand to show her you love her. But the Deobandis here, they take everything that was ever said by their elders in the subcontinent as if it had been cast in stone. In India they do not label people 'Deobandi'; there it is seen as just a town and a school, because there are so many different types of people who came from there." His declaration was unpopular; the Bahishti Zewar is a widely read Urdu-language treatise written primarily for women by Maulana Ashraf ʿAli Thanawi (d. 1943), a highly respected Deobandi graduate.[16]

Leicester as a whole has a majority of Indians among its Muslim population, and Indians are the strongest Deobandi supporters in Britain. The city has twenty mosques (half of them Deobandi), three Deobandi seminaries, eight Muslim day schools, and many mosque-based schools for the very young after hours. The Deobandis have a firm hold on the city's Muslim school system, and consequently more radical groups have found few inroads.[17]

For Ibrahim, the hardened lines opposing Deobandis to Barelvis run counter to the true Deobandi teachings, which welcome Sufism. Indeed, we drove by another, smaller Deoband mosque that has its own Sufi lodge (*khānqāh*). A few minutes later we suddenly pulled over on a small business street and entered a shop selling Islamic books and sundries. Ibrahim introduced me to the owner, who has run the shop for fifteen years. Ibrahim asked him, "Tell him [me] who your sheikh is, to whom you have taken a *bayat* [oath]," and the owner answered, "Sheikh Yusuf Motala." Ibrahim wanted to show me that a Deobandi such as this man could have a Sufi sheikh.

As he explained after we left the shop, Sheikh Motala had been the pupil and follower (murīd) of Muhammad Zakariyya al-Kandhalvi (d. 1982), a Deobandi scholar who was a major figure within the Tablighi Jamaʿat (and the nephew of its founder). In 1973, Sheikh Motala established the Dar al-ʿUlum in Bury, Lancashire, which today is the largest Islamic seminary in the UK (and from which Ibrahim graduated). The Bury seminary reflects the more Sufi-oriented stream of the Deobandi movement, and Motala traces a spiritual lineage (silsilah) within two of the major South Asian Sufi orders, the

Naqshbandiyya and the Chishtiyyah. Ibrahim's point was that Sufism and Deobandi teachings were in fact part and parcel of the same heritage, but that British mosques, defining themselves by opposition to others, had forgotten this lesson and instead had hardened the boundaries between the two movements.[18]

To drive the point home, we continued on our drive, pausing opposite some unremarkable terraced housing. "Watch those boys there," he said, pointing to five young men dressed in white gowns who were gathered outside a door. "That is Sheikh Adam's house." Sheikh Adam was Ibrahim's own teacher, and had been the pupil of Sheikh Motala. Ibrahim Mogra thus had his own spiritual genealogy, stretching from Sheikh Adam through Sheikh Motala to Sheikh Zakariyya. The boys eventually left, but Ibrahim thought they might have been waiting to carry Sheikh Adam to his car; they often do this because he is so frail and they are devoted to him. "They observe the silsilah, part of Naqshbandiyya."

He recalled his own days as Sheikh Adam's pupil: "Fifteen or twenty years ago, Sheikh Adam was very anti-English, but then he changed. He is no longer against technology, adds less fire and brimstone to his sermons, and adds more love of God. We are the fruits of his labor," he concluded. "I used to be afraid of him, but teachers are no longer like that." Indeed, as we kept walking, we encountered a young girl, about six years old, who was one of his own pupils at his school. She cheerfully ran up to greet him. Remarking on Sheikh Adam, Ibrahim said, "We don't see him as holy but as enlightened; he can help us out of this hole we are all in here. He was why I studied Islam. He never preached against Barelvis. I wish the Barelvis could appreciate this. He loved his Rumi, and his Ghazali." We finished our tour at the Barelvi mosque, near the train station, and because of that location, well known to Leicester residents. "If only they, the Barelvis, knew how much Sufism there is in Deobandi teachings."

A similar sentiment was expressed later that day when I went to nearby Nuneaton to visit with Qamar Bhatti, the Pakistani kin group leader introduced in chapter 2. He is a Barelvi Sufi, and thus provided me with a complementary perspective to Ibrahim's, in that he, too, was likely to cross the line separating the two movements. The mosque nearest to his house in Nuneaton is run by Deobandis, and consequently, that is where he and his family worship. "We go there; it should make no difference: legal views should not be an issue; what happens at the people level should." I asked Qamar about the Deobandi-Barelvi disputes and specifically what differences he notices between Deobandi and Barelvi mosques. He explained that "the Deobandis will be wearing shorter trousers, have bushy beards, and say the final 'amīn' out loud; the Barelvis will have longer trousers and say the 'amīn' to themselves. I think that the Prophet said the amīn sometimes out loud and sometimes silently, so we can choose."

I asked him why, if the differences were so trivial, there was so much anger? He responded, "I think that too often people seek division in order to impress others so that they can remain leaders. I have tried to change this attitude, but it did not work, because they like to follow. The older generation will hang on to control of the mosques; we will just have to wait until they get too old to continue. The young people in Birmingham go one of two ways. Those with more education want these distinctions to go away; they just want to pray at the local mosque and wish the older people would stop talking about these juristic [*fiqh*] differences. Those with less education want stability and certainty, and some go toward Salafism and toward making distinctions based on fiqh."

Our excursion to Leicester highlights the difference between a relatively complex relationship toward Sufism on the part of some teachers, and the hardened, diacritic opposition between Deobandis and Barelvis as two opposed camps. But even for these two camps, the Islamic topography of Britain is still more complex.

Building Niches and Networks

Across the Midlands and the North, the rising number of South Asian Muslims has led to an institutional specialization that has permitted, and indeed encouraged, the emergence of religious cleavages. This specialization has operated through constructing particular kinds of networks for Barelvi and Deobandi streams of Islam.

We have already seen that as more families came to Britain, local associations arose to meet demands for Islamic goods and services, such as the provision of halal food and Islamic materials for state schools. At first, immigrants structured these associations along ethnic or regional lines, in part because British government policies favored working with or giving aid to bodies defined in these ways. But by the mid-1980s, mosques and other religious organizations, rather than ethnically defined bodies, were playing a more prominent role than before.

This change occurred for two reasons. First, the ethnic-based organizations that had played this role had depended on the state for funding, and Margaret Thatcher's government severely cut back such funding. Mosques had never enjoyed state funding and so were left relatively unscathed. Second, religious leaders encouraged British Muslims to give greater emphasis to religious learning and practices. They did so at the same time that more British Muslims were raising children and were reflecting on the best way to educate those children in their homeland religious and cultural traditions. By this time Muslims also began to mobilize at the national level around religious issues, for example, in 1985, when Muslim and Jewish organizations together headed off a bill that would have phased out exemptions granted to ritual slaughterers from animal welfare provisions.[19] Eventually, other national Islamic innovations saw the light of day, such as shariʿa banking and Islamic schools. These innovations were within established institutions, however: banks, schools, and food preparation. And although the efforts to organize politically at the national level have continued, they have met with little success.

More important in shaping religious space were local mosques, schools, and their networks. As more mosques were built, they began to map in a more fine-grained way the religious divisions of the homelands. Communities imported religious teachers and preachers who saw things through their particular Islamic lenses. By the mid-1980s the patchwork of communities continued to be defined by ethnic or regional labels, but within these communities religious organizations played increasingly important roles.

Bradford

Bradford, in West Yorkshire, provides one of the best-studied cases. Bradford rose to fame in the nineteenth century for its woolen mills, but South Asians arrived to work just as the woolen mills were closing and industry was shifting to new areas. Known as Britain's "curry capital," in 2011 it had the highest percentage of Pakistan-origin people in England (20 percent) and the fourth-highest percentage of Muslims (25 percent).[20]

The first Bradford mosque was built in 1959, and worshippers came from different places and schools of thought. By 1969 there were six mosques in the city, and by 1989 thirty-four. Worshippers tended to frequent nearby mosques, but because they had settled with religious and ethnic identities in mind, the mosques increasingly reflected one or another South Asian religious stream.

Most notably, of the 1989 mosques, eleven were associated with the Barelvi Sufis and twelve with the Deobandis. Smaller numbers were affiliated with the Pakistani movement Jamaat-e-Islami (JI), the Ahl al-Hadith, Shiites, and the Ahmadiyya.[21] The Barelvi mosques tended to be run by people from Mirpur district, while the Deobandis came from Gujarat and Attock districts in Pakistan or from Sylhet in Bangladesh. Internal differentiation went further, however: for example, Muslims who came from Gujarat by way of years of residence in East Africa eventually split off from Gujaratis who had come directly from India. Their differences included the former's better command of English and commercial skills, as well as the two populations' participation in distinct kin groups. They worshipped separately.

Through the 1970s and early 1980s, immigrants formed Urdu-language cultural groups to read poetry, burial societies tied to particular districts in Pakistan or India to enable funds to be quickly raised to send bodies home for burial, and youth societies associated with different ethnic communities. State funds were available for these associations. Pakistani political parties also opened branches in Bradford, as did the movement for the liberation of Kashmir. Indeed, a majority of Bradford Muslim councillors were from the Azad Kashmir region, and Kashmiri political interests surfaced in the form of official invitations to pro-Kashmiri groups in Pakistan to visit Bradford.

Barelvi Mosques and Deobandi Schools

Let's stay in Bradford to examine the two quite distinct types of networks that have shaped Barelvi and Deobandi worlds in Britain. The relative ethnic homogeneity of the Barelvis has facilitated coordination among the many mosques that follow that orientation. The critical force for unifying these institutions came from the work of one sheikh, Pir Maroof Hussain Shah. Pir Maroof created an association for the preaching of Islam, which a majority of the Barelvi mosques and religious schools joined.[22] He also created seminaries in Pakistan to train their imams, extended loans to mosques, and founded the Barelvi World Islamic Mission in Bradford. The conical structure of a Sufi movement, with the sheikh at the top, facilitates this coordination by giving him religious legitimacy. Although Pir Maroof set up a college in Bradford, it does not appear to have produced teachers.

Across Britain, Barelvi Sufi mosques are often the most visible, probably because of the greater ease of amassing the resources needed to build large structures. As I noted earlier, visitors to Leicester are most likely to see the Sufi mosque near the train station. In Birmingham, the two mosques with the highest profiles and greatest physical visibility are the Sufi Ghamkol Sharif Mosque and the unaffiliated Birmingham Central Mosque.[23] Both attract worshippers from diverse ethnic origins. These two mosques are, along with the Bradford Barelvi mosque, the three largest mosques in Britain. Indeed, of the ten largest mosques in Britain, measured in terms of dedicated prayer space, six are Barelvi and only one is Deobandi. The visibility of the large-scale Barelvi mosques gives the impression that most British Muslims are Sufi in orientation.

But if we simply counted mosques, the winners would be the Deobandi and related Tablighi Jamaʿat orientations. One widely used source estimates that of the 1,667 active mosques in Britain in mid-2013, 45 percent were Deobandi, 25 percent Barelvi, 6 percent Salafi, and much smaller percentages were affiliated to other groups. Crosscutting these differences are ethnic identities of mosque administrative boards: in numbers, Pakistanis are in charge of 360 mosques, Bangladeshis of 226, and Gujarati Indians of 94; other ethnic groups show up as governing much smaller numbers of mosques.

If Barelvis have a smaller number of large mosques, structured by their places in a particular spiritual hierarchy, Deobandis have a network of many more mosques and schools, united by what their leaders see as shared pedagogies and theologies. Both the Barelvi and the Deobandi contours are transnational; both derive energy by their sense of opposition, and this sense varies in importance from place to place.

Coordination among Deobandi schools and mosques in the Bradford area comes from their ties to the two oldest schools at Bury (fifty miles west of Bradford) and at Dewsbury (ten miles south). Bury boasts the Dar al-ʿUlum school established by Yusuf Motala in 1973, which was mentioned earlier. The Bury seminary is the largest in the UK and, either directly or through its affiliated schools, dominates the world of British Deobandi seminary training. Bradford's Deobandi mosques regularly send people to study at Bury. They also send students to the school at Dewsbury, founded in 1989; this school also serves as the center for European activities of the Tablighi Jamaʿat.[24]

By 2003 there were about twenty-five Islamic seminaries that had registered with the government, required because they taught pupils under the age of sixteen. (Many more schools and mosques provide Islamic education only to older students and so do not need to register.) Sixteen of the schools were Deobandi and five were Barelvi. The six largest schools, all Deobandi, were in the North at Bury, Dewsbury, Bradford, Blackburn, and Lancaster, or in the Midlands, at Kidderminster. They turn out the vast majority of scholars ready to take posts as imams or as teachers in Islamic schools. Until recently, their seminary training mainly took place in relatively isolated worlds, where interaction with the broader populations was not encouraged, but since the 1990s, some efforts have been made to link a few seminaries to British universities to allow students to sit for A-level exams and then to obtain advanced degrees, and to encourage a few graduates to continue studies overseas or to take up work as chaplains.[25]

What sort of boundaries do the seminaries create? If we look at their graduates, we see both those committed to dialogue, such as Ibrahim Mogra, and those who emphasize the boundaries between Muslims and others. For example, the approach of Deobandi graduate Sheikh Riyadh ul-Haq, who has officiated at prayer services at several mosques, has been described as containing an "almost Manichean" view of Muslim/non-Muslim relations.[26] Some of these graduates go on to teach at Muslim primary or secondary schools, whether private seminaries or state-aided schools. For example, the well-known seminary Ebrahim College in London offers A-levels at their sixth form in economics and law. It is headed by a Dewsbury graduate who continued his Islamic studies in Bangladesh and received a master's degree in Islamic studies from the University of London.

To this point, we have traced the creation of religious boundaries and networks that draw on pathways stretching back to South Asia and that were facilitated by chain migration and the renewal of kin ties through close marriages. We now turn to East London and reverse the focus, to explore the social ecology of one mosque in terms of its niche, its competition, and how it has shaped the space around it.

An East London Religious Ecology

We note right off the contrast in social ecology between the two largest Muslim populations in Britain. If Pakistanis live in many distinct cities and neighborhoods, and form linkages across them through schools and mosques, Bangladeshis are concentrated in one place, the Tower Hamlets borough of East London. Statistically, Bangladeshis are also more segregated than are Pakistanis—and Indians less segregated than either. About one-third of Bangladeshis live in areas where they form at least half the population. Within Tower Hamlets, Spitalfields has the highest concentration of Bangladeshis, to the point where the sermons at the local Brick Lane Mosque are given in Sylheti Bengali.[27] Socioeconomically, Bangladeshis in Tower Hamlets include a poor working-class population, and also a smaller elite of younger men and women who benefit from the proximity of the City and the broader commercial potential of London.[28]

Some British Bangladeshis have belonged to UK-based branches of Bangladeshi political parties, which serve as local patrons, easing practical issues for Bangladeshis traveling between the two countries. Their numbers are continually replenished with new arrivals in Britain from the homeland. Even by the early 2000s, because many of the party activists had recently migrated to Britain after marrying a British resident, the intensity of the political dimension of the circulatory social imaginary had not diminished.[29]

Among political parties, the secularist Awami League has benefited from its history of spearheading the fight against racism in Tower Hamlets; some of these activists from the 1970s' struggles later entered the Labour Party and became community leaders. Working with borough associations and government-funded agencies, they sponsored an array of secular Bangladeshi cultural events and revived the market areas of Spitalfields and Brick Lane. Many of them had also participated in the struggles for Bangladesh's independence, and they were part of the move to create a monument to the martyrs of the 1952 Language movement in Dhaka, the Shaheed Minar (martyrs' tower). In 1995 one such monument was built in the northern city of Oldham, and in 1999 a second was built in Altab Ali Park, near the East London Mosque.

The Awami League's importance in Tower Hamlets has placed it in contest with the East London Mosque, which presents Islamic alternatives to the secular league. This competition has shaped the mosque's strategy of institution building.

Political Activism and the East London Mosque

I focus on this mosque because of its particularly strong social and religious role for East London Muslims. At the turn of the twentieth century, many men from the British East Indies (especially Sylhet) had taken up dwellings in East London, and asked for prayer spaces. In 1910, Syed Ameer Ali (d. 1928) established the London Mosque Fund to minister to their religious needs. Syed Ameer was a noted Islamic jurist from Oudh, who in the 1870s had joined London's Inner Temple and in 1909 had become the first South Asian to be named to the Privy Council (the second joined only in 2009!). He also promoted the anti-British Khilafat movement.

The fund was not a structure but a way to make worship possible by renting halls in East London. Eventually the fund purchased three houses, which in 1941 were inaugurated as the East London Mosque and Islamic Cultural Centre. It was not until 1985, however, that a "purpose-built" mosque was finished, with aid from the Saudi king. Prince Charles led a subsequent campaign to build the London Muslim Centre next door, which opened in 2004; the Maryam Centre, for school facilities and women's prayer, opened in 2013.[30]

The East London Mosque (ELM) has been a center for shifting configurations of religious and political activism. In the 1960s Pakistani followers of the Jamaat-e-Islami met there to discuss the ideas of the movement's founder, Abul Aʿla Maududi (1903–79). Maududi had founded JI in 1942 as a movement to promote Islam in India and then Pakistan (which at the time included today's Bangladesh).[31] In 1962 JI leaders created the UK Islamic Mission (UKIM) at the ELM, and in 1973 two followers of Maududi, Khurshid Ahmad and Khurram Murad, created the Islamic Foundation to publish and teach Maududi's ideas. Since then the foundation, now located in Markfield near Leicester, has become a major publishing house of Islamic thinkers and gives courses, in particular, on Islamic economics, to an international group of students.

In 1984, UKIM in its turn created a youth wing, the Young Muslims UK (YMUK), which ran camps and sports events and taught Islamic fundamentals. (As YMUK leaders grew up, they founded the Islamic Society of Britain in 1990.) The YMUK offered an attractive mix of English-language religion and politics, plus fun, to young Muslims chafing at the Urdu-language lectures of the uncles and aunties. Many of those young Muslims later became adult activists.

As young Muslims have grown up in Britain, they have often tried out a number of different religious orientations and social organizations.[32] I wanted to find out more about how an individual had moved through JI organizations, so I arranged to meet Tahmina Saleem, formerly a YMUK activist and now a leader of the gender-oriented Islamic organization Inspire. On May 14, 2013, we sat in a Debenham's department store in Luton, just a thirty-minute train ride from London. Luton was a production center for the Vauxhall automobile industry, the birthplace of the mall (it says), and in 2009 it also spawned the anti-immigrant English Defence League (EDL). With a 20 percent immigrant population, mostly Pakistani (because of the goodly supply of factory jobs), the EDL had plenty of local targets.

Tahmina had been brought up in the north of England, in Huddlesfield, located halfway between Manchester and Leeds. Her family lived in an ethnically mixed area, and for a time she attended Catholic school, an experience that led her to doubt her family's Islamic faith, until a Catholic friend gave her an English Qur'an and she decided that she did indeed believe what was in it. She began university at Birmingham in 1989, and that was when she first saw women wearing tighter head scarves than those she was used to; she thought they looked odd. At that time she and her friends were "shopping" for the right Muslim group—they even tried the separatist Hizb ut-Tahrir—and soon joined the YMUK. When she went back home, she was wearing a *hijab* in dull colors and the flowing covering called the *jilbāb*, and her mum could not understand why she would dress in that way when she went out. For Tahmina, it was about submitting to God, not about "showing my identity."

At Birmingham, she and her friends became active in the university's Islamic student society (ISOC). They distributed leaflets and engaged in outreach (*dawa*). "We gave our lives to this": they would work feverishly to find housing for others coming for weekend camps, sometimes two to three thousand young people at a time. From thinking of themselves as British Pakistanis, they now saw themselves as members of the global *umma*, the Islamic community. These were years when many young British Muslims were making the same readjustment in their sense of who they were. The year 1989 was pivotal, signaled most visibly in Britain by the burning in Bradford of Salmon Rushdie's *Satanic Verses* and the "death sentence" proclaimed against Rushdie by the Ayatollah Khomeini. It was also the year when anti-Islamic sentiment began to grow in much of Europe, as the fall of the Berlin Wall symbolized the end of one polarization and opened up the field for a new one.

Reflecting on their choice of the YMUK, Tahmina said, "What I adopted then probably was the most progressive alternative at that time." YMUK leaders had come from Pakistan, "and they wanted us to be involved in politics in Pakistan, and there were the Islamic Foundation [Markfield] people, and there were Ikhwanis [Muslim Brotherhood] who wanted us also to pay attention to politics in Egypt and to read their founder [Hasan al-Banna]. The leaders' ideas were jarringly different from ours, because we did not care about Pakistani politics."

The élan of the movement soon began to fade for Tahmina and her friends. The Ikhwan branch left the YMUK, taking a number of activists with it. Tahmina continued to be inspired by Maududi, "although when I read what he had to say about women, I did not think very highly of it. The YM segregated us; there were separate sisters' and brothers' organizations, and at the *sura* [council] there were women representing the sisters but they could not vote. It is still segregated in that way." As they grew up, they shifted into the adult grouping, the Islamic Society of Britain (ISB), but some of them began to leave the organization. "For me the change came in 2005, when I was spokesperson for the ISB at the time of 7/7 [2005, the London bombings]. Muslim leaders did nothing to stop the denial by Muslims that these events were the work of Muslims. When we gave grassroots seminars, the first hands that went up were from people who said: 'yes but we know who really carried out the bombings' and for them it was the Jews."

Finally, in 2009 several of them started the organization Inspire in order to promote more progressive ideas of Islam. Tahmina finds that they are losing the battle with the Salafis, as evidenced by more *niqabs* and more *halal* (unregistered) marriages, but they continue to pressure leaders to adopt progressive views. "We act as a catalyst, to force others to talk about these subjects. We got the Muslim Council of Britain to designate 20 percent of their leadership positions for women." Their past dissatisfaction notwithstanding, they find support in the current leadership of the JI.

The importance of the JI may lie primarily in the past, in its activism. The Islamic Foundation in Markfield now publishes a wider range of thinkers than before, most popular among them being Tariq Ramadan. The East London Mosque remains the JI center, but even there the influence of the movement, and of Maududi, have been diluted by other teachings. For example, the Bangladeshi *khatib* and primary imam of the mosque, Abdul Qayum, spent time with JI but thereafter went to the University of Medina where he learned Salafi approaches, and today he also draws on *fiqh al-wāqiʿ*, a jurisprudence of reality, invoking in discussions with me the idea, associated with Yusuf al-Qaradawi, that under situations of emergency (*darurah*), which can include the unavailability of Islamic institutions, you have to adapt to English conditions.[33]

A Polyvalent Mosque

From the mid-1980s on, the nature of the ELM's activities and involvement have significantly changed. The ELM is an interesting case of adapting to an English social and political niche while maintaining transnational ties. The ecological particularity of the ELM, its signal status in Tower Hamlets, and its active roles in domestic and transcontinental politics make it both highly visible and highly suspect, and it is the object of frequent journalistic attacks for its political organizing.

Because the mosque has always been a focus for East London Bangladeshi activities, it has had multiple affiliations. Broadly speaking, it has been the pole for Islam-based community organizing, which in the 1980s meant opposing the groups organized by Bangladesh's Awami League. To compete with the league and to appeal to Bangladeshis, in 1978 the Pakistan-focused UKIM created a parallel Bangladeshi organization, the Dawat ul Islam, with a youth wing, the Young Muslim Organisation (YMO), both located at the ELM. Their leaders were largely rural people from Sylhet. A distinct organization, the Islamic Forum Europe (IFE), attracted more educated Bangladeshis and has partnered with the YMO (after the 1988 departure of the Dawat ul Islam from the mosque). The IFE cultivated ties to Tariq Ramadan, Yusuf al-Qaradawi, and others. Although small, the IFE took control of the ELM, and in 2006, one of its former presidents, Dr. Abdul Bari, became general secretary of the Muslim Council of Britain.

Like most large mosques, the ELM offers a range of classes for all ages, distributes zakat, and, of course, holds prayer services. About one thousand children study each week in evening classes, and there are separate boys' and girls' day schools. But it goes beyond most other mosques in the range of social services centered there. Muslim Aid is housed at the center. The Tower Hamlets Council funds one full-time staff worker to coordinate health services with clinics and hospitals. Clinics set up in the mosque offer diabetes screening, blood pressure readings, and vaccinations. The Made in Europe business rents space in the center; in 2013 they were engaged in campaigns to encourage use of fair-trade products and to replace bottled water with tap water. A separate Somali center features a program for drug users; their director has a diploma from the University of Medina. A school is adapting sign language for the 350–400 men and women who are deaf and come to pray. A pro bono law service, staffed mainly by non-Muslims, works out of the center, handling immigration and family law cases. The mosque attracts other Islamic businesses: numerous restaurants in the area follow the ELM's lead in featuring the relatively stringent Halal Monitoring Committee's food inspection service (preferred because they do not allow stunning). A funeral service is located next door and works with the mosque. The Islamic Bank of Britain lies across the street.

The twinned trajectories of religion and social services may seem contradictory to some British commentators, but they make sense from an Islam-based service-oriented perspective (one not unlike that adopted by the Muslim Brotherhood). In 2013, Dilowar Hussein Khan, the director of the mosque, gave me a tour of the mosque and center. He stressed the Islamic character of the ELM's broad outreach: "The Prophet's mosque found employment for people, resolved disputes, did not just serve as a place for religious rituals. We have the community living around us and attend to a wide range of their needs. Our largest prayer attendance is at *zuhur* [midday], with around fifteen hundred people, because so many work right here, Bangladeshis and Somalis." Dilowar's remark is pertinent. In most mosques, the midday prayer attracts small numbers because men are working away from the mosque.[34] Here, they are likely to work in the neighborhood.

We can understand these mosque activists' enthusiasm for social projects as a way to maintain the mosque's presence in a local landscape once occupied by secular Awami activists. The appeal of the YMO to local Bangladeshis is in part as a lifeline held out to those young men and women suffering from unemployment and drug abuse.[35] The mosque's energies in tackling domestic abuse and the opening of the new Maryam Centre bolster its appeal to women.

The IFE and the YMO also link the ELM to local politics and at the same time to global Islamic networks. The IFE aided George Galloway and his Respect Party for elections and in his opposition to the Iraq invasion, and also helped politician Lutfur Rahman in his campaign to lead the Tower Hamlets Council and to become the first directly elected mayor of Tower Hamlets in 2010. (In 2014 he was reelected mayor, but in 2015 the election was declared void and Rahman was removed from office.) These links between religion and politics make the ELM the object of frequent attacks in the press. "The *Telegraph* columnist is in contact with a segment of our community, secularist Muslims who are allied to the governing party in Bangladesh, and who are unhappy that we succeed at anything," claimed Dilowar Khan. Indeed, over the span of Rahman's tenure, the *Telegraph* and other media have charged that he was running the council as a Bangladeshi Islamic operation, in league with the radical Islamists of the IFE.[36]

Burial

To be a truly "full-service" mosque in a British urban context means attending to death as well as to life. Muslims living in Tower Hamlets receive a council subsidy of 225 pounds per body because the borough does not yet have any Muslim burial sites. This extraordinary feature of local political life allows the center to partner with a cemetery farther east, in Hainault (Ilford), where many Muslims now bury relatives. Dilowar Khan explained: "Because burial has to happen quickly, they call the mosque or the adjoining burial services quickly. Our tenant Taslim Ali, now deceased, ran the services, but it is a family business. This is the oldest Muslim funeral service in London, dating from the early 1960s. Taslim Ali's family gets the body and prepares it and takes it to the cemetery. We have about two *jenazahs* [services] here in the mosque each day. We have cradle-to-grave services: we might have an *aqidah* [birth ritual] in one room, children's education elsewhere, prayers, organizations meeting, and a jenazah all at one moment!"

In May 2013, I took the train to Hainault and made the long walk to the Gardens of Peace Cemetery. I spoke with director Mehboob Patel in the office.[37] "Up to recently," he said, "it was difficult for Muslims to find places to bury their dead in an Islamic way. Councils insisted on burying in caskets, and, even today, some councils that allow Muslim areas in graveyards do not allow them to align the graves to face Mecca. Some people sent bodies home, but it is a long ways to India or Pakistan, and sometimes there would be no one there to pick up the body."

In 2003, the land came up for sale, and Patel and others, all Indian Gujaratis who came by way of East Africa, like Ibrahim Mogra in Leicester, won the bid. It was zoned for forestry or burial, and it was part of the Green Belt, so they could use it for a cemetery. The local council was not happy, and neighbors were worried about all the Muslims next to them, "but there has been no noise and now everything is fine. But it was the Home Office and not the council that gave us permission to bury in shrouds, not caskets. They were Labour, and they wanted us to help preserve the Green Belt."

The cemetery has adopted a strategy of shaping funerals in ways that will lead to the fewest religious objections. They only allow small granite markers on the simple hills that mark the burial place. "In Saudi Arabia, if you go to the tomb of the Prophet's daughter, you see only this simple marker; we brought this practice here." Signs say there is no reason to leave flowers and that anything left on the grave will be gathered up and kept by the cemetery. "Women are not allowed at the burial itself, because this is [found] in Islam, and people from South Asia know this, and few [women] come to the service. They pray first, at the East London Mosque or at another mosque, and then they come here. They prepare the body first, perhaps at the services at the East London Mosque. We can do it if there is an emergency. People can pray here if they want but usually the larger prayers are at the mosque and then a smaller number of people come here. Look, I have a funeral this afternoon and there are only ten cars." They charge £2,100 to bury an adult, £600 for a young child, and £100 for a stillborn infant.

The East London Mosque has adapted to a number of locally specific conditions in Tower Hamlets: competition with the Awami League, the opportunities furnished by the density of Bangladeshi residents, and the possibilities in Britain of forming networks with a wide array of social services and political structures. It is precisely this polyvalence, including mixing of the religious, economic, social, and political domains, that has both permitted its institutional rise and attracted attacks. Its context is both highly local and highly transnational.

Conclusions: Profiles of British Islamic Institutions

So far I have emphasized ways in which migration and settlement have shaped local-level Islamic institutions in Britain. State policy also shapes Islamic institutions. To explain the transition from ethnic-based to Islam-based local services, we have to consider changes in UK immigration policies that led to more family-based immigration and hence more demand for religious and school services, and the withdrawal of state aid for local associations, which indirectly favored the mosques because they had never depended on state aid. Britain's willingness to fund faith schools favored the development of Islamic schools (to be discussed in chapter 12).

The several streams of Islam that were transplanted to Britain defined their positions vis-à-vis each other partly with reference to shariʿa. As British Islamic institutions were under construction, they sought to preserve their distinctiveness by maintaining strong links to an Asian seminary or movement. The concentrated nature of settlement, reproduction of transcontinental ties, and strong boundaries between distinct religious orientations together facilitated the reproduction of older Islamic social forms from South Asia—seminary curricula, authority structures, and shariʿa practices—even as schools, councils, and other associations adapted in form and function to their British environment.

There are also Britain-wide Islamic institutions, of course, including the Muslim Council of Britain (MCB), the Muslim Parliament, and the Sufi Muslim Council. Their stories have been told elsewhere. The MCB, in particular, has fallen in and out of favor with successive British governments, caught as they are between a desire to keep close to their base and the government's expectation that they "manage" Muslim reactions to British foreign and domestic policies. The result is instability, as it is not possible to satisfy both constituencies at once. This instability has plagued corresponding efforts elsewhere in Europe. As a result, the major dynamic of French, German, Italian, and British Islam continues to be that of local efforts to teach, organize prayer, run for office, or secure halal food, on the one hand, and movement along transnational webs of migration, marriage, and authoritative Islamic knowledge, on the other.[38] British Islam does organize nationally, but as networks of local organizations: Deobandi schools, Barelvi mosques, or, as we shall discover in chapter 4, shariʿa councils.

PART 2

PRACTICES

CHAPTER 4

Background to the Shariʿa Councils

IN 1982, A COLLECTION OF ISLAMIC SCHOLARS MET IN BIRMINGHAM TO CREATE a new Britain-wide shariʿa council. The scholars had hoped to deal with a wide range of religious issues, from banking and mortgages to standards for halal food. But few of these issues were brought to their doors. As one of the founding scholars, Suhaib Hasan, said later, "We intended that the council provide decisions for the Muslim community on any and all matters, but pretty soon it became clear to us that we were spending all our time giving women divorces. This was not what we set out to do, but there was a vacuum in the community and we filled it."

Why Is Women's Divorce the Issue?

Marriage is central to an Islamic religious life, but some marriages do not work out. In Islam, marriage (*nikah*) is a contract, requiring both parties' consent, whose primary effect is to render legitimate sexual relations between a man and a woman. Most Muslims take very seriously the idea that proper religious marriage is required to avoid sin. When a marriage has broken down, ways must be sought to allow the woman and the man to remarry.

In most majority-Muslim countries, from Egypt to Iran to Indonesia, religious acts of marrying and divorcing are intertwined in various ways with civil procedures. Most often, a marriage or a divorce that follows Islamic requirements must also be registered or involve a court for it to be recognized by the state. Conversely, Islamic scholars in those countries attest that when a state-appointed judge declares that a divorce has taken place, the couple has been freed to remarry in the eyes of God as well as according to civil law.

If Islamic marriage has certain specific features—in particular, its contractual framing—marriage and divorce are central topics of debate and reform across most, if not all, religious traditions. Anthropologists and historians show that across most societies, marriage, property, and lineage form highly structured systems that are profoundly disrupted by divorce or death. In Western Europe, the Church developed regulations of marriage in a way that channeled property into church coffers while prohibiting divorce.[1] Indeed, even if one can say that "there has never been a society where divorce, or its functional equivalent, did not exist," legally and religiously recognized divorce is a very recent phenomenon in Western Europe. Divorce rights also index the relative capacities of women and men, and since the 1960s, Europe and North America have witnessed both a reframing of marriage and divorce in contractual terms and an enhancement of women's legal and economic autonomy during and after marriage. In some respects, (post-) Christian regimes of marriage and divorce have become closer to Islamic ones.[2]

For Islam, the Qur'an and the hadith make clear three things concerning divorce. First, divorce should be avoided and mediation sought to help a marriage to continue. Second, if a marriage cannot continue, then it should be ended. Third, men have the right to divorce their wives. They should "retain them honorably or set them free honorably" (Q. 2:231).[3] The ambiguity concerns precisely how a *woman* can initiate a divorce. And this ambiguity has given rise to loud debates and contested legislation throughout the Islamic world—and has provided most of the work of shariʿa councils.

Talaq and *Faskh*

Classical scholars in the Sunni tradition agreed on certain main features of divorce. Men had a prerogative to divorce their wives within certain limits. A man could pronounce a talaq, or unilateral divorce, and normally the divorce would become final at the close of the *ʿidda* (the mandatory waiting period, normally three menstrual cycles). He could take her back anytime during that period. After the end of the ʿidda, the couple was divorced, but they could conduct a new nikah and reunite. The husband could divorce (and perhaps reunite) a second time as well, but after the third talaq, the divorce was final. The only way to reunite after that point would be if the wife married a third person and that new marriage was consummated and then terminated by divorce or death. Scholars disagreed across the legal schools on the "felicity conditions" for this performative act. What if the husband said the three talaqs all at once? What if he was so angry he had lost his mind? What if he did not intend a divorce but said the words?

The wife's only way to initiate a talaq was if the husband had delegated it to her. For example, at the time of marriage or later on, he might have given the power to divorce to his wife, to be used if and only if he were to take a second wife. He could take an oath to the effect that, were he to remarry, this talaq would automatically occur. Later on this "delegated talaq" (*talāq tafwīz*) was to appear on some marriage contracts, whereby the husband made this conditional form of divorce a formal part of the marriage agreement.

A wife could also approach a judge and ask that an annulment (*tafrīq* or *faskh*) be pronounced. The conditions for annulment were quite narrow in classical writings. Impotence was clearly a reason, because the purpose of marriage was to produce a lineage. Insanity and some other physical defects were accepted by some, as was the husband's disappearance, on which the Maliki legal school was the most lenient, requiring an absence of only four years. A woman so divorced had the same rights as a wife divorced by talaq, including the full payment of her *mahr*, the "marriage gift" from the husband to the wife (often not paid in full at the time of marriage), and maintenance during the period of ʿidda.

Our earliest solid evidence for judicial practice comes from records of the Ottoman Empire from the sixteenth century onward. Ottoman judges, who followed Hanafi legal traditions, recognized abuse, lack of support, and desertion as grounds for dissolving the marriage. They did so in part by recognizing doctrine from other legal schools when doing so would permit the end of a disastrous marriage, and, in part, by "bundling" abuse with blasphemy—a true Muslim would not beat his wife, therefore a man who did so was not a Muslim, they said.

The *Khula*

So far we have discussed the husband's pronouncement of divorce, the talaq, and an annulment (tafrīq or faskh). A great deal of ambiguity surrounds the third kind of divorce, the khula (*khulʿ*). Everyone agrees that the main idea of khula is that a woman who wishes to have a divorce propose to her husband that he divorce her in exchange for a payment of some amount. But how much should be paid? Is the divorce the same as a talaq (because pronounced by the husband) or is it a distinctive form with distinct ramifications? Must a third party, such as a judge, recognize or pronounce the khula for it to be effective?

The scriptural basis for this practice does not clarify matters. There are several relevant Qurʾanic verses ("no fault in them for her to redeem herself," Q. 2:229), and, most important, a hadith in which a wife approached the Prophet and said that, although she found no fault with her husband, she feared she might stray beyond the bounds of marriage were she to stay with him. The Prophet said she should return to him the garden he had given her, and then told the husband to divorce her.[4] In versions that shariʿa council scholars have related to me, the Prophet simply told her she was released from her marriage vows.

But questions remain. In the hadith in question, what was the role of the Prophet? Did he dissolve the marriage or merely facilitate an act performed by the husband, a talaq? Does the hadith imply that whatever had been given to the wife was the appropriate amount for her to give the husband to obtain his divorce? Would this include any gifts or be limited to the mahr? Or is the amount entirely a matter of negotiation between the husband and the wife?

Because most of those seeking a divorce at a British shariʿa council come from regions traditionally following the Hanafi legal school, we are particularly interested in Hanafi positions on these questions. Among classical Hanafi scholars, some considered that unlimited bargaining over the khula divorce was allowed, even though it would be morally reprehensible for the husband to ask for more than the amount he had given his wife as mahr. Together with scholars from other legal schools, they said that if both the husband and the wife wished to end the marriage, the divorce was in a completely different category, that of *mubār'a*, or divorce by mutual agreement, with different financial implications. (Hanafis differed among themselves as to precisely what those implications were: whether all obligations then dropped out or if the husband would still owe unpaid mahr.) But if the husband had pushed his wife to ask for a divorce, for example, by ill-treating her, then it was a talaq, not a khula, and he then clearly owed his wife any unpaid mahr plus maintenance.

There remained the question of whether a "proper" khula, with no pressure from the husband and at the sole initiative of the wife, was a kind of talaq (because the husband performs the speech act) or a kind of faskh or annulment (if a third party, such as a judge or scholar, were involved). If the latter, then it would be logical to argue that a judge or court should pronounce the divorce. But most jurists agreed that the husband's consent was required for a khula to take effect, thus limiting the role of a judge to ensuring that the procedures had been followed, for example, that a husband was not trying to turn a talaq into a khula in order to avoid his financial obligations. These seemingly endless debates are consequential in that financial consequences follow from a category decision. In a talaq or faskh, the husband must pay any remaining mahr; in a khula, the wife either gets no mahr or must repay mahr she has already received.

From eighteenth-century Ottoman court records, we know that khula had become prevalent throughout Ottoman lands, and that it exhibited what have since become standard features. If reasons for ending the marriage are given in an Ottoman court, they are usually of the "our marriage is over" sort. The wife usually forgives all debts and payments due her by her husband and returns any mahr already paid. The appearance in court is to register the divorce; the husband has performed it. His consent is, therefore, presumed to be part of the khula process. Practices at this time indicate that khula was not a way for a woman to obtain a divorce against her husband's wishes.

Divorce Reform

During the nineteenth and early twentieth-century discussions of Islamic reform, scholars tended to put forth faskh rather than khula as the appropriate mechanism for expanding women's autonomy. Following this logic, judges did not need the husband's consent to dissolve a marriage. Reformers recognized that judges already had been dissolving marriages in cases of lack of support or abuse; some scholars proposed that the mere incompatibility of the couple should also be taken as sufficient grounds for faskh. A number of newly independent states also passed laws requiring that talaq be approved by a judge, and in some cases allowed judges to grant damages to the wife if abuse was found.

In South Asia, courts have recognized the validity of marriage contracts in which the husband delegated to his wife the right to perform a talaq under certain conditions. These conditions varied, but sometimes included incompatibility and his failure to treat her kindly. The Ayatollah Khomeini proposed the use of such contracts in Iran in order to give the wife broader powers. In modern Indonesia, marriage contracts include a place for the couple to write down such conditions. In all these places, however, families are usually reluctant to countenance marriage breakdown at the moment when they are performing the marriage.

More productive has been the tendency to write new law codes that empower a state judge to dissolve the marriage through faskh if the husband has committed one of a specified number of actions. The actions that warrant dissolution typically include failure to provide material support or causing his wife harm (*dharar*). These codes have drawn from several of the Sunni legal schools. In particular, they have taken from the Maliki school the broad sense of what constitutes harm, and from the Hanafi school the preference for trying to mediate or arbitrate the dispute. But their effectiveness depends on the willingness of judges to enforce them, which varies considerably across judges and across countries.

In the 1917 Ottoman Law of Family Rights, if a wife approached the court to request a divorce, the judge would appoint an arbitrator from each side to investigate and report. If the judge found fault to lie with the husband, then the marriage would be dissolved (tafrīq) and outstanding mahr paid. If he found the wife to be at fault, then the action would be deemed to be a khula, and she would forgo the mahr. Similar laws were passed in Egypt and Tunisia. Today in Indonesia, if the wife requests a divorce, she may be retroactively awarded child support and maintenance. Indonesian judges have discretion to set payments based on their evaluation of the moral quality of the husband's and wife's behavior. (The question of mahr does not enter directly into Indonesian judgments because it is usually a small amount that is paid at the time of the marriage.) In Pakistan, the Supreme Court ruled in *Khurshid Bibi v. Muhammad Amin* (1967) that judges may overrule the husband's objections to a divorce.

These rulings and practices are a change from the earlier period. From the standpoint of classical scholarship, khula is a process that leads to a talaq. The husband not only must agree, he performs the divorce speech act. The wife must pay him something to induce his action. No grounds are necessary, because a husband, in this classical view, does not need to justify a talaq pronouncement. Faskh or tafrīq, however, is a dissolution carried out by a judge on grounds that were once quite narrow, and only over time, and in some places, have broadened.

When modern states grant to judges the right to grant a khula or a faskh, they leave the agency of the husband unclear. If under khula rules the husband performs the divorce that begins with the wife's request, then it is difficult to see where the court's power lies, except for verifying that it really is a matter of khula and not a talaq. Such were the objections to the 2000 law in Egypt that permitted awarding of khula without the husband's consent.

But if the judicial determination is one of faskh or annulment, a finding that the marriage never properly took place, then how can the husband's actions after the marriage be grounds for divorce? We saw above that early jurists suggested that certain actions might be taken as evidence for apostasy and thus annulment, because being a Muslim is required for there to be a valid marriage. I have heard British Islamic scholars suggest other ways of bridging this logical gap: for example, that because marriage is a contract, and a contract presumes certain conditions (honesty, among others), if the husband violates one of these implicit conditions, the marriage automatically ceases to hold, and a shariʿa council merely notes that fact. In Lebanon, in the Sunni courts a wife brings actions for divorce (tafrīq) usually on grounds of discord (*nizāʾ wa-shiqāq*), and for some judges, the suit itself is clear evidence of discord, particularly if the husband's response does not refute the claim that discord exists. (In the Lebanese Shiite [Jaʿfari] courts, by contrast, a judicial divorce is very difficult to obtain, and so inducing the husband to grant a divorce is the major strategy.)[5]

The Colonial Background for Shariʿa Councils

Back to India. In the nineteenth century, British rulers decided to govern marriage affairs within each of the religious communities under their rule by the traditions and laws of those communities. As they extended legal recognition to more and more of them, they created a set of regulations for each that judges and administrators would apply. This process indeed resembled Britain's actions at home, as the government expanded the list of religious communities empowered to perform marriages. By the nineteenth century, Britain had accorded to Anglicans, Quakers, and Jews "at home" the right to regulate marriage in their own communities. Britain first recognized civil marriage in 1837 against this preexisting background of religious marriages. Religious marriage rights were extended to others from an Anglican starting point; the extension was motivated by a policy of promoting toleration.

An additional wrinkle to these British policies continues to reverberate across the subcontinent. Indian personal status laws were conceived not as merely positive law, the legal force of which would arise from their enactment, but as restatements of already existing practices. In theory these laws derived their authority and legitimacy from the "ancient traditions" that they were supposed to translate into a usable form. The laws were "digests" of material available elsewhere, not "codes" with the ex nihilo force of statutes. In today's India, this legal fiction—that law is a window into independently existing religious norms—permits judges to directly inspect the "ancient traditions" to evaluate what they say and how they might be reinterpreted. The 1985 Shah Bano case (*Mohd. Ahmed Khan v. Shah Bano Begum* [1985 SCR (3) 844]), where a Hindu chief justice looked into the Qurʾan to critique the existing Islamic code, is only the most famous instance.[6] With state judges presumed to master Islamic law—codified as Muslim Personal Law—religious scholars became superfluous.

The duality of the jurisprudential theory behind personal status laws—a legal form but a scriptural source—has, however, allowed and encouraged religious scholars to create their own alternative tribunals. A critical moment occurred in 1933, when the scholar Ashraf ʿAli Thanawi called for the creation of local councils of scholars to give women religious divorces—to stop them from apostatizing in a desperate attempt to dissolve their marriages. The Deobandi scholars united in calling for legislation to establish these tribunals, and many religious schools created such schools on their own. Much later, in 1973, Muhammad Tayyeb, the first president of the All India Muslim Personal Law Board (AIMPLB), called for separate state Islamic courts that would adjudicate cases regarding Islamic personal law, on grounds that current state judges did not have the requisite training to apply shariʿa. The board also proposed a model marriage contract that stipulated that couples would bring marital disputes to such a court.[7]

In parallel to these (unsuccessful) efforts to create state Islamic *courts*, religious scholars began to successfully create nonstate Islamic *councils*; such a council is generally known as a *dar ul-qaza*. The first such organized set of councils emerged in the state of Bihar in 1921. Muslims constituted about 10 percent of the Bihari population during this period, in contrast to other northern provinces where they formed a majority (Sind, Punjab, Bengal). Some Muslims in Bihar saw themselves as obligated to govern the affairs of the community by creating councils. A governing body, the Imarat-i Shariʿa, was established in 1921,[8] sponsored by the Jamiat Ulema-e-Hind (JUH) in Bihar, because there the influence of Muslim leader Maulana Abul Kalam Azad was strongest.[9] The leader of the Khilafat movement and an advocate of a united India, Azad proposed that each province in India select its own leader (the Amir-i Shariʿat) and council to protect Muslims from the majority Hindus. The Imarat created a system of dar ul-qazas, as well as a treasury and other administrative offices, and conducted campaigns to induce Muslims to give up liquor and remember their daily prayers. Intriguingly, for what would develop later in India and in Britain, the Imarat largely stayed clear of sectarian differences. Indeed, the Sufi centers in the province provided the initial Imarat leadership.

By one count, thirty-three of these shariʿa councils operate today in the three states of Bihar, West Bengal, and Orissa; twenty-eight of them are in Bihar. A smaller number operate elsewhere in the country, most of them under the aegis of the AIMPLB. They vary in how they approach the khula/faskh issue. A study of a dar ul-qaza in Patna found that most often women brought requests for dissolution of their marriages, or faskh, in which the judge may award maintenance or compel the husband to pay the mahr that he had promised but not yet paid. Much less frequently, they requested that the court oversee the khula process. Women who requested faskh were better educated and more aware of their legal rights. By contrast, a Mumbai dar ul-qaza (associated, as it happens, with the Deobandi schools) awards judgments of khula, but if it finds the wife was not at fault, she keeps the mahr.[10] But the dar ul-qazas have no enforcement powers, and judges are unable to compel husbands to comply with an award of mahr or maintenance. Only by taking a case to the civil court can a husband be forced to comply.

The institution of the dar ul-qaza in India was part of the background knowledge of scholars who later moved to England. These Muslims brought with them ideas and habits about personal status that had been developed under British rule of the Indies. They assumed that Muslims could and should work out matters of marriage and divorce among themselves, and that although ideally their judgments would be enforced by the state, their legitimacy did not depend on the state. In effect, by transposing their Asian experiences to Britain, the Islamic scholars who created shariʿa councils brought colonial ideas of personal status back home to their legal source.

The Islamic Shariʿa Council, London

This quick review of the history of women's divorce should make clear that there is no single set of rules, no "book of Islamic law" that can be pulled out in a court or other setting. There is a history of Islamic jurisprudence, in which differences remain across the several legal schools, and there are many ways to integrate or articulate those traditions with state courts.

This is the jurisprudential background for the creation of shariʿa councils in Britain. That initial 1982 meeting in Birmingham reflected some but not all of Britain's Islamic diversity. Deobandi and Ahl al-Hadith scholars were there, as were followers of Maududi's Jamaat-e-Islami and representatives of the UK Islamic Mission (UKIM), founded at the East London Mosque in 1962.

The Saudi-funded Muslim World League also attended, bringing the Salafi teachings that were already well known to South Asian scholars who had studied in Medina or Riyadh. The group left out the leaders of Sufi movements, as well as Shiites and Muslims from other countries. In short, they reproduced, rather than transcended, the fault lines of South Asian Islam as transposed to Britain. Internally, they were not theologically united but formed some strategic alliances. Doctrinally, the core combined the Hanafi scholars from the Deobandi tradition with scholars affiliated with the Ahl al-Hadith movements and who generally had a Salafi background. The few prominent scholars of other backgrounds played only a temporary role. Even the alliances represented at Birmingham were not all long-lasting, and some of the Salafis ended up attacking their doctrinal bedfellows in the Ahl al-Hadith movement as being insufficiently rigorous. These attacks remind outsiders of Freud's reference to the "narcissism of small differences."[11]

Those attending the meeting created the Islamic Shariʿa Council (ISC). They chose Syed Mutawalli ad-Darsh (1930–97) as its first chairman and Mahmud Ahmad Mirpuri (1946–88) as secretary. Syed ad-Darsh was an Egyptian trained at Al-Azhar, and in 1971 had been sent by that institution to London to serve as an imam at the London Central Mosque near Regent's Park. In 1980 he left the mosque to work in journalism, in particular, at the progressive Muslim magazine *Q-News*. He died in 1997.[12] Mahmud Mirpuri was the leader of the British branch of the Indian Ahl al-Hadith movement, based in Birmingham. He and the movement were dedicated to reforming those Sufi practices followed by a majority of Midlands Muslims that they saw as illegitimate. Of South Asian origin (as his name suggests), Mirpuri studied Salafi scholarship at the Islamic University of Medina.[13] He presided over the Green Lane Mosque.[14]

The framework and procedures of the shariʿa council were worked out by two scholars, Khalid Mahmood and Suhaib Hasan. Mahmood was educated at the Dar al-ʿUlum in Deoband, and founded the Islamic Academy of Manchester in 1974. In 1970 he received a doctorate in comparative religion at the University of Birmingham. Suhaib, about whom we will hear a great deal, grew up in Pakistan and studied at the Islamic University of Medina, where he was influenced by some of the key figures in Salafi Islamic thought, including ʿAbd al-ʿAziz ibn Baz (d. 1999), who was Grand Mufti, and Sheikh Muhammad ibn al-ʿUthaymin (d. 2000).

Within several years of the 1982 meeting, Mahmood was called to Pakistan to become a judge on the Shariʿat Appellate Bench, ad-Darsh became involved in journalism, and Mirpuri died, leaving Suhaib as the council's leader. In 1988 he officially moved the office to London, but from the very beginning, the council held their formal meetings in London because it was more central and because they tried to have a large number of scholars—the goal was seven to ten—when making decisions. They first met at the Muslim

FIGURE 2. Suhaib Hasan with Clients, 2010

World League–owned mosque on Goodge Street, where Suhaib sometimes gave sermons. Suhaib had started a mosque in 1984 on Frances Road in Leyton, eastern London, where he was the regular preacher (khatib). In 1997 they were able to build a new Leyton mosque and to open the council office in the old mosque premises.

If, as noted above, the council has ended up dealing primarily with women's divorces, at the beginning they also responded to requests for nonbinding legal opinions (fatwas), many of which arrived by e-mail. The first requests concerned matters of home mortgages (because Islamic banking was not yet developed), conflicts arising from schools about girls having to attend swimming and gym classes, and the matter of the standards to use for halal meat. "Many scholars said that any meat killed by ahl ul-kitab ["people of the book," referring to Jews and Christians] was acceptable," recounted Hasan. "Some of the Arab scholars agreed regarding Jews because they remained faithful to their kitab, but not regarding Christians because they had not done so. We thus needed a collective fatwa." On that issue, the ISC posted a fatwa allowing Muslims to eat meat slaughtered by Jews, because Jews retain a focus on God, but not when it is slaughtered by Christians, because Christian animal processing "is totally commercialised and has no regard for naming Allah at all."

Leyton, 2015

Today, the ISC offices are located in Leyton, an ethnically mixed town of single-family housing in the eastern area of London. The offices are in a converted house on a quiet street, and just across from a Sikh temple. Major construction work done in early 2010 created a functional setup with separate waiting areas and about six rooms for consultations, plus a sizable back office. The entryway leads to a waiting room with a receptionist behind a window, and, set off by a closed door, a narrow hallway. Three rooms line this hallway: a large interview room with a raised dais (Suhaib's idea, to give the proceedings more solemnity), then two workrooms, with three or four staff answering phones, looking for files, and giving advice to one another, and the chief clerk's office.

Stairs on the other side of the reception room lead down to the basement and up to the second and third floors. On the second floor the stairs lead to a hallway with two restrooms and a small kitchen at the end. Turning to the left at the top of the stairs leads up a few more steps to two interview rooms, where often one or more junior scholars field questions and decide whether a client should be sent on to speak with a senior scholar. (The office calling system routes callers to whoever is free among the staff; they then field the question or transfer it to the clerk or a junior scholar.) The stairs bend around to the left again and send you to the attic, a quiet, pleasant room with windows on two sides and a view across the east end to the Gherkin in the City. In 2010, when I was working through the council's archives in the attic, I could easily follow the construction progress of the Olympic Park facilities not far away.

Once a month, usually on the last Wednesday, the senior scholars and the chief clerk meet for formal deliberations in a building adjoining the London Central Mosque, located on the west side of Regent's Park. Other scholars join them for these sessions, mainly corresponding scholars who live elsewhere in England, hear clients in their home cities, and travel to London to participate at these sessions. They are reimbursed for their expenses. Other scholars may also participate in these sessions; every now and then scholars appear from other countries and are invited to give their opinions.

The Scholars

Three senior scholars work regularly at the Leyton office: Suhaib Hasan, the secretary of the council; Abu Sayeed, its president; and Haitham al-Haddad. Suhaib has served as secretary and functional leader of the council since the beginning.[15] He was born in India, near Delhi, but when he was seven, the family had to move to Pakistan as part of the partition; he remembers the violence. They later moved to Nairobi. His father, Abdul-Ghaffar Hasan, was an important scholar and teacher who taught in India and then Pakistan, and was recruited to teach in Medina as a replacement for the well-known hadith scholar Muhammad Nasiruddin al-Albani. Suhaib studied at the Islamic University of Medina, starting two years before his father's arrival. After his graduation, the Saudi government sent him to Kenya to start a school. In 1976 he traveled to Britain.[16] He achieved a doctorate from the University of Birmingham in hadith studies, with a thesis on the use of hadith regarding the imam Mahdi.[17] He considers himself to be of the Ahl al-Hadith school, and to be Salafi.

Suhaib founded and has been chairman of the Masjid Tawhid in Leyton, within easy walking distance of the ISC offices. Until 2012, he served as one of the three regular sermon-givers at the mosque, rotating with his son, Usama Hasan, and his fellow council scholar Haitham al-Haddad. The mosque erupted in controversy over Usama's championing of evolution—he holds degrees in scientific fields from Cambridge, King's, and Imperial—and as of 2015, rival factions continue to dispute control of the mosque (see chapter 11). Suhaib has carried on scholarly activities outside the mosque and the ISC. He writes books on Islamic topics published by the Al-Qur'an Society, housed in the same building as the ISC. For years he gave a cycle of weekly lessons at the mosque on Islamic topics: on the Qur'an, on books of hadith (in 2010 it was a Maliki text), or on the first four caliphs. He gives weekly lectures on two television channels: in English on Islam Channel, and in Urdu on Iqra', where in 2010 he discussed the signs of the end of the world, *alamat al-qayām*. He also sits on the European Council for Fatwa and Research, where he tends to uphold Salafi positions over and against the arguments of Yusuf al-Qaradawi.[18]

As the council secretary, Suhaib is the leader and makes the ultimate decisions, in meetings and at the council more generally. He writes the fatwas, takes the lead in reading and summarizing cases at sessions, and often speaks for "how we do things." In his absence the others will say, "Sheikh Suhaib always says that . . ." His manner is sharp and humorous, and he listens intently to what people say in interviews.

Abu Sayeed is president of the ISC. He comes from Bangladesh and was formerly imam at the East London Mosque. His English is not as precise as Suhaib's, and in the council's formal deliberations, he generally intervenes only to ask for the final decision or to make sure that someone's point was understood: he is more on top of things than his general reticence would suggest. Abu Sayeed is grandfatherly and well disposed toward women petitioners. He usually recommends dissolution of the marriage after interviewing the wife. But his manners can make it seem that he does not really hear what they are saying in interviews: he chews his tobacco, speaks in somewhat stilted English, and asks what must appear as rote questions.

Clients probably think they've had a better hearing from Suhaib than from Abu Sayeed. But the latter's reports on cases are sympathetic to the woman petitioner; among other things, he scrupulously writes down what she says.

In Bangladesh Abu Sayeed studied in a Deobandi seminary, following the Hanafi legal school, but he joins the others in ruling according to distinct opinions. For example, Hanafis consider the triple talaq—three divorce pronouncements made at once by the husband—to count as all three talaqs and thus to disallow reconciliation. This issue arises frequently in office exchanges. On March 15, 2010, between cases, Abu Sayeed took several calls. One caller asked whether the triple talaq counted as one or three divorces; he said it counted as one, but "if not reconciled within three months, it becomes an Islamic decree absolute." After the call, I asked him how he could say this and hold to Hanafi views. He replied, "Yes, but on the Shariʿa Council this is what we decided, because it is Sunna. Abu Bakr counted it as one. It was Umar who made it count as three, perhaps so people would take it more seriously. Most scholars around the world now follow Ibn Taymiyyah, even though Hanafi, Shafiʿi, and others say that it counts as three." As this example indicates, but also more generally in his tone and his role on the ISC, he is a consensus player.

The third London-based senior scholar is Haitham al-Haddad. Of Palestinian origin, he was raised in Saudi Arabia. When speaking with clients, he self-consciously draws on his Arabic directness to, as he puts it, "give them all a hard time." He studied in Medina with a student of Sheikh ʿUthaymin, and obtained a civil engineering degree in Sudan, and in 2010 he completed a doctoral degree at SOAS on the idea of a fiqh of minorities. He has a rather rule-book approach to things, upholding shariʿa over and against custom (*ʿurf*) or practical considerations—let the procedures take time if that is the right thing to do in Islam. He also is the champion of the dads, the skeptic concerning the women's testimony. He joined around 2003 as part of Suhaib's efforts to give Salafis a greater voice in deliberations. He speaks his mind freely in public circles about "Islam" in general, which leads him to takes stances against homosexuality, for different rights for women and men, and other unpopular positions. He is the British Muslim the *Daily Mail* online most loves to hate—and indeed, a figure whom many in Britain see as extremist.[19]

These three scholars live in London and each week spend one or more days at the Leyton offices answering questions about a range of issues and hearing clients who wish to have an Islamic divorce. Several other scholars live in other cities in England and hear clients at those cities on behalf of the ISC. Some of them regularly attend the formal London sessions.

The most regular participant from out of town is Khurram Bashir. Khurram comes from Pakistan, where he spent time at their Union Councils, which process divorce claims. He has a doctorate in Islamic Law from Birmingham. He often refers to Pakistani realities, usually in opposition to Haitham's references to Islamic textual principles. He and Haitham are easily the most vocal contributors to the deliberations. In August 2011, I visited him at his home and office in Birmingham. On the second day of the fasting month, he had a steady stream of visitors who brought questions about Islamic law, divorce procedures, or how best to deal with a police matter. Once a week he has a one-hour radio call-in show, but during Ramadan he has three: two shows in English and one in Urdu. He grew up in Lahore, where he obtained his first degree, and then spent five years in Riyadh: the first year and a half to improve his Arabic and then three years completing a master's degree in Islamic studies. From Riyadh he came to London in 1984 and started work right off at the Leyton mosque as an imam; he already knew Suhaib. He then moved to Birmingham to join his parents, did his doctoral work at the university, and worked at the Birmingham Central Mosque, where he remains a trustee. He was working at the care service but then was recruited to be imam of the mosque at Edinburgh, and did that for one and a half years but found it too much of a commute, as his family remained in Birmingham. He works as a chaplain in hospitals and mental wards. If people come to him for a divorce, he just interviews them and sends the interview along to London.

Three others often attend the London sessions but play quieter roles. Hafiz Abdul Aala Durrani is from Pakistan, and spent four years in Medina studying fiqh. He lives in Bradford, where he interviews clients, and he is an Islamic leader in the city, having founded a school and working as imam at the Keighley mosque near Bradford. Shafiq ur-Rahman now lives in London's Bethnal Green; he also studied in Medina after growing up in Bangladesh. Abduh Hadi lives in Birmingham and serves as imam at the Green Lane Mosque. Green Lane also has a shariʿa council, but without the necessary staff, they often simply send cases on to London.

These are the regulars; other scholars may attend. Most important in this category is Mufti [Abdul Qadir] Barkatullah. He is from India and studied at Dar al-ʿUlum at Deoband, and as an Indian Muslim, he is sometimes considered neutral between the Pakistanis and the Bangladeshis. He also receives a certain degree of respect for having studied at the original Deobandi school. He is active on Islamic finance boards in England and has been a member of the ISC since 1982, when he attended the founding meeting as the representative of UK Islamic Missions. During the period I was attending ISC meetings, he appeared only once; his general absence was due to a falling-out over his efforts to write a "model Muslim marriage contract" (see chapter 11).

Other people come from time to time, such as scholars working at the London Central Mosque. Choukri Majouli, the mosque's imam, is from Tunisia; Dr. Ahmad al-Dubayan is director general of the mosque (officially of its Islamic Cultural Centre), appointed by the Saudi government. The only female scholar ever in attendance when I visited was Dr. Rosheen Shahzad-Raja, a Muslim of Afghan and Irish descent who had been asked by al-Dubayan to develop a uniform set of procedures for the councils. She also heads a volunteer legal aid society that provides legal assistance to women who, for example, are sponsored by their husbands and so do not have access to public funds. As we shall see in the following chapters, visiting Islamic scholars or, sometimes, lawyers, will appear and will be invited to take part in formal deliberations.

Institutional Differentiation

Although several English organizations opposed to the spread of shariʿa routinely claim that there are eighty-five shariʿa councils in Britain, no clear number can be established.[20] When I posed the question of numbers to Suhaib in 2010, he said there were probably about a dozen across the country. Other shariʿa scholars (including Shahid Raza, below) have given similar answers, estimating twelve to fifteen established councils across England; there may be additional, less visible councils operating out of other mosques.[21] The best known after Leyton are the Muslim Law (Shariʿa) Council (MLSC), located in the western suburbs of London but with a second home in Leicester; a well-established council in Dewsbury; and two councils in Birmingham. The ISC in London has what one might term "friendly relations" with the western London council and with Birmingham's Green Lane Mosque council, in that each considers the other's procedures valid. Given that the clientele and most of the scholars at the western London council are Sufi, this agreement on procedural validity is worth noting. By contrast, Suhaib did not mention either of the two Midlands institutions to be discussed in chapters 7 and 8, nor did either of them speak warmly about the London council. Here or there, it may arise that an individual imam will dissolve a marriage, but little is known about these practices.

The Muslim Law (Shariʿa) Council, UK

The second major shariʿa council to appear in England was created by the Islamic scholar who, though deceased, still probably commands the widest respect among British Muslims. In 1978, Zaki Badawi became director general of the London Central Mosque, where he worked as imam. Born in Egypt and trained at Al-Azhar, Badawi came to London in 1951, where he studied psychology and obtained a doctorate in modern Muslim thought in London. In 1986, he founded the Muslim College in Ealing and set up a shariʿa council in the same building.

In May 2013, I discussed the story of this council with Maulana Muhammad Shahid Raza (OBE), now the executive secretary of the council.[22] Born in India, he studied at the Dar al-ʿUlum in Muradabad, and is a Barelvi Sufi. When I spoke with him in May 2013, he was working out of an office of chartered accountants at Wembley. The council files are there and people must come there for interviews. They had just had to vacate the space they had been in since the beginning, at Ealing, because the building's owners, the Libyan government, had asked for its return.

Shahid Raza described the MLSC's beginnings: "By the early 1980s, Zaki Badawi and other imams would help women but there was no way to get divorces; women were left hanging. In October 1985 he called a conference at the mosque; it lasted two days and had 250 people: imams, mosque officials, scholars, and they agreed that there should be a shariʿa council, like the dar ul-qaza in India. The major problem was that none of us knew how to do this, there was no precedent. And we had a lot of suspicion from the community; people thought we would endanger the family structure, encourage women to divorce their husbands. We would be walking down the street and people would say: 'There are the people who want to attack families.' They called us 'feminists.' Now there is hardly any suspicion of the council from the community."

The initial group included other Egyptians, a barrister from South Africa of Indian background, people from the Deobandi circles, and Iraqi Shiites. Most of them were Barelvis, however, from Pakistan or India. "The Deobandis were reluctant to go along, not for any theological reasons but because of general suspicion, but eventually they formed their own councils," explained Shahid Raza. Mufti Barkatullah told me a slightly different version: "When we tried to set up a meeting to set common procedures, here at the London Central Mosque, Zaki Badawi had already moved to Ealing, and accepted the Barelvis, and he would not come to the meeting because he saw that the ISC was dominated by the Salafis."[23] Whatever the precise story, although relationships between the two councils remain cordial and respectful, the Deobandi/Barelvi rivalry made it impossible for them to join forces. Once more, the South Asian oppositions produced hardened interinstitutional effects in Britain. These rivalries may also complicate efforts to establish a national board of shariʿa councils with an appellate structure. Beginning in about 2010, the director of the London Central Mosque, al-Dubayan, invited fourteen councils to discuss a proposal for such a board. As of 2014, ten had attended at least one meeting but without a concrete result.

An Open Field

The story of the first shariʿa councils is one of differentiation along several lines. First, the two earliest and best-known councils, both in the London area, were set up by two distinct groups of scholars. One, Ahl al-Hadith and

→ division of schools → divisions of classes

Deobandi, formed the Islamic Shariʿa Council in eastern London. The other, largely Sufi and including Egyptians and Shiites, formed the Muslim Law (Shariʿa) Council in western London. The east-west divide maps onto socio-economic contrasts between wealthier Arab and South Asian populations to the west and poorer South Asian (and now also Somali) populations to the east. Each council has its own network of correspondents around England. As noted above, the two councils acknowledge and respect each other, and they follow much the same set of procedures. The theological divisions have not prevented a practical convergence.

Most other shariʿa councils in England developed for geographical reasons: Dewsbury serves a broad section of the North, for example, as does Birmingham for the Midlands. The North is regarded as underserved. Mufti Barkatullah of the ISC said that in the broad northern belt from Manchester to Bradford, no one has dared set up a new council because the party that loses threatens the scholars.[24] "Abu Sayeed once was verbally harassed and we called the others and went to the Crown prosecutor's office, to have a united front, but there was not enough evidence of a case. So we desisted from the case. The woman came to see me and said that the case was all set and what could she now do? I said 'Look, consider yourself divorced'; I took it upon myself to do it. But in the North, it is worse; one man's house was torched in Bradford after he dissolved a marriage." He explained that the Dewsbury shariʿa council head, Yaqub Qasmi, had been in that capacity for forty years and so was somewhat protected from attack.

Other Muslim communities have their own procedures regarding divorce and, more generally, settling disputes. The Kurdish Peace Committee in the UK functions as a general dispute-resolution body, in which divorce disputes are mediated as conflicts between families.[25] A few law firms tailor services to Muslims (see chapter 10). Shiʿa Muslims have a number of distinct centers in the London area (generally to the west and north), each with its own ties to Iranian or Lebanese scholars, and they each have their own rulings and procedures regarding marriage and divorce, including *muta* (temporary) marriage.

Other, more marginal shariʿa councils are set up from time to time and, indeed, doing so is a way for an extremist group to proclaim its entry onto the scene. As Mufti Barkatullah said, "When people saw we were attracting lots of cases, many started setting up councils, but they had no training. Even [al-Muhajiroun founder] Omar Bakri did this; it was just him deciding by himself. People would come to us as a kind of appeals body from his 'council.' One woman had insisted she and her husband—they had been married by Omar Bakri—register their marriage, but the husband refused. She came to us to ask for a divorce, and the question was: Is this [the husband's refusal] sufficient grounds for divorce? And we said yes. Bakri sent a legal representative to urge us not to do this, but we did it anyway."

Two other councils stand out because their specific histories have strongly shaped the way they proceed. The Birmingham Central Mosque, examined in chapter 8, developed out of a women's crisis center, and retains a focus on women talking with women. The Hijaz center for mediation and arbitration near Nuneaton in the Midlands is a complex of institutions centered on the grave of a Sufi sheikh, and we turn to it in chapter 9.

We have seen that South Asian divorce institutions took on a particular shape in response to British colonial policies, and as a way of preserving Muslim life in minority situations. They were then transposed to Britain and, in the close-knit urban communities, where religious ties and authority structures had, by the 1980s, taken on important roles, they found audiences. They were then easily adapted to the new environment, in ways that we will examine in chapter 5.

→ colonial influence on Shari'a

CHAPTER 5

Improvising an Institution

IN THIS CHAPTER WE FOCUS ON EVERYDAY PRACTICES AT THE ISLAMIC SHARIʿA Council, London (ISC). In succeeding chapters, we will examine the tensions and choices facing these scholars before turning to two other councils, and then, in part 4, we will broaden our focus to ask how the councils fit in the context of British ideas, institutions, and demands.

ISC scholars do what judges do in courts throughout the world: try to arrive at a reasonable outcome in a way that is consistent with their own procedures and with their understanding of the relevant law. But the ISC scholars do so in a global context of Islamic jurisprudence and of transnational movement: clients come to them from dozens of countries, many of them will return to those (or other) countries, and from time to time Islamic scholars from prestigious religious faculties drop in to observe. Understandably, the scholars on this and other councils discuss whether their practices fit with those of Muslim-majority countries and with positions taken by those prestigious Islamic scholars. The situation is even more complex, because the council scholars are working in a media-saturated Western country, one not always friendly to the idea of shariʿa in their midst.

The council's ways of working lie at the crossroads of two temporal rhythms: one that grows out of the logic of files and documents and another that follows from the open-ended nature of office life. I start with one, and then turn to the other, in order to give a fuller account of the institution.[1]

Files cry out, "Sequence!" When a file is opened, a case begins. An ISC file exists as a cardboard folder with a case number. It contains letters, notes of interviews, and documents. As the folder fills with documents, a sequence of events emerges or can be reconstructed from the documents. During a formal deliberation, scholars must often undertake such a reconstruction in order to make sense of the case. When I spent weeks in the council's attic studying their archives, I had to do precisely the same thing. The council's chief clerk writes decisions taken by the council upon the folder itself. With files there is a beginning and, unless the petitioner drops the case, an end, and a logical sequence in between. Files lend themselves to spreadsheets and to smooth narratives: one thing leads to another. From the files, the council appears to be like a court, with cases and calendars and causality.

By contrast, offices shriek, "Chaos!" People drop in to make appointments, seek advice, argue in front of a scholar or a clerk, or ask about getting a divorce. Office experiences are anything but linear. There are appointment calendars, but they bear only an approximate relationship to what anyone is doing at any moment of the day. The staff is deluged with calls and visits by husbands, wives, uncles, policemen, solicitors, and salesmen, who may be inquiring, complaining, cajoling, or demanding service. Scholars both senior and junior are meeting in different rooms with clients, speaking any one of a dozen languages, and discussing insurance, sex, fasting, interest rates, and, most often, marriage and divorce. Few of these discussions lead to the opening of a file. In the office, the council appears to be like a crisis center or a government office.

We need to take account of both temporalities. If we look only at the paper trail of a formal organization, we will see the elements of the working day that fit its own conception of itself, the "flowchart." For a body that only works from written documents, such as the French Conseil d'État, the isomorphism of files and procedures allows the ethnographer to focus entirely on files, and on what judges do in their formal deliberations—although this approach means that the case remains flattened down to its formal features.[2] But most legal and quasi-legal bodies handle some combination of written files and arguments, on the one hand, and a continuum of more or less formal encounters, on the other. Much of the anthropology of law has been devoted to thinking through the methodological implications of this complexity.[3] At the ISC, the written documents do not contain the arguments and reasons. You only learn those by listening to the scholars' deliberations and later on questioning the players. Furthermore, much of the argumentation is "meta" to the case at hand: triggered by it, but concerning the council's very right to issue judgments. None of this is ever written down.

Of course, if all we did was to drop in to see what happens at the council offices, we would see dispute, confusion, and anger, but we would miss the flow of events and the reasoning processes that eventually move cases along. Most office events have no conclusions: someone gets advice and leaves, and we don't know whether she is satisfied; a couple disputes what went wrong with their marriage until their time is up; a woman requests a divorce and we don't know what will happen next.

We need, therefore, to attend both to files and to office life.

Files

Each organization has its own "politics of files." A Pakistani bureaucrat interviewed by Matthew Hull claimed that he never read any of the files he had to handle. Files were useless in clarifying matters but constituted a "material infrastructure," formidable roadblocks to any actions he might wish to take.[4] ISC files have no such constraining power. They circulate only within the network of scholars, and they have no civil-legal effect. Reading and responding to them is central to the scholar's sense of responsibility.

Life at the Leyton office of the ISC consists to a great extent of moving the file along its assigned path following rules of procedure. These rules start with the identity of the client. If a husband seeks a divorce, it is considered a talaq, and he will receive a certificate to that effect from the council but must pay any outstanding mahr to his wife. If the wife seeks the divorce, it is considered a khula, and she must return or renounce her mahr. Mahr may be quite substantial and include money and gold. If her husband does not contest her action, then the divorce is given quickly; if he does contest it, then it requires the full procedure.

Following procedures subtends bureaucratic claims to legitimacy. The first thing a visitor sees when entering the ISC office is a large flowchart posted on the opposite wall. It shows how a case moves from filling out the application for divorce, through stages of notifying the husband and arranging for meetings, to the final determination of the case at a formal meeting of scholars. The flowchart would suggest a rather certain and near-automatic set of stages. Indeed, the council put it there to reassure potential clients that there is a regular process with many stages—that it may take time but will produce an outcome. Many of the changes I have seen at the council since 2007 have been efforts to forestall complaints, and this is one such instance. Now, things do not work exactly as shown on the wall, for reasons I will explain, but the *idea* that this is how they work is part of the ISC's effort to claim legitimacy. The visitor is supposed to think, "If I do what is required of me, the outcome is the divorce certificate." This interpretation sees the council as an input-output machine.

The file examined in a formal deliberation of the ISC always contains an account of an interview conducted with the petitioner (usually a wife) by a scholar based in London or by one of the corresponding scholars who receive petitions and interview petitioners in Bradford, Leeds, Manchester, Birmingham, or elsewhere. The report is usually written by hand, either in Urdu or in English (more rarely in Arabic). Some scholars are known for their poor penmanship or other idiosyncrasies, and this is noted by the assembled scholars. For example, Abu Sayeed is criticized for using what grammarians would call the "free, indirect style," such that claims made by the wife could be mistaken for his own judgments.

Usually the file contains other documents as well. These could be reports from other interviews (of relatives, for example), letters written by a solicitor or a welfare agency, documents proving that the address to which letters have been sent is indeed the husband's current address, attestations that the couple has lived apart for at least one year (these days, with at least two signed witnesses), and sometimes an exchange of letters between the husband and the wife through the mediation of the council secretary.

The same file could lead to quite varied discussions, as we shall see in chapter 6. For example, if the scholar Haitham al-Haddad is present at the deliberation, he is likely to raise evidentiary questions: How do we know that the couple has not had sex for a year (required for divorce)? Has the wife given her husband an affidavit that he will be able to visit the children? He is quite likely to suggest that he call the wife or the husband right then and there, as he also will do if the husband has never replied to their letters, which is often the case. Files are not sovereign; interviews and telephone conversations have (at least) equal weight. If Haitham is not there, then it is more likely that the chair of the session will propose that they dissolve the marriage on condition that the wife return any mahr she has received and that the others will agree. The group is particularly likely to agree with this suggestion if the wife has obtained a civil divorce.

Beginnings

Files may not have closure but they all have beginnings. Usually the file is triggered when a woman writes to the council to request an Islamic divorce.[5] She composes her opening salvo in an effort to persuade the council that their marriage is finished; often the writers compile grievances against their husbands. Here is one woman's particularly dark story:[6]

> In February 1997 I was taken to Pakistan for a holiday without my father; it was my mum, brother, and I. A month later my father arrives to meet his ill mother; during the six weeks that he stayed there he used a lot of violence on me because he had no power to do so in England. He asked me to marry his nephew when he knew that I didn't want to marry him . . . after he had left my mother started emotionally blackmailing me . . . in a way I felt sorry for my mum and that I should keep my mother happy, because after all she was the one who gave birth to me and raised me. I didn't even say ye[s] when I heard that the marriage was going ahead, it was just too late to express my feelings to my mum that I didn't really want to get married. I talked to my mum's sister who understood me more than my mum and explained about what was happening, she just told me to go ahead with it and that it was just for the best. My own brother, who supported me in England, turned a blind eye to what I wanted and was with everyone else getting the marriage arranged.

She goes on to say that the Islamic marriage was held in Pakistan, and that her new husband beat her. After two weeks she returned to England. She told her parents about what had happened but they were not helpful. "The main thing is that they can't take the fact that I've been honest in expressing my feelings; they say I've been disrespectful in telling them that I want a divorce and that I couldn't continue like this." She talked to social workers and friends and decided she must divorce. "My parents don't know that I am writing to you and I know they will become extremely violent if they were to find out." She was in sixth form, the last level of high school, and had "all the teachers behind me." She used her school address to communicate with the council, but she never sent the divorce form back to the council. This letter rings all the frequently rung alarm bells about violence and forced marriage among British Pakistanis.[7] It also points to the council as a way out, although in the end, for reasons we do not know, she did not pursue the case.

This case is atypical for the degree of violence but not for the basic pattern.[8] Most of the women and men involved in cases brought to the council were born in Pakistan or Bangladesh, or they are of South Asian ancestry; Somalia provides the next largest category of petitioners. The women petitioners are much more likely to be born in the UK (42 percent) than are their husbands, the respondents (20 percent). The wives are much more likely than their husbands to be British citizens and to reside in the UK.[9] But nothing prevents women from conducting their cases from afar or from visiting Britain just to obtain an Islamic divorce.

As we saw in chapter 2, British children and grandchildren of immigrants from Pakistan often marry persons living in Pakistan, and often they marry first cousins, as in the above case. For Pakistani parents living in Britain, finding a spouse "back home" from among a sibling's children is not the blind continuation of a backward custom but a way to negotiate the strains of holding an extended family together across a very long distance.[10] Not infrequently, the son or daughter is taken to Pakistan for the marriage. Sometimes the spouses welcome the arranged marriage; in other cases one or both suffer from physical or psychological coercion.

Of course, a sample of divorce cases will give us a skewed picture of marriage, but at least it can give us an idea of the distribution of complaints. Of 178 cases brought to the ISC where women petitioners advanced reasons for divorce, 23 cases included a claim that the marriage was forced. Sixty-three cases, the largest category, involved claims that the marriage had broken down because of irreconcilable differences, separation, or desertion; 10 additional cases had claims that the husband failed to provide material support; in 40 cases the women emphasized violence and abuse. Ten cases involved a marriage "only to get a visa."[11]

Usually, transcontinental marriages will lead the UK spouse to apply to bring the new spouse into the country. In ISC cases it is nearly always the wife bringing the husband, and it may go badly, as in the following case.

The wife married a Pakistani man in Pakistan. She wrote that once he got his UK nationality, "I was practically thrown out of my house." He asked her to sign papers for an English divorce and promised that once it went through, he would give her a talaq, but "he is a liar, cheat, and a deceitful person and not to be trusted. I therefore wish to apply for a talak from the Shariʿa Council, as I know he will not give me a talak . . . I have been advised by my solicitor to write to you and to acquire a talak. My husband has an English woman living with him at the moment and that is why he is pestering me for a divorce, as he wishes to marry her."

Now, husbands can pronounce an Islamic divorce (talaq) on their own, without the need of the council. In the above case, the husband was "pestering [her] for a divorce." Why would he not simply divorce his wife? The answer lies in the different consequences of the two types of divorce. If the husband initiates the divorce, then he must pay his wife any mahr still owed her from their marriage, but if she initiates the divorce, even if in the end he pronounces the talaq, then she forgoes any mahr due her and indeed will be told to repay any she was given as part of the marriage. Strategically, then, a husband may try to induce his wife to start an action for khula (as was probably the case here). Conversely, a wife might seek to goad her husband into divorcing her, in which case she can claim unpaid mahr.

Women learn about the ISC or other shariʿa councils from friends, family members, or religious officials. Two earlier studies focused on the women who sought divorce at a shariʿa council. Samia Bano (2012a, 142–228) interviewed twenty-five British Pakistani women. In their accounts of their desire to divorce, Bano found themes of "being controlled" and of a lack of empowerment in their new households (ibid., 194). Her interviewees began by asking relatives or local religious leaders about how to resolve a difficult marriage; these contacts then directed them toward a council. Some only learned that they had the right to initiate a divorce after they visited the council. Typically, they called a council and either followed up with a visit or tried a different council, or scholar, depending on the kind of response they received. They mentioned preferring a council that used Islam to "correct" certain culturally specific ideas about women's rights held by members of their family (2012a, 200–207). In this way, councils were extensions of the community but also provided checks on the community.

Sonia Nurin Shah-Kazemi (2001) interviewed twenty-one women who had applied to the Muslim Law (Shariʿa) Council, UK, then in Ealing. These women were of diverse ethnic backgrounds. The majority described their marriages as "arranged," and most preferred arranged marriages. Because of this council's regulations, the women had contacted the council by letter, and most often the entire process took place by correspondence. Shah-Kazemi found that many of these women had made efforts to reconcile with their husbands before approaching the council, and that their direct access to the council gave them some leverage in family discussions (2001, 35–39). When we recall that many of these marriages are with close cousins, and that divorce means a rift within the immediate family, we can understand the importance of having access to an outside religious authority who is not part of the applicant's immediate community.

Procedures

Once a wife has sent in the form requesting divorce, the council sends a letter to the husband to inform him that she has filed for divorce; if he never replies, a second and third letter, each one a month apart (or two months if he lives abroad), follow. A copy of each letter goes to the wife.

Atif Matin, the chief clerk for about eight years, explained how he handled these exchanges: "Once there is a response, then we let them have one exchange of letters before calling them in for interviews. But if the husband is not going to come, for example, he is overseas, then I let the exchange go on a bit longer, because then they are *less likely to be angry at us later on* [his emphasis]. We might repeat interviews but usually only in London." Many of Atif's procedural innovations were based on trial and error: if he thought that changing procedures would reduce the frequency of haranguing telephone calls from husbands who were upset that the council ended the marriage, or from wives who were tired of the delay, then he would urge the council to adopt them.

After the series of letters and perhaps one or more interviews, the matter is ready to go to the panel for deliberation. Here, too, Atif exercised some discretion: "After all this we send a final notice with the certificate of talaq [*talaqnama*] to the husband and the letter of confirmation to the wife, just before going to the panel. After the panel decision, sometimes I will send him the divorce certificate but not the letter with the panel's decision, because if he gets that [the letter] then he thinks, 'oh alright I still have a chance to protest this' and he calls me up and I try to avoid that. If I feel that someone challenges a lot, then I make sure to give him more opportunities to come in, so that later I can say, 'Well, we asked you to come for a meeting; did you come?' If he refuses to come to a single meeting, why ask him to a joint meeting? I don't think we need to do that."

When the husband does respond to the council's notice, bargaining may ensue and may involve complex intrafamily dynamics, as in the following case. The records on this case allow us to follow it through to an ending; it also stems from the most frequently given reason for seeking divorce, namely, the breakdown of the marriage.

Case: Waiting for Grandmother

In September 2007 a woman wrote asking the council to dissolve her marriage. She had been born near Manchester, the husband in Pakistan, both in 1981. They married in Kashmir in 2001 and moved to the UK, where he became a UK citizen. They never registered the marriage. They had separated in 2004. In June 2009 she applied for a civil divorce, apparently because someone at the council office told her that she needed it because she had been married in Pakistan. She cited irreconcilable differences and his behavior as reasons. They are first cousins (she is his father's brother's daughter).

The file shows that the divorce process started well enough. The first letter was sent in September 2007 and the husband replied two weeks later, asking the council not to proceed because their grandmother was trying to resolve the differences. There was another exchange of letters and apparently the family was very busy in the matter, because in March 2008 the wife wrote to the council saying this had dragged on too long: "It has been three years and six months since we separated, during the separation we have had over ten to twelve different meetings within the family regarding reconciliation, members of my family from Pakistan, Nottingham, and Luton have tried to reconcile us, BUT the answer has always been no. *I want to confirm that I have no intention of going back to [H]*" (emphasis in original). She said that she had called the council and was told that her husband had asked for a pause in the procedure because their grandmother was coming in four weeks.

At this point, council procedures required that the couple be interviewed, either in London or close to where they lived: at a joint meeting if possible, otherwise separately. Letters in the file attest to efforts to set up several meetings: in Manchester, Bradford, or London. It seems that they did attend meetings in Manchester separately, because the wife mentioned this in a letter from July 2009, where she accused the council of letting her husband delay matters on grounds that their grandmother would arrive from Pakistan and settle their differences: "It has been exactly one year and three months and she is not here . . . It seems to me that you are listening to him and in my opinion wasting time." Indeed, the husband traveled to Leyton at one point to ask Atif to put the case on hold while they awaited Grandmother. Grandmother did arrive that October, and the wife wrote to ask, "Please, could there be no more delays."

The council considered the dossier at their monthly meeting on January 27, 2010. In the meantime, Hafiz Abdul Aala, a regular attendee at the London deliberations (who also serves as imam at a mosque near Bradford), had interviewed the wife, and they began by considering his report of that interview. Apparently, the grandmother had not succeeded in resolving the dispute and returned to Pakistan. In the interview, the wife added that twelve reconciliation meetings had been held, with relatives coming from throughout the north of Britain as well as from Pakistan; she and her husband had attended a mediation session as part of their civil divorce procedure, her husband had threatened her family, and divorce was now going through civil court.

Because the civil divorce was under way, it was clear that the council would eventually dissolve the Islamic dimension of the marriage. The council required proof that the couple had been separated (meaning had not had sex) for one year, and in the files there was such a document, signed by two witnesses attesting to the separation. The marriage was dissolved in exchange for the return of the mahr, which had been paid in the form of gold jewelry. In formal, procedural terms, this meant that the council sent the husband their "letter of intent," stating that if they had heard nothing to change their mind within the month, the marriage would be dissolved. When the month is up, normally the council secretary sends a certificate of dissolution to each party.

However, in this case the husband's solicitors quickly wrote to the council, in a letter dated February 2, 2010, to say that "our client objects to the Islamic Marriage being dissolved as he does hope to reconcile with his wife. His wife has English divorce proceedings which she has decided not to finalise. We therefore would urge you not to finalise the Islamic Divorce which allows parties time to consider their marriage further. If his wife decides to proceed with the English divorce only after it has been finalised my client would further consider entering into an Islamic Divorce." The husband followed up three days later with a letter urging the council to help get them back together again. He enclosed a wedding photo (where he is the only one smiling; perhaps he could have made a better choice) and love letters between them.

This letter was quickly relayed to the wife (with, as often happens, the council serving as intermediary), and her parents replied, saying that no such delays were on the table: "As you know, every parent wants their offspring to have a happy and prosperous life. Naively without investigating too much on this man's personality we arranged this marriage. The husband is our nephew, her paternal cousin. Very quickly we realised this mistake, regardless we called him over to the UK and got him his British nationality thinking and hoping things would improve." But they agreed with their daughter that it was time to end the marriage. What of the grandmother? "Once grandmother arrived, on having a few meetings within the family and [the wife] she realised there is no chance. She then tried to make him understand this. She also witnessed his behavior and at this point she decided to leave for Pakistan." The father had talked this over with Hafiz Abdu Aala. The wife also wrote, assuring the council that she would be concluding a civil divorce "in the near future." She sent the jewelry, knowing that such would be required for the divorce.

The wife also sent along a letter from her solicitors addressed to her but clearly intended for her to show to the council. The letter said that "you have consistently instructed us that you seek a divorce from [your husband]," and that "you have been unable to progress the divorce due to legal aid not being available for a contested divorce case." As it had been five years since the date of what she claims was their separation, they could file afresh for a contested divorce. (English law requires a five-year delay if the divorce is contested.) They also said they were aware that the Shariʿa Council received a letter saying that the divorce "has been cancelled," and that "as a result the Shariʿa Council are not prepared yet to finalise the Islamic divorce." They explained that she never took steps to stop the divorce nor did she say she had changed her mind, and "you require the Islamic divorce to be finalized and request the Shariʿa Council to proceed to do this." They continued: "Overall, it would seem that [the husband] is intent on using every possible delaying tactic to prevent a divorce from taking place and there are strong grounds for believing that in trying to achieve this he is not being truthful to the Shariʿa Council as he has apparently claimed that you and he are reconciled or seeking to do so, which is plainly not true."

This duel by proxy had no discernable effect on the council's procedures. The file contained a note that the mahr was deposited with Atif in March and that the council issued the certificate of marriage dissolution on April 22. We do not know what happened to the jewelry, which included two earrings and a necklace, but if the husband had not reclaimed it within three months, Atif would have returned it to the wife, or, at her instruction, would have donated it to a charity. (These dispositions are not recorded in the files.)

In this case, three processes were under way at the same time. First, the family had been engaged in massive mediation efforts since well before the case was brought to the ISC. Relatives came from throughout the north of England, and everyone was caught up in the drama of "waiting for Grandmother" to arrive from Pakistan. These were family efforts. For the approximately one-half of British Pakistani marriages that involve first cousins, a divorce does not push away a set of in-laws; it threatens the unity of the family from within. It also threatens the continuity of what may have become well-worn ties with family members back in Asia. These ties are often economic and social as well as familial, and a divorce could have serious repercussions for joint business ventures or future marriages. The shared grandparent will often have a serious role in attempting to keep the family together.

Second, the two teams of solicitors had their own negotiations regarding a civil divorce. Because the couple had married in Pakistan, and Britain recognizes marriages conducted in Pakistan, they needed to file for a civil divorce as well. As Pakistani-born family lawyer Aina Khan explained to me, if the woman had married in English law and had a civil divorce, a "mirror order" for the divorce would be sent to the Pakistani registry. Aina had never heard of problems arising in Pakistan in those cases. "If a woman was afraid of problems, she could go right to a *qazi* [judge] in Pakistan and ask for a divorce, showing the English certificate. Or if she were to remarry there, she would have no problem: the imams there want to marry people, any chance they get." On a khula granted in England, she said, "If that was all there was, because the couple had never registered their marriage, it could be challenged in Pakistan, but I have never heard of such cases."[12]

As the ISC explains to women seeking Islamic divorce, if they have arranged a visa for their spouse, there is a record of their overseas marriage at the Home Office, and if they remarry without a civil divorce, they risk being prosecuted for bigamy. (That such prosecutions do not seem to happen does not eliminate the sense of potential threat.) Many clients first learn they must file for civil divorce because of an overseas marriage when they apply to the council and are told they must begin the civil divorce procedure before their case may be taken up. Clients are more likely to know the rules if they married in the UK and registered their marriage. Civil divorce does not require a court appearance, but if one party contests it, the other party either must prove fault or wait for five years, as was the case here.

Third, the council was following its own procedural rules: sending letters, interviewing the parties separately or together, and deliberating. The council always tries to arrange for joint meetings, and these meetings figure on the official flowchart as steps to a divorce, but more often than not, they fail to occur. Couples who have separated don't want to meet; one may have threatened the other or even obtained a court order preventing contact. More often, as here, the two parties are interviewed separately, or the husband fails to respond to the three letters sent by the council.

These three processes were not independent. The numerous family mediation sessions and the long waiting period for the civil divorce bolstered the husband's claims in his discussion with the ISC that they should not proceed hastily. Many cases are like this, in that the shariʿa council proceedings are embedded in complex family and legal webs of accusation and bargaining.

Delays

The council procedures are intended to increase the possibility that the couple will reconcile, and the scholars see value in delay—much to the irritation of women trying to end their marriages quickly. Indeed, when a husband complained that they did not need a joint meeting because they had already tried mediation, Atif replied, "Having a joint meeting is part of procedure; it is not mediation," meaning that their joint meetings were required even if the couple had sought outside mediation.[13] The council scholars say, correctly, that building in delays is precisely what the English legal system does with its one-year and five-year waiting periods, and that Islamic courts throughout the world include mediation as part of divorce procedures.

Sometimes the delays come in ways not formally part of procedure. On August 18, 2010, I was in the office when Atif fielded a call from a woman wanting to know why she had not heard back from the council about her case. Atif said that if she wanted to pursue it, she had to take the next step herself. After the call, I said that I had noted gaps of several months between letters going out to husbands and the ISC bringing a case forward; could this step not be taken automatically after a short wait? "I have thought about this for five years [the time he had been chief clerk], and we could do it," he replied, "but I decided not to, especially as we now have the new phone lines here so it is easier to contact us. It is because the courts do it this way too; you have to initiate the next step each time. If we were to go right from sending out letters to bringing the case forward, we don't know what is going on with the marriage, if they are reconciling or discussing, and each case is so different we cannot have a single rule. So we let them decide if they want to move forward and then contact us." When a case simply ceases, with no formal deliberation by the council, it is because the wife did not take the next step. Note that Atif explicitly models their procedure on that followed by the civil courts.

The council also responds favorably when a civil divorce procedure appears to be moving along smoothly. To differing degrees, the scholars take the progress of a civil divorce as indicating that the marriage is over and that they should hurry up and let the woman get on with her life. Because of this sensitivity of the ISC to the civil procedure, solicitors can slow or speed up the Islamic process by reporting on what is occurring in the courts. In the grandmother case, each set of solicitors tried to shape the council's procedure; the wife's side seems to have prevailed, with its statement that because the five years were up, the civil divorce would continue. This argument fit the dominant logic at the ISC: delay and give time for reconciliation, but in the end, if she persists, give the woman her freedom.

Petitioners sometimes try to play the courts and the council against each other. On April 4, 2013, I was in the office for a discussion between a young woman and Suhaib Hasan. She wanted the council to dissolve her marriage and to say that she had the right to take their children to the United States. She planned to remarry there. She was in the process of obtaining her civil divorce from the courts, and she was in the middle of a hearing on her rights to take their children out of the country. The civil courts were to issue a judgment on this question on May 8; the court order would be legally binding on the parents. Suhaib stated that the council would await their courts' decision on all matters before issuing an Islamic marriage dissolution, and that they did not wish to get ahead of the courts. For about thirty minutes, he reiterated his decision, and she refused to accept it; in the end, she stormed out of the room, an unusual occurrence. It was clear to Suhaib that she was hoping to use a statement from the council to affect the civil court judgment—such an outcome was highly unlikely, but Suhaib wished to avoid any such entanglement.

The time elapsed between filing and a decision is highly variable: the petitioner may respond quickly or not; the couple may try to reconcile in the middle of the process, the husband may stall, or be unavailable. The figures from a sample of eighty cases on which the council made a formal decision during 2007 to 2010 give a sense of the wide range of time to decision. The delays fall into three clusters. Thirty-four cases were decided in six to eight months, thirty-two cases were decided in ten to nineteen months, and nine cases were decided over much longer periods, from twenty-three to forty-one months. (Five cases had missing data.) Resolving the case takes longer when more complex issues arise, when the husband disputes the claims made by his wife, or when there are children. Disputes over repayment of marriage goods can also prolong the process. Six months is a fairly short time to complete the procedures, quite comparable to an uncomplicated civil divorce procedure.

Procedures drag out when the council asks one or the other parties to come for a meeting and one or both live far away, or postpone the meeting, or simply refuse to come. Usually the council asks the husband to take the action of granting his wife a divorce, and he may delay his answer. The council may ask the wife to provide a statement that she and her husband have been separated for at least one year, or one that says that she will let the father see their children. Very frequently, delays come from the unwillingness of the husband to respond to letters. The council sends three letters to him, asking for his opinion on the matters in question, and if the letters meet with no response, they ask the wife to try and verify his address in one way or another—much as does the English civil court. It may take many months to either produce a response from the husband or decide that they must proceed without him. A concern with procedural fairness is at work here.[14]

To sum up our files-centric view: the scholars on the council consider whether the marriage has irremediably broken down (which leads them to grant a divorce), whether there are children (which may lead them to seek assurances that the father will be able to see the children), and whether there is documented fault on the part of the husband, such as a court order against him or a jail term on drug charges. Although the scholars weigh the versions of events provided by the man and those provided by the woman, they are not a court and have no subpoena powers, and usually do not see the husband. Moreover, they do not need to engage in a long process of fact-finding, as in a trial, for if they can assure themselves that the marriage is over and that the father's rights and children's rights are considered, they will almost always dissolve the marriage.

Office Life

Let us start over with an ethnographic "dropping in" to the Leyton offices of the ISC. From this vantage point, the council no longer appears essentially as a divorce court. Muslims come to pose questions and to seek advice about a range of personal matters, most, but not all, having to do with family life.

I write from my notes on a visit to the Leyton office on May 6, 2010. The council had been meeting in the Leyton mosque while renovations on the office were carried out. My visit occurred on one of the early days after the reopening of the office.

For the first two weeks after the office reopened, it had been chaos. For one thing, there were no chairs, or very few, because until the day I dropped in, they had remained stored in the mosque, on the other side of the A12 motorway. Clerks dragged chairs back and forth between rooms as clients entered and left. For another, they had not yet hired enough clerks, and the new ones were, much of the time, clueless. As I sat in the waiting area that day, a pair of young ladies complained to me about how one of the clerks (a newly hired, young, smoothly shaved man) had explained why they had had to come back three times, saying about one of the younger scholars, "He is a scholar, so he does not know anything about divorce." In addition, the scholars didn't seem to have settled into a routine; there was one scholar when there should be two, or two when there should be three, so the waits were long and the people were irritable. Small children, made to wait longer than the ten minutes most of them were capable of managing, were appealing to their moms to leave. The moms were doubly irritated because of the wait (with the young ones tugging on their skirts) and because the precise appointments they were assigned ("come Thursday at 3:45") bore no relation to when they were finally seen.

One of the two young ladies had been sent back twice to her husband to get his signature on forms, something hardly pleasing to a wife when she is living apart from her husband and they are angry with each other. Her friend played this to the hilt, as the wife was an English convert (whose father hailed from California); the friend said to the clerk, to try and speed up the process, "Brother, she's a revert, and she's likely to go back to . . . if you don't work things out here."

The busiest days then were Monday and Thursday, because Suhaib Hasan was there on those days and had many clients. Indeed, most of the available chairs were now in the waiting room, with half a dozen people sitting at any one time, waiting to deliver a form, to see a sheikh, or to find out what was up with their application.

A Pakistani woman in her early thirties waited with her five-year-old son for almost an hour before she was able to see Suhaib. With her permission, I went in with her. She supervised an IT group, was married (only the nikah), and her husband lived in Pakistan. She seemed at ease with Suhaib. Her husband had converted to marry her. That was five years ago, and now the marriage had fallen apart over his behavior—"he takes drugs"—and over her suspicions that he had not really converted wholeheartedly to Islam. They had a solicitor work out their dispute over property, and that was in the courts, and she wanted a divorce at the ISC. The husband had not responded to the three letters from the ISC; now she had brought proof that he really lived at that address so that the ISC could take the case forward. He told her that he would divorce her, but he never did; he said, "I cannot say talaq; that is not my language." Suhaib wanted details on any jewelry he had given her; some had been destroyed in a fire, she said.

Out in the waiting area, a wife's father, Mr. Khan, was waiting to drop off the confirmation letter that his daughter wished to continue the divorce procedure. He explained the situation: his daughter had married his brother's son, but "the boy went crazy, won't give her a divorce because he is stubborn, and once took a gun and pointed it at her head, but she was able to grab it and force it upward so it shot a hole in the roof, and she got burns on her hand." She had been here in England for three years; she couldn't go back and get a divorce in Pakistan because she was afraid of him. She married here in England, a civil marriage, and needed the Islamic Council certificate because otherwise the Pakistanis would say, "Well, that is just an English divorce; it is not the same as a Pakistani one." It was just a matter of paperwork, but she would need it back there. And she was about to marry again here: "We had scheduled the hall for June but had to forfeit the deposit because we can only hold it three months and the council keeps sending more letters—now even if they give the divorce to her next month, then three months later we will be in fasting month!"

In another case, an Arabic-speaking man was waiting to hand in his request for a *talaqnama* (divorce certificate). When asked by the clerk what the reason for divorce was, he said, "Differences; that is all I can say." The clerk said they would then send it to his wife and wait thirty days before issuing it to him. "Brother, I cannot wait that long; I will go and have her sign it and bring back her passport, not just a copy but the real thing, and her driver's license and you can make a copy here." He said he would be back on Monday, and they said he should ask for Yahya, who worked then. "I will do it, brother."

The chaos was soon calmed—the chairs moved back to the office, the new clerk told how to respond to questions—but the focus on, and sometimes impatience over, office procedures continued to characterize life in Leyton. Although there was a daily appointment book for each scholar, sessions could easily go on well after the allotted time had ended. In the rare case that the husband and wife appeared together, the scholar was reluctant to let them go before he had tried to convince them to reconcile, or convince the husband to give his wife a talaq and avoid continuing the ISC procedure. (Neither effort was likely to succeed.) Prayer times offered momentary disruptions, although because the staff prayed together in the basement, the pauses did not last more than ten or fifteen minutes. Usually the scholar would urge the couple to try to work out their differences while he prayed; on several occasions, as he left the room, Suhaib asked me—with a bit of a grin but not much hope—to "try and get them to resolve things."

Elsewhere in the offices, one or two of the three regularly present senior scholars—Suhaib Hassan, Haitham al-Haddad, and Abu Sayeed—might be meeting with clients. Another senior scholar might've dropped in to meet with a client who spoke Somali or another language not mastered by the three regularly present scholars—whose languages include English, Arabic,

Urdu, Punjabi, and Bengali. One or more junior scholars might be fielding basic questions—about how to pray or fast, loss of faith, or sexuality—and the office staff of four to five young men were answeringing the telephones, arranging the scholars' schedules, finding files, and handling paperwork. As of 2012 a young woman served as receptionist and brought files to the scholars. In 2013 an office manager was hired, and Khola Hasan, Suhaib's daughter, began acting as media spokesperson.

Many, perhaps most, office sessions had no clear outcome. When they involved both sides of a dispute, they might have served to clear the air, or played a part in a long-term process of settlement. Often Islamic law had little bearing on the issues in question. In these cases, the council served as mediators. For example, in 2012 a young couple, divorced in civil law, came to work out whether or not he owed her unpaid mahr. He planned to give her a talaq and wanted a certificate of talaq from the council. But the council replied that he had to pay any mahr due her, and they notified her to get her side of the story. Neither questioned the principle that unpaid mahr must be paid upon divorce; the only issue in question was whether the mahr debt had been implicitly part of the financial settlement arranged in court. Without powers of subpoena or enforcement, all Suhaib could do was to try and find a middle ground. Valiantly he tried, but in the end, failed.

Case: Talaq for Dropping Charges

Suhaib had more success in an interview held on April 29, 2013. A husband came for what was supposed to be a joint meeting, bringing a friend with him. Suhaib stated that the wife was not coming, and that he had received a letter from her solicitors. In their letter, her solicitors referred to a finding by social services that she should keep their son away from his father. The solicitors added that because the mother had difficulty getting child care, were she to travel to London for a meeting at the council, she would have to take her son, and that doing so would contradict the social services' directive. The solicitors also stated that the wife claimed that the husband had stolen jewelry from her. Suhaib read from the letter to the husband and his friend. Turning to me, he said, "You saw this letter; they say we don't listen to the police or social services; we get letters from them all the time." A very negative, privately produced program on the council had just aired on the BBC, and Suhaib was responding to the general charge that shariʿa councils acted outside the law.[15]

In response to the letter, the husband told Suhaib that he had already verbally divorced her. Suhaib noted that the wife had begun khula proceedings with the council because she did not know whether the talaq would be sufficient. Suhaib then called the wife on his speakerphone. They entered into a long back-and-forth with the husband's friend acting as his spokesperson. The wife finally said that she would drop the allegation of stealing jewelry if he would agree to the divorce. He agreed and signed an affidavit in Suhaib's presence saying that he divorced her, and his friend signed as a witness. Suhaib explained to them that once the council received the written statement from the wife dropping the allegation, they would release the khula certificate, and that no further joint meeting would be needed. Suhaib's role here, as in many cases, was to facilitate bargaining pursuant to a judgment.[16]

Adapting Procedures

In 2013 I asked Suhaib about their early efforts to standardize procedures at the ISC, and how these procedures evolved.[17]

JRB: How did you know what to do? Did you have models?

Suhaib: I drafted the procedures, and I did not have any models. So I wrote the models for letters that we send husbands, and we still are using them thirty years later! But we should probably revisit them. The second letter lists things husbands might have done, such as being absent, not giving support, but the husband then can say none of that applied, that there was no justification for divorce. So we need to add new reasons, such as domestic violence. [He brought over the ISC computer database, which lists all the justifications mentioned by women.] We found that about 30 percent of the women mentioned abuse in 2010 and 2012, and now we entered the 2011 records and it is about the same. [He showed me the highlighted passages, all counted as domestic violence, including mental abuse.] You see, we don't send women into domestic violence; they come to us for divorce because they suffer domestic violence. This is one of their major reasons.

JRB: How did you decide to send out three letters?

Suhaib: I had no models. Shariʿa says to give three chances, as in the story of Moses and Khidir, in Sura al-Kahf, where Moses tells him not to speak, and he does, and then again, and then after the third time, Moses says, "That's over and we will go separate ways." Only later did I see that British courts also send three letters. Also, later on I saw books of the cases the Prophet decided. . . . We added procedures from time to time. For example, we added *talāq tafwīz* [delegated divorce] as another form of divorce.

JRB: How often do you find those?

Suhaib: Almost never! In the Pakistani *nikahnama* [marriage book] you have the option of following that, but everyone just crosses them out.[18] We also added the solemn declaration [that the mother would let the

> father visit the children], and we added the opinion that if the man initiated the civil divorce, or if the wife did and the husband did not defend [contest] it, that this is an Islamic divorce—but not if the husband is absent from the proceedings, or if he says nothing.

The ISC publishes procedures on its website. Indeed, as the flowchart posted at the entryway to the Leyton office suggests, the ISC devotes considerable attention to public demonstrations that it has clear, fair, and transparent procedures. This attention also helps explain why it makes both client interviews and formal deliberations open to visitors, including journalists and anthropologists (with the permission of the parties involved).

The concern with procedure goes beyond publicity, however; it rests on a sense that legitimacy to a number of different publics will be aided by an emphasis on procedures. Indeed, as the flowchart suggests, one can almost say that if a client follows certain steps, and is able to provide the right sort of documents along the way, a divorce will be granted. But a focus on procedures can lead to multiple outcomes. For example, as we shall see below, Haitham al-Haddad has urged the others to resist granting a divorce if they have not been presented with correct forms of proof, whereas the others are more willing to grant a divorce if the wife has followed the correct steps.

We have seen mention of four major procedural requirements. First, the scholars require that there be a civil divorce proceeding if the marriage was registered in the United Kingdom or conducted abroad. Although they do not necessarily wait for the completion of the civil divorce process to finalize the Islamic divorce, if a final divorce decree, the "decree absolute," is granted, the scholars are likely to proceed quickly to granting the wife's request; they say that the marriage is over and there is little sense in prolonging its Islamic dimension. They also wish to work in a way that complements the workings of the civil courts, in the hope of future, closer linkages between the two bodies. They know of the existing collaboration between rabbinical tribunals and family courts based on the Divorce (Religious Marriages) Act (2002), which allows civil judges to suspend divorce proceedings between the decree nisi and the decree absolute (which mark the two stages of a civil divorce proceeding) if there is an ongoing religious divorce. The law was motivated by the observation that even after a civil divorce some Jewish men refused to grant their wives religious divorces. Currently the law only applies to Jewish proceedings, and in any case, the issues facing Muslim women differ from those facing Jewish women. However, some Islamic scholars believe that the law suggests that English courts might someday recognize their own judgments as having legal effect, and it leads them to value steps that would bring their own procedures closer to those followed by civil judges.

Second, they require that the two parties have been separated for one year, though some urge that there be a two-year separation if the divorce is contested. As with the first requirement, this rule is invoked for practical reasons, as a way of determining that the divorce request is serious. It is a lower bar to clear than are the two-year and five-year separation periods required for most divorces in English law (depending on whether the divorce is not, or is, contested by the respondent) but follows a similar logic.

Third, if the children live with the mother, and the father has indicated that he has difficulty getting access to them, they usually ask her to give an affidavit that she will allow him to see his children. In recent years the wife often swears to this undertaking in the presence of a solicitor. The ISC requires the undertaking in part to converge with what they think a family court would do in these circumstances, and in part because they consider it to be an Islamic norm that both parties be able to see their children. Some scholars believe that English family courts tend to give insufficient weight to the father's need to see his children (a claim also made by some English fathers) and that consequently they need to pay particular attention to this issue.

Finally, they may ask the wife to return any mahr that she has already received. Usually they propose that she give it to the ISC for safekeeping and notify the husband that he may come and collect it. If he does not respond in six months, then they return it to her (or donate it to a charity in cases where she so requests). Often the wife has also received jewelry. Sometimes gold jewelry is clearly part of the mahr, and in those cases they require her to return it. Otherwise they make no ruling concerning its eventual disposition, on grounds that the jewelry and other goods given by one party to another around the time of the wedding obey local social logics of reciprocity and are not the responsibility of the shariʿa council.

Attesting Separation

The council changes procedures as their members develop consensus around a particular issue. For example, scholars have long considered the couple's prior separation to be a critical element in establishing the seriousness and validity of the divorce request, but only in 2009 did they ask for written attestations with two witnesses. In January 2010, Atif explained to me how the council came to adopt the rule and how it complicated his life:

> Atif: We have a rule that the woman has to prove separation of at least one year with two witnesses. Haitham urged us to add this rule six to eight months ago. I wish they had not adopted the rule, because now I have to specify who does and does not count as a witness; it cannot be family members, but perhaps those are the only people who know about the matter. English people, they say, "We do not like to air dirty laundry," and they [the couple and their families] keep these things to

themselves. Why do they [the scholars] need two people to attest to it? Well, when the scholars discussed this issue, they said, well, judges require two witnesses, and that is what you need for a talaq.

JRB: So it was a *qiyas* [an analogy, here referring to the talaq procedure]?

ATIF: Yes, a qiyas, so we have two witnesses here too. Haitham insisted on this rule in cases where the husband has not responded to our letters. If he responds and does not contest the fact of separation, okay, but the other scholars were assuming that even without a response they could tell from the case, from what the wife said, that there was separation. But perhaps, said Haitham, she is lying and she sneaks out and they have sex? There may be one case in two hundred like this, but now we have to make a general rule, and then that will just lead the one case to do some other trick.

JRB: Why require one year?

ATIF: Well, the scholars said yesterday that many jurists had different views about this: some said sixty years, some ten, some five, some one, and they took the easiest number. Those jurists' rulings had to do with the cases where the husband has disappeared, but the scholars now apply it to the length of separation.

The following week, on January 27, 2010, this issue came up during the formal deliberations about a divorce petition. The wife had initiated proceedings with the ISC in June 2008, reporting that they had already been separated for six months. The husband refused the invitations of the ISC to attend a reconciliation session. The wife was told to begin the procedures to obtain a civil divorce, which was finalized in August 2009. The issue before the ISC was whether they had sufficient grounds to grant her a religious divorce.

The scholar chairing the discussion of the case, Abu Sayeed, pointed out that the English courts granted a decree absolute if, six weeks after the decree nisi, the other party had not responded. But Haitham al-Haddad, the scholar who had been adamant about the need for proof of separation, objected to giving her the Islamic divorce right away. "We have not yet asked her to prove that they have been separated since that time," he said. "This is important." Atif, who was studying for his law degree, noted that the granting of the decree absolute proved that they had been separated because English courts require that this be established. They continued the exchange, with two other scholars, Suhaib Hasan and Khurram Bashir, joining in:

HAITHAM: In so many cases they say that they are separated, but they meet from time to time [and have sex]; we can't just act on emotions.

ABU SAYEED: They are living at different addresses.

HAITHAM: We have countless cases; here, she said [they separated] one year ago, and then we asked when they last had relations and she said two weeks ago. Because this will make our life easy [if we just believe her]. . . .

Abu Sayeed: The recommendation is to end the marriage, so can we add that we do so if she provides independent evidence of separation?

Suhaib: Here is proof. In a July 2008 letter, the husband says, "She took all my goods and did not speak to me since December; I am not allowed to see my son; I am required to pay child support. I do not want to divorce so I can see my son."

Abu Sayeed: Here I am going with Sheikh Haitham. There is still room for suspicion; perhaps they still sleep together.

Khurram: The husband himself says there is no contact [between them] and there is already a civil divorce. What else do you need? . . . Must we as judges try to prove [all] things that are not before our eyes?

Abu Sayeed: In these matters, we have to be strict [in following rules].

Haitham: The physical thing has not been established; we want physical evidence. We cannot say, "This means . . ." We cannot assume that civil divorce is proof of separation. I admit that the letter proves that he admits [that they had not had sex].

Haitham wanted the council to follow clear rules of proof, in this case, about the separation. The others argued that the absence of such explicit attestations should not keep them from dissolving the marriage because (1) they could infer from various statements that the couple had been separated for some time, and (2) the couple was already divorced legally, so the council should let them get on with their lives.

The discussion continued, and it became clear that Haitham was mainly concerned with making the general point and would allow the marriage to be dissolved, and, indeed, this was the action the council took—with the proviso that the wife must provide proof of separation. But this proof would simply be noted by the clerk and not require council approval, which meant that it would not be scrutinized very strictly. The scholars reminded themselves that they must be careful, and to that effect they cited an oft-quoted hadith that two of three judges will be in hellfire, and only the third will make the correct decision.

Practical Convergence

Recall that the other early shariʿa council, the Muslim Law (Shariʿa) Council, UK, has been largely directed by Barelvi Sufis. And yet despite the doctrinal differences between Sufis, on the one hand, and Ahl al-Hadith and Deobandis, on the other, the two councils work in very similar ways. Indeed, each presumes the other's judgments to be sound.

As the western London council's executive secretary, Maulana Shahid Raza, explained, when they began, they also improvised procedures: "At first we had no procedures or forms; it would take us hours to draft a letter. Each letter and each divorce certificate we would draft each time. We would call the husband and ask him to come to meet with us. He would either curse us or, more rarely, come. For the first two years we worked like that, with no records. . . . We used to put the reasons for the divorce on the certificate itself, but women came to us and said, 'We came to get a divorce certificate; we did not come to be certified as quarreling all the time; these became a charge sheet against me.'" Now they would not put that in the certificate, but they do mention grounds such as failure to support, or a long separation, or that a civil divorce has already taken place, or that efforts at reconciliation have failed.

As with the ISC, they have consultations ("surgeries") both at the central office (once in Ealing, now in Wembley) and at mosques throughout the country, including in Bradford, Leeds, Birmingham, and, especially, at the Leicester Central Mosque, the Sufi mosque near the train station that welcomed Ibrahim Mogra when "his own" Deobandi mosque would not—and where Shahid is the imam. Their delays are three to twelve months long, a range close to that of the ISC. They send three letters, allowing for responses, as does the ISC, and Shahid gave the same reason for three as did Suhaib, from the Islamic tradition of giving three chances, as shown in the story of Musa and Khidir. They have the same difficulties of ever getting mediation to work: "If the wife comes here, it is her last thing; no one can stop her from getting a divorce. We also offer the possibility of arbitration, drawing up a contract, about access to children, or property, but rarely does this happen. No one has ever taken such a contract to a civil court for enforcement." Nor do they ask about assets; if the husband raises the question of assets and child custody, they send him to civil court, as does Suhaib. They also offer the husband the option of giving a talaq upon the wife's agreement to let him see the children.

Clients do note differences between the two councils, but these are rather particular. Shahid mentioned two issues. First, his council follows Hanafi rulings, including the judgment that saying the talaq three times means that all three talaqs have been pronounced. He said, "Muslims here who are Hanafi come to us because they know what we follow." That may be true, and the two councils do differ on the triple talaq issue, but Abu Sayeed is also Hanafi-trained, and in many issues the Leyton council also follows Hanafi doctrine.

A second difference regards the weight given to men's and women's interests, but this is a question of individual tendency.

Shahid: Some clients believe that the Leyton council is more oriented toward the husband.

JRB: Perhaps this regards Haitham al-Haddad in particular.

Shahid: Yes, that is true, for example, one woman came to us and we asked the husband by telephone if he were willing to have mediation,

> and he said yes, as long as Sheikh Haitham was the mediator! Some clients know that Zaki Badawi [their founder] was seen as liberal and progressive, and so think that we might be more "liberal." But we also have differences among us: some are more conservative and want to delay proceedings and contact the husband again, and so on, whereas others want to finish it now, saying that the marriage is over and so let us give the divorce today.

If Britain's mosques have a tendency toward hardening theological differences (see chapter 3), it is not surprising that shariʿa councils would converge on procedures. The shariʿa councils face practical questions regarding resolution. They work in recursive fashion, revising their procedures and doctrinal stances as a result of interaction with clients and with multiple publics, including the legal system.

Conclusions

Although at its founding in 1982, the ISC scholars thought that the council would undertake a wide range of matters for British Muslims, it quickly came to focus its formal deliberations on matters of religious divorce, although the individual scholars also give daily informal advice on a range of spiritual and social issues. The ISC has become a tribunal, and indeed looks to the procedures found in English courts for some of its own rules.

The council founds its legitimacy on its procedures, the promise that if a client does this and that, she will get a divorce certificate. The council has adapted its procedures in a recursive relationship to three audiences: clients, English courts, and judges in Muslim countries (especially Pakistan). Clients' behavior has led the council to retreat from making declarations about child custody and to require attestations that a father can see his children, or that a couple has been separated—and with witnesses and signatures added as time went on. English courts have offered a model of procedures, and council scholars see their willingness to revamp procedures "in the shadow of" the English civil procedures as steps that might win them eventual recognition as competent to deliver divorces with civil effect. That this is highly unlikely to ever happen does not diminish the appeal. Concern that their judgments be accepted overseas has led them to ensure that clients know that they should have the judgments stamped by the Pakistani Consulate in London.

These continuing adaptations are made against the background of a twin anxiety that runs throughout the council's reasoning and debates: Does what they do produce the desired religious effect? And, how can they most appropriately justify their procedures to these multiple publics?

CHAPTER 6

Unstable Performativity

IN CHAPTER 5 WE LOOKED AT WHAT THE ISLAMIC SHARIʿA COUNCIL DOES IN ITS everyday interactions and in its management of cases. But we can now ask what it does in a different way: What is the act performed by the council? What is their argument for having met the conditions for a successful performance of an Islamic act? What justifies dissolving marriages at all?

Institutions depend on their capacity to change the world by decreeing, stating, affirming, announcing, baptizing, pronouncing, or doing other acts that we call "performative" for their special quality of announcing and at the same time creating a new state of affairs. "I pronounce you" announces and marries; "I give you an A+ for the course" communicates and grades. Marriage and the university depend on the shared understanding that the world has changed when the right person says the right words under the right circumstances. Of course, we change the world in myriad ways by speaking, but the special character of these "explicit performatives" lies in their dual form of announcing plus changing.

An early formulation of this idea comes from the philosopher J. L. Austin (1962), who queried performatives' "felicity conditions," that is, the conditions under which the announcing brings about the changing: the person "pronouncing you husband and wife" has to really have "the powers vested in me." But as Jacques Derrida (1988) pointed out, these conditions are not prelinguistic features of the world but a matter of the shared intentions of those concerned by the act in question. Furthermore, they are constantly subject to challenge and change.[1]

We ascribe social value to the idea that performatives are fixed and predictable—once married always married until death or divorce—but we also know that they are not always so. Prizes can be withdrawn, marriages annulled, course grades changed. When these things happen the performative is obliterated. Indeed, a whole branch of private international law—one that concerns us here—concerns precisely when getting married does not mean staying married when a couple travels across jurisdictions.[2]

Performativity can be distributed in differing ways between religious and state authorities. We are used to the idea that a religious marriage may have legal effects, because in many countries such is the law. Once a few papers are signed, an Anglican priest, a Jewish rabbi, or a Muslim imam can change a couple's civil status in, for example, England or the United States. Conversely, in many countries with Islamic courts, a court divorce is also, immediately and automatically, an Islamic divorce, because the laws say so.

The shariʿa councils do not have that legal legitimacy. They make no claims to legal authority, and their religious authority is self-proclaimed, albeit based on the general principle that Muslims, as a community, should create the conditions that enable individuals to live within the limits ordained by God. No state laws back them up, and the religiously performative quality of their acts is nowhere made explicit.

We can go further. Why are doubts not also present for state-based Islamic courts? By what delegation of authority did the Indonesian or Pakistani state receive a divine performative power that they could in turn hand over to the state courts? The uncertainties around shariʿa council performativity thus point toward a much broader problem regarding the capacity of a state to say when a religious act has taken place.[3]

How Does a Divorce Occur?

We can recognize three competing theories about what happens when, at the wife's request, a shariʿa council dissolves a marriage.

One theory has it that the council has the Islamic authority to dissolve a marriage: their pronouncement has a performative value in that it causes the marriage to end. The council scholar would then be functionally equivalent to an Islamic judge (*qadi*). Let's call this idea *judicial performativity.* It corresponds to the widespread practice and idea of judicial dissolution of marriage found in Muslim lands, mentioned in chapter 4.

A second theory is that the council mediates an agreement between the husband and the wife, whereby the wife repays or foregoes her mahr and the husband grants a talaq. This is the classic idea of a khula. All performativity would be found in the husband's agreement. Let's call this the *husband's performativity*. In a technical sense it assimilates the khula to the talaq, but in a procedural sense, it is distinguished from a talaq by the fact that the wife brought a divorce demand to the council, as she might come to a court in a country with Islamic law.

A third theory is that the council attests to the dissolution of the marriage contract, certifying something that has already occurred. Through their behavior, the couple has caused the marriage to fail. That failure might be proven by the completion of a civil divorce. This theory depends on the idea of marriage as a contract, which can dissolve due to nonperformance by one of the parties. We can think of this theory as one of the *couple's performativity.*

Three theories, then: judicial performativity, husband's performativity, and couple's performativity. The shariʿa council dissolves the marriage, or it facilitates the husband's divorce pronouncement, or it certifies an already-existing marital collapse. In chapter 4 we saw how the first two theories have coexisted uneasily for centuries in Muslim countries.

Each theory resonates in different ways with different publics. Many British Muslims, including some who use a shariʿa council's services, are unsure of how well the scholars grasp English life, or why they have the authority to grant divorces. Husbands, in particular, fail to see how the councils can issue divorces without their consent. Many non-Muslims join in that skepticism; some argue that the councils perpetuate the subjugation of women and subvert the unity of the law. A bill before Parliament as of 2015 would punish shariʿa council personnel who make erroneous claims about their services. The theories that impute performativity to the husband or to the couple would plausibly reassure these audiences, as a council would merely facilitate an arrangement between two persons.

For officials in Muslim countries, the theory of judicial performativity is more convincing because it corresponds to how they see their own role. Some women who seek divorces from shariʿa councils plan to return to Pakistan or another Muslim country and remarry, and they, along with the ISC scholars, want to make sure that the council certificates are recognized as valid in those countries. Pakistani judges require something like the certificate of divorce given by a shariʿa council for a woman to remarry in Pakistan. They recognize the ISC certificates once they have been stamped by the Pakistan Consulate in London.[4] The Saudi embassy reportedly accepts ISC documents as Islamic documents of marriage and divorce required of Muslims wishing to travel to Mecca. So if the shariʿa council act is assimilated to that of an Islamic court judge (qadi), then these matters are easier to negotiate: an ISC divorce certificate is functionally equivalent to a Pakistani divorce certificate.

All three theories appear in the words and deeds of the scholars on the ISC and at other councils. However, and this is the central argument of this chapter, no single theory can be held and proclaimed across all discursive contexts because they are not mutually compatible. Each theory performs a certain function in the social life of the councils, but no one theory can perform all such functions. The performativity of shariʿa councils is, I argue, *intrinsically unstable*, and this leads to areas of ambiguity.

↳ main argument of the chapter

MANAGING THE KHULA

At the heart of the problem is the khula. Recall that a khula occurs when a wife persuades her husband to divorce her by giving him something. The "something" is often assumed to be the mahr: if it has been paid, it is returned; if unpaid, it is forgiven. That the mahr is the appropriate payment for the khula is a convention, with support in the hadith, rather than a fixed element of shariʿa.

Table 6.1. Major types of divorce

Talaq	Husband divorces wife, pays *mahr*.
Khula	Wife gives husband a gift (often the mahr) and in return he divorces her, with or without the intervention of a judge.
Tafrīq, faskh	Judge separates the couple/annuls the marriage, and the husband pays mahr.

Note that in the theory of the khula, the husband agrees to the divorce, as represented in table 6.1. But how do we know when he has done so? If he pronounces the divorce, then the matter is clear. But if the husband does not give a talaq, can the scholar infer his agreement to divorce from another action he has taken? The shariʿa councils look either to the husband's failure to contest a civil divorce, or his failure to respond to the council's letters, as a basis for making such an inference. But he may not agree. Let's see how these considerations arise in cases.

Case: Does Civil Divorce Imply Religious Intent?

On April 4, 2013, a young woman came with a friend to see Suhaib Hasan. Her husband had divorced her in civil court, "and now he says he is not a Muslim, [saying:] 'so far as I am concerned, I have given you a divorce,' but I am practicing, even if he is not, and I want to clear the air, and in case there is a new person, I can show him a certificate." The husband had paid the mahr and kept the gold; they did not seek the return of the gold. Suhaib said, "He just has to pay the mahr; we cannot deal with the gold."

Suhaib called the husband on the telephone; he answered and said "yes" when Suhaib asked for him by name, and then when Suhaib explained that he was calling from the Islamic Shariʿa Council, the husband said, "You've got the wrong number" and hung up. Suhaib stared bemused at the phone, chuckled, and turned to the two women. Because the husband was the petitioner in the civil divorce case, Suhaib said they would send him a letter, and if he did not reply, they would issue the certificate.

FRIEND: But why do you need his consent?

SUHAIB: This is a matter of procedure; when there is no reply in a month, we will issue the certificate.

FRIEND: No, you should not ask him, you should say that they are divorced, because she just needs the certificate.

SUHAIB: We must have something in our record saying that we asked him. Intention is intention, but divorce should be in writing, that "I divorce you."

FRIEND: It *is* in writing.

She referred here to the civil divorce. The wife stood up, approached Suhaib's desk, and picked up the civil divorce papers that were in the file. She began to read aloud from the court's decree nisi, and then from her solicitor's letter. Suhaib said, "Now, there are two ways of doing this. We can send him the letter, and then issue you the certificate [and he shows her a certificate], meaning we followed the procedure, or I can write you a statement saying that the civil divorce constitutes an Islamic divorce as well." The wife and her friend indicated that they liked the second option.

> Wife: Am I divorced in the eyes of Allah?
> Suhaib: Yes.

He wrote the statement while they waited. They talked among themselves in hushed and excited tones.

> Friend: The statement tells you that it is all over, in the eyes of Allah.
> Wife: I'm clean!

Suhaib explained that "you are free once your ʿidda [three-month waiting period] has ended."

This case began as a straightforward, if truncated, divorce case: Suhaib inferred the husband's intent (*niyyah*) to divorce his wife from the fact that he petitioned for the civil divorce. Indeed, he had pronounced what could be taken to be a talaq. The husband's behavior on the telephone made Suhaib little inclined to continue any exchange with him. All Suhaib needed to do is to write the husband and, after the husband predictability failed to reply, issue a certificate of divorce. From my many conversations with and observations of Suhaib, I would say that he believes that the husband should divorce his wife religiously if he has divorced her in court, and that the husband's act of signing a civil divorce agreement constitutes, at the same instant, a talaq. Another scholar at the Birmingham council (to be examined in chapter 8) put it this way: "If he agreed to the civil divorce in court or signed his agreement, then it is a talaq and they do not have to come here at all to be divorced."[5]

The friend pushed the question, however, saying that if her friend was indeed already divorced "in the eyes of God," then Suhaib should just issue her the certificate then and there. Suhaib agreed with her on the substantive point: the friend was divorced. However, he informed her that the council's procedures require issuing the certificate only after they have tried, and presumably failed, to elicit a statement from the husband. He offered a quick alternative, a simple statement affirming that, given the nature of the civil divorce, she was indeed divorced on the Islamic dimension as well: a fatwa.

But not everyone would agree with Suhaib. The ISC senior scholars generally do agree that if a husband states that he agrees with his wife's petition for a religious divorce, then the divorce should be granted in near-automatic fashion. His intent is clear. But not all are convinced that failing to contest a *civil* divorce implies intent to grant a religious divorce.

More broadly, the case raises the issue of the relative roles of intention and utterance in performing the talaq, an issue that has been a matter of debate among Muslim scholars for centuries. As we saw in chapter 4, Islamic scholars have disagreed among themselves on the felicity conditions for this performative act. What if he was so angry he had lost his mind? What if he did not intend a divorce but said the words, for example, while dreaming? There is general agreement that an act is necessary, but there is considerable leeway as to the words that need to be uttered. The ISC scholars frequently accept that words such as "it's over" clearly communicate a talaq intention. Across a wide array of Islamic practices, the right intent, niyyah, is critical for the practice to succeed. An oft-quoted hadith says, "Actions are but by intentions." And part of the efforts to reform Muslims' worship practices is always insisting that worshippers have the right intent. Part of this injunction has to do with the importance of sincerity to the accomplishment of pious acts. Part of it has to do with the practical issue of determining what action you wish to accomplish: go on the hajj or just visit Mecca? Divorce your wife or just argue?

Atif Matin explained how these concerns make it difficult to infer a religious intent from a civil action: "Sometimes, even if he did initiate it [civil divorce], he will not agree to a khula. He will say that he intended to divorce her only in civil fashion, that he did not formulate an intention to give her a religious divorce. And so we have to give the wife's request the full formal examination; we have to contact the husband. And if then he asks for a full refund of mahr, we will require it."[6]

Atif's last remark could be puzzling unless we recall that the form of divorce (talaq or khula) is determined in wholly proceduralist terms: Who started the ball rolling? From this perspective, and regardless of what happens in civil court, once a woman initiates a proceeding with the council, it is a khula procedure and will require a request for the husband's opinion and the eventual repayment of mahr. Put another way, procedurally, the Islamic divorce is a khula if the wife requests it, but a scholar can also infer a substantive talaq from the husband's civil-court behavior.

But not everyone accepts this proceduralist view, as in the following case, which highlights the instability of the theory of *couple's performativity* versus that of the *husband's performativity*.

Case: "But your website says the divorce already occurred!"

The ambiguity of the council's theory of performativity sometimes leads to objections on the part of women seeking divorce. On one occasion in

February 2010, I sat in on a consultation with Suhaib, held at the Leyton mosque because of the ongoing construction at the council offices. In the third case heard that afternoon, a young woman who was born in Pakistan but who now lived in Canada came accompanied by a female friend from Malaysia. The first woman had petitioned for a civil divorce from her husband, who also had been born in Pakistan. He did not contest the divorce, and she had the final divorce decree (the decree absolute) in hand.

The previous May she had come to see Abu Sayeed and had asked him, "Now that I have my English divorce, why can't I get an Islamic one?" Abu Sayeed had instructed her to begin the proceedings. She told Suhaib that she had never received the promised mahr even though her husband claimed to have paid it in full. They had a number of financial disputes that had been heard by the civil court. Suhaib informed her that because her husband did not contest the civil divorce in court, he should consent to an Islamic divorce, but also that he had the right to take back any mahr he had given her.

Suhaib asked the wife, "Can he prove it [his claim that he had given her the mahr]?" She indicated no. "No? Well then, just swear that you do not have it. Will you do that?" The wife said that she would. Suhaib said, "We are not required to write to him because he did not contest the [civil] divorce, but it is a matter of khula, so he does not have to pay you the mahr."

The woman then read aloud a passage from the ISC website that says that if the husband does not contest the civil divorce, the divorce is valid under Islamic law as well. She asked why, if so, he did not have to pay the mahr. Suhaib responded by quoting the next section from the website, which states that if a woman comes to the ISC for a divorce, then it is a khula. He reminded her of what that means: that she loses her right to mahr. This went back and forth until the woman turned to me and asked, "You speak English. What does this mean?" She handed me the printout of the website. It did indeed say both of these things. I waffled and said that perhaps the ISC is saying that a woman has been freed from her marriage by an uncontested civil divorce, but if she wants to undergo the ISC procedure, then certain consequences would follow. She indicated her frustration with the whole procedure but said she would take the next step.

Suhaib was ready to presume that the husband agreed to a khula divorce because he had not contested the civil divorce. But he also reminded the petitioner that although the civil divorce allowed her to get on with her life, if she wished to complete the ISC procedures, she would have to renounce any claim to mahr. One might find this in contradiction to the notion that she could be considered already divorced under Islamic law, as indicated on the website, and indeed that is how the woman interpreted the situation. This portion of the website suggests the third theory of performativity, namely, that the collapse of the marriage, as evidenced by the civil marriage, automatically brings about the collapse of the marriage on its Islamic dimension as well.

To the extent that Suhaib is applying the theory of "couple's performativity"—that the marriage collapse brings about the divorce—then issuing the certificate is not in order to carry out the divorce but merely to have the certificate in case it should prove useful. He indicated as much when giving the woman in the first case above the choice between waiting for a certificate and accepting a simple statement from him. In any case, God already considered her divorced. But then, why should a woman be asked to forgo or return her mahr as a condition for receiving the certificate? Suhaib's response was purely proceduralist: because agreeing to forgo the mahr is a prerequisite to completing the procedure for getting a certificate.

Suhaib's insistence may seem formalistic, but there is a practical reason for it. The rule that asking for a certificate from the council frames the divorce as a khula, and that therefore the mahr must be returned or forgiven, provides the ISC a way to forestall husbands' objections to the legitimacy of their wives' claims. Husbands who are irate that the ISC has divorced them at their wives' behest sometimes call up to berate the clerk, claiming that the ISC has no right to do so. They are less likely to protest if there has been a civil divorce and if the ISC has said that they were free of the obligation to pay outstanding mahr.

Parrying objections to council procedures requires some fast footwork. Atif suggested that while the council sees itself as dissolving a marriage, the second theory retains a backup status: "Sometimes the husband just ignores the whole process, but when he receives the divorce decree, then he knows there is no more he can do, and someone might tell him, 'Hey, you know you can get back the mahr,' so he comes by and then we give it to him. So it is sort of a 'halfway khula,' to cover our backs, so that if the husband complains, we can give him the mahr."

The following case involved such skillful parrying, and presents one of the more sustained critiques by a husband of the ISC.

Case: Virginity and an Irate Husband

The case file was opened in September 2009, and the clerk noted that the wife was born in Lahore and the husband in Bradford, that they married in Bradford in 2006, and that by the time the file was opened, they had been separated for eight months. The husband had paid one hundred pounds in mahr. The wife had French nationality; the husband was a British national. They had not yet obtained a civil divorce. She claimed that the marriage was never consummated and that there was no guardian (*wali*) at the wedding, which some scholars would see as making the marriage illegitimate. At the time of the formal deliberation, they continued to live in Bradford. The husband had responded to the council's letter but did not agree to a joint meeting.

The wife wrote to the council on October 1, 2009, to explain that she went through the nikah just to prove to his family that she would not leave him, and that they had never consummated the marriage. Two years after the marriage, she returned to France. She included a letter from her father saying he was not present at the nikah and that "I do not recognize this nikah to have any significance." She also enclosed a certificate of virginity from a doctor in France.

The ISC sent its usual first letter to the husband, transmitting the wife's letter. He replied with a lengthy, eloquent account of his mother's long illness and death, and his search for someone to love, and how he found his wife working in a restaurant. When she suggested they do nikah, he took her to see Sheikh Siddiqi of Hijaz College, who had regular sessions in Bradford, and who also was a barrister (and whom I profile in chapter 9). He asked one of Siddiqi's people to do the nikah.

On October 7, Haitham wrote a report for the files, saying that her father's consent was not given, "which is a prerequisite for a valid Islamic marriage according to the vast majority of scholars." He wrote a letter to this effect to the husband, who replied (on December 3), stating that "We are followers of the Hanafi school of thought," according to which "a woman—like men—possesses full legal capacity to marry without her guardian's permission. When presenting such a ruling, you cannot simply write a short e-mail stating that we go by the majority of scholars. Are you stating that the Hanafi school of thought . . . is wrong and has no bearing?" He offered to swear on the Qur'an that they did have sexual intercourse. He upped the ante, threatening to "expose the shariʿa council for its prejudicial stance." Presumably, it was he who later did so in an anonymous blog entitled *Exposing Shariʿa Council*, posted on January 23, 2011.[7] Letters were exchanged back and forth, always via the council. The wife sent a CD with voice message clips in which the husband insulted her.

The case was discussed at the Regent's Park Mosque's monthly meeting on July 28, 2010. From the file they read that the wife claimed the marriage was not consummated and they produced the doctor's certificate saying she was a virgin. (The certificate came from a doctor in Marseille; I translated for them.) The discussion was very brief. Abu Sayeed said, "We cannot read the whole file: if the marriage is not consummated, she can ask for dissolution, and if the wali is opposed to the marriage, then by all the schools, including Hanafi, he can cancel the marriage." Another scholar, sitting in on the meeting, asked, "Yes, but how does that bear on [the matter of] khula?" Atif gave his view: "It is a checklist, and shows that they don't get along." To which Abu Sayeed responded, "The husband did not provide a contrary medical report, so we should dissolve it, for all these reasons."

They dissolved the marriage, requiring that she return the jewelry and the mahr, on the grounds that the marriage was not consummated and it was carried out without the approval of her father. The bulk of the file bore on the decision in a way expressed by Atif: the couple clearly did not get along and the claim that there was no consummation gave the scholars a clear justification for ending the marriage. They wrote out the certificate on July 28, 2010, and sent the husband a letter with the decision on August 4. The files show that the wife left the hundred pounds mahr and one ring at the ISC; they sent the husband a letter attesting to the receipt of jewelry on August 16, 2010.

But the matter did not end there. I happened to be in the office on August 19, when the angry husband called Atif to say that he did not see how they could divorce him from his wife when he did not consent and they did not prove the wife's claims—in effect, that the felicity conditions for neither khula nor faskh were present. He had words with Atif for about twenty minutes. I heard Atif's side, a series of justifications for issuing the divorce without the husband's consent. (Ellipses in parentheses indicate when the husband is talking; after the conversation, Atif told me the gist of the husband's statements.)

> If a woman says she does not want to live with you, do we force her to do so? (. . .) As human beings, she cannot ignore her parents. I have heard this [the husband's complaints that the council did not prove anything] a lot of times; at the end of the day, Allah will hold us responsible. The Qur'an says, don't keep them in limbo. (. . .) Yes, yes, it is there (. . .) She said there was no consummation and her father said he did not give consent. After eighteen years of bringing up a daughter, what do you want: to marry her off in a respectable way, or have her show up and say she's gotten married? Will any Muslim, of the one billion, prefer that? I have seen hundreds of cases of this nature. "No marriage without the wali's [guardian's] consent" [he repeats it and then cites the Arabic]; it is a hadith, brother!
>
> What is the solution, brother, how can you move forward? She provided a doctor's report; you provided no evidence to the contrary. (. . .) We asked you for interviews, did you come? We invited you to a joint meeting, did you come? [They never come to these meetings, so when Atif responded by reciting procedure, it put him at an advantage.]
>
> It is up to the husband to reconcile; she provided copies of all your e-mails and you are so rude, how do you expect her to reconcile? Read what you wrote, brother! The etiquette a person has, it has nothing to do with a master's degree. Are we supposed to have a magic wand to reconcile you? [The husband starts criticizing the wife.] Why do you want to keep her with you as your wife, then? In Islam, "either keep them nicely or leave them nicely." We go into the basics here. (. . .)
>
> She is saying "no intercourse"; if you were in a judge's shoes, what would you say? [The husband raises the possibility that hymen reconstructive surgery had been done.] You are saying she has done this just to get

> a divorce? She has come here personally, once in Bradford and once to London; this shows her intent to have the divorce; it is not her parents pushing her. Okay, if for the sake of argument, brother, she were lying, what would you want us to do for the future of the marriage? [He starts complaining about her behavior again.] She accepts she wasn't forced into the marriage, so what? What is the future, so that neither party falls into *zina* [fornication]?
>
> You can send us an e-mail and we will forward it back to her, about what you want to do. But otherwise we dissolve it on grounds that the marriage cannot go on. The decision on the divorce won't be final until September 15. We will see if [your] wife is willing to come to a joint meeting on the 15th [he ascertains that the husband can come], but I will need to ask a senior scholar.

None of Atif's advice for going forward was taken, and the divorce was declared final. Atif had cleverly relied on procedural justifications—"you didn't show up"—and on various scriptural texts about freeing the wife. These tactics usually work to quiet down husbands, as does the fact that the wife is asked to return any mahr paid her, which the woman in this case did do, and the husband collected it. (More often the husband does not do so and it is returned to the wife, or, if she prefers, donated to charity.) This is the social function of the "halfway khula."

The issue of proving her virginity—and the general difficulty of proving anything—vexed the council, as they were dependent on documents submitted by and testimony from the parties involved. Atif dealt with the problem by invoking the absence of proof from the other side and the likelihood that because it was her body that was in question, a judge would side with her. He avoided the question of how to assess the balance of evidence; doing so could take the council into an evidentiary battle that they could not enter.

This case and all cases in which the matter of the husband's agreement is invoked raise the second tension, between the theory of *husband's performativity* and that of *judicial performativity*. Given the complexities of the theory of the husband's performativity, why does the council not just say to everyone that the council arrogates to itself the judicial authority to dissolve a marriage? This stance would render irrelevant the consent of the husband. It also would correspond to the general development of Islamic jurisprudence in states applying Islamic family law. As we saw in chapter 4, during the nineteenth- and early twentieth-century discussions of Islamic reform, reformers saw that judges already had been dissolving marriages in cases of lack of support or abuse, and proposed that incompatibility may also be grounds for faskh.

In accord with this idea, when they discussed these matters with me, the ISC scholars referred to what they do as a faskh or judicial dissolution.

Khurram Bashir explained what they do as an attempt at khula followed by an inevitable determination of faskh:

> KHURRAM: Most of what we do is faskh.
> JRB: But the council's information refers to khula.
> KHURRAM: Well, the husband *might* agree to give his wife a divorce. But as the same moves along it becomes evident that he will not, most of the time, and then we dissolve the marriage, faskh.[8]

However, if the council were to proclaim their judicial performativity and speak of faskh, they would make themselves into an Islamic law court, and doing so would raise at least three questions. First, it would be difficult then to justify why the wife should give up her mahr if the husband was at fault. Such a sacrifice is part of the deal for a khula but not for a faskh. Second, if they were a court, they would be able to summon witnesses, and if they decided that the husband was at fault, they might award the mahr to the wife. But they are not a court and have no such powers, and they don't really think they can prove much of anything. For that reason they never use the terms "qadi" or "faskh" in speaking with clients or on their website. Third, for many Muslims, faskh retains a sense of "annulment," implying that the council finds that a valid marriage never took place, and, although sometimes (as in the case just examined) they do so find, in most cases they do not.

These dilemmas of performativity lead to the instability we have seen in the process of interacting with clients or deliberating among scholars. It is structural, not reducible to attributes of particular scholars. It is found in Islamic jurisprudence, but is exacerbated by the specific condition of constructing a quasi-judicial institution without a legal base. A similar instability seems to characterize the workings of the nonstate tribunals in India, called dar ul-qaza, or at least has led to legal challenges to their legitimacy.[9]

Do the other councils experience the same dilemmas? I discussed the issue with Maulana Shahid Raza, the executive secretary of the Muslim Law (Shariʿa) Council, UK.[10]

> JRB: Were there discussions about when a divorce was by khula and when it was by faskh?
> SHAHID: Yes. We discussed what the husband could ask for in khula: Demand more than he paid? Only valuables, or also clothing, furniture, or other items given to his wife? And could there be a khula if he were in Pakistan and could not be expected to respond?
> JRB: Did anyone say that you could not really prove grounds for faskh?
> SHAHID: If the husband had been in prison or had committed violence and she had reported it to the police, then we have proof. Or if he took a second wife without telling her, and there was a contract [a "delegated

talaq" signed at the time of the marriage]. Or perhaps there was no contract but he did not treat them equally, so it was grounds of injustice.

JRB: What about if the marriage was really over?

Shahid: We used to have many cases of noncompatibility, when one person was a farmer in Pakistan and the other was brought up here, but now there are not so many spouses from overseas, so that reason has declined. There is also less parental interference than before, either because parents have realized that interfering produces bad results or because today's parents themselves were born here and so they understand. Now new issues arise: drug use, gambling, drinking, and having affairs. Recently we have heard complaints about "cultural clash," when people marry across ethnic lines. After several years of marriage, issues start to arrive, about where to spend holidays, attitudes toward in-laws, and so forth.

JRB: The Leyton council says in about 30 percent of petitions, the wife alleges abuse.

Shahid: Oh, easily 30 percent here, perhaps more . . . But to give a faskh, there always must be a fault, according to shariʿa.

JRB: Does the husband's mere refusal to divorce constitute a fault?

Shahid: It could. We always ask the husband to pronounce the divorce. If he refuses, and they are separated, and he does not support his wife, then he is refusing to let her continue with her life, and that is a fault, so we can issue a faskh.[11]

In the end, this council falls back on a theory that they can find the husband at fault and dissolve the marriage merely on grounds that he refuses to divorce his wife although the marriage is over, a form of judicial performativity but without a very high standard of proof of fault.

Transnational Instability

This instability has repercussions for the trans-state legibility of the divorce certificates, as the following incident suggests: I went to the Leyton offices of the ISC in the afternoon of July 13, 2010. Haitham joined Atif and me in the upstairs kitchen, where Atif was tinkering with their new espresso machine. Haitham sat on the edge of a table in the by-then crowded space and puzzled over the folder in front of him. "Where is the original, the one the Jordanian judge would have seen?" he asked. "I worry that, seeing that we gave a faskh, he will make an unfair decision."

I had been confused for months about just what sort of Islamic divorce women were obtaining from the ISC, and this confusion was emerging here in a concentrated, tense way. The case Haitham was fretting over concerned a couple from Jordan who had been divorced by the ISC in 2005. Now, in July 2010, the husband had appeared in Leyton, reporting that his wife had gone before the Jordanian tribunal to ask for a settlement of 10,000 dinar, on grounds that the divorce was a faskh and thus she was due her mahr. "What do I write? There is no Arabic version of the divorce decree," complained Haitham.

There never are Arabic versions, Atif explained: "You have to say that the wife came to us to get a khula, that is what the procedure is, but because the husband never agreed to give her the divorce—he imposed unacceptable demands—it was the shariʿa council that awarded her the divorce. But we explained—this is what you write—that this is just because the husband would not agree, you do not get the mahr." "If only the ISC were well organized," lamented Haitham, "all this would be clear."

But it would not be clear, indeed could not be, because the ISC's ambiguities are built into its structural dilemma. In this case, moreover, two of their perennial problems converged into a perfect ISC storm. First, the decision that concerned Haitham was written as a khula but in substance it was a faskh because it was given without the husband's consent, and thus the wife had the right to ask for her mahr, which she was now doing. Second, there is no "international, private Islamic law" that would resolve difficulties across jurisdictions. Haitham has no way of knowing what the Jordanian judge is reading or thinking, and thus does not know what to send back. Atif tells him that he can print out an original of the judgment from the database, and he does so, one that looks just like the 2005 document, with "Duplicate" stamped in red. But this does not resolve the matter.

The next day, Haitham told me that the husband in the case had said to him that "If I had known that the wife could ask for money from this divorce in Jordan, I would have given her the khula." He did not know what the different categories of divorce meant. Atif remarked, "But we tell them, they are on the form."

Conclusions

The legitimacy of the ISC is attacked by irate husbands, by wives frustrated at delays (which usually follow from the husbands' efforts to stall the procedures), and by many in the media and various think tanks who see in them a creeping replacement of English law by Islam. The London council responds by establishing and continually adding to rule-like and "court-like" procedures. They even have a wildly complicated flowchart on the first wall you see when entering their offices. But rules require translations from the practices of judges in particular countries and run into a contradiction between a universalistic view and a context-sensitive view of marriage and divorce.

Furthermore, the rule-like procedure ignores the claim that either husbands should consent to a divorce or the council should be able to prove, in court-like fashion, the wife's claims.

The instability in what the council does hints at an instability at the heart of all attempts in Islamic countries to decide by statute what Islamic jurisprudence says on a matter, given the inherently pluralistic nature of jurisprudence—one says commonly there is no pope in Islam but there is no Supreme Court either, only supreme courts of this or that positive-legal system. The English case just accentuates this instability because, shorn of state backing and vulnerable to anti-Islam criticism, it has to scramble to make foundational claims. On a theoretical plane, this case recalls Derrida's critique of Austin on performativity: namely, that "felicity conditions" are never assumed; they can always be challenged.

CHAPTER 7

Competing Justifications

THE SHARIʿA COUNCIL'S PROBLEMS WITH PERFORMATIVITY COME FROM ITS status as a nonstate tribunal. But it shares with state Islamic courts elsewhere the challenge of arriving at a common judgment from diverse starting points.

Indeed, this challenge is exacerbated for a British shariʿa council, as it lacks a shared set of laws or jurisprudence on which to base decisions. Each scholar has his or her own repertoire of texts and traditions, practical knowledge (of Britain, Pakistan, or elsewhere), and ideas about rights and fairness. The scholars come from different countries: the three senior scholars on the ISC come from Pakistan, Bangladesh, and Saudi Arabia. They have different educational histories and have developed individual theological allegiances to different Islamic legal schools and to different ways of interpreting scripture. They also differ in what legal scholars call judicial temperament: how to weigh multiple criteria, such as the value of precedent, the practical effects of a decision on litigants, and the intent of lawgivers.

Shariʿa council scholars, as well as Islamic court judges elsewhere, must also choose among several possible ways of justifying a decision. At times they must decide whether it is more important to let a woman get on with her life by dissolving her marriage or to uphold Islamic moral principles by refusing to reward improper behavior on her part. Judges and scholars may also find that there is a textual admonition in the Qurʾan or hadith that would outweigh either of those two concerns. I have found judges in Indonesian courts continually engaged in this kind of balancing.

In cultural sociology and political theory, modes of justification have become objects of analysis for two reasons. First, by studying how people justify their evaluations and actions, social scientists can account for differences by referring to other factors: national political traditions, positions in social networks, and so forth. Second, normative theorists can derive from such empirical accounts a normative basis of "spheres of justice," in Michael Walzer's phrase, for criticizing, for example, a transgression of marketplace logics into the sphere of family or ethics.[1]

However, much of the practice of justification involves, not a clash of broadly defined domains, such as morality versus economics, but variable weighting of alternative elements in a repertoire of ideas, values, and rules. Should we rely on a chart or on direct observation in making a medical diagnosis? How do we weigh different sources of authority—witness testimony, forensic evidence, written documents—in a courtroom? In these two cases actors might refer to distinct epistemological arguments about reliability, or distinct procedural arguments about the rules of the game. To capture these practices of justifying decisions, we need to adopt a microlevel approach.[2]

In our case, the debates are moral and theological as well as epistemological. How does one weigh the interest of a woman requesting a divorce with the tenets found in scripture? How can one decide whose testimony to rely on, or, given the unreliable nature of such testimony, should one just work for the "common good"? To look into these debates, we turn to the formal deliberations held monthly at the Regent's Park Mosque, and sometimes as additional "mini-meetings" at the Leyton offices. Although we will continue to take our point of departure from cases, we now focus less on the substantive outcomes reached than on the alternative reasoning processes or logics that provide the conditions of possibility for reaching any outcome.

Harm versus Haram

ISC scholars often find themselves debating about the relative importance of increasing welfare (*maslaha*) and minimizing harm vis-à-vis protecting the rights of God, his *haqq*, by avoiding an endorsement of forbidden (*haram*) acts.[3]

Case: Must She Return the Children?

On February 24, 2010, the scholars considered a case involving a Somali couple. In 2005, the wife and their four children were admitted to Britain from Tanzania, apparently as refugees; the husband was not admitted. In June 2007, a Somali-speaking junior scholar, Sheikh Abdullah, interviewed the wife in person and the husband by telephone. Haitham then took over the case and in July 2008 interviewed the wife in person, and the husband by telephone, with Abdullah's linguistic help. In his report of July 9, 2008, Haitham reported that the husband said he wanted her back and the wife admitted she could rejoin him. "The case should be closed; if she does not go back she is committing *nushuz* [disobedience]; we should not under any circumstance dissolve the marriage." Then, on October 14, 2009, Haitham interviewed her together with her brother, and they insisted on ending the marriage. Haitham wrote that the wife agreed to send the three daughters (ages four, seven, and eight) back to Tanzania and to let the boy, age fifteen, decide whether he would stay or go.

The council sent the usual letter to the husband to inform him of his wife's request, and when, after nine months, he had not responded, Atif inserted it into the day's agenda. Haitham opened discussions by challenging Atif on why he brought the case forward, as Haitham thought it closed.

HAITHAM: Why did you bring it?

ATIF: Because three months and he has not responded, and, Sheikh, you wrote this letter yourself and asked him to respond.

KHURRAM: The wife and husband agreed that she goes to the UK with the four children; she did not run away.

HAITHAM: They agreed, and then he could not come, and said, "As I am unable to come, you come back."

KHURRAM: This is the final report; listen to your own report [here in the report Haitham quotes the Somali scholar's initial interview]: "The husband never tried to travel to UK and he told her not to return to Tanzania with the children. The home office refused her application for asylum and [she] cannot travel abroad because she has no travel documents. Therefore I recommend her case for khula because separation of three years, no hope for family reconciliation, and no help or respect from the husband's side." Now it has been seven years, so how long does she have to suffer? This is our final report from our member [Abdullah]! We have to have respect for our members!

HAITHAM: She is the one who escaped, who did not want to come back. I met the case! I am dealing with this case.

KHURRAM: We cannot linger on [with] someone suffering like that.

HAITHAM: She committed the crime; why should we destroy the future of the children? She is the one who ran away, escaped. I don't want to continue because all this is being recorded.[4]

Haitham usually tries to slow down what he sees as overly hasty efforts to grant divorce requests. He was irritated that Atif did not follow his recommendation that the case be closed and no divorce granted. Khurram and Haitham then entered into the substantive issue: Did the wife fail to accede to her husband's request that she return to Somalia with the children, which could fall under the category of nushuz or disobedience? Or did she simply do what they had agreed on by traveling to Britain with the children? Should they require that she return to her husband or just let her get on with her life? Haitham felt himself getting worked up and, mindful of the presence of my recorder, decided to pause at that point.

Then they moved the debate to another level, which concerned less what the couple did than the principles on which the scholars' judgment should be based. Should they seek to prevent harm? And if so, what particular harm? Or should they adjudicate on the basis of the Islamic obligations of a husband and wife? At issue would be the charge of the wife's disobedience, a charge that, although it could be levied against a man as well as against a woman, has generally been used to penalize a woman who disobeys her husband, including leaving him without his agreement. In this case, Haitham saw the woman's refusal to return to Tanzania as obliging the council to refuse her petition for divorce.

Khurram argued that a woman should be able to end a failed marriage. But then he reframed the issue as a matter of preventing the haram act of fornication by allowing both people to remarry. Haitham refused this framing and insisted that they judge the wife's actions on the basis of shariʿa, and on God's rights and requirements, his haqq.[5]

Khurram: They will go to haram, if a man cannot give divorce. Women can seek khula without giving any reason, and we have to take environment and everything in consideration. This is January 2005.

Haitham: I spoke to him [the husband], and he said that "We agreed that we [would] go, and she went [to Britain] and I did not manage [to follow her] and I told her come back so why does she not want to come back, at least she should return the children to me because she breaks the agreement," and if she breaks the agreement we should help her to continue?

Khurram: She is asking khula and has the right; she has to pay the gold back. So, give the gold back and that is it.

Haitham: We want to give justice; you're stuck on this word "lingering on, lingering on."

Khurram: It is difficult to establish nushuz.

Haitham: We want haqq.

Khurram: We all want haqq; we all spend time and resources for haqq; you think we don't want haqq?

This exchange could have continued without resolution, and indeed the two scholars frequently do engage in prolonged debates over the question of what kinds of justifications should be given priority. Haitham agreed that steps should be taken to prevent people from committing forbidden acts, but he wanted the council to enforce shariʿa-based conceptions of the family. These were God's rights. Khurram emphasized that women had the right to seek a divorce, and in today's world, the council could not require that they prove that their husbands did something wrong in order to have their marriage ended. He did not disagree that acts of nushuz violate God's law but did not see how the council could prove such accusations.

At this point in the discussion, Suhaib intervened to try and bring the debate to closure by reverting to the original report. But this attempt turned the discussion to the matter of the children. Who had the right to child custody, and what could the council do in this regard?

Suhaib: We should have some consensus on this issue. Another report from Sheikh Abdullah, what does he say?

HAITHAM: Maybe we get an agreement with solicitors, to return the children.

KHURRAM: We cannot decide that it goes against the laws of this country, we have our boundaries and limitations; we can ask that she lets them visit him.

HAITHAM: This is something else. . . . We cannot even apply half of the medicine.

SUHAIB: Because they are grown children, they should be asked where they live.

KHURRAM: They are fifteen years now; she is eighteen. We cannot go in that [degree of] detail.[6]

ATIF: We cannot draft that kind of letter.

Suhaib's effort to reach closure did not immediately yield results, as Haitham sought another way to resolve the case within what he saw as the requirements of shariʿa: that the council bring in solicitors to draw up a binding agreement that the wife return the children to their father. He was no doubt encouraged in making this proposal by the wife's willingness, as reported in his written report, to let the younger children rejoin their father. Khurram and Atif both objected, pointing out that the council had no jurisdiction over child custody and could not order the children's "return."

This debate indicates the scholars' sense of the limitations of the council's actions. Even if Haitham was only proposing that a contract be drawn up regarding the children, the scholars knew that these have no weight in a court of law; judges would always consider the best interests of the child regardless of parents' prior agreement. Suhaib did not even agree with Haitham on the substance: he preferred that each child live where he or she chose. He suggested a compromise:

SUHAIB: We ask for [a] sworn statement that she will let the children return to [the] father if they so decide. No solicitor will write it; ask her for a statement. That way the burden will be on her; if she violates her statement, then she is in the wrong.

HAITHAM: So if a person insists on drinking wine and does not want to leave it and he comes to us and we tell him it's halal?

KHURRAM: She has the right according to khula.

HAITHAM: Khula!! This is shariʿa! There's a condition that the man must accept the khula.

SUHAIB: *La dharar wa la dharār* [no harm, and no necessity left unmet].

HAITHAM: Yes, but we are causing harm to the husband and the children.

SUHAIB: Sworn statement.

HAITHAM: If we create the conditions for them to stay in this country, and one of them apostates, then we would be the cause.

KHURRAM: But they were living in Tanzania; they could not do that there? They were already here; if we bring them here, that's another story.

HAITHAM: As long as you write down my firm objection to this matter in your report. If you are willing to take this in your necks, go ahead; I am not going to take the responsibility for this.

The council agreed, with Haitham abstaining, to dissolve the marriage, as long as the wife agreed to let the children decide what to do. Haitham launched into a series of hypotheticals: Would the council simply approve anything if it was already happening? He also invoked the alternative understanding of the khula, discussed in chapter 6, that it involved the husband agreeing to divorce his wife in exchange for the return of the mahr. No one picked up this point, as the success of council procedures depended on ignoring it. Haitham and Khurram continued to argue; Haitham said that angels were damning the wife as long as she did not return to her husband, and Khurram said that they needed to allow her to move on. They then reached a conclusion.[7]

HAITHAM: Do we tell all the people of Somalia then to come here?
KHURRAM: And once children are eighteen, no one can stop them. So write down that Sheikh disagrees with us; you've got the right.

The exchange ended there. Suhaib and Atif discussed the content of the letter they would send the wife. The written case file shows that the council wrote her on February 24 to say that the marriage would be dissolved upon receipt of the gold jewelry her husband had given her at marriage. She had already signed a statement that she would let the husband see the children. (The file states that the statement was made and sworn before a solicitor, but no document is included.) The wife replied to the council that the gold had been spent on the children, and, consistent with the council's usual procedures, no further mention was made of it. (This decision was usually made by Atif, often with Suhaib's consent.) The council sent her a letter with the certificate of divorce on March 10, 2010, which brought the procedure to a close.

Haitham's frustration stemmed from what he saw as simply dissolving marriages at a wife's request without properly determining the harm that could come to the children, or to the father, or, in the afterlife, to the wife—or for that matter to the scholars. He wanted to draw on English legal resources to compel the parties to obey shariʿa. Haitham is the one who most often urges a procedural reform on the council, sometimes to ensure that the husbands get a fair hearing. Khurram and, to a slightly lesser degree, Suhaib, do not necessarily disagree with Haitham on substantive points of law, but they are more concerned with freeing women from failed marriages. They tend to respond to statements or pleas from solicitors or social workers, but they see little point in trying to use the coercive potential of English law to achieve shariʿa ends, if the parties cannot be compelled to follow their agreements.

How to Justify Divorce?

In chapter 6 we analyzed the inherent instability of performativity regarding divorce. But some also challenge the very right of any shariʿa council or court to dissolve a marriage. On what can claims to legitimacy be based? Is it relevant to refer to practices and judgments issued in a particular country? In the following two cases, we see this issue emerge with respect to Pakistan and then to Saudi Arabia. The debates play out on two levels: Should this divorce request be granted, and, on the metalevel, should we be doing this sort of thing at all?

Case: Shariʿa versus Pakistani Courts

Running throughout the council deliberations are the tensions between appealing to a timeless and placeless shariʿa and appealing to the judicial practices of a country whose laws draw on Islam. Many of the council's cases come from people with connections by birth or marriage to Pakistan. What relevance does Pakistani judicial practice have for deciding a divorce case in Britain?

On January 27, 2010, the scholars deliberated a case coming from a woman living in Oldham, in northern England. Her husband had never left Pakistan, where they had married in 2003 and separated immediately thereafter. She had not seen him since. She went to see one of the corresponding scholars for the ISC, Sheikh Karim in Manchester, who recommended that they give the husband one month to pronounce a talaq, and if he did not do so, that they dissolve the marriage, because it was a forced marriage. She had not seen her husband for six years and did not love him. She had also been ill, she thought because of black magic. She had returned the jewelry to her husband, which was stated by the sheikh in the dossier. She thought that the husband was prolonging the marriage in order to come to the UK.

Khurram: And he admits himself that it was not a marriage but an "engagement," a "nikah." It never was consummated and he remains in Pakistan. She has no need to get a civil divorce, because they never were married.

Suhaib: In a letter addressed "to whom it may concern" dated July 1, 2005, he says that in Islam divorce is a bad action, and "I do not wish to break my engagement and am willing to sit down and solve any problem with her personally," and that she is not married but is his fiancée. He sent a letter received from a Dar al-ʿUlum, says he "received a fatwa" from them.

Khurram: For Pakistanis, "engagement" means "fiancée," not consummated; we should just dissolve it.

At this point the case seemed clear: the nikah was not consummated, and although still a nikah from an Islamic perspective, in Pakistani practice, it was considered only an "engagement" and would not have involved sexual intercourse. But Khurram's admonition to "just dissolve it" did not follow from these facts; furthermore, the husband's opinion had not been fully presented, as Haitham pointed out:

Haitham: But what did *he* say?

Khurram: Read it! She has not gone back for all this time.

Suhaib: The husband rejects her demand for a khula because the nikah was done by an agreement between the two of them. He writes that "there is no defect on my part" and asks, "Are you authorized to give khula without any reason? She was seventeen to eighteen years old and that was a right age to marry, and this is why I reject *talaqnama* [the divorce certificate mailed to him by the ISC]. If khula is done I will go to the Pakistan courts and will have a case against her where she has to appear." [The husband is arguing that there is no ground for annulling the marriage, the classical understanding of faskh, because the felicity conditions for a nikah were met.]

Khurram: He could apply in Pakistan for a restitution of conjugal rights, so we will advise her to stay away from Pakistan for the near future. If she goes then he can claim her as his wife according to Pakistani law. The family sides with the husband.

Haitham: In the past you have said they have recognized our decisions.

Khurram took the position of acting in the wife's interests against steps the husband could take under Pakistani law, but Haitham pointed out that Khurram usually claimed that Pakistani judicial practices could be a normative basis for what the ISC does, as we will see below. If Khurram held that view, how could he reject Pakistani legal procedures here?

Khurram: Yes, if she gets a civil divorce here then they accept it according to Pakistani law.

Haitham: But even if she did not, and she got our dissolution . . . ?

Suhaib: He would have to go to the Union Council [in Pakistan]. They would help her if she had our letter as a supporting document. Pakistani High Commission told me that if we add her Pakistani ID number to our letter, this helps. [The Union Council acts as a marriage registrar and is reported to accept ISC dissolutions of marriage, if they are stamped by the London Pakistani Consulate.]

Khurram: In Pakistan it is done at random. The Union Council is like a local council; they are deciding cases every week. . . . She had gone in 2003 to Pakistan for her sister's marriage and her parents married her off.

Suhaib: He got this fatwa, and he says that according to Hanafi rules, if the man is unwilling to divorce, the court cannot give khula without the consent of the husband, and asks: What is the jurisdiction of the qadi and the court? According to Imam Abu Hanifah, the total consent lies in the hands of the man in khula; the qadi serves as an arbiter, and according to Malik ibn Anas, if the spouses disagree, then a qadi can appoint a two-member arbitration committee, and if they come to an agreement, that is well and good, but if it is not possible, and if both arbiters want khula, then the qadi can dissolve the marriage. But the main point is . . .

Haitham: But this is not accurate even about Malik . . .

Suhaib: We are not discussing the right of the qadi. When can the qadi dissolve? Is there no right of dissolution? He is speaking about khula. Yes, khula cannot be done without the consent of the man, but can the qadi give talaq or not, this is the question?

Khurram: Every day there are hundreds of dissolutions in Lahore.

Haitham: This is what we discussed in the seminar, that the *jumhur* [majority of scholars] don't approve of marriage dissolution, and Hanafi don't have it: Maliki, only one opinion that says so, more lenient; Shafiʿi, no, except for cases of impotence and in some cases. This is really important.

Suhaib: Divorce against his will . . .

Here the three scholars cited different kinds of authority. Khurram repeatedly referred to the banal nature of judicial dissolutions in Pakistan in order to say that the practice was now normal in Islamic terms. Suhaib agreed on the propriety of dissolving a marriage without the husband's consent, but he wanted to have a basis in jurisprudence, and he distinguished between the claims of the husband concerning khula and what Suhaib saw as the clear right of the Islamic judge to dissolve a marriage. Haitham disagreed with both of them; for him, except in rare cases, judicial dissolution had no basis in jurisprudence. The details of which legal school (madhhab) takes which position were not at issue, as none of these scholars required that one madhhab be followed; the issue was whether they were jumping past classical jurisprudence in doing what they do regularly, namely, dissolving marriages. Haitham was questioning the very foundations of what they do. (Another council scholar, Hafiz Abdul Aala Durrani, had been silent but contributed to this exchange.)

Haitham: They want to escape the word *yafzaʿ* [to fear, as of God]. Thirty years ago in Saudi Arabia there was no dissolution of marriage; until Sheikh Muhammad Ibrahim asked the Committee to look at the matter again and they found that some of the *tābiʿūn* [second generation of Muslims] dissolved [marriages]; then they wrote to the courts saying they now could do it. But from a shariʿa perspective, marriage dissolution is the weakest option, should be the last resort; the qadi should be cautious, should delay as much as we can. In Saudi Arabia, I asked them, "What do you do?"; they said they approach the husband, try to persuade him: "She will give you money, divorce, she will give you money, blah, blah," if he is adamant; then we exercise this, okay?

ABU SAYEED: In Egypt . . .

KHURRAM: Pakistan, with the 1961 ordinance . . .

HAFIZ: The judge can decide. If there is harm against the women, *dharar*, if the judge confirms it, then dissolution, khula.

HAITHAM: Dissolution, not khula.

ABU SAYEED: Yes, in Egypt it is khula.

KHURRAM: But in Pakistan it is nikah, 1961 ordinance.

Here Haitham, too, cited judicial practices, but this time in Saudi Arabia, where, according to him, allowing faskh at all is relatively recent, and because it has a weak normative basis, the judges try to persuade husbands to give a talaq. Other scholars began to cite statutes in other countries that permitted judicial dissolution, sometimes, and confusingly, using the word khula; the reader will recall the discussion in chapter 6 of this confusion.

SUHAIB: The husband had a fatwa.

HAITHAM: Is it addressed to us?

SUHAIB: If he showed it to any Pakistani court, they would reject it completely because all the Pakistani courts. . . .

KHURRAM: To the 1961 family ordinance, allows judge to faskh, became ordinary: impotence, separation for a longer time, four years thereabouts, hundreds of cases of dissolution every day.

HAITHAM: Reason: she claims she dislikes him, or claimed, this is a matter of dispute, otherwise impotence, or if the arbiters agree on marriage dissolution. All the *madhāhib* [legal schools] agree but differ on the period, four years, two years, or one year.

KHURRAM: Yes, sixty years, fifty years separation.

ABU SAYEED: No, no, you are giving the wrong impression.

KHURRAM: Malikite law, sixty years, the original position

ABU SAYEED: But the latest Hanafi position, four years. All the India scholars adopted Maliki on this question, the latest position, all the Hanafi scholars of India adopted the Maliki madhhab as far as this situation is concerned.

This exchange reprised a discussion heard frequently about the length of time a couple has been separated before the marriage can be dissolved on those grounds. The ISC has adopted a minimalist position of requiring proof of one year's separation, a period arrived at on sheer practical grounds, but they frequently revisit the question of the legal schools' varying positions on the matter in order to (I think) make their own one-year period seem no more arbitrary. Abu Sayeed expressed his concern that Khurram's references to very long waiting periods would make Islamic rules seem unreasonable, perhaps to me.

HAITHAM: The Dar al-ʿUlum, do they accept dissolution?
[THE OTHERS SAY "NO."]
HAITHAM: They don't accept it . . . If someone believes in Dar al-ʿUlum and does not believe in Pakistani courts because he believes they are secularized or whatever, will he, and he goes to Dar al-ʿUlum and will they say to him your dissolution is invalid?
SUHAIB: They can't say that.
KHURRAM: If the court has made any decision they would accept it, even the Dar al-ʿUlum, they accept it.
SUHAIB: But the fatwa has no legal . . .
HAITHAM: But their fatwa goes against it. But what will he or she do? Will she say that my marriage is invalid? Like here [in England], she got a civil divorce but does not think that her civil divorce makes her Islamically divorced so she will come to us, so similarly in Pakistan if she got the divorce from Pakistani courts will she still apply to Dar al-ʿUlum to feel confident?
[CHORUS OF "NO."]
KHURRAM: Dar al-ʿUlum has no legal status, point ooooooo, never; Pakistani courts are final authority; Dar al-ʿUlum can issue whatever they like.
SUHAIB: As far as Muslim personal law is concerned, that is, shariʿa law: that is upheld by all the courts, they are deciding according to the shariʿa, so there is no question.
KHURRAM: Even if according to one fiqh, it is not according to their fiqh, but that is the last word.

At issue was a question posed in many Muslim countries: What if there is a difference between opinions issued by religious scholars—here represented by the many Dar al-ʿUlum schools—and the position of the country's state-appointed judges? Suhaib wanted to minimize the problem by saying that, in any case, the courts apply Islamic law. Khurram concurred but held that in any case only courts pronounce legal opinions. Haitham, in rather clever fashion, basically said, "If you think that way, then how is it that we even exist, that British Muslims are not satisfied with British law?" He did not pursue the matter.

ABU SAYEED: So what are we doing here?
KHURRAM: We are dissolving this, no point keeping it on.

HAITHAM: When did he send this fatwa to us? I just want to confirm something. Is there any way that proof from his side or from a third party that the marriage was not consummated, that he left her for four years or six years, and they never lived together?

KHURRAM: The fact that it is engagement shows it is not even marriage. It is ʿurf [custom] in Pakistan; people have nikah but do not live together, this is not "marriage."

HAITHAM: But is there any proof?

KHURRAM: The proof is here, he acknowledges himself that this is "engagement": "She is not married to me," he says.

HAITHAM: He never admitted that he has been away from her for four years or six years.

ABU SAYEED: It's common sense; he would have said that they had been living together if he had any evidence in his favor.

HAITHAM: He could say this if he first saw her claim that they had been separated and is objecting to it, but if he is taking it for granted that she is his wife and she has come from time to time and they have slept together, then he would not say anything.

In the end they dissolved the marriage. Haitham argued on two levels. First, they did not have a statement from the husband saying that the marriage was not consummated, and they could not infer from the absence of a reference to the matter that this was the case. They had seen this sort of debate in earlier cases. The others argued that such inference was perfectly reasonable, and Khurram, in particular, claimed that saying "nikah" commonly meant "engagement" in Pakistan; it was a matter of Pakistani custom. Second, Haitham disputed the others' claims that they should dissolve marriages as frequently as they do; we can see his objections on the evidence as a kind of continual guerilla action against the council's general habits. Haitham cited Saudi Arabia as a more rigorous place where dissolution of marriage was not common, but he had a surprise one day, as shown below.

Case: What Do the Arabs Do?

One month later, on February 24, 2010, four scholars and the clerk began the meeting shortly after lunch. After less than an hour of deliberation, Dr. Ahmad al-Dubayan, director general of the Islamic Cultural Centre, appointed by the Saudi government, entered the room, escorting two guests. One was Sheikh Abdullah al-Mutlaq of Riyadh, a senior advisor to the king on Islamic affairs. He was accompanied by an Islamic scholar from Bahrain. Sheikh Choukri Majouli, a Tunisian scholar and one of the mosque's three imams, also entered. They discussed proposals to create an appellate structure for the councils and the many problems resulting from the absence of control over what imams do in Britain. Suhaib then suggested that they return to the council's business: "Let's take advantage of the sheikhs' presence and take up a case."[8]

The sheikhs' arrival presented Haitham with a golden opportunity to bring up his continual concern that the ISC dissolves marriages too readily. He often argues that faskh or dissolution is really annulment, and thus should be reserved for situations where the scholars find that the marriage is flawed. This is a position that has strong bases in Islamic jurisprudence, but, as we have seen, it is not the approach favored by others in the council, for whom the more complex mixture of khula and faskh is practiced. The case we just examined was one of many where Haitham was frustrated in his position.

HAITHAM: We have a matter, Sheikh, concerning faskh. I reviewed some of the decisions and I found that faskh was not pronounced in Saudi Arabia until recently, at the moment when Sheikh Muhammad Ibrahim asked the committee to write a report and they decided to annul marriages, and they wrote to the courts to legitimate decisions of annulment. Does this not make a person to be careful and reluctant when it comes to faskh to a large degree?[9]

AL-MUTLAQ: I know what you are saying, but it's been there in fiqh from the beginning. Faskh is tied to harm [*dharar*].

[SOMEONE INTERJECTS: "shortcomings," *ʿuyub.*]

AL-MUTLAQ: Harm, whether the woman or the man is harmed, and khula, as you know, has financial consequences less severe than faskh. With khula the man retrieves a portion of his money; with faskh he gets nothing, and the ʿulamaʾ have looked into difficulties with maintenance [*nafaqa*], with shortcomings in nikah, and with severe harm in long separations. In all these matters that they have looked into, there is no remedy but faskh. Faskh is one of those circulating problems these days, regarding the qualification of *nasab* [relatedness] and violence. So the matter of faskh has been there from long ago.

CHOUKRI: I don't think he means . . . he is speaking about its presence in fiqh; he is not talking about acting upon it in courts in Saudi.

AL-MUTLAQ: The Saudi courts have implemented it from ancient times. They were previously ordered [to] not leave the matter until they had arrived at exhaustive explanations and convincing explanations, with evidence from *al-kitab* and *sunna*, and justification [*taʿlil*]. And now the matter has widened and we have books from Ibn Taymiyyah, Ibn ul-Qayyim, and books from the four legal schools. It has become easier on people. In the past, the judge would rule and would only have one book . . . He memorized it and that was it.

SOMEONE: This is the best kind of judge.

AL-MUTLAQ: If I gave you this book and told you to copy it, you could sit for five years and not finish. Now, *alhamdulillah*, matters are easier, printing is easier.

The sheikh came out quite forcefully for the use of faskh to correct situations where one or the other party experiences harm. (The suggestion of "shortcomings" may have been an attempt to push faskh toward the notion of annulment.) Choukri seemed taken aback and suggested that the sheikh could not be discussing courtroom practice—but he was. "Printing is easier": it's the twenty-first century. Haitham continued his effort to minimize faskh:

HAITHAM: There are two master's dissertations, Sheikh, by Hufa and Zubaida, on the separation between two partners and faskh. They say that faskh wasn't pronounced until about the year 1370 in the Kingdom, not until Sheikh Ibrahim or Sheikh ibn Baz asked for an inquiry into this, and the decision came out number such and such and such, to dictate to judges to do faskh for the marriages if the matter calls for it.[10]

AL-MUTLAQ: No, this is not true; these people don't understand anything; in the past they acted upon nushuz, then King Faisal, God bless his soul, saw with his advisor that this was not a [good] decision. Do you know what nushuz means? The woman if she leaves and goes to her parents' house, and did not justify or give reason for this, the judge will rule that she is nashiz [disobedient] and she will be without *nafaqa* [maintenance], no talaq and no faskh, because no harm came to her. So if she leaves, it's called nushuz. So King Faisal said this is not a remedy; if she *nashazat*, she is *tukhallā* [separated, ripped out]. If she does not have the evidence to do khula, find another way. This is not a remedy for nushuz. They strongly meant this point.

Again, the sheikh delivered a rude shock to the assumptions some had about Saudi rulings. If the wife left the home with no reason, there must be a way to settle the matter and allow both parties to continue with their lives without pronouncing faskh, because that required finding harm, but also without refusing to declare a divorce on grounds of disobedience, as Haitham had urged in some council cases, because that was too violent an act toward the wife. "Find another way."

HAITHAM: "May God be kind to you." With nushuz we receive some cases where the woman herself runs away. The *nafaqa*, according to what the *fuqahā'* [jurists] agreed on, she does not deserve it. Alright, the children; does she take the children? [Recall this issue emerging in the case described above.]

AL-MUTLAQ: The children, God save me with you all, you know the legal schools [*madhāhib*], but the prevalent opinion among us and the one that is acted on by us in Saudi, is that custody is the right of the small one, not the father or mother. And the judge looks into who is protecting the right of the little one and gives that person the custody.

CHOUKRI: Whoever works for the *maslaha* [welfare] of the child.

AL-MUTLAQ: So if he sees that the mother is more deserving, then . . . and that's why for us now that the custody is given to the mother in most cases, then, to the mother of the mother, then to the father. So the mother of the mother is preferred over the father because the father is going to hand over custody to his wife and he won't care for the child himself.

[SOMEONE]: Who says this, Sheikh?

AL-MUTLAQ: This is what is acted upon and this is what Ibn Taymiyyah and Ibn ul-Qayyim say, and it is a strong case in the legal schools.

Once more, the sheikh surprised: even the wife who committed nushuz might get custody of the children if doing so was best for them; the best interests of the child took precedence. He drove the point home by citing the most prestigious scholars from the Saudi perspective.

[SOMEONE]: And the story between Abu Bakr and ʿUmar bin al-Khattab, and the mother is more deserving and then the mother's mother.

[SOMEONE]: Sheikh? The mother, it is *mahfum* [understood]. It may even be consensus, but it is one of the rights of the child.

AL-MUTLAQ: No, it is a right for the child. What is the purpose of custody? [Unclear] If the mother is seen, let's assume that the mother is frivolous and that's why now we have among the cases that are raised. The mother, if she becomes a teacher and gets married, why does not she deserve the custody? . . . But a mother who does not work and waits for husband to give her [things] cannot care for her children without him. But if the mother is an employee and got married and placed a condition on the husband, that her children remain with her and she provides their subsistence and does her duty toward them, why should we prevent her [from having] custody when she is able? If she married she was cut off from work, in the old days, and now, no, she can marry with the condition of [being able to] work.

KHURRAM: But Sheikh, the shariʿa council did not see that . . . in the British courts . . .

AL-MUTLAQ: What you have here is a fatwa, like what we have, a fatwa. I am talking about the *haqq musharraʿ*. Your council gives fatwa. Alhamdulillah, you are trying to show haqq [that which is right].

Women now worked and could ensure that their marriage contract mentioned the right to work, and in those cases there was no reason why the wife and mother could not have custody of the children. This way of thinking is a far cry from the usual formulas, which award presumptive custody rights by the age of the children. In the end the sheikh sounded closer to an English family court judge than to a more traditional expositor of Islamic family law. He reasoned from the welfare of the parties and then argued that one could find a basis for rulings in the texts.

Conclusions

These exchanges reveal continuing debates on the relative weight to be given to distinct kinds of justification. They bring out two basic "metajurisprudential" tensions. One concerns justificatory reasoning based more or less explicitly on the welfare of the parties concerned, versus attention to possible violations of particular rules that form part of Islamic law, such as instances of nushuz or a couple's failure to separate prior to asking for divorce. In practice, particular scholars combine these arguments: Haitham argues that rules about proving separation must be followed, but also that overly lax reasoning will lead to improper behavior and thus should be condemned for its consequences.

A second tension lies between arguments based on the consensus of the scholars versus those based on the common practices in the courts of a particular country, often Pakistan. Here the case of Saudi Arabia plays a shifting role: Haitham cites it as evidence for how the most prestigious scholars have ruled, without explicit reference to court decisions. The visiting sheikhs then shift the discussion to current Saudi judicial and governmental policy.

This metalevel of debate—what types of reasoning should we highlight or most heavily weigh?—is not peculiar to Muslim societies in minority situations, but it is particularly prominent in those situations because scholars or jurists do not have positive law to fall back on, nor do they have an established body of scholars to deliver a single, prominent fatwa. In these debates across the European and North American Muslim diasporas, scholars ask about the limits of accommodation—not British or Canadian accommodation of Islam, but Islamic accommodation of British or Canadian social realities. Two broad approaches seem to have emerged, each involving diverse theoretical arguments.

The first approach, the best known, seeks to develop new normative bodies of knowledge. It takes a number of different forms. One form is that developed by the European Council for Fatwa and Research, and in particular by its leading scholar, Yusuf al-Qaradawi, who has called for developing a "fiqh for minorities" (*fiqh al-aqalliyāt*), a distinct jurisprudence that would apply to Muslims living as minorities in non-Muslim societies.[11] Al-Qaradawi also speaks of *fiqh al-wāqiʿ* (fiqh of reality), which entails bringing knowledge of empirical matters into the normative sphere as matter for reflection, as when the relative rates of rents and mortgage payments were taken as relevant to the normative issue of whether sometimes Muslims may accept bank loans.[12] Closely related is the idea that Muslims should evaluate their normative statements over and against what they see as the overall "objectives of God's revelations," the *maqāsid ash-sharīʿa*. Those who advocate this "maqāsid approach" draw on a long tradition of thinking about the interest and welfare (*maslaha*) of Muslims.[13] Their pragmatic focus is on adapting the

Islamic traditions to a new place. This approach is widely discussed and developed in France, where for various reasons the North African intellectual leadership has favored this direction of thinking.[14]

This approach has been much less successful in England, for reasons that by now should be apparent. British Islamic institutions have developed under conditions that produced more conservative lines of thinking, perhaps rendered more conservative and entrenched by the mutual opposition between Sufis and Deobandis. The shariʿa councils are dealing with women and men who travel back and forth from the homeland to Britain. Their pragmatic focus is on devising instruments that would constitute an embryonic "international private Islamic law," fragments that might ease those movements across state borders.

This second broad approach, one that emerges from the practices of the English shariʿa councils, focuses on both social and legal practices abroad—especially in Pakistan—and on the workings of the English social and legal system. It does not lend itself easily to theorizing—indeed, I argued in chapter 6 that it cannot do so because these practices involve an inherent instability. Quite unlike the debates I recorded in France, those found in Britain concern how to assign weight to distinct criteria for making a legal judgment: practices in Pakistan, practices in putatively "more Islamic" Saudi Arabia, the likely consequences of a divorce for a husband or wife, and the many, diverse scholarly sources. The debates that result look a lot more like those in English common law and a lot less like the more highly theorized debates across the Channel. Perhaps this is a sign of Islamic legal debates adapting to French or English legal styles, respectively.

Of course, many common elements can be found across these countries. For example, Islamic scholars in France and in Britain find it useful to invoke certain legal maxims (*al-qawāʿid al-fiqhiyya*) that were collected during the early period of the development of Islamic law. We can see in the exchanges between Khurram Bashir and Haitham al-Haddad, as well as the interventions of the visiting sheikhs, the effects of the maxim "harm should be removed" (*al-ḍarar yuzāl*). Khurram tends to plead along the lines of the classical maxim "customs determine the legal disposition [of a case]" (*al-ʿāda muḥakkama*). I have heard more often in France variations of the maxim "hardship brings about facilitation" (*al-mashaqqa tajlib al-taysīr*). These maxims are commonly and widely accepted by scholars across Sunni and Shiite contexts, even if most scholars would not use them to overrule an explicit rule found in scripture.

Classical jurists, too, were involved in balancing competing rules and principles,[15] as are judges on contemporary Islamic courts. In Aceh, Indonesia, for example, judges on the Islamic appellate court invoke three kinds of justificatory material: scripture (Qur'an and hadith), the Indonesian Islamic law compilation, and several commonly used texts of the Shafiʿi legal school—as well as their own ideas about fairness. They work in an environment where other actors emphasize one or another of these sources. Their superiors on the Indonesian Supreme Court emphasize the importance of following the law compilation. Acehnese scholars heading up influential Islamic boarding schools (the *tengku daya*) stress the Shafiʿi tradition, and villagers who approach the legal system will have drawn their ideas from those scholars. Certain Islamic law professors, some of whom also serve on government boards, have their own ideas about developing more socially progressive forms of Islam, and they tend to draw directly on the Qurʾan—for example, in arguing that husbands as well as wives could be considered as nushuz (disobedient). They are the most likely of any group to invoke maslaha or the objectives of shariʿa as grounds for their arguments.[16]

So even in this reputedly most "shariʿa-oriented" part of Indonesia, multiple forms of justification are in play and invoked. Such was the case in fourteenth-century Moroccan courts as well, and comparative scholars of Islam have traced the competing fortunes of modern maslaha-based reasoning and older forms of fiqh.[17] Debates about justificatory forms are part and parcel of Islamic legal reasoning and not the product of a diaspora situation. But the particular weights of these forms in specific contexts, as seen in the France-Britain contrast, underscore that sociohistorical trajectories shape the forms of deliberation to be found in contemporary Islamic institutions.

PART 3

VARIANTS

CHAPTER 8

When Women Rule in Birmingham

SOME OF THE MOST TRENCHANT CRITICISMS OF SHARIʿA COUNCILS IN BRITAIN or elsewhere concern male scholars' attitudes toward women, and a perceived weakness of procedural protections for women. Do things differ when women play a major role?

To find out, I spent time in the Birmingham Central Mosque. As the name implies, the mosque is centrally located, indeed, hard to miss for anyone driving through the middle of the city. It is "central" in another sense as well, in that, unlike the other major mosques of the city, it is not identified with any one religious orientation. The mosque opened in the late 1960s, and is thus one of the oldest, as well as one of the largest, mosques in Britain. Until his death in 2014, the chair of the mosque's trustees was Dr. Mohammad Naseem. Born in British India, Naseem studied in Pakistan before being trained as a medical doctor in England. He developed a reputation as an independent religious leader who both opened condolence books for non-Muslim victims of the Madrid train bombings and strongly criticized Tony Blair and the London police force after the 7/7 London bombings. In the early 2000s, as he tells it, he decided to create a shariʿa council where women would play a prominent role, so as to create an environment more welcoming to women.[1]

For that, he turned to another medical doctor, Dr. Wageha Syeda, who, together with Saba Butt, had been directing a Family Support Service in Birmingham, which included a help line for Muslim women experiencing family difficulties. Beginning in 1996, Wageha had worked with Khurram Bashir, whom we met on the London-based Islamic Shariʿa Council, on a mediation service at the Birmingham mosque. Quite often, women who came to them for help also wanted an Islamic divorce. Khurram and Wageha would refer these women to the London Islamic Shariʿa Council, and Khurram would consider the case during the London monthly meetings.

Although this arrangement provided a pathway to divorce, some women complained that Khurram tended to take the husband's side. Wageha went to see Naseem to see if they could establish an independent shariʿa council in Birmingham. He thought this a good idea, and indeed had been thinking along those lines. In 2004 he set it up, with himself and one or two other scholars sitting to hear cases. In 2006, he added Amra Bone to the council, the first woman to sit on such a council. Amra was born in Pakistan but was raised in Kuwait. She studied mainly in England, with two years spent in

FIGURE 3. Birmingham Shariʿa Council, 2010

Cairo, and is the only member of her natal family who speaks Arabic. Despite the novelty of her position, she has never heard of opposition to her position among the Muslim men attending the Birmingham mosque, "and I would hear it because my brother worships here," she told me in July 2010.

INTAKE

The Birmingham council began as a place for women to find advice and help, and only later transformed itself into a shariʿa council, and this origin is apparent in how the intake procedures work. Wageha has retained a position as "key advisor on all cases," and she and Saba screen petitioners and prepare cases for the council to hear.

Wageha grew up in Hyderabad and did her first two years of medical training there. Because her father could not afford the last two years of fees, he sent her to his brother in Pakistan. In 1970, after the delays many Indian nationals faced, she completed her studies and came to England: first to London and then after six months to Birmingham, where she practiced gynecology in hospitals. Then she switched to pediatrics, in part because her husband, also a medical doctor (from Turkey), did not want her to work nights. After he died and she lost her sister, she left that work and joined Khurram Bashir at the mosque. In 1997 she brought in Saba to assist her. Saba had worked as an education welfare officer; she would investigate when pupils were repeatedly absent from school, and if she found abuse at home, she would take the family, or the father, to court.

In the days before the clinic added its shariʿa council role, "people would come mainly for counseling," explained Wageha in July 2011. "At first it was only girls; they were getting beat up at home, their husbands took drugs or were mommy's boys and listened only to their parents, or gave their wives no support. Some were not allowed to go out: girls brought here from Pakistan were kept in house by the boy's family as a maid; usually they were all related." In 2001, Wageha obtained a degree in Islamic studies "so I could sit up there and not have people say I did not know the Islamic side."[2]

By 2011, Wageha and Saba each worked two days a week in the council room at the mosque, receiving appointments, taking telephone calls, and handling paperwork. Saba explained that 70 percent of their clients are women and that most cases involve women born here who were married to men in Mirpur, usually illiterate men, sometimes in forced marriages and sometimes not. "The third generation—because I have been doing this for fifteen years—they know about their rights, but the older generations do not; they do not have education."

Women may come or call for a variety of reasons, and they may speak either with Saba or Wageha. But many who contact them regarding a divorce are turned away because of a rule adopted several years previously by the council. The council had been hearing all cases where a woman wished to end her marriage, until one day when they granted a woman her religious divorce, only to have her turn around and stop cooperating with her husband on the civil divorce. She only wanted to remarry in Britain with a nikah, which she now could do (or so she said), despite being legally married to her husband. He, however, wished to remarry in Pakistan, for which he would need the civil divorce. This unfortunate consequence of their divorce judgment led the council to only accept cases where the civil divorce, if one was needed, had been completed, so that women could not keep their husbands from remarrying. "The rule was great," said Saba, "because it cut my work in half!"

Telephone

One afternoon in July 2011, Saba was fielding telephone calls in the office. She received calls from women seeking advice, and often sought to negotiate with the husband via telephone. The tone of her calls was friendly and collaborative, a sharp contrast to those fielded by the London ISC chief clerk, her closest equivalent on that much larger and more fully staffed institution.

I followed one series of calls carried out by Saba on that day in 2011. She called a woman who had begun divorce proceedings after interviews with Saba and Wageha. Saba began by asking after the woman's health, and upon hearing she had an ailment, she said, "I hope you are taking something for that." She explained that they had sent the first of the three required letters to the husband (their procedures are the same as those followed by the London council), and that he had then called Saba. Saba then told the wife what he had said (ellipses within parentheses indicate when the other party is talking to Saba on the other end of the phone):

> He is happy to have you back but on condition that you break off contact with your family and with one of your friends; he feels you are influenced by these people: "She listens to them more than to me," he said. I explained to him that he had to be reasonable: "How could you expect her to give up her family; how would *you* feel?" He said it is not his family that is causing problems. He is not happy to come here and resolve issues. (. . .) Yeah, I understand that, I know, and were things any better then? They weren't. That's what he said. (. . .) The conditions need to be reasonable; it sounds that he is saying this because he knows you will reject them. I told him you've made up your mind and are applying to the shariʿa council for a divorce. (. . .) I will call him and let him know that I've passed on the message and you don't agree. (. . .) The case will go forward after Ramadhan; wait for a letter for an appointment. (. . .) I won't say that to him, don't worry.

Saba then called the husband and said:

> I passed on the message but she is not agreeable; she says that she does not feel her family played a role in the breakup of the marriage, and how would you feel if she asked you to leave your family? (. . .) I don't know whether that is true or that is not true. What chances are there of making this marriage work? (. . .) She is not agreeable to that condition. (. . .) Sorry? Is it not possible for your father to contact her? Anyone else in your family? Sounds to me that you don't want a divorce, am I right in saying that? (. . .) Yeah? If not, deep down she doesn't want either, although she has. (. . .) [She] keeps asking, "What does he want?" but you're not coming together and talking directly, at a neutral place, coming to the mosque, with somebody neutral, sometimes how would you feel if you had a conversation with her? (. . .) Her mum's uncle? (. . .) Sometimes other people don't want to get involved; shall I give her a call back and ask her? You can't cut blood ties either; any request you make has to be reasonable. (. . .) But she says something different, that you are setting up a stalemate situation. (. . .) *Wa ʿalaikum salam.*

Then Saba called the woman:

> I don't really think in his heart he wants a divorce, and the same with you, you feel [you're] being pushed into this; what he says is he does want reconciliation but wants your mum's uncle to go down, [that he] has a good relationship with him. (. . .) Sometimes when they receive an official letter, they notice, change attitude, realize you are serious. A chance, one last try at this? (. . .) Talk to your family and at least you'll know that you've tried everything; he does not feel comfortable coming down here. I will ask what is a convenient time, and see if you could go down at that time. Have a discussion with your family.

While Saba waited for the woman to try her mum's uncle and call back, she explained to me that the issue that led to their separation about a year previous was his refusal to register the marriage; he had said, "Why bother?" Saba thinks that nonregistered nikahs are on the rise.

The woman called back and said that she preferred to come to the mosque but would discuss other possibilities. Saba asked her if she and her husband had ever lived with her in-laws, because that can cause problems.

Saba then called the husband to report on the negotiations.

> Many people tried going to your home and no one ever opened the door, so she [his wife] feels it a waste of time sending someone there, and no one [else] wants to go there, but she is happy to talk with you at the mosque, so you can talk face-to-face as opposed to getting other family members involved. (. . .) Yes, but if you keep on talking about that (. . .) seem to be misunderstandings. (. . .) What things need to [be] sort[ed] out? Last time she did that? This year, right, has not been contacting you since then, does not have your number. You need to talk to her. (. . .) Living with your parents after the marriage? (. . .) What's happened has happened; we need to move forward. [Had you] talked with each other prior to your marriage? She feels [it was] promised prior to the marriage [that they would register it] [the] reason [being] the commitment, that you'd be committed to the marriage. (. . .) That's good. (. . .) If you do change your mind. We won't be taking sides. I know it's a bit daunting coming in like that.

Saba called the wife, but the line was busy. She stepped out of the office to make some photocopies, and while she was out, the woman called back and left a message with a new offer.

I don't know how this case turned out, but Saba seemed to have had some luck in working toward a compromise, at least on where and how they might meet. I had never heard this sort of conversation take place at the London council. When London staff initiated a telephone call, it was usually to track down a nonresponsive husband or to follow up on an appointment. When they received a call, it was either a request for information, usually about procedures, or a complaint about delays. We saw earlier the type of exchange the secretary was likely to have with a husband. By contrast, Saba was engaged in mediation on two levels: on the issues dividing the husband and wife (family interference, marriage registration), and on the conditions each side posed for having a meeting.

Why this difference? The London staff sees their work as part of a bureaucratic machine, with fixed rules and procedures leading to predictable outcomes—remember the flowchart. Those scholars see themselves as facilitating encounters between the parties in the hope that they might reconcile and then, when that effort fails (as it is expected to), debating among themselves about the Islamic grounds for dissolving the marriage. The London scholar sees himself as first and foremost a giver of advice and an administrator of justice, as a mufti and a qadi. The scholar is the one to lead the inquiry; he is the first step in the intake process, once the petitioner has filled out the necessary forms. The London council has its heritage in the quasi-judicial bodies of British India, the dar ul-qaza, and has adjusted and adapted in the shadow of the English law court.

Birmingham, by contrast, began life as a center for receiving complaints and mediating in family problems, and only later added on an Islamic law component. Saba and Wageha are the first step in intake, and they engage in nearly all the dialogue with petitioners. They follow procedures the scholars have established, invoking elements of Islamic law only as references to opinions already arrived at by the scholars. Their work concerns trying to bring the parties together and establishing the facts of the case as best they can. Only when they have screened the case and prepared the dossier for the council do the scholars learn about the case and interview the petitioners. The time the scholars spend on each case is far less than for the London council, because they step in only at the last minute to dissolve the marriage.

The difference between the two institutions became even greater in 2013, when the Birmingham council decided that in cases where the civil divorce had been completed and the husband did not contest the Islamic divorce, the matter did not even have to be considered by the council but could be handled as an automatic divorce by Saba. They thereby elided the major issue that complicates deliberations in London, namely, whether the husband intended to agree to the religious divorce. For Birmingham, a civil divorce makes Islamic divorce quasi-automatic, and if the husband does not object, truly automatic.

Clinic

During the week, clients, sometimes with members of their families, can arrange to see Wageha and Saba to discuss domestic problems or the need for divorce. If the case goes to the council, the important questions will already have been asked at these clinic sessions, and often the two women will have given out legal and Islamic advice, and the clients resolved their problems, without appearing before the council.

On one weekday morning in 2011, four clients appeared in the office. A young wife came with her father to obtain the original divorce certificate issued by the council. She planned to remarry in Pakistan, and had learned that the Pakistan marriage board would accept such a certificate and give it a stamp, which in turn would be accepted by imams. (Wageha confirmed the wife's idea of how things worked there.) Saba urged her not to bring the new husband back to England right off: "Don't give him the stay right away this time; get to know him better first; you don't want to make the same mistake twice."

Next client: a husband had brought his wife from Pakistan and was unhappy with their marriage. Saba and Wageha repeatedly expressed their wonder as to why he allowed himself to be pressured into the marriage, and told him that he could simply write out a statement of talaq and have it witnessed, and once the civil divorce was over, the council would issue him an official divorce certificate. But, they told him, a civil divorce is sufficient unless you want to remarry in Pakistan.

Then they heard from a woman who had been separated for a year and wanted "a halal divorce"; the husband physically abused her and her son. Unlike most of the cases the council sees, their marriage was without the parents' knowledge. She came with her sister, who acted supportive but also reminded everyone that the family had known it would turn out badly. I entertained the sister's two young children with drawing paper and pencils. Saba and Wageha told her what she must do but also took down details of the physical abuse. They emphasized that they would interview him as well, but at a time when the wife was not there. Saba told her that it was not her fault and that she had "a lovely son; something positive came out of it."

The final client was a woman with a somewhat more complex case. Her family and her husband's family were neighbors in Pakistan, and they married there in 2004. They did not have a child (she had had three miscarriages), and his family wanted the divorce for that reason. She and her husband obtained a civil divorce in March 2009, and her husband did not contest the divorce. One month later, she approached the council for an Islamic divorce, but then the husband pronounced the talaq three times and said to her that this was sufficient, so she did not continue her case with the council.

But one month later, he proposed they remarry, which they did over a Qur'an, with no one else present, "with the Qur'an as our witness." Her husband said that because it was within three months of the talaq, it was legitimate, but their local sheikh said that it was not, that the Qur'an was insufficient as a witness. However, "they say in the community that we are married because we remarried over the Qur'an and within three months we became close again." (The husband had confused the temporal limits for *rujuk*, reconciling without the need to remarry, and a remarriage.)

Saba replied that the civil divorce made them divorced in Islamic terms as well: "Don't pay attention to them; you are divorced, but the main thing is to make sure that if you ever are pregnant again, you see a gynecologist; there is no reason you cannot have a child." They set the start of the ʿidda period (the three months before she could remarry) at the date the civil divorce was final.

But their calculations fell apart a moment later when the wife revealed that she had slept with her husband after their divorce, the last time being in 2010. Wageha told her to give some money to the poor because of the sex, and that now she had to observe the ʿidda period after the Islamic divorce was granted because she had had sex after the civil divorce: "The civil divorce has no practical effect because you had sex, so you need the religious divorce." They told her to pay £150 for the divorce, and that the husband would not have to appear because he had already approved the civil divorce, but that they would have to inform him.

Note two aspects of these discussions. First, Wageha and Saba gave out social and medical advice: pay no attention to the neighbors, see a gynecologist, don't be in a hurry to bring a husband into England from Pakistan. This sort of advice would be highly unlikely to be given in the London offices, in large part because there the advice-givers would be male Islamic scholars, but also because they do not see such matters as their major concern.

Second, the two women also provided the state of Islamic law on a variety of issues: when a civil divorce counts as an Islamic one, when the ʿidda period should start, when the husband's opinion does and does not matter. They spoke not as muftis or qadis, Islamic scholars or judges, delivering judgment or interpretations of the sacred law, but as active members of the council who are well aware of what have become the standard rules and practices applied by that body. For example, the council had already voted to consider three pronouncements of the talaq to count as only one talaq of the three that would require remarriage, thus making the couple's remarriage in the case just above a reconciliation (rujuk). Other Islamic scholars, including one of this council's scholars, opposed this interpretation, but once decided, this rule could be simply applied in the clinic.

At the London council, all of these pronouncements would be made by the scholars at the formal deliberations. Because each can involve issues around which there is not universal consensus, each can give rise to long debates, as we saw in the previous chapters. But the Birmingham council, by formulating them as simple rules, sometimes applied in the clinic, sidesteps such debates. Shortly, we will see what happens when one such rule emerges at a Birmingham deliberation. At this point, however, what needs to be emphasized is that these differences between the London and Birmingham councils are institutional ones regarding procedure and authority, and are not doctrinal ones. For example, the three-talaq rule is the same at the two councils. It is the mission and inspiration of the two councils that gives each its specific character.

Sessions

When the Birmingham Shariʿa Council gathers to deliberate on divorce requests, which in the 2010s they did at most once a month, they meet in an inner room at the mosque. You reach the room either by cutting through the prayer room (which the women prefer to do) or passing through the men's ablutions area. A table comfortably accommodates four scholars seated in a row along the back with Wageha at the end; four visitors can sit in a row facing them. Saba sits at a desk to one side, where she accepts petitioners' payments and ensures that she has their addresses so she can send along certificates.

The scholars generally occupy the same chairs from one session to the next. Amra sits at one end, nearly opposite Wageha. She takes the lead role in greeting petitioners and in posing the first questions. She is able to convey her sympathy for the plights in which the wives often find themselves, as well as give reminders of how they ought to behave "next time." Unless he is ill, Naseem sits next to her. He has good English but a soft voice, and speaks in conclusions rather than by thinking out loud; these two characteristics mean that often petitioners find it hard to instantly grasp what he says. The others generally defer to him on matters of legal interpretation.

The sometimes dissonant opinion is supplied by Sheikh Mohammad Talha Bokhari, who studied at the Dar al-ʿUlum school in Deoband and hews to the Hanafi legal school. He plays a less prominent role in exchanges between the petitioners and the scholars, or those among the scholars themselves. The first is due to his relatively poor English; the second due in part to his temperament, as he is easily fed up with irrelevant points and finds himself rebuffed in his attempts to invoke Hanafi opinions. At times he would turn to me with a smile, shrug his shoulders, and say, "that's not grounds for divorce" after a divorce had been agreed on.

By 2013 a new scholar had joined the council. Sarfraz Mohammed was born in Birmingham and studied at a Deobandi school in England before obtaining a degree in chemistry at Manchester University, with an eye to combining Islamic studies and science. Indeed, he has done so by working for the Halal Monitoring Committee in Leicester. But he also took the four-year fatwa course in Karachi with the noted scholar M. Taqi ʿUthmani. Although he and Bokhari share Hanafi training, Sarfraz tends to be more pragmatic and thus closer in temperament to Amra and Naseem than to Bokhari.

Amra is usually the one to open proceedings and to frame the case. She often emphasizes two points: that English law is the only law of the land, and that couples who have English divorces do not really need to obtain Islamic divorces to satisfy God, even if the divorce certificates are socially and perhaps legally useful.

In one case heard in July 2011, Amra welcomed the petitioner, a Birmingham-area woman who, accompanied by her father, had come to request an Islamic divorce. The couple had married in Pakistan and the husband had recently returned there. The wife claimed that her husband neglected her and in any event could not father children. They had approached the council office a few months earlier and said they were not going to bother with a civil divorce, but were advised that, because the husband had entered Britain on a work visa, they were obliged to do so. Now civil divorce was under way. This upset Amra and the others because they do not like to grant a religious divorce before the civil procedure is completed. As she said to the wife, "You must complete the civil divorce; civil law is supreme here." But they decided to grant the religious divorce in any case, because the wife had come to them before she had initiated the civil procedure. They said that the husband's failure to support his wife and his decision to return to Pakistan justified a decision to separate them, tafrīq. As Amra then explained to the woman's father, even though the woman could have just remarried without coming to them, "Not everyone is aware of how shariʿa works. If you marry again some people will ask you if you got a divorce from a shariʿa council. It is a good idea to have it; you have to consider how society sees you."

Amra and Wageha regularly sprinkled advice to the wife into their questions: "Register your marriage next time," "Join a gym and make yourself healthier." The manner in which they welcomed the women (and, less often, the men) made it clear that the shariʿa council was mainly there to advise women and help them to move on with their lives within an Islamic framework.

Case: Do Rules Need Reasons?

At the session held on April 2, 2013, the council heard thirteen cases, and in all of them, the wife was the petitioner. None of these cases had undergone mediation because in all of them the wife had decided on divorce. In all but one case Wageha had seen them together with Saba for the intake interview; in one case, it had been just Saba. In every case Amra opened up the questioning. Sarfraz played a secondary role, and Bokhari and Naseem, both ailing physically, played still less prominent roles.

But Naseem still held the upper hand on matters of how best to interpret Islam in practical situations, as this case demonstrates. The client was a woman from Syria living in the Midlands. Thirteen years ago her husband left her and took their daughter with him to Kuwait and then, she had heard, to Syria. She notified the police right after he left. They arrived too late to arrest him at the airport but they ordered customs officials to arrest him should he try to return. She thus knew that he had not been in Britain for the past thirteen years. The girl was now fifteen.

She did not do anything about divorcing all this time because she did not care, but now she wanted to marry someone, and the day of the hearing, she gave everyone the impression of being in a great hurry to have the divorce settled. She came supplied with all the documents that could be requested: his Syrian ID, their marriage certificate, her birth certificate, and their Syrian family certificate.

Amra: If he came back now, would you consider reconciling?
Wife: What do you think?
Amra: I think I got my answer!

The council's problem was how to categorize the divorce, which they clearly wanted to give (as they did in all cases heard that day). The husband had said to her, "If you step outside the house without my permission, I['ll] give you a talaq." She did indeed leave the house on her own, and then he left. She had no evidence of his pronouncement, however. Amra said to the others, "We take their evidence; we don't ask them to take an oath. He is missing, so we will declare a divorce, but we cannot ask him to pay maintenance, which we would do if he were here."

Speaking now to the wife, Amra said, "He has disappeared; we say 'he has deserted you,' and so we can dissolve the marriage. We do this based on your evidence. If later this is found to be untrue, the certificate will be invalid. After three months you will be free to remarry." Notice how different this resolution is to parallel discussions at the ISC. For Amra, the wife's statement is accepted as provisionally true; if it turns out to be false, then God will respond—saying the certificate is invalid does not mean that Amra and Saba will recall it.

The wife told them that she would need the certificate of dissolution to reenter Syria. Saba said she would send her the certificate and keep the husband's copy in case he ever returned. All was done and she rose to leave, but then turned before walking out and said:

Wife: Could I just ask a question? Why do I need to wait for three months, as it has been thirteen years? In shariʿa, after four years the marriage is over.

Sarfraz: That's a very good question; it is because in shariʿa, we consider you married until this moment, and in the Qur'an it says that you must wait the ʿidda period of three menstrual cycles. You have to ask the court to dissolve the marriage, otherwise perhaps you would not have wanted a divorce and yet after four years it would have occurred automatically!

AMRA: Is there a reason you want to marry quickly? Allah does not want to put hardship on you. With Dr. Naseem we have decided cases where there was urgency, based on proof that she had not seen the husband.

WIFE: I can provide evidence from the police.

SARFRAZ: Leave it with us.

BOKHARI: This is haqq Allah! [He means that the waiting requirement is absolute and only God knows the reasons.]

WIFE: For a reason!

BOKHARI: No, for the ʿidda there is no reason in the Qurʾan, no statement of "here is the reason." ʿUlamaʾ are divided on this: for some, it is because of the Rahim [ascertaining the contents of the womb] whereas for others it is haqq Allah.

AMRA: But in the Qurʾan it says that if there has been no consummation of the marriage, then there is no ʿidda [implying a reason for the waiting period].

Saba entered the room at this point having talked with Naseem to report that "Dr. Naseem says that you don't have to wait for ʿidda, as with nonconsummation." Apparently Amra had asked him and Bokhari earlier about the cases and both had said that she could dispense with the wait.

SARFRAZ: A simple assertion won't do.

AMRA: If she wants to have children, she is old enough, won't want to wait.

SABA: She waited thirteen years before coming here because she only cared when she decided to remarry.

After a pause, Naseem joined them and they brought up the case.

NASEEM: I propose that she take pregnancy tests on three consecutive weeks, and if they are negative, then we issue the certificate, to protect the new husband and ensure him that she is not pregnant.

JRB: But following your logic, you should make all couples do that before they marry.

NASEEM: Yes, that is my position.

Bokhari takes a posture comparable to that adopted by Haitham al-Haddad on the ISC, namely, that when it comes to rules—both men phrase them as "God's rights"—we do not call for reasons or apply general maxims or principles, such as general welfare (maslaha). We just apply the rules. The difference between the two institutions lies in the respective distributions of authority. Bokhari occupies a marginal position, and Naseem, with his own views on these matters, gets to call the shots. At the ISC, Haitham is one among equals and is rather forceful, and finds allies at times. Bokhari will join the discussion on a particular issue or complain from the sidelines about departures from the Hanafi legal school. Haitham carries on a continual and consistent argument for not overly adapting to considerations of what benefits women in Britain. His is a coherent argument and receives a respectful hearing, even if his is usually not the decisive voice.

Performativity

Let's look more closely at the ideas of performativity at work here. This council faces the same basic evidentiary problem as does their London counterpart, but they approach it in a different way. As we saw earlier, councils cannot gather evidence in a convincing way: they cannot subpoena the husband or compel testimony, and so must rely on the evidence voluntarily supplied, which generally comes from the wife. And yet the self-ascribed role of these councils is to dissolve marriages or perform faskh, which is a judicial act, and in Muslim legal systems, the court would have proper evidentiary scaffolding.

The London ISC's response to this dilemma is to frame what they do as certifying the couple's divorce by khula, and to fudge the issue of the husband's presumed consent. This is the "halfway khula," as the London clerk put it. Birmingham also starts by calling their action a khula, but they finish somewhat differently. As Amra explained to me, "It does refer to 'khula' on the website, and people come here thinking in those terms, but that is not necessarily how the Shariʿa Council will decide." Most of the decisions are called tafrīq, separation, another term for judicial dissolution. Amra explained: "Khula is when the husband and the wife are able to work something out on their own, and every now and then it happens that they do so at the time they come to the council. Most of the time they don't, though, and then we dissolve the marriage." I asked, "So do you phrase it as 'khula' on the site in the hope that they do work it out?" "Yes, that's it," she responds, "we hope they will settle."[3]

When the Birmingham council does dissolve the marriage, they frame their action among themselves using the terms tafrīq or faskh, and when speaking to the petitioners, they speak of dissolution or annulment. They also add, as in the above case, that the act's performativity depends on the veracity of the wife's testimony. This is quite clever: the council's act only concerns the relationship of the couple to God, not to Britain, so they can leave it at that, as a matter of conscience. They also produce a certificate for the wife, but condition its validity on her truthfulness. Compared to the London council, they seem less concerned with the legitimacy of their certificate in the eyes of, say, a Pakistani official than in the eyes of God.

These considerations concern divorces initiated by the wife. And here is where a gender dynamic shapes the Birmingham council's judgments. Even when the husband takes part in the proceedings, the Birmingham scholars avoid finding that he has performed a talaq. In the above case, if they were going to believe the wife on the matter of consummation, then they could have also believed her when she reported the husband's statement of a conditional talaq. But, in stark contrast to the London council, they generally prefer to dissolve the marriage themselves. Amra explained the reason to me in a conversation held in July 2010: "If we let the husband say the talaq, then we are empowering the men, and we don't want to do that, because then he can say, 'I did it, it was up to me!' whereas if we dissolve the marriage, it was at the behest of the wife and empowers her. Now, true, that if it is a talaq then the husband gets nothing [and must give the wife unpaid mahr], but these matters of mahr don't come up very often, so that doesn't really matter." Here, then, is an important difference with the ISC in London: if they (to a great extent at Haitham's urging) focus on the rights of the fathers, the Birmingham council places much greater emphasis on empowering the wife within the broader community.

As these practices suggest, the council as a body tends to look for practical solutions, sometimes with some internal dissension. In the above case they applied an innovative way of thinking about the mandatory ʿidda waiting period. Naseem's judgment here triggered an expression of the deep divide between him and Bokhari. For Bokhari, one cannot ask why God ordered such and such and then say, "'Well, today we have a better way.' We cannot know for certain what His reason [the divine *ʿilla*] may have been, and so we must follow His directive literally." Naseem's reasoning is completely the opposite: we *do* know the reason for the ʿidda rule; it is to avoid doubt as to any eventual child's paternity. Although normally we would enforce the rule as it is, when another consideration presents itself—in this case the wife's urgency to remarry, combined with her claim that the marriage was never consummated—then other ways of meeting the purpose of the rule can be countenanced. And because the council cannot be sure that the wife is truthful in her claim of nonconsummation, Naseem proposes the three successive pregnancy tests. During a different hearing, Naseem said during a break in the proceedings, "If the Prophet had had pregnancy tests, he would not have imposed the three-month waiting period. It is about the ʿilla."

Running throughout these exchanges, here as in other cases, is Amra's leading role, buttressed by Naseem's legal rulings. As with most cases, she requests input from the others but orchestrates the sessions. She often speaks for, or at least together with, the wife, who is usually the main party present.

Both Amra's particular role and the issue of considering the reason for the ʿidda rule come up in numerous cases. On July 5, 2011, for example, they heard a Somali woman whose husband had left her after their nikah, and returned twice, once the previous year after she had given birth to a baby girl. He asked that a DNA test be run because he doubted that he was the father. The contrasting reactions of Bokhari and Amra can stand for numerous interactions I have observed on the council. To the demand for DNA testing:

Bokhari: And did you [agree to the test]?
Amra and the wife, simultaneously: "She's/I'm not going to do that!"
Amra: A case of abandonment . . . why not register the marriage?
Wife: Too busy with work . . .
Amra: She cannot be left hanging . . . [turning to her left to face the others] Are we happy with that?
Bokhari: Yes, now, these times, information, in old days, took long to find someone [he strings together an incoherent series of phrases by way of saying that times had moved beyond the old rules about length of time needed to wait].
Amra [speaking to the wife]: This council has decided to dissolve the marriage, because in Islam you have the right to live in companionship.

The three scholars—Amra, Naseem, and Bokhari—then had a discussion over when to start counting the ʿidda period. Amra asked to see the woman's passport, and said that ʿidda could start from when the couple was last together, because his failed application to stay and her passport, unused for foreign travel, showed that this period had been more than three months, so the ʿidda could be declared to be already over. But Bokhari argued that the ʿidda was not only to ensure she was not pregnant but that they didn't know the other reasons, and so they couldn't reason from its purpose but must follow the rule. So they decided the ʿidda would count from the current meeting. Naseem added that this must be the decision, because they had no evidence that the couple had not been together. Amra asked the wife, "[Is there] someone you wish to marry soon?" to which the wife responded, "No, no!"

Case: The Triple Talaq

The differences among the scholars in ways of understanding fiqh emerge with regard to a number of issues. Around 2010, the council made a policy decision to take the position that a talaq pronounced three times on one occasion, the "triple talaq," counted as but one divorce. This position is also that adopted by the London council, and it follows the teachings of Ibn Taymiyyah against the Hanafi position that the triple talaq counts as three divorces and that reconciliation is then impossible. As Saba explained to me, the vote allows her to say to anyone who asks that "the shariʿa council position is this, even if some individual scholars say that."

Nonetheless, the issue never goes away, because Bokhari never accepted the decision. Here is a case where the issue emerged. On July 5, 2011, a husband and wife came to see the council. The wife petitioned for divorce. Her husband had concealed a previous marriage from her. Both marriages were only the nikah. The council spoke first with the wife, then with the husband.

AMRA: Some women do fine with a polygamous marriage; is that what you want?
WIFE: My issue is that he stays nights here, that I am here just to satisfy his needs.

The husband admitted that he had pronounced the phrase "I divorce you" to his first wife but claimed that he did so only to show what he would say were he to divorce her. He said it three times, but, in any case, this would have counted as only one divorce. Bokhari picked up on this issue:

BOKHARI: Why did you think that pronouncing the talaq three times equaled one?
HUSBAND: You have different people with different ideas, and you have to read them and then decide, and this is what I decided.
BOKHARI [SHOWING HIS ASTONISHMENT]: But why do you think that three equals one?

The others ignored him. Later on the husband left the room and the wife reentered:

WIFE: He said "I divorce you."
AMRA: Even if he did divorce you, you were back together and had sexual intercourse within three months.
NASEEM: He doesn't admit it; I don't consider it divorce.

Bokhari kept repeating sotto voce, "clear words, clear words," meaning that because the husband pronounced the divorce formula, regardless of his intention, the divorce occurred, and furthermore, it was a final divorce, a triple talaq, meaning that the couple could not reconcile. Therefore, while the couple's reunion "within three months" would be a licit reconciliation for the majority of the members on the council, to Bokhari it was sex outside of marriage. Amra said, to no one in particular, "There is a difference among scholars, two opinions [on the triple talaq]." Bokhari, looking at his watch, muttered, "Move on," but it is unclear whether he thought they should declare them divorced or just drop the case with no resolution. In fact, they did not resolve it.

In April 2013, I spoke with Bokhari and Sarfraz about the dar ul-qaza in India, which preexisted the British shariʿa councils. I asked if the first of these, in the state of Bihar, had formulated a clear rule on the triple talaq. I asked this knowing that Bokhari defended the Hanafi position against the others.

Indeed, he immediately and vehemently criticized the view that the triple talaq only counted as one divorce: "Even Ibn Taymiyyah's own disciples did not accept his view. It counts as three everywhere in South Asia except for the Ahl al-Hadith. The idea of counting as one came from the Khawarij, those Shi'a who hated [the caliph] Umar, who had said it counted as three. There is only one source for the Ibn Taymiyyah view, a hadith that has only one transmitter, Ibn Abbas, who himself said that if a man says the talaq a thousand times, then three separate him and his wife for life, and the rest are on his neck. So, the hadith needs to be interpreted not in a literal way."[4]

Reporting

At the session on July 5, 2011, a reporter from the Sunday *Telegraph* attended part of the session and asked questions between cases. During one break, he had time to follow up with the scholars.

Telegraph: How do you have the power to dissolve marriages if they are not registered? [This question reflects a common misunderstanding, that the council performs legally relevant divorces. However, Amra interprets it differently, as closer to a challenge, frequently made, as to the propriety of the council interfering with what is a state matter. She and Naseem answer in a way that minimizes the importance of the council's role.]

AMRA: As British citizens they have a contract with the state. When they have a civil divorce, then the contract is broken, and they do not have to come here to us.

NASEEM: If it becomes clear to us that the marriage is unsustainable, then we dissolve it.

[AMRA THEN REHEARSED THE BASIC WAYS OF DIVORCING: talaq, khula, and dissolution.]

NASEEM: In this court, the view is that the marriage is by consent, and if one party withdraws the consent, then we have no choice but to grant the divorce.

AMRA: We try to make the other person understand that the first does not want to live with her.

Telegraph: Does the husband get all the money?

AMRA: If he initiates the divorce, then he has no right; even if the marriage was not consummated, the wife still keeps half [she was referring to mahr, but the reporter had no idea what she was talking about]. If she initiates, then it is not clear-cut but depends on how long they have been married [and] other factors.

Telegraph: And are some of these arranged marriages?

Naseem: Yes, but it is not like the olden days in England, when someone would say, "You marry her!"

In the end the *Telegraph* coverage was fair regarding Birmingham but characterized the sympathetic woman, Amra, as the "good" Muslim scholar who is fighting against the patriarchal religion, epitomized by the London council and "bad" Muslim scholar Suhaib Hasan.[5] Quite incorrectly, the article stated that the two councils followed quite distinct "theologies," which, as we have seen, is not the case.

This rhetoric is familiar, however: frame the situation in terms of good versus evil forces, a "liberal" view in Birmingham and a "fundamentalist" view in London. As is always the case, the hundreds of anonymous comments on the article posted on the *Telegraph*'s website reached not even this level of subtlety as they jousted with each other over who could denigrate shariʿa and Islam most brilliantly. They seemed to settle on Islam as "Dark-Ages camel herders' myths."

Anticipatory Measures: The Fiqh Council

Of course, the tone and policies of the Birmingham Shariʿa Council represent just one of many ways of responding to questions and requests. We have seen how the London council adopted a proceduralist approach to its mission—do this and that and you will get a certificate—and how its particular intake procedure means that establishing Islamic grounds for divorce is the first and major topic of exchanges between scholars and petitioners. The Birmingham council begins with counseling and introduces the Islamic scholars at a later stage. The case is first framed as a family problem, with the legal dimension taking its place among other dimensions. The difference in gender between the two councils further differentiates the two settings. In chapter 9 we turn to a third, even more different institution, one that grows out of Sufi practices and ideas.

I emphasize that these differences are mainly in the structuring genealogies of the respective institutions, more than in theology or legal school. London and Birmingham include quite similar debates about how to think through divorce matters. Both councils are composed mainly of people of South Asian backgrounds, and both accept petitions from any and all Muslims who present themselves. In terms of rulings, there is little that is more "liberal" about Amra Bone's statements than those of Suhaib Hasan. Their differences have much more to do with age, gender, and how each has adapted to the institution in question. Suhaib has, increasingly, shaped the London council as a self-functioning organization—with procedures, files, and flowcharts—as a rational bureaucracy. Amra and Naseem have taken the Birmingham council in a very different direction.

Still other permutations are possible. We can in a sense "control" for personalities by looking at how Sarfraz Mohammed, the newest addition to the Birmingham Shariʿa Council, operates in a different context. When not sitting on the Birmingham Central Mosque council, he sits with a different group of scholars: the Fiqh Council of Birmingham (FCB), headed by Mufti Abu Zafar.

Abu Zafar, Sarfraz Mohammed, and some others associated with this Fiqh Council studied in Pakistan with the former judge of the Shariʿat Appellate Bench of the Supreme Court of Pakistan, M. Taqi ʿUthmani, at his Dar al-ʿUlum in Karachi. Sheikh ʿUthmani was born in Deoband. He is recognized as a major authority on Islamic finance. He cites as one of his teachers Muhammad Zakariyya al-Kandhalvi, the scholar associated with the Tablighi Jamaʿat, and he was the teacher of Yusuf Motala, whose influence among Deobandis we discussed earlier in the discussion of Leicester in chapter 3.

The Fiqh Council differs markedly from the Central Mosque on the rules and procedures for divorce. For example, it follows a more consistently Hanafi line of reasoning. On their website they stipulate that the triple talaq counts as three divorces, not one. They also make clear that their acts of dissolution of marriage are faskh and not khula, as khula requires the consent of the husband. They also reserve all determinations of performativity to the Fiqh Council, clarifying, for example, that a civil divorce does not automatically mean an Islamic divorce.

If the Fiqh Council is more Hanafi in doctrine, Sarfraz sees it as allowing for particularly creative ways to keep marriages from ending. He mentioned some of those to me in April 2013.[6]

SARFRAZ: In one recent case, the husband was carrying on an affair openly. At the dinner table he would be here, his wife across from him over there, and the other woman down the table, all eating together. He had a drinking problem as well. They had three younger children, ages five, seven, and nine, and they wanted to find a way to move on without ending the marriage. So we drew up an agreement that he would end the drinking, stop seeing that woman, and attend a full series of weekend retreats that a mosque here has for cases like his. And if he failed to do one of the things, she would have the power to bring about the talaq, with the FCB as the sole arbiter if he disagreed that he had failed.

JRB: Is this like a *talāq tafwīz* [delegated divorce]?

SARFRAZ: Yes, a tafwiz. So far, he is doing what he should. We told him: "The evidence is here to give a faskh straightaway, but due to your wife's generosity, she is willing to let you try this. Not your generosity!" In a second case, the marriage had broken down, and the husband said that if his wife wanted to end the marriage, he would agree, and he signed an *ikhtiar* agreement that the wife had the right to end the marriage. But he did not want to pronounce the talaq himself. He did agree

> to delegate a *wakīl* [representative], so he wrote out a statement making his uncle his wakīl. We called his uncle in from the other room—he had come with him—and he was angry because he did not want to take the responsibility, but he did it. The third case involved a first-cousin marriage; both fathers came to the session. The couple had been married for five or six years but were separated most of that time. They were getting older and could not get on with their personal lives, and no one wanted to begin a divorce, because of the repercussions for the family. [Here he relates how he told them the hadith about the garden as mahr.] We drew up a statement for both to sign that said that there is no blame to either side, which either of them could show to others in the future. The husband did not want to issue a talaq because this would make it harder for him to remarry in the future and would lead to accusations within the family. The FCB advised him to pronounce one talaq. He did.

These cases likely would have looked very different had they been brought before the Birmingham Central Mosque council. Each would have first been discussed with Saba and Wageha, and in those discussions, the focus would have been what the wife wanted to do. Only if she decided to end the marriage would the matter have reached the scholars on the council, and the question would have been framed as "divorce or not." I never encountered the kind of anticipatory agreements described by Sarfraz, which derived from the tafwiz agreement, often called the "delegated divorce," which empowers the wife to trigger a judicial awarding of a talaq. The Fiqh Council is less procedural than the London council, but also more fiqh-oriented than the Birmingham Central Council.

In the end, then, it is the character of the institutions that matter. The Birmingham Central Mosque's shariʿa council preserves much of its initial inspiration in its tone and procedures, as do the London council and the Fiqh Council mentioned above. This point will become even more apparent when we turn to another institution often cited as a shariʿa council—the Muslim Arbitration Tribunal—located elsewhere in the Midlands.

CHAPTER 9

Sufi Encompassments

"ONCE YOU STEP ONTO THE LAND, HE IS LOOKING OUT FOR YOU." I WAS AT THE rural site of the "blessed seat," where the living sheikh and saint, and his entombed, still-sanctified father and predecessor, welcome and protect visitors, particularly during weekend family days and at the annual Blessed Summit. These eighty-four acres, located a few miles from the small Midlands town of Nuneaton, house the Hijaz community. Physically, the community consists of a collection of buildings used for schooling and visitors, plus a graveyard. Spiritually, it is the protected space surrounding the tomb of Muhammad Abdul Wahhab Siddiqi. Mediation and arbitration occurs in this space, but it is part of a larger array of activities, all carried out under an umbrella of sanctity.

What happens when one constructs a shariʿa council within an explicitly and visibly Sufi world? At Hijaz, the current leader and sheikh, Faiz ul-Aqtab Siddiqi, dispenses advice and blessings to Muslims living in Britain and, sometimes, abroad. He is also a barrister and has sought to include the mediation activities of his Muslim Arbitration Tribunal (MAT) within the community. If the London ISC scholars seek to base their legitimacy on correct following of jurisprudence and adherence to explicit procedural rules, MAT is based on Sufi sanctity.[1] Here, shariʿa, understood in the broader sense of God's plans for Muslims, is invoked in much less court-like ways. Because the specific difference of Hijaz regards the multiple activities of its sheikh, and because Hijaz is indeed so different from the other cases, I begin with a broader account of legitimacy and practices in the institution.

The Hijaz Umbrella of Sanctity

If you walk the kilometer or so from the Nuneaton highway up to the college, you first come upon a sign telling you that you have entered "Hijaz College, Blessed Seat of Spiritual Renaissance." You see the graveyard on the left and, between it and the college buildings, the mausoleum, where Muhammad Abdul Wahhab Siddiqi is laid out in a coffin in the center of the room. The shrine building or mausoleum (his *mazar* in Sufi terms) is as important as the grave. By building a shrine above the grave, the site becomes a house within which the body dwells, creating and signaling the presence of the

FIGURE 4. Children at Hijaz, 2010

saint in the world. In July 2010 when I attended the Hijaz annual Sufi gathering, the Blessed Summit, one man explained to me that I could follow events equally well anywhere on the eighty-four acres, "because when you enter the grounds, you are in his domain," pointing to the mausoleum. "He looks after you."[2]

The saint's coffin is draped with red embroidered tapestry and garlands of artificial flowers. At the head is a column with small tiles on it wrapped with white sheeting, thicker near the top, which serves as a head post. On the walls are a plaque that traces the saint's spiritual genealogy (*silsilah*) back to Abubakar Siddiq, the temporal successor to the prophet Muhammad. Another plaque shows his family lineage. "Some non-Muslims come here just to meditate," explained Farid, my guide. Anyone is allowed to visit the tomb, but only adepts (*murīds*), followers of the saint, are permitted access to a private area. They may descend a stairway hidden by wood lattice and guarded by a coded, locked door. Behind the door is an area set aside for them to meditate. Some visitors spend days mainly meditating in this room, explained Farid. He would like to do this but cannot find the time, because he is always on call as Siddiqi's assistant. He took a few minutes to pray while we were there.

The Hijaz community encompasses a wide (and often changing) range of activities, but its central significance for the area's Muslims is as a place to seek advice and blessings from the sheikh. Boys attending local schools live in the buildings, as do others who work at Hijaz. Before 2012 these boys attended day school on the campus. The school offered GCSEs (General Certificate of Secondary Education) and A-levels in the sciences and humanities alongside a religious studies curriculum. It also offered a three-year BA in Islamic law and theology, and a four-year LLB (bachelor of laws) course that prepared students for careers as barristers or solicitors. When I visited in January 2010, there were around one hundred people in residence at any one time, mostly pupils aged eleven to eighteen, but some older boys following the BA program in law also resided there.

By 2013, the day school had closed. A smaller number of pupils lived at the site and attended classes in Islamic subjects in the evenings and on weekends. Siddiqi's brother-in-law, Sheikh Tauqir, had been the school director and was an enthusiastic teacher of science and Islamic subjects, with a large telescope perched on his desk, but in April 2013, he expressed few regrets for the closing: "Now the pupils who used to be at our school attend local schools, and we have let go all the teachers. This is better; the school had been shrinking, and this way the kids get better instruction and they meet with English kids, because this is a pretty white town—except for the area just around the town mosque, which is mainly African Asians, and we don't talk with them often."

The spiritual line focused on the shrine of Muhammad Abdul Wahhab Siddiqi is a branch of the Naqshbandiyya order (*tariqa*) that has long been based in the village of Ghosuhr near Lahore and traces its spiritual lineage through Sheikh Ahmad Sirhindi (d.1624).[3] In 1972 Siddiqi moved to Britain and established a mosque in Coventry. He retained his base in the Midlands but traveled throughout Europe, where he developed followings. He was particularly successful in the Netherlands, and I have met Dutch Sufis who have traveled to the Blessed Seat in order to seek consultation with his son. Notably among British Sufis, Siddiqi focused on promoting education along two tacks: the classical Islamic curriculum (the Dars-i Nizami) and British professional training. In 1982 he established a religious school in Coventry and sent his four sons into law and medicine. Three of them today cooperate in the Hijaz venture. So committed was he to establishing in Britain what he saw as the moderate mainstream of Islam, the Ahl al-Sunnah wal-Jamaah, that Siddiqi asked to be buried there rather than in Pakistan. When he died in 1994, his body was maintained in Coventry until a mausoleum could be built on the land he had purchased in Nuneaton for the new college. To the best of my knowledge, this site is still the only Sufi tomb shrine in Britain, and it may be the only one in Western Europe.[4]

In July 2011, I asked Sheikh Siddiqi how he first learned that he would replace his father. "It was in July 1993, at the Summit, that he announced it. I already knew, because he had discussed with me about three *khalifah* [deputies] whom he wanted to appoint: Would they be alright with me? He would not have done that unless they would be working under me. I think he could not find anyone else than me!" This way of working was unusual, he continued, because usually a council meets to decide on a spiritual successor. "But I never developed those three khalifah; they are of his generation and I am working with the next generation." I asked him, "So you appointed others to be khalifah?" He responded, "No, I have not done that; I don't want to have a hierarchy here. We have a practical division of labor: Zeenat working with the community and Ameerah with some of the MAT issues, but that is not as if someone is speaking for me on spiritual issues."

As this narrative suggests, Siddiqi has kept direct control over a wide range of Hijaz projects, appointing assistants to work on one or another project. Over the five years I visited Hijaz, from 2009 through 2013, the personnel and their duties were in near-constant rotation, all dependent directly on the sheikh. Siddiqi's relaxed manner and smooth discourse coexists with a top-down leadership style that matches his spiritual status. One is reminded of this status when assistants enter his rooms walking backward, or when visitors approach him with bowed heads. Siddiqi's assistants often refer to him in the plural: "Do you want to see them?" One assistant explained that "we say it out of respect." She added, "We take on the ways that we speak to each other in the community, and new members do also; we call each other brother and sister, or auntie and uncle."

But at the same time, Siddiqi is a barrister, and he made English legal training the special brand of the college. His younger brother Noor ul-Aqtab Siddiqi works as a solicitor in Birmingham, as do (at a different practice) his brother Zain ul-Aqtab Siddiqi and his brother-in-law Maulana Arif Awan. Several other men training to be solicitors also contribute service to Hijaz.

Although Siddiqi has been mediating in family conflicts for a long time and continues to do so, it wasn't until 2004 that he decided to create MAT in order to be able to resolve conflicts among Muslims in ways that would be contractually binding. These conflicts vary from disputes between rival mosque groups over leadership to conflicts within small businesses. The presence of lawyers at Hijaz also means that the same person might mediate a family conflict, propose a religious divorce, and act as solicitor for a civil divorce. Although Siddiqi insists that "we do not want to do the work of the Islamic Shariʿa Councils" and take on religious divorce work in a systematic way, the Hijaz site has provided religious and legal services for some young women, as we shall see below. Siddiqi receives people on days when he is "at home" in his spacious Hijaz office, he makes formal appointments to resolve disputes, and he travels to cities in the Midlands and northern England to hold similar sessions whenever warranted by the volume of requests. These sessions are mainly consultations and requests for general advice about life and sometimes business or legal affairs. Formal arbitrations consume only a small portion of his time. Nonetheless, on the basis of his movements, the British tabloid press and several ill-informed think tanks claim that there are multiple MATs in England. On a number of occasions Siddiqi arranged to have me interview those visitors who were willing to speak with me after their consultations, as well as to set up interviews with parties to arbitrations. The cases discussed in a subsequent section give some idea of the tone of these processes, in which it is Sufi legitimacy more than any quasi-legal dimension that is on offer.[5]

The spiritual aura surrounding the saint is not limited to the grounds of Hijaz. One night I was escorted home from a meeting in eastern London by two young adepts. Each told me how he came to know the sheikh. One had a baby daughter whose heart difficulties baffled doctors. He lost faith; he wrote to Islamic sources of authority all over the world. One sheikh in Saudi Arabia wrote back with verses from the Qur'an, "but I had lost faith, I did not believe in the Qur'an, so what good did that do? But Sheikh Faiz ul-Aqtab Siddiqi answered every question I had. And I thought through the issues, and how everything had to have a maker, and that had to be God. I came to that conclusion myself, and then the sheikh convinced me of the truth of Islam." The other man told a story of failure in his personal and professional life. "I had nothing, and no hope, and then I found Sheikh Faiz ul-Aqtab Siddiqi, and since then I have received blessings, and now I am a qualified engineer. I have been blessed many times."

Some of the mantle of sanctity extends to Siddiqi's brothers and brothers-in-law. Sheikh Tauqir married Siddiqi's sister and ran the school. He regularly receives telephone requests for advice and help. In January 2010 he explained to me that many of these questions concern spells that others have placed on them. "I get these all the time." He prescribes talismans (*tawīz*) and insists that the afflicted do exactly as he says. A call came while I was there. A woman described her child's illnesses. He asked, "Is there *ikhtilaf*, division in the family?" He asked about dreams and other signs; later he told me that it was clear to him from her answers that others were putting spells on the family. He said to her that he would write a tawīz, and said that the entire family needed to say prayers often, as this would bring them closer to God, but he also told her not to tell anyone that she had called him, as that would just increase the tensions. "I can help 80 to 90 percent of the people who are possessed, as long as they do exactly what I tell them."

Hijaz People

With Sheikh Siddiqi as the pole of the Hijaz community, who else participates? There are, first, his relatives: his brothers and brothers-in-law, in particular, Tauqir and the solicitor Arif. They can claim the title of sheikh or maulana, and bring their professional areas of expertise to bear on Hijaz activities: two brothers plus Arif are solicitors, for example. Then there is a changing army of assistants: the women and men who work at fixed jobs, such as secretarial or personal assistant roles, or who show up on weekends to help guide the mass of visitors through the site. We will meet some of them below; they often gravitate to Hijaz out of a specific personal issue that led them to seek Siddiqi's intervention.

There are also a smaller number of people who are community leaders in their own right and who have more or less close ties with Hijaz. Qamar Bhatti is one such person: head of an extended Pakistani kin group, and based in Birmingham, we encountered him in earlier chapters. During my years of visits to Hijaz and to him, he drew away from direct involvement and focused on the needs of his own larger, extended social group. A second such person is Shamim Qureshi, who works as a district judge in Birmingham, and was one of the first Asian judges appointed to the bench.

In May 2010 Judge Qureshi talked with me about some of the ways he relates to other forms of Islam. For about three years, when he lived in Bristol and worked as a lawyer, he traveled with Tablighi Jamaʿat, the piety-focused *dawa* group that grew out of the Deobandi movement (and that we encountered in chapter 3). He enjoyed those activities: "Professional people tended to join, lawyers and doctors, because it gave us a chance to do something. We would go and sleep in a mosque and then be handed lists of addresses to call on and invite people to come to the mosque. These would be Muslims who were not avid mosque-goers. But once I rang a doorbell and a white guy answered and said, 'Why do you people keep coming back again and again; that fellow moved out years ago!' And I asked the guy in charge if we could not develop a database so that we could mark when someone had moved. He said no; that was un-Islamic because the Prophet did not have a computer. We have this kind of thinking, not willing to change."

Qureshi's attitude is similar to that which we heard earlier from Ibrahim Mogra, namely, that the divide between Sufis on the one hand, and Deobandis and the Tablighi Jamaʿat, on the other, was overstated in the British context. "I liked the TJ because we were doing something, talking to people who did not go to the mosque," he said. "The problem I have with the Sufis is that they talk amongst themselves, all people who do go to the mosque, and what good is that?" Qureshi was first posted to Wolverhampton, and in 2009 to Birmingham; he and his family live in nearby Coventry. His elder son Ahmad was already attending Hijaz College when they were in Bristol, and that was the beginning of his relationship with the Hijaz community or "HC."

The Blessed Summit

The peak moment of performing sacrality comes at the annual gathering at Hijaz called the Blessed Summit. I was invited to attend in July 2010. The setting is conducive to letting members of the community mingle freely, as the grounds are protected by neighboring fields devoted to cattle or to pond fishing. The gathering lasts Friday through Sunday, with the events picking up in the afternoons and on the first two nights, extending till around three a.m. with prayers and *dhikr* recitations. You pick up the brochure when you register, which takes a much more devotional tone than do the other forms of Hijaz communication and includes the details of the dhikr. "This is not a public event," explained Sheikh Siddiqi, "we don't advertise and expect people to come in from the outside." Word is spread through their mosques and the website. Hundreds rather than thousands attend, and they are mainly families and young people.

The site was turned over to the summit for the weekend. School was over, so the "sisters," all the women visitors who wished to spend the nights there, could be housed in the dormitory spaces, while the "brothers" slept in the larger of two tents. This tent was also used for worship and lectures; a smaller tent was used to serve meals and to hold some goods for sale, including books and CDs of Qur'an readings by one of the Siddiqi brothers, homemade nonalcoholic perfumes, and cards with simple calligraphic designs. At mealtime people sat in the main tent and chatted, holding a meat and sauce dish and bread, with sweet rice, Pepsi, or water. You could purchase other snacks at stands near the site's main buildings. In 2010, for the first time, there was also an ice-cream seller parked in the main area.

The saint's grave watched over all. The mausoleum had been decked out in lights, and men and women were gathered around the tomb reading scripture and chanting or just meditating. Friday afternoon they changed the covering of the tomb. This year the covering was handmade in Mauritius; in previous years it had been mass-produced. Bhatti explained that "there is the summit inside the tent, and one outside, because when you enter the grounds you are in his domain," pointing to the mausoleum. Sultan Mahmoud, as he called the deceased saint, "looks after you, and you can participate sitting anywhere; that is why we have the loudspeakers everywhere, so you can hear." Judge Qureshi was particularly happy because one of his sons had graduated from the Hijaz School several years previously, another was to finish that year, and another was coming up. The afternoon and evening were filled with *naat* songs, speeches, interviews, and one full hour of dhikr.[6]

Women were dressed in a variety of colors, nearly every man in a white gown and white pointed cap. (I stood out in all aspects of my appearance.) Many were saying to each other, "I have not seen you for so long," and the summit was an opportunity for those who are active in the Hijaz community to see one another. But it also gave some the opportunity to see Sheikh Siddiqi for the first time; when people arrived, they registered and filled out a form with their name, mobile telephone number (so they could be called to his office when it was their turn), and e-mail (for further contact). The forms were stacked up at the office (the "blessed seat"), and people were shown in, one after the other, to see the sheikh.

Siddiqi's office is half of a very large room, with wood screens separating the back area, used for his living room and prayer area (with the bedroom through a farther door) from the front area, which has his desk on one side and a carpeted area on the other. The carpeted area has low couches along the far side. When receiving, he sits on a low seat at the end of the carpeted area, his back to the wood screens. When working (or discussing issues with colleagues, or with me), he sits at his desk, which featured the largest computer monitor I had (as of 2014) ever seen on a desk.

"We are on the floor today," he said in greeting when I came in. Siddiqi sat on his low couch and his guests sat across from him on a slightly lower cushion. Only people who had not previously seen him were permitted to sign up for a slot this weekend, but most had been in contact with someone at Hijaz previously, often with someone in one of the major cities they work in, including Bradford, Manchester, Birmingham, and Coventry. The visitors generally do not come with practical questions, explained Siddiqi, as I had first thought (I had assumed that marriage and work would top the list) but more "philosophical" ones, such as "How do I figure out what to do with my life?" He explained that "I explore with them how they should think about where to get where they want to be." He stays out of events taking place outside the office until late in the evening when he leads the collective dhikr chanting.

In the main tent, four older men who had studied with the sheikh's father sat on the stage and exchanged stories about his wisdom. One related the story of a woman who came to see him and said she had been kicked out of her house by her husband and had nothing. She wanted a talisman from the sheikh, who gave her an envelope and told her not to open it until she reached home. The sheikh told his pupil (who was telling the story) that it contained at least a week's expenses: "She does not need a talisman but a way to get on in life." The narrator commented: "This shows he was concerned with both the spiritual and the practical."

Over the course of the many hours in the main tent, from time to time one of the more revered men in Hijaz would enter the tent and the speeches would stop so that all could properly welcome him. Around nine o'clock that evening we could see Siddiqi approaching the tent from the direction of the office. His acolytes held umbrellas over him and he wore a shawl. At the sighting, one of the younger men who formed a group to the left of the stage stood up and pronounced the *takbīr* (Allahu Akbar), at which moment the eminent speaker instantly stopped and many of the younger people stood up and made their way toward the entrance to greet him, stooping low and kissing Siddiqi's hand. The dhikr then resumed and lasted late into the night.[7]

Surgeries

Siddiqi's core activity is receiving visitors in what are called surgeries, held at Hijaz or elsewhere in England. One weekend in May 2010, I showed up at Hijaz for a surgery. At noon there was as yet no one waiting, but in the office, his assistants, Zeenat and Farah, were working over the lists of people who had signed up. They hold a general surgery there about once a month, and people find out about it by word of mouth. There is no web announcement or e-sign-up; people connected to the Hijaz family seem to make up a goodly share of those who make appointments. If they hold surgeries in another city, say at Bradford or Birmingham, then they let a local person know, and he or she sends out text messages. For today about thirty people had signed up, though many had canceled, and others were phoning as we sat; many just came as walk-ins. This was a relatively quiet day. Each person is allotted about ten minutes, but Siddiqi won't make them stop if, for example, it is a divorce case and they need to keep talking.

Sister Zeenat, as she is called, had been here for two years. She had lived in the north all her life, growing up in Bradford, and attended university in Liverpool, obtaining a degree in pharmacy and then three years of finishing her diploma and building up clinical experience as a specialist in monitoring doses and responding to queries from hospital staff about drug doses. She wore a white hijab and had a pronounced Yorkshire accent. She found herself rising up into management but not liking it as much—"Could I see myself doing this when I am sixty or fifty-five or fifty?" She was in Bradford, where she still is when not living at Hijaz, and had heard about Siddiqi, but "I figured he was just like the others, the hierarchy that looks after us, where men do the talking," so she offered to pick him up from Hijaz when he next came to Bradford, figuring that maybe a sister couldn't do that. But he agreed, and then she realized how far it was—two and a half hours—but she had committed herself by then and so drove him, and realized this was someone she really trusted. So she began to come to Hijaz.

She decided she would have to balance out "*din* and *dunya*," religion and worldly things, and decided to work outside just enough to make ends meet and to spend more time at Hijaz. She stayed on campus and looked after Siddiqi's relationships with outside people (such as me) and was building up the Hijaz community: "Right now that means developing seven to ten people in each of several cities, Birmingham and Bradford, for example, so that eventually they will be able to mentor people who might be in trouble." None of this had happened in 2010, nor had it at my last visit in May 2013.

I sat in the separate building used and designated as the "waiting room." A succession of people filed in and out, although others just walked around in the fine weather. A Dutchman, born in the Netherlands to Pakistani parents, had come to ask a question about theology. Another, older Dutch-speaking man showed up as well. (The two did not know each other.) They exemplified the strong ties that Muhammad Abdul Wahhab Siddiqi had built up in the 1970s between his order and the Masjid Noeroel Islam in The Hague, where the two Dutch visitors worshipped.[8] Two men who had left Tanzania for Britain also showed up. One spoke an American-accented excellent English from his years of earning his first degree in Wichita. He was in business and wanted to eventually move to Tanzania, but his son was still only ten and the family did not want to leave London. He was there to ask about business matters; his friend about matrimony.

A few days after the above surgeries at Hijaz, I returned to the Blessed Seat, arriving as Siddiqi was in discussion with two men from a Coventry mosque, rather Deobandi in orientation, over a dispute between them about their relative responsibilities for running the mosque's education program. "It is like a couple married for twenty-five years and then they cannot stand each other," he said later. They signed a contract to abide by the arbitration, with him as the lawyer, and then ate lunch together with Siddiqi in his office to make peace.

We then drove to Coventry to stop by the bank—he was leaving for ten days in the United States—to his house in a leafy area of Birmingham, not too far from Birmingham Central Mosque, and then to the offices of his new venture, Muslim Insurance Services offices, in Snow Hill Plaza in central Birmingham. During the drive he held telephone meetings, including a scheduled three-way conversation with the financial officer and a lawyer from one of their would-be major insurance brokers. When we arrived at the office building, he donned his more formal turban and long brown coat, and we took the elevator to the twelfth floor. He had to have two assistants punch in the door code. "See, I run this company but I don't know how to get in; I don't carry keys." I asked him, "You're leaving for the US; what about money?" and he replied, "No money, just credit cards."

On the twelfth floor, members of the Hijaz community mingled in the large common office area. They included several younger men working on the insurance project. I spoke with Rizwan Ali, who was born in Britain but grew up in Pakistan with his father's brother. Until recently, he always thought about religious matters in the Urdu language, and, as a result, he found it a bit hard to respond quickly at his British university when he would be drawn into arguments about Islam. "Some people would argue with great certainty, the Jamaat-e-Islami types, 'Brother, do this and you are a kafir,' whereas the Sufis would say, 'Try a little harder,' which is rather soft. So the more hard-line young activists win over quite a few." He was brought over to Muslim insurance from Hijaz and would shortly leave for Chicago to talk to some imams of mosques to get them to be on the board of the company.

For the surgeries, Siddiqi sat alone in a room and people entered one by one to discuss issues with him. An assistant asked people as they came out if they would be willing to talk with me and quite a few people were. I was told to sit in the adjoining room, and had a steady stream of "post-Siddiqi" visitors.

Muna was a "revert" from Hinduism (three years previously). She and her husband run an optician service, and she had come to drop off glasses ordered by some of the brothers and sisters, who take their business to her. She often comes to talk with the sheikh, to pose questions about practical life. She worried that because wine and other drinks were served in the same glassware in restaurants, the glasses would be tainted. Siddiqi assured her that the forms of the glasses are different, and that in any case, because juices come in cans or bottles, she could ask for them that way. She worried about contamination in general. For example, in Subway sandwich shops, she wondered whether they changed gloves between handling pork and salad. Siddiqi said that they should, and that it is fine to ask them to, and that otherwise the produces are not mixed; they don't drop the salad onto pork and then serve it, for example. But, he continued (as she reported to me), if you worried about every possibility, you'd never eat! "Now it is easier because I live just down the road and most people are Muslims but before that in shops they never would have heard the word halal and not understand my request." She and her family come to Hijaz often; they like to sit in the mosque in the mausoleum and pray or meditate. She attends surgeries once a month or so, sometimes just to see the brothers and sisters.

In the halls many families were talking and walking around. Some had been waiting for hours, including a number of younger children, some carried by their mums. A friendly man in his thirties came in to talk with me, accompanied by his wife and two-year-old daughter, Aisyah. His wife wore a dark face veil with a multicolored headscarf. She is an English revert. A friend had brought her to the Blessed Summit and she chose Hijaz as the place to recite the *shahada*, the confession of faith that signals entry into Islam. She asked Siddiqi whether it was permitted to attend celebrations of the Prophet's birthday (Mawlid). "Some have told me that it was forbidden to attend, but others said I had to, and he told me that it was up to me. Or about whether I could talk to men: again I heard people tell me never to do it and he explained that it was fine as long as not in the wrong way, not joking [In my mind, I quickly reviewed my own interaction with her to see whether I had made any jokes]. He said, we get confused, you hear all these opinions, but he gives us the reasons, not just says yes or no, plus he tells us what to read, they are a bit long, but that's good. We are not educated, so we need this. . . . People talk with us here, with women, we're not educated and sometimes people won't do that. He is the only one who will talk with women."

In April 2013, I was back at Hijaz for another surgery. I was immediately ushered into the separate building that serves as an (unheated) waiting room where I chatted with visitors. A bit after eleven a.m., the two assistants invited everyone into Siddiqi's office. They were trying a new procedure. They used to keep everyone waiting and then usher them in one after the other into the office. Now they all sit together in the carpeted receiving area, the women along the right and the men along the left, with some babies ricocheting back and forth from mum to dad. Siddiqi sits on his slightly raised couch at the end of the area, and calls people forward. They sit, often kneeling, and speak with him. He speaks very softly, sometimes placing a healing hand on someone. Most people, when through, back out of the room. Some don't, and no comments are made.

For most people, he reaches into a drawer for a small piece of paper, or uses one of the large sheets stacked to his left. They have *doa* written on them, prayers that are effective as spells; the one large printed sheet has instructions, for example, to repeat the phrase of praise *subhanallah* a certain number of times. Or he writes specific prayers for people; sometimes they are to dissolve them in water and drink the water, explained Arif (with whom I sat for a while). He did this three times for a family with a boy who appeared to have Down syndrome. Siddiqi was dressed all in white, with cap and long shirt, with a black robe over his legs and waist. He played with the children who came up as part of a visit. An old-fashioned but gold-plated telephone sat next to him, and quite a few silver or gold objects surrounded him, conveying a sense of luxury.

A young man sat next to me. His wife, very pretty and more expressive than were most in attendance, sat across from us. Their three-year-old daughter was with dad for most of the time and then with mum. (Mum and daughter had a terrible time in the changing room later on, with much crying.) He told me he had come many times to see the sheikh: for advice about how to find a job, about how to marry, and so on, as well as for guides for spirituality. He was born here, but his wife was born in Pakistan and lived in the city, and was, well, "Modern?" I ventured. "Yes, modern, so I wanted her to come here and see the sheikh. And also, our daughter has not been healthy. The sheikh gave them doa." He had brought his friends to see the sheikh as well. They live in north London. I asked him what he did—"work in a bank, operations"—and I pursued this by asking, "Does that ever give you pause, with loans at interest?" "No," he replied, "I have never worried about it; perhaps I should, but I am just in the operations part, not that I am trying to justify it, but . . ." his voice trailed off.

Arif, Siddiqi's sister's husband, told me a bit about his own history. His family came from Nairobi. The Asians who had spent twenty to thirty years there at most had completely changed their outlook, such that "When we came here after Idi Amin threw us out, we started East Indian societies wherever we went, shops, kept in touch with each other; whereas those from Pakistan directly, they maybe just met in the mosque. There is a real difference, plus very few of us marry someone from Pakistan, almost always it is with someone born in Britain. [In] my family, all the children became engineers, doctors, lawyers." He explained that most people who come to see the sheikh have marital problems, or a general lack of meaning in their lives: maybe they have a job and family but it feels empty. Arif himself went up to see him with his wife and three daughters.

Many of Siddiqi's surgeries are held away from Hijaz, at other cities in the Midlands and the North. For example, he travels from time to time to Bradford in the North. A small community center is sometimes used for the surgeries; a Bradford man who is a follower of Siddiqi organizes the surgeries and lets Siddiqi's office know when sufficient numbers of people have signed up for the saint to make the trip.

Mediating, Divorcing, and Arbitrating

The surgeries are the heart of Hijaz. Siddiqi, as saint, dispenses wisdom and amulets. All else that he does draws at least some of its legitimacy and appeal from the saintly role. As we move from practices defined by spiritual potency to practices ostensibly concerning worldly matters, we must keep the spiritual dimension in mind, however much it might remain in the discursive background. And indeed, when we move to the domain of arbitration, we switch radically from a spiritual frame to one of law and contracts. The irony of Hijaz is that they employ a public rhetoric of high legal performativity, of binding arbitration, to encompass a range of practices, almost none of which have any legal effect. To non-Sufis and, more importantly, non-Muslims, Siddiqi underlines his status as barrister and his role as arbitrator, and most people know of his activities under the rubric of MAT. And yet rarely, if ever, have the activities framed as "MAT work" ever involved courts.

You will have already read several references to MAT in the above conversations, without its functions being made very clear. Much of the confusion in public policy debates in Britain regarding shariʿa and law rests on a misunderstanding of what is meant by "arbitration." Commercial and some other kinds of disputes may be resolved through binding arbitration under the terms of the Arbitration Act 1996, as can, as of 2012, financial and property disputes arising from a divorce.[9] If a proper contract is drawn up in the presence of a lawyer and freely agreed to by the parties, then one party may ask a court to enforce the contract's terms. The act limits the conditions under which either party may appeal: basically, and not unlike the situation in the United States, appeals are allowed on grounds that the procedures followed were unfair or misleading. Nothing prevents a religious body from supervising such an arbitration procedure (either in Britain or in the United States), as long as proper contractual procedures are followed. MAT's webpage on procedures accurately presents how a binding arbitration works. Divorce, however, must involve the English legal system. Granting an Islamic divorce has no legal effect in and of itself, and so the language of contracts and enforcement does not belong there.[10]

The Hijaz lawyers, and, in particular, barrister Siddiqi, know the difference between arbitration and other forms of mediation quite well. But because they use the term "Muslim Arbitration Tribunal" to refer to cases that can be subjected to binding arbitration *and also* to cases that cannot, such as divorce, confusion reigns.[11] In what follows, I first look at marriage and divorce, and then at cases where binding arbitration is possible.

Dissolving Marriages

Productively confusing is the way in which Siddiqi uses the instrument of a contract, not to prepare the way for a future lawsuit but to lead a husband and wife to take what they are doing more seriously. On May 9, 2010, I interviewed Meena on the Hijaz campus, where she then lived. She was twenty-four years old and had grown up in Yorkshire, in a relatively small community of people with a Pakistani background. Her parents arrived in England in the 1980s and, as she put it, "My mum is very stuck in Pakistani values." As with many young people born into these communities, Meena first spoke Punjabi and learned English only after she entered school. As she was growing up, she saw that other girls had relationships with boys, but she knew she would not be allowed to do so. She went on to university, reading law in Manchester.

Meena knew from when she was very little that she would marry one of her first cousins, because that was what girls around her had done. "I could figure it out and see that this one boy would be him," she said. He had no education and lived in Pakistan, near Jhelum; he was her mother's brother's son, and her mother wanted to help him. "She would send remittances," Meena explained. "It is hard over there when you are here in England, and she could repay favors this way." Meena's sister had managed to refuse all proffered spouses and married someone she had chosen. "Somehow she got away with it," Meena said. In 2008 Meena was married off to the Pakistani cousin. They had only met once, three years prior to the marriage. Since then they had chatted over the telephone, and she had tried unsuccessfully to find shared interests or ideas. After the religious ceremony (nikah), held in Pakistan, they did not take the next step that completes the marriage process—going to the groom's house to eat and consummate the marriage (*rukhsati*). Instead Meena and her parents left for a three-day holiday in Dubai without the groom and continued on to England. The parents arranged for the cousin to get a visa to join Meena in England.

She continued to speak with her new husband by telephone. Although her family is very close-knit, studying away from home allowed her to withstand the ensuing family pressure to make the marriage work. Two or three months after the nikah, she concluded that she and her cousin could not succeed as a couple. Her sister, who had already married "for love," said that Meena could get divorced and that they could cancel the visa. In Manchester she met a woman who knew Sheikh Siddiqi and who brought her to Nuneaton to meet him. She quickly felt confidence in him; she could no longer trust her family, so whom could she now trust? Her sister had been her confidante but now sided with her elder brother, and both insisted that she give the marriage a go and wait until the cousin did something wrong before divorcing. "But why should I wait if I know I cannot live with him?" she asked. Siddiqi said she should move to London from Manchester to further escape pressure. He said that he could easily give her a religious divorce (khula) because the marriage had not been consummated. The Hijaz solicitor, Maulana Arif, told her to cancel the cousin's visa, and after some difficulty, she was able to do so.

Meena did move to London and stayed there for three months, but, she says, "life is too fast-paced there and I came from the north." At that point she was invited to move to Nuneaton and live at Hijaz. MAT lawyers arranged to have the marriage dissolved in England and have a khula divorce declared by the courts in Pakistan. For a while she traveled regularly to London for law courses, but by 2012 she had abandoned her law studies and worked at MAT. She had, however, met and conducted a nikah with another man. She decided not to register the new marriage as an English civil marriage. "Why do that?" she asks rhetorically. "We can always register it later if we wish. Registering just complicates things." She thinks it is better to marry someone who already lives in England because "people from abroad are just not compatible with us here." Her cousin was an illiterate farmer, and there is the problem of male pride. "For me, Islam is a box," she says. "It is not culture. He would have brought in Pakistani culture with its male dominance. They use rituals adopted from Hindus there."

On the same occasion I also spoke with Sarah, whose first contact with Hijaz was when she came to the July 2008 Blessed Summit with her small daughter "and very pregnant with my son." She came with a friend who, like herself, had converted to Islam. On that occasion she met Siddiqi. She then took the general Suyuti course on Islam that was offered at the Hijaz site.[12] Maulana Arif was her teacher in Hanafi fiqh. She began coming often to surgeries, seeking advice on her spiritual journey to come closer to Allah and also on her practical life, her divorce.

> I had been married about a year, to a Muslim man (born in the UK), but he did not want to be part of the Hijaz, did not practice, and we grew apart and I wanted to divorce him. I work in parent support, as a counselor, and I do not earn much. I realized it would take me five months to save enough to pay a solicitor, so I asked the Sheikh and he said let MAT handle it, so they said that Maulana Arif was a solicitor, and I worked with him. He drew up the letter to my ex-husband, on his firm's stationery, and that meant my ex-husband took it seriously; he had said that he would not pay attention to sheikhs. They did it free of charge but I have then been giving freely to the Hijaz community twenty pounds a month; I can do that.

Finally, her husband did sign the divorce decree (talaqnama). Sarah shared: "We had separated months earlier, but I did talk with him and tried to be even and kind. He felt very isolated and angry. He was angry because he did not think that we should divorce, also because I turned out to have backbone and that I had initiated it, and because the grounds were serious." They had not had a civil marriage; she used a solicitor because, as she explained it, Siddiqi told her, "If you want to take care of all dimensions of it, then do this." Sarah continued:

> As it happens, my ex-husband is a follower of the Sheikh but had not had anything to do with him. His father had been his murīd before; I do not know how that began. So I hope that they can talk and that he can feel less isolated and angry. I come here often, [and] when I turn off the main road, I feel tranquillity; ordinary cares disappear. I come with my children, and they play with others, and we have a picnic; even if the weather is bad, it does not matter.

Cases such as Meena's and Sarah's resemble other marriage cases resolved at Hijaz, in that they learned of Siddiqi through a mutual friend, sought advice, and then were given a religious divorce. To what extent did the involvement of a solicitor make a difference? Sarah was not in a civil marriage and, although she said that having the letter to her husband sent on legal stationery made him take notice, even had he ignored the letter, she would have received her religious divorce. Meena had married in Pakistan and therefore she needed to have it dissolved in Britain (or in Pakistan). In her case the "full-service" dimension of the community probably made things easier, in that Arif handled both the religious and the legal sides of her divorce. The shariʿa and spirituality dimensions of these women's lives were the main agenda. In these two cases, both women became regular visitors to Hijaz, and for some time Meena worked as an employee of the insurance company and resided at the college. In 2012, Meena was put in charge of managing MAT requests, including divorces. She was living at Hijaz and charged with establishing a centralized numbering system for cases. By 2013 she was no longer involved and it is unclear if the filing system was ever created.

The Legal and the Religious

In May 2010 I visited Arif at his law practice, Saints Solicitors, in Birmingham. It was in a house on a side street in south Birmingham; the neighborhood had boarded-up shops. The waiting room had pictures hanging on the walls and and modern renderings of a mosque. An assistant came down and escorted me to a second-story conference room consisting of a large table in an attic room fitted with nice windows all around, the top edges open to let in air. Atif bounded up a bit later. He explained that he handled mainly property and commercial cases, not family issues; others did that. The firm accepted the entire range of civil cases. They only began work in 2007, and because they had not been doing family cases, they didn't have an established practice in the field. A few divorce requests came their way each month. They didn't advertise or go to mosques; people found them, although they planned to do some marketing for their Islamic services at other law firms. He saw the MAT approach as superior to those of the shariʿa councils. "Clients who don't speak English as their first language go there; they feel more comfortable," he said, but "the councils don't have lawyers and don't know procedures."

MAT religious divorce procedures are the same as for the London and Birmingham councils. If the husband comes to them to ask for a talaq, they tell him that he does not need their services, that simply telling his wife or writing her will do, but if he wants something written up, they do that, as it might be useful for a consulate. "If the wife comes," Arif said, "then we send him a letter and give him three months [to respond], but usually he responds and we invite him to work to figure out a khula, what she might give him in compensation, the mahr or other. If he does not respond, then we could call witnesses, if she had mentioned people, and annul the marriage, a faskh; but [we] have not done that [as] he always responds, so we never have to make a decision. Grounds for a faskh would be domestic violence, not giving maintenance, [and so on.]." I asked, "Over any particular period of time?" and he replied, "No, we don't fix a period; we look at the circumstances and see how severe the situation is; perhaps it was only two weeks but she really suffered."

He explained that about half their clients—"we don't call them clients, in fact," to distinguish solicitors' work from MAT work—are already part of Hijaz. He is concerned not to seem to profit from the MAT role, so when people come to him through MAT, he proposes they find another solicitor, and he doesn't do the legal part, but if they come to the solicitors' office, then he proposes that they help with the Islamic side as well because they don't profit from that. In a case they were currently handling, a Birmingham man came to them. "He had married a woman in Pakistan, who clearly married him just to get over here, and once she did so, she left him. He came to MAT to ask about a divorce, and they suggested he use a local solicitor for the legal part." But more recently the "one-stop shopping" idea seems to be less the case: Arif avoids handling the legal side of divorces to avoid conflicts of interest, and by 2013 he told me that they were "outsourcing" them.

For years Siddiqi had been trying to set up relationships with solicitors, whereby he would provide the Islamic component and they would carry out the civil divorce part. He had tried to interest the barrister Aina Khan (who by 2012 was working at the prestigious Russell King firm) to provide him with these services; she was not interested and has since set up her own "full-service" Muslim legal services shop within the firm.

Although Siddiqi talks of their success in producing family agreements that then lead to court orders by consent, it is unclear how often this happens. Not only are there no centralized records but Siddiqi himself recognizes (as do the other shariʿa councils we have examined) the limits of nonlegal tribunals. In May 2010, he told me that "on ancillary relief [monetary awards], here it is harder to get them to agree, they have competing interests, and we are not as successful, and then we just tell them to go to court and get an order." Indeed, Arif indicated that there is very little interface with the civil courts. "Now, regarding divorces," he said, "we could see couples drawing up contracts as a result of mediation about finances or children, and then going to court with them, but it never happens; it's a law of emotions that they never would want to arbitrate divorce; if there is a dispute, they are angry and go to court." He has seen couples litigate over goldfish or a potted plant.[13]

Domestic Violence

Around 2009, Siddiqi and others tried to present themselves as the best answer to domestic violence (often called DV) among Muslims. In March of that year he presented a very progressive view to me: "In domestic violence cases we can tell the woman that this is forbidden in Islam." I asked, "What about the '*daraba* verse' in the Qur'an, which allows the husband to strike the wife?" He replied, "It is ignorant people who cite this: it recounts a process of conciliation, and the last step, only if all else fails, is to move your hand in the way you do to ward off something, saying 'leave me alone' [he moved his left hand outward, slowly]. The Qur'an limits what you can do with that gesture. The commentators were clear that the Qur'an forbids wife-beating."[14]

But this interpretation, dismissing a widespread view of what the verse in question says, is difficult to convey convincingly. Later the same year, Hijaz organized an event to discuss their ideas with practitioners: Muslim and non-Muslim men and women working with police, in law firms, or in hospitals dealing with issues of domestic violence. The gathering was held on October 4, 2009, in the Assembly Hall in Walthamstow, an eastern London district with the highest concentration of Muslims in London. There was a stage, about a dozen tables, and perhaps a hundred people.

The discussion focused on forced marriage in the morning and domestic violence after lunch. For each of the two themes, brief lectures were followed by a Q&A session and then a one-hour discussion group period, where people gathered at the tables, and each table was asked to address questions about how MAT might improve what they do and how they could better communicate their message.

I arrived from Heathrow just as the first Q&A session was beginning. MAT speakers emphasized that they try to reconcile the couple and to seek the root cause, such as other relatives' "winding up" one or the other of the parties to end the marriage.

Tauqir took the stage and spoke about three cases. One was from Glasgow and involved emotional abuse of the wife. They asked her if she wanted to save the marriage and she said yes. They found that his mother was trying to break up the marriage. "We then followed the Qur'an, which says that if there is a chance that divorce will happen, you should try to reconcile the parties. We did that and succeeded." In the second case, "the wife came to us with marks on her face and said her husband had beat her, but we called her husband in. She had this la-dee-da expression on her face and we were unsure. When we told him what she had said, he pulled out a large knife and said 'she attacked me with this to try and kill me,' and that he had slapped her to stop her. So here he was acting in self-defense. The mother again was winding up her daughter." The third case concerned a couple from Dubai, and there was a history of serious violence against the wife. "We explained to the man the limits of what he could do, that Islam does not allow abuse of any kind in marriage. He complained that his wife would get angry at him; she said she just wanted to tell him about what was on her mind. We said, just sit down and let her do that," Tauqir said. People phone him often and ask for advice, and he usually suggests "cooling off, just listen to one another."

He then turned to the infamous "daraba verse" in the Qur'an.[15] (Later he told me, "Some said I should not bring this up, but people will go there anyway.") He said, "Here Allah says that if your wife will not listen to you and she is doing something she should not, then first you admonish her, and then you deprive her of physical love, say I am going to sleep somewhere else, and only after that do you give her a gentle tap, like this [tapping his arm], or a push—no permanent marks, no show of anger."

When written questions were brought to him, he was irked that some of them suggested that he had advocated violence against wives under certain conditions, and he repeated several times, "Islam does not allow violence; how many times do I have to say that?"

Q: So why can't wives similarly tap their husbands?

Tauqir: I think wives do not need a verse to attack their husbands.

Q: Why not get the police involved?

Tauqir: We have done that, but often the wife does not want the husband in jail. Sometimes I say to leave the house, or in one case leave the country. [He later explained to me that it was a case where the husband would lock the door; even with the family alerted they could not get to the wife.]

Q: How can you tolerate violence?

Tauqir: Islam does not allow violence, but if the wife is tossing pans around and then you have to push her a bit, then push her a bit!

Q: What about getting social services involved?
Tauqir: We do sometimes, but the extended family works better.

At this point a woman raised her hand from the floor. She is a matrimonial lawyer I later talked with, and she began an exchange with Tauqir:

Lawyer: So why cannot the wife give the tap also? We feel that you trivialized DV in your talk, with your jokey answers. Will women approach a shariʿa council if she thinks that Islam allows physical force?
Tauqir: Men and women are equals, but justice comes before equality, and you cannot treat different people in exactly the same way. From one-quarter to one-third of the people on MAT are sisters [I later determined this does not mean judges but personnel and sometimes the state solicitors].
Lawyer: How do you get the husband to stop abusing?
Tauqir: We get to the root cause; often there is outside interference.

Later, when speaking with me, Tauqir explained that sometimes the root cause is possession by evil spirits, causing the husband to commit DV. "I can see it in his eyes," he added. "I can resolve those cases by giving the family prayers to recite, but when there are social workers involved, they don't let me do it."

During the discussion period, I sat with ten women around a table. Two of them were solicitors who worked on issues of domestic violence; the others were activists on the issue; a majority were Muslims. A woman in a colorful headscarf, wearing something akin to a niqab but with a white scarf pulled across the face, sometimes worked in surgeries with women who had suffered abuse, and she said that when the sheikhs come, they always tell the women to go to the police.

In subsequent meetings with MAT people, I had contrasting assessments of the session's value. The following May, Siddiqi told me that "The DV initiative is moving ahead; some of the people who came to the meeting are working with us. A woman in Bethnal Green [East London] who serves as a go-between with the police and social services asked if it would be alright for her to go to the mosques on our behalf, and I said go ahead—because they would just toss her out if she went on her own. We realize we have to work with the police. We try to persuade them that the cases we deal with are not ones that they would have had instead, but new ones. We get it from both sides: the people in the mosques say we are too liberalized, and the others say, why do you have the wife beaters deal with wife-beating?"[16]

But about a year later, Bhatti, also present at that session, said that a person from the Justice Ministry delegated to DV issues had been at my table and told him later that the meeting had been a complete disaster, and that she had no interest in the Islamic approach to DV.[17] Tauqir's levity had not been appreciated by any of those present, and, as one Hijaz person present told me, with Tauqir, MAT really lost ground, as he—and thus they—seemed to defend wife-beating; the meeting made taking an Islamic approach impossible for many of those present.

The Muslim Arbitration Tribunal

Now, Siddiqi presents MAT as producing arbitrations performed according to the provisions of the Arbitration Act. What this means in practice was explained by Arif, the solicitor, over dinner in April 2013. Arif does sometimes draw up arbitration agreements for commercial partners, in which they agree to have any disputes arbitrated by MAT. They have drawn up perhaps twenty or thirty in the past few years. However, he said that no one has ever approached MAT to request that a dispute be formally arbitrated. He thought that people would be more likely to lie to a secular judge than to an Islamic body, and so they don't get to the arbitration stage; they work it out among themselves. No one involved in MAT had ever heard of one of their arbitration agreements going to court.

If MAT does not seem to engage in formal arbitration, or at least to do it often enough that Arif knew of cases, Siddiqi certainly does intervene in disputes and employ legal-looking documents. When families approach him to ask for help in resolving their problems, he fills in an "order form" that says that "we want to keep our marriage intact and that in order to do so we will do the following things, and we agree to return to see Sheikh Siddiqi to ensure that we are both complying," Siddiqi told me in April 2013. In one case, he had ordered the couple to take a walk together, see a film, that the husband should cook a meal for his wife, and so on, each with its own temporality: once a week or once a month. They were supposed to return every six months to let him know that they were abiding by it, until things were resolved.

I asked Siddiqi what the Islamic elements are in arbitration, and he replied, "These cases are commercial cases—leases, shop arrangements, investments—and a judge will ask for written evidence of any claim, whereas we will ask what was said and what can be inferred from what was said. These also count. So if one party says to the other, 'Here, run the shop, and pay me back as you go,' and this is the pattern, and then the other says he was given the shop, the judge will ask where the proof is, whereas we will ask what words were said, and also is it reasonable that the shop would be given away? Under what conditions would that be reasonable? Maybe long ago something happened that makes it reasonable. Judges don't follow out the logic of these inferences; they just ask for written evidence."

Resolving the Linen-Hire Succession

Here is an example of a commercial case that shows how things are resolved in a way that mixes Islamic and business advice. On March 4, 2010, I interviewed a young man who had asked for contractually binding arbitration from MAT. Usman, of Bangladeshi origin, was twenty-six years old but seemed older. "My father used to take me with him to meet people," he explained. "It made me at ease with different people." He owned a linen-hire business in Birmingham, renting napkins and tablecloths to hotels and restaurants. His father ran this business for nineteen years, but had died sixteen months earlier. "He was an important man in the community; those are hard shoes to fill," Usman said. He and his family had a 60 percent share in the business, another man who worked in it held 20 percent, and a third had 20 percent but was a silent partner. The second partner died around the time Usman's father did, and that man's son, Ridwan, a few years older than Usman, had previously worked in a similar enterprise and wanted to play a major role in the business. Usman refused. "I was selfish," he admitted. "I wanted to be the boss."

Usman had heard about MAT from a friend who was working with the Hijaz community outreach program. It didn't mean much to him that they were Sufis; his father had never paid much attention to the difference between Deobandis, Sufis, and other streams of Islam, and Usman worshipped at a mosque that was conveniently located. It happened to be a Deobandi one, but he thought about worship as an individual matter; as he put it, "It is just me here." Talking with his friend sparked his interest in learning about these differences. He wouldn't have accepted guidance in business matters from the imam of the Deobandi mosque because that man thought about religion and business as separate things. Usman asked Ridwan what he thought about approaching MAT, and Ridwan agreed. Indeed, the two of them had been childhood friends, had never argued, and felt awkward talking about financial matters. The generation before them would have asked community elders to mediate, but, Usman said, "For our generation, we don't trust the elders. They don't seem to have much experience or success, so how would they know?"

When they arrived at Hijaz, Fiaz Hassan, a barrister in training who works in the community, interviewed each of them separately and then in a joint meeting, and had them sign a contract indicating they would abide by the outcome. "I was not sure how things would come out," Usman explained, "but I said to myself, 'I'll just trust the system.'" Then they met with Siddiqi. He had read the notes of their intake interviews, summarized how he saw the case, and then asked them if they agreed. They did. At their final session, now with both Siddiqi and Fiaz, Siddiqi told them of his decision, and then gave them guidance. He said they should have the same pay because they did equal work, and that Usman would be managing director, in charge of the company, while Ridwan would be a senior player, with a mission to develop new business and to carry out marketing, because these were his skills. Of course, the profits would still be split along the lines of the shares (60/20/20), but there had been no profits to split from the previous year and only negligible profits up to that point in 2010.

Usman shared what happened next: "Sheikh Siddiqi then gave us guidance—business and investment advice—but also said, 'If you run the business only for profit, where then is the spiritual benefit?' He asked us to give back to the community. He asked us to serve as role models for young people working in the Hijaz community. There was no fee for the mediation, he said, but added that if we found a way to contribute to Hijaz, that would be fine."

Indeed, they donated a little bit from the business each month, and a person from the Birmingham Hijaz community outreach program had contacted Usman to ask him to mentor younger men. He said he would once he got his business together. Ridwan also said he would do this; in the meantime, Usman went to weekly events for these young people and played badminton with them. In subsequent visits to Hijaz, I often encountered Usman there, still helping out.

I asked if the experience was particularly Islamic in any way, and Usman replied, "Sheikh Siddiqi explained how I had to offer my sister and mother their share of the inheritance, that it was their right. But how can you divide tangible assets? He suggested that we involve my mother more in the business, that she play a role. And it was a really good idea, because we are young, and she is an older figure in the Bangladeshi community; she has a presence, a PR person. And we thought the resolution was fair. Within the Asian community, we have all been brought up together, have faith in each other, [so] we did not want to screw each other over. I thought I would have a problem, but it has been alright."

Now Usman chooses his mosque carefully. He thinks of himself as a Sunni and Sufi, "What you would call Barelvi," he explains. He worships at the Ghamkol Sharif Masjid on Golden Hillock Road in Birmingham, which he refers to as an Ahl ul-Sunna mosque. It is also the one closest to where he lives and the only one open around the clock. This mosque is a center for a major Sufi figure in Birmingham, Sufi Abdullah.[18] Usman continues, "I am a very analytical thinker, always taking things apart. I have been reading books, looking at the shops around Birmingham. But I also recite the litany [*wirid*] of Sheikh Siddiqi's father, and doing this helps me to turn off all this analytical thinking." On the day we spoke, he had come to Hijaz with his wife to spend the day, and he intended to meditate at the mausoleum. "All this changed me. I had the beard before this [indicating piety], but now I feel more connected with God."

Ten days later I followed Siddiqi to Birmingham, where he held the nighttime surgery described above. Among the people who came to see Siddiqi and who agreed to speak with me afterward was Ridwan, Usman's partner in the linen-hire business. When I asked him about Siddiqi, he replied:

> When I first heard about him, I thought it was a cult. These guys were growing beards and praying all the time—kind of weird. Two years like that and then I heard him speak, and he talked about purifying the heart, not about Islam per se, and six months later I am a father and I think, "Now I have responsibility and I want to get closer to God." So I come to Hijaz. When I saw Sheikh Siddiqi I told him I thought it seemed like a cult, and he did not get mad but said, "I am sorry it seems like this. Sometimes the brothers hang on every word, but they are supposed to think for themselves, not just come to me for everything. If someone has run a business and asks me about how to do that, I will say, 'Well what did you do before? Did that work? Why ask me?'" Tonight I talked with Arif [the solicitor] about fiqh [legal] questions. I don't bring those to Sheikh Siddiqi because he [is] so busy; I go to see Arif. I talk with Sheikh Siddiqi about matters of spirituality and also life's problems. Every couple of months I come. I ask his advice on business also.

In this case Siddiqi played the role of spiritual and business advisor, and incidentally resolved the dispute between the two partners, but in a manner that, despite the signing of an agreement to abide by what he said, seemed rather informal. Indeed, Ridwan did not mention the arbitration; he had moved on to other things. Hijaz ended up recruiting two new acolytes as the outcome of the dispute, just as Meena had become a member of the community. Disputes often begin with practical concerns but then lead some individuals toward spirituality.

Unlike the London Islamic Shariʿa Council, Hijaz is neither an office nor a council; it is a spiritual center with a full panoply of activities, MAT being but one. MAT is perhaps best seen as a legal-sounding framework for what is really an age-old process of seeking guidance from a spiritual guide.

The Mosque Dispute at Waltham Forest

When I first met Judge Qureshi in October 2009, he and others were still working to resolve a dispute over the control of a mosque in Waltham Forest, in northeast London. "These [disputes] are very common: when two groups fight for control of a mosque, usually all from the same origins and same beliefs, sometimes families are split by the dispute," he said. At the time, fights would break out at Friday prayers, and the local police were called in on occasion.

The immediate issue was that new elections for the mosque committee were overdue. Mosques are registered under the Charity Commission, and that body requires that elections be held every three years. It is in the interest of a mosque to register, because then and only then can they have their real estate taxes rebated. One of the parties to the Waltham Forest dispute asked MAT to intervene. Qureshi asked the Charity Commission if they would approve, and they did so on condition that it be a mediation and not an arbitration, on grounds that only then would both sides feel that they agreed to the decision. Qureshi agreed.

I asked in what ways Islamic knowledge or authority was involved in settling the dispute. He replied, "I had to know something about Islam to get them to agree. The side challenging those in power wanted to make sure that only Barelvis voted. Now, anyone can join the mosque; they sign up and pay one pound a year. The elections stipulate that only those in the borough may vote, and only those there as of a certain earlier date, so that no one gets people to sign up just to vote. But maybe the side in power had some non-Barelvis in the mosque; the opponents wanted voters to have to hold the Qur'an and say that they were Muslims of the Ahl al-Sunnah wal-Jamaah, and followers of Abdul Qadir Jilani."[19] They reasoned that holding the Qur'an would ensure that they would not lie. The side in power said, "No, we should just ask for an affirmation" by signing a piece of paper. So Qureshi gave each part of what they wanted: voters would not have to hold the Qur'an, but they would have to say "before Almighty God" in their attestation, which would bind them to tell the truth just as holding the Qur'an would do. He could not have done that without knowing about Islam.

Qamar Bhatti participated with Judge Qureshi, and he remembered the old guard as proposing a "Barelvi test." He explained: "I asked them about the features of Barelvis, and they named two or three, but I said there are many more, and if there was a test, then none of you could even be members of the mosque. So we decided on a simple statement that members would sign saying they were Barelvis, and that they said that 'by Almighty God.'" Bhatti had approached a local (white) policeman, who had intervened in the disputes that occurred after Friday prayers, and who therefore knew the people involved. "And I asked him to chair the meetings with the two sides and appoint an independent scribe, so it would not be us taking the minutes. At the first meeting I did not tell the two sides that the Charity Commission had put us in charge but asked them if they might like us to help resolve the problems. That way we were asking them to approve us, and they said fine." The mediators were paid by the mosque at five hundred pounds per hour, explained Bhatti, "but then we donated it back to the mosque." Because of the way charges were figured, the mosque officials would urge them to finish before the hour was out! In the end it required two sessions of two hours each.

Judge Qureshi picked up the narrative: "The younger group won the mediation in the sense that both sides agreed to hold elections, but the old guard managed to delay them once, and then on the day the elections were to be held, at the mosque, the old guard was trying to put them off again. They went to the court to demand an ex parte [only hearing one side] injunction, saying that the new slate would be taking the treasury and the membership lists so that the matter could not wait until both parties could come to court. Then they filed suit in court to challenge the election on grounds of fraud, but the Charity Commission wrote to the judge saying that they could sue only with the commission's approval, as they would be using funds of the mosque (over which the commission has supervisory powers) to pursue the suit, and the judge threw the suit out. The young group handily won the election." But in 2010, Qureshi cautiously concluded his account by saying, "But we will see how well it holds." As of mid-2013, things were quiet. "Every time we take on a case, we make one group of Muslims mad at us," he said.

Leadership Style

In contrast to the file-keeping done at the London shariʿa council, with carefully numbered and filed cases, it is difficult to know when a case has "occurred" at Hijaz. Ponder my perplexity during a two-day stay I had at Hijaz when, on April 9, 2013, I discussed the workings of MAT with Siddiqi, and he told me that "MAT has always heard thirty to forty cases a year; just last Sunday I heard eight or ten. It isn't a regular schedule." The Sunday cases concerned family disputes, domestic violence, and forced marriage; generally, "no one topic dominates." Divorces do not enter the picture, as these are all treated by Arif or someone else.

"In DV cases, if a wife comes to us, it is not for protection but for resolution of the conflict, so we might ask them how their lives are, and maybe she is bored so she yells at her husband and then he hits her. So I said, 'Why not take a walk together; when was the last time you did that?' 'Never,' they said, so I put that in the document and said, 'Let me know how it goes,' and the wife tweeted back and said it worked well. They had signed an arbitration agreement as in all MAT cases because this makes them take the guidelines we propose more seriously: it is written out, perhaps weekly times you do this or that." These "arbitrations" are in fact counseling sessions, where Siddiqi's saintly status adds to his credibility and to the likelihood that the couple will take the advice and return for follow-ups.

The next day I spoke with Fiaz, a barrister in training, who had been appointed by Siddiqi to be in charge of MAT cases: appointments and records. "People might contact one of us directly, and an arbitration might be handled very discreetly, even as part of surgeries, if it seems to Sheikh Faiz [Siddiqi] to be appropriate." Fiaz never learns of such cases because they enter via a surgery. "But since January there have been no MAT cases that I know about." I said, "But this past weekend, Sheikh Siddiqi said he had handled a number of them." Fiaz replied, "Yes, well then, that's true, on the weekends people come for consultations, and he might treat them as arbitrations; I am not here on the weekends. But in the formal cases, someone mails in a signed form; they can get it from the website, and then there is an appointment, and [they] usually meet there where the sheikh sits, and then he writes up a judgment, and then they all sign. These often are commercial matters; I recall one where there was a dispute over finances, and one party, when they were to sign the contract saying they would abide by the arbitration, said he could not lie and that he was at fault, and that was it." He added that he had "never heard of an arbitration agreement from MAT going to court; of course, I would only know if one of them wrote to us, or if it was nearby. People fear what will happen on Judgment Day. And Sheikh Siddiqi will say to them before they sign: 'Make sure that what you say is the truth.'" I was struck by how new he was and yet was in charge, just as I had been in an earlier visit, when I learned that Meena was to handle records. Arif has kept any records of divorces he handled at his law office; there are no records of divorce cases at Hijaz.

The Hijaz people, from Sheikh Siddiqi down to the various assistants, always welcomed me enthusiastically and encouraged me to spend time on the grounds. They also selected people for me to interview, and some of those stories have been shared above. My sample maps onto the object of study: a top-down structure, controlled by sanctity. This close control also helps Hijaz stay out of the news (which in the Britain of the 2010s was a good thing). Coverage of Islamic institutions is rarely positive. Siddiqi knows how to speak with the media: he emphasizes their fight against extremism, his status as a barrister, and his constant use of solicitors—exactly the points on which the London council was attacked in 2013. Ironically, it is the relative openness of the London council that has exposed them to criticism. At Hijaz, by contrast, everything passes by way of the sheikh.

On nearly every visit to Siddiqi, he has been engaged in a new project. In 2008 he started Muslim Insurance Services to try and capitalize on demand for shariʿa-compliant insurance products. By April 2013, the company was renamed Iman Insurance, and Siddiqi was targeting the United States and Africa, an operation that remained quite hypothetical. In 2011, he set up his own halal certification service, Halal Authority Board (HAB), to compete with the older such ventures in Britain.[20] The HAB received national press in 2012, when Siddiqi conducted a MAT deliberation on the use of the mechanical blade, pronouncing it unacceptable.[21]

Conclusions

Speaking with Siddiqi feels like having a conversation with someone who sees the world in a way that combines how he finds it and how he would like it to be. In my early interviews with him in 2009, he described the Hijaz community as if it were a well-honed organization, and that it worked through "the fifty or so mosques that work with us." He described a series of recent arbitrations, but the person supposedly in charge of these events did not know of them. He said that MAT "had arbiters in major cities," in pairs, with a solicitor and an Islamic expert, but by 2013 he told me that he was still setting up an arrangement with a solicitor, who would be the first to play such a role. Often, his desire to keep things under his personal control meant that, intentionally or not, no one else had a very precise idea of what the community was doing.

Maybe none of this matters. The purpose of the Hijaz community is to reproduce the sacred structure of authority that gives people answers or certainty, or promotes education, and so on. Hijaz is not procedural at all except for rules for seeing the sheikh.[22] All depends on the relationships of clients, who may also be adepts, with the saint, who also may be the barrister. The main point is maintaining, expanding, and drawing on those ties.

PART 4

Boundaries

CHAPTER 10

Shariʿa in English Law
The Argument So Far

WE BEGAN THIS BOOK BY TRACING THE HISTORICAL PATHWAYS ALONG WHICH South Asian Muslims arrived and settled in Britain, and how patterns of settlement shaped the Islamic topography of the nation, including the reproduction of boundaries and the exploration of specific socioreligious niches. British Islamic institutions—mosques, schools, and shariʿa councils—emerged in communities defined internally by spatial concentration of people with shared origins, and externally by strong oppositions based on distinct religious heritages. They were able to flourish as they did in a Britain that allows for, and indeed encourages, the development of religious communities.

We then focused in on the development and workings of three shariʿa councils in order to explore three questions. First, and mainly through our analysis of the Islamic Shariʿa Council in Leyton, London, we analyzed how shariʿa scholars deliberate on cases and on the issues of performativity and legitimacy that are at stake. Second, by contrasting three distinct councils (with brief excursions into two others), we were able to see how their initial inspirations continue to shape the quite distinct manners in which they work—a feature that we could see only by exploring contrasts. Third, we looked to see how the distinct starting points of each council also involved distinct attachments to broader communities.

Origins clearly matter. The ISC in Leyton grew out of a scholarly alliance of Ahl al-Hadith (or Salafi) and Deobandi scholars, and an institutional attachment to the London Central Mosque near Regent's Park. This alliance and this attachment keep them open to interventions from scholars from Saudi Arabia and the Gulf states, where the Hanbali legal school has its center. At the same time, the South Asian origins of most of the scholars and clients mean that case discussions involve reference to Pakistani everyday life. One result of these disparate origins is the tension between attention to custom and attention only to texts, which we saw in chapter 7. Finally, the relatively broad array of scholars' educational backgrounds means that they reach decisions only thanks to their prior agreement on procedures. We saw their "proceduralism" on a number of occasions; the upshot is that the Leyton council tries to be a kind of court.

For its part, the Birmingham Central Mosque's shariʿa council grew out of a women's crisis center. To this day, the staff combines social work and medical concerns with their knowledge of Islamic legal procedures as they field calls and conduct intake interviews. Scholarly deliberation by scholars over divorce comes only after these investigations, and in cases where a civil divorce has been granted, this deliberation no longer occurs at all. The council remains women-centered. It also mainly attracts people from nearby in the Midlands, especially Birmingham itself, which makes repeat visits possible, something that is more difficult for the far-flung clientele of the London council. Birmingham deliberations take place in the presence of the clients; London ones do not. The Birmingham scholars, led by Amra Bone, reach resolution but also give the women practical advice about bettering their lives.

Finally, the Hijaz community is primarily a sacred space that incorporates people through the power and practices of its sheikh, Faiz ul-Aqtab Siddiqi. At the heart of Hijaz are private sessions with followers; resolving disputes and granting divorces are but two of many additional activities. Everything hinges on the sheikh's spiritual position: people become clients because they seek his aid and advice. To label the whole operation a shariʿa council, or, as is current in the media, the Muslim Arbitration Tribunal, plays up Siddiqi's status as a barrister, but ignores a large Sufi forest for a few scraggly judicial trees. The community in this case consists of those individuals and families attracted to Hijaz who may, by the by, ask the sheikh to resolve a dispute.

Even though origins matter, these and other councils converge on similar practical schemas. Striking here is the nearly complete overlap in procedures and Islamic references between the Islamic Shariʿa Council and the other major London-based council to the west, mentioned in chapters 4 and 7. The ISC is Salafi-Deobandi; western London mainly Sufi, but they decide matters in roughly the same way, and indeed respect each other's decisions. Birmingham also converges in its grounds for divorce on the other two. This practical convergence across doctrinal differences is in part because all these scholars know that judicial dissolution of marriage has been practiced in Muslim-majority countries in certain ways. The ambiguities of khula and faskh, explored at length in chapter 6, are part of a long, shared Islamic tradition. The scholars also share certain principled concerns, such as taking pains to ensure that a husband has a chance to reply to his wife's case. Finally, all these institutions are adjusting to the same English social and legal environment.

In part 4 we examine the social life of shariʿa in that broader English environment. Fears and accusations circulating in England about Islam focus on one of two contentions. The first is that English law has "recognized" shariʿa, a worry given credence by the 2008 remarks of Rowan Williams, then archbishop of Canterbury. The second is that Islamic institutions are keeping Muslims from fully integrating into English, or British, society.

sharia legitimazed

by preserving their religium

Are these fears well founded? We begin by asking whether shariʿa councils find their judgments enforced by civil courts, and whether shariʿa and English law intersect or converge. Here we must dive into some of the intricacies of English civil law.

Does English Law "Recognize" Shariʿa?

In his widely discussed February 2008 remarks, Archbishop of Canterbury Rowan Williams explored ways in which the legal system might "recognise shariʿa." He observed that doing so would require "access to recognised authority acting for a religious group" and mentioned the Islamic Shariʿa Council, London, as such a body. Despite the storm of media criticism, he was joined later that year by Britain's highest justice, Lord Phillips, in saying that English law should recognize certain elements of shariʿa, since shariʿa seemed to be here to stay.[1]

A number of organizations and newspapers reacted sharply. Many cited a report by a small organization called Civitas, which claimed that "Shariʿa law has already become quite entrenched in Britain."[2] The dailies upped the ante, as is their wont, regularly blaring headlines such as "Islamic shariʿa courts in Britain are now 'legally binding,'" and "Shariʿa courts 'as consensual as rape,' House of Lords told."[3]

The archbishop and chief justice's speeches gave a stamp of approval of the most authoritative sort—to something. They left most readers confused as to what it might mean to "recognize" shariʿa. The archbishop mentioned both commercial arbitration and family law, and this juxtaposition confused matters because in England and Wales these two areas of law have had different degrees of openness to private resolution.[4] Commercial disputes are clearly subject to resolution under the Arbitration Act 1996, and there are few obstacles in the way of a religion-based body carrying out binding arbitrations of commercial disputes, as long as a proper contract is drawn up in the presence of a lawyer. As we saw in chapter 9, the Muslim Arbitration Tribunal already carries out some arbitrations—even if they are done informally and even if none have gone to court.[5] The value of such an approach has earned official recognition: we saw that the Charity Commission for England and Wales, the government body responsible for the smooth functioning of registered charities, including religious institutions, called on MAT to assist in resolving a dispute over the administration of a mosque.[6] But any legal force that agreements arbitrated by MAT might have rests entirely on the contractual agreement between the two parties and not on any element of shariʿa, even if in some cases an Islamic moral tone plays a practical role in moving the parties toward agreement.

It is rather in the domain of family law where suggestions that private Islamic bodies might take on a function of the civil courts raise the greatest degree of legal and social concern. In England the state retains an interest in marriage and divorce in the name of protecting public welfare. Marriage must be registered to be recognized in law. Religious buildings may apply to become places of marriage registration, but most have not done so, and in any case, many Islamic marriages take place in homes. Even when it is uncontested, divorce cannot be carried out through private arbitration but must involve the English legal system. More importantly, if marriage is a contract, "it is also a status."[7] The state's special interest in the welfare of children adds to the difficulty of delegating any element of family law to private religious bodies. Even when parties arrive at private arrangements for child residence and the division of assets, such arrangements may be challenged in court. Public bodies such as city councils may also intervene if they suspect that the child's interests are not adequately met, and their intervention may lead to a court hearing.

Although some Islamic scholars have urged Parliament to create formal linkages between law courts and Islamic shariʿa councils, these councils carry out no actions that have the force of state law. For the moment, then, the main possibility for legal "recognition" of Islamic law in England would be if civil courts were to act on some elements of an Islamic divorce proceeding.

English Divorce and Private Arbitration

To see how shariʿa could intersect with English legal proceedings, we have to understand something about the latter. Two kinds of courts may be involved in civil divorce: family courts handle issues of residence and care of children, and civil courts handle assets and the divorce itself. In England, after five years of separation, a divorce can be requested without the other party's consent (ex parte), and during that time of legal separation, the court takes responsibility for issues of children and assets.

But most divorcing couples never appear in court. Mavis Maclean, academic advisor to the Ministry of Justice on family issues, estimates that fewer than 5 percent of divorces are contested, and perhaps 10 percent of divorcing couples see a lawyer about child contact or residence issues, and "an extremely small percentage get a court order."[8] You can get a divorce decree by mail without appearing in court if there are no contested issues and if there are no children. But by 2015, decreased legal aid funding in Britain has meant that those couples who do seek legal advice for settling child custody and division of assets are less and less able to get such advice, and face pressure to seek private arbitration or to ask a judge to write an order.[9]

Whether or not the couple appears in court, it is a court that dissolves a marriage. It does so in two stages.[10] It issues a "decree nisi" (Latin for "unless," meaning unless someone objects) and, at the second stage, a "decree absolute." At the nisi stage, they ask: Is the marriage valid? Is there a financial arrangement to be made? Has the couple met one of the five grounds for divorce—adultery, unreasonable behavior, desertion, two years' separation (if the divorce is uncontested), or five years' separation (if it is contested)? Do they have children? Do they need to resolve child issues? The court will state the arrangements regarding the children's residence and support, but unless there is a clear reason, for example, because of a social services report, the court will not give an order. The Children Act of 1989 contains a "no order" rule, that the court only orders a certain rule for residence and visiting if it is in the best interests of the child to make one. Family obligations and situations are so complex and varying that courts consider it best for them to work it out, and in the vast majority of cases, there is no order.

The law governing marriage and divorce, the Matrimonial Causes Act 1973, gives judges the discretion to consider religious norms and outside mediation when they decide on the child's residence or on financial matters. At issue may be a parent's request to circumcise, to take a child away for religious education, or to change the child's residence.[11] Each parent may introduce specialist evidence here. Although the judge prefers to have a single witness of the court, a single imam or rabbi, for example, lawyers sometimes persuade the judge to allow each side to provide their own experts. The court decides on the grounds of the child's best interests, not the interest of the parents. In addition, if there are difficulties regarding child custody or the quality of child care, the local municipality will get involved.

The couple may sort out financial issues themselves or with a solicitor, or ask the court to do so. Unless asked, the court does nothing. Until recently, judges and lawyers interpreted the 1973 law as preventing divorcing couples from submitting financial matters to binding arbitration because doing so would "fetter the court." However, in 2012 a private body, the Institute of Family Law Arbitrators (IFLA), proposed a set of rules, the IFLA Scheme, for the arbitration of financial and property disputes for divorcing couples under the terms of the Arbitration Act. Although this new approach would seem to allow arbitration in shariʿa councils, the Scheme stipulates that the arbitrator may only decide the dispute in accord with the law of England and Wales, that is, not elements of Islamic law, Jewish law, or foreign law.

This sharp legal shift occurred in typically English fashion, when, without benefit of legislation, IFLA's private initiative met with approval from some key judges. Of particular importance was a recent decision by Sir James Munby, president of the Family Division of the England and Wales High Court. In the case, *S v. S* [2014] EWHC 7 (Fam) (14 January 2014), a divorcing couple asked the court to approve (give legal force to) the agreement resulting from an arbitration conducted under the IFLA Scheme. Justice Munby wrote that because the petition was from both parties it was easy to approve it, and noted that it fit with the general trend in English law toward holding parties to their agreements.[12] He added that even in cases where one party contested an arbitration, the court would probably approve the agreement and that "the parties will almost invariably forfeit the right to anything other than a most abbreviated hearing" (para. 25). However, he said, the court would approach the agreement differently if gender-based discrimination were suspected (para. 27), a clear reference to shariʿa councils.[13]

A second recent case concerned a Jewish tribunal, and has still more direct implications for shariʿa councils. In *AI v. MT* (*Alternative Dispute Resolution*) [2013] EWHC 100 (Fam), the High Court endorsed and facilitated an Orthodox Jewish couple's wish to arbitrate under rabbinical law at the New York Beth Din. Justice Baker stipulated that the Beth Din could not "oust" the jurisdiction of the court, especially concerning decisions regarding the couple's children. But he approved the agreement, noting the rising approbation in England for family arbitration. He argued that ruling in favor of the best interests of the child need not exclude paying attention to the child's cultural and religious background. We should remember, however, that in the end, it was the judge who issued the legal ruling.

These recent decisions signal a partial opening of courts toward private arbitration of divorce, and even to arbitration conducted by religious bodies, but with the proviso that the court has the last word, and that principles of equity and the child's welfare prevail. These cases concerned marriages that were legal in English law. I asked family lawyer Sarah Anticoni what actions a judge could take regarding an Islamic marriage (nikah) that was *not* registered. She replied that one answer lay in informal mediation:

> Briefly, if there are children—even a one-day-old baby—then the judge can issue an order regarding income and assets, but if there are no children, then there is very little he can order regarding finances. . . . There is a huge movement to have more mediation. The laws are way behind the changing ways families conduct themselves. We use memoranda of understanding in family mediation; these are not binding but set out clearly the expectations. By the late 1980s mediation was catching on, it started with family matters and then expanded. Now, judges suggest or can require that the parties in a family dispute go off and seek mediation, however they wish to do it, but it should be with trained mediators, who may be solicitors or not; they include many Muslims.

In a number of discussions with family lawyers I had during 2010–12, this theme was echoed frequently: that mediation is always better than court orders, because it produces better consequences for the persons involved, and to the extent that Islamic bodies chose to do so and do so fairly, all the better. (Such is how most of them interpreted the archbishop's 2008 address.)

To get a better sense of the interplay of court actions and informal agreements, on several occasions in 2010 and 2011, I sat on the bench with Shamim

Qureshi, a judge who often adjudicates family disputes at the Birmingham County Court and, as we saw earlier, sometimes participates in Hijaz activities. As he explained to me, family law has public and private dimensions: private when matters are to be sorted out between the mother and father, for example, a contact arrangement or residence, but public when a local council or the state is involved, for example, a care order when a child has been taken from its parents. But the state also has a general interest in working for the best interests of the child, such that much of what happens in family court involves sorting out the relative competence of the mother and father to care for the children.[14] As he explained,

> We almost never have to issue an order for residence [child custody]; they always work something out. The only time would be if we think they should share residence and the mom does not want to. But usually the wife has residence because the husband really is not set up to do so. We never interview the children, only read reports from Cafcass [Children and Family Court Advisory and Support Service] reports, and those workers cannot really assess claims made, such as when the mom says the dad has mistreated her or the child. But it is not all that complicated; you can tell if the mom is telling the truth in court.

Sometimes Judge Qureshi does end up issuing orders, as in the following case, in sessions on May 24 and 25, 2010: The mother and father appeared before the court, separated by their respective solicitors, two young women. The parents were disputing contact rights. The file told only some of the story, and several documents were not in his file, and in any case, the judge did not remember the entire file from the brief period in which he had to read it, so he had to ask the solicitors to rehearse the issues.

The couple had a five-year-old daughter. The father had once a month supervised contact for two hours, at a contact center near the mother's residence. He came up from London and changed trains at Birmingham, quite a journey, explained his solicitor. He wanted to "move forward"; his solicitor kept repeating that word, and it worked; she had noticed that the judge was using it as in "We have to move forward," meaning gradually giving the dad more contact. The mother contested any unsupervised visits and dug in her heels. Judge Qureshi told them that if they could not work things out, they would "be in court until she turns eighteen, for the next thirteen years," and that if he had to order something, one side or the other would be unhappy: "I could order that dad has frequent rights with no supervision or I could order that he sees her no more than now; one or the other will be unhappy." He urged them to work it out and then adjourned. "This is the second time we have adjourned this case" he told the courtroom, indicating his displeasure that they had not yet worked it out. It gradually emerged that the mother was fine with more frequent visits, "so he gets to know her, they hardly know each other," her solicitor said, but not at all fine with unsupervised contact; dad had an alcohol history. She began to give reasons for refusing unsupervised contact, and the husband's lawyer then just said that these claims were disputed, and Judge Qureshi said, "We are not going to adjudicate these matters here."

Judge Qureshi only had the Cafcass report to go on, and kept saying, "the Cafcass person has interviewed you and [your daughter] and says we should move forward" and held to that, indeed, decided before we went in that such would be his ruling. But for the moment, he let them work it out and propose something. He gave them alternatives: he suggested one hour supervised with another hour unsupervised, but the mother could come on the hour and view them from afar to see if the daughter looked okay, and that way the contact center people could report if there was a problem, or if dad had alcohol on his breath. To all objections from the mother, Judge Qureshi fell back on the report, as he had no other knowledge and could not assess claims. They went on till six that evening on the matter. The next morning he wrote the order, which called for two-hour contact sessions alternating with one-hour ones.

Islamic Contracts in Court?

Courts make the decisions regarding financial matters and children's welfare, even if they encourage informal agreements and may approve the results of arbitration, if those results are consistent with legal principles and rulings. But shariʿa councils sometimes interact with legal bodies in other ways. In some of the cases we examined in earlier chapters, solicitors and shariʿa councils were in communication. Solicitors may write to a shariʿa council in order to affect the council's proceedings, as when, in the "waiting for grandmother" case discussed in chapter 5, the two sets of solicitors cited the state of the civil divorce proceedings to try and either hasten or delay the shariʿa council proceedings. These efforts sometimes do lead the shariʿa council to expedite the awarding of the religious divorce, on grounds that the marriage is already over. In other cases, a solicitor might lead the shariʿa council to change its plans to hold a joint meeting, if the solicitor points to a court order against the husband, usually because of a police record of domestic violence. (In any case, these joint meetings rarely occur.) But no action taken by the shariʿa council produces a legal effect.

Given the recent trend to consider the outcomes of financial arbitration, are there scenarios where a shariʿa council document could end up in court? Critics of councils often suggest that shariʿa council meetings lead couples to enter into binding agreements that are later enforced in court. No examples are produced of this occurring. Indeed, we have seen that the three major councils do not generate documents of this type. In chapter 9, we saw that MAT leaders did not know of cases arising in court from their own arbitrations. Arif, the Birmingham solicitor working with MAT, said although theoretically a couple could draw up a contract concerning finances or children, he knew of no such instances.

Now, even if an ex-spouse did produce an agreement in court and the judge gave an order for its application, it would not be an instance of "recognizing shariʿa" but of enforcing a legal contract. But could this occur? In March 28, 2013, I put this question to Judge Qureshi. He began by noting that of the many Muslim couples that have come before him, only two or three had their marriages registered; nearly all had either held only an Islamic marriage, or they had married overseas, usually in Pakistan. For those couples, family court proceedings would concern children, and in those cases, judges are particularly concerned to make their own judgments.

JRB: Have you ever seen an Islamic mediation be referred to later in court, or a document from a mediation produced in court?

Qureshi: No, and it would be unlikely to happen, because they have solicitors, and the solicitors would have told them that the court is secular and that such a document would not be accepted. And if they still agreed to something, they would not come to court. The court might accept an agreement for child residence but only if it seemed reasonable on other grounds, not religious ones. For example, if they agreed to have the child stay with the mother until age seven and then leave and go live with the father, I would ask Cafcass to look into what the reason was, and it would not matter that a religious authority had told them to do it. It would be too sudden for the child and I would not approve it. . . . The closest case to what you are asking was when a mum and dad had a five-year-old boy and she did not want him circumcised and he did. She said she belonged to a group that only followed the Qurʾan and not the hadith, and her imam had told her that there was nothing about circumcision in the Qurʾan. Well, that's true, I said; it is in the hadith. I told them to go off and try to reach an agreement, and she ended up agreeing to the circumcision.

JRB: But if they had not agreed?

Qureshi: I could not have ordered the circumcision. I would have said wait till he is eighteen and let him decide, because at five it is really painful and recovery takes a long time.

JRB: Those supporting the Cox bill [to regulate religious arbitration] say that sometimes a woman is pressured to agree to something at a shariʿa council and then it is ordered by a court.

Qureshi: It could not happen, because you would have to have an unusual combination of circumstances. The wife would have to be willing to

> give in to the husband and there would have to be concerted pressure placed on her, and the shariʿa council not be acting correctly, and the judge would have to not judge fairly. Residence is almost always granted to the mum, unless she is unable to take care of the child. The most the dad can then ask for is shared residence; more often he has rights to have the child once or twice a week.

I posed similar questions to Sir Peter Singer, for years a judge in the High Court of Justice and a prominent authority on family law. He said, "About money, we are very paternalistic, likely to say 'that's not fair' even if the wife has agreed to it. This is not an area of contractual certainty; the adults are not competent to bind the court, and the courts will be reluctant to agree to a settlement where the wife surrenders her right to come back and ask for maintenance, or for more maintenance, at a later stage, should conditions change. At the same time, one of the principles of the law is that we try for a clean break in a divorce, section 25 (a). We would find that a 'fully entitled wife,' where the marriage had lasted awhile, should get half."[15]

I have made other efforts to find instances of a shariʿa council agreement surfacing in a courtroom, without results. In 2010, I was invited to speak at the annual retreat of the UK Family Law Bar Association, and I asked any of the many lawyers and judges present who had even heard of such an event to please let me know. None had. Speaking hypothetically, some said that were there to be an agreement that had emerged from shariʿa council mediation and presented by one party in court as the proposed basis for a court order, it might be accepted if it was close to what the judge would have decided on in any case. But this is complicated. I asked family lawyer Sarah Anticoni whether a judge would consider a shariʿa council–mediated settlement. "Yes," she replied, "he or she might look at it and say, 'yes, that looks alright.' But he would pull it apart and use the bits that correspond to what he does: take out the child residence provisions because he is not going to issue an order there, and that would leave the bits regarding division of assets and income. Then it would depend on whether those financial arrangements fell within the range of what the court usually does. If they did not, he would call the parties in and say so. Now, they might then give reasons and both parties might stay with what they had said, and he might accept them."

I have discussed these issues on several occasions with Aina Khan, the family lawyer we met earlier who specializes in legal matters affecting Muslims and who now works for the prestigious London firm Duncan Lewis. She often attracts Muslim women who wish (and have the financial means) to take their husbands to court for a divorce or to retrieve property. She sends them to the western London shariʿa council for the shariʿa dimension of the divorce. On August 3, 2011, she summarized the new family law rules and their implications for this question:

> With respect to children, things are tightly controlled and judges don't rubber-stamp agreements, impossible for a shariʿa council settlement to "sneak in." There is always a hearing, either in private law or, if a local authority is involved, public law. Finances are a different matter. What judges prefer is that the parties agree on a division of assets in the form of a consent order, a two-page form they fill out, with income, assets, pension, and so forth. Courts insist that they sign off, though. The fee is low, a forty-five-pound court fee. Each is, in theory, to have his advisor, with full disclosure of assets. But this never happens, very few cases, because the two parties cannot agree. But when these do come through to the judge, he sits in his chambers, he has a big stack of these, and he does always accept them. They would have to be really one-sided for the judge to refuse a consent order, and, of course, the parties would not sign one. So it never happens. Very little chance that shariʿa councils would lead the two parties to an agreement that then would be rubber-stamped by a judge.

Shariʿa councils do not, then, produce documents that are rubber-stamped in civil court, as some charge. Judges accept, indeed encourage, agreements between husbands and wives about children and assets, but judges inspect such agreements to see if they are fair and in the best interests of the child. English justice abides by its own rules and principles.

On other matters, legal contracts could replicate what might be the determination by an Islamic scholar. For example, in 2014, the Law Society, which represents solicitors in England and Wales, pointed out that, as British citizens are free to divide their estates as they wish, and as solicitors were increasingly approached by Muslims wishing to follow Islamic law, it would be useful to provide guidance. Despite newspaper headlines of the sort: "Islamic law is adopted by British legal chiefs,"[16] the Law Society had simply circulated an information sheet. Nonetheless, later that year, and after heavy public criticism, the society withdrew the sheet.[17]

Jewish Parallels

The parallels with Jewish divorce law, discussed above, are intriguing. The Divorce (Religious Marriages) Act of 2002 was passed at the urging of Jewish family lawyers to provide an incentive for Jewish men to deliver a religious divorce certificate (the *get*) to their wives.

Eleanor Platt QC was the chair of the Family Law Group of the Board of Deputies of British Jews, who organized the effort to represent to the government the need for a statute to help deal with this problem of "limping marriages." She explained to me:

> Not only would men refuse to deliver a get, but wives sometimes refused to receive them. In that case, if the husband could get a hundred rabbis to sign a letter, then he could marry again and the rabbis would hold the get until such time as the wife accepted it on grounds that it was in her interest. The consequence [of no get] was that the children of a subsequent marriage would be considered to be *mamzer*, without the religious right to marry another Jew (but they may marry another mamzer). So the law now says that after the decree nisi in civil court, one of the parties may ask the judge to hold up the decree absolute if there is a religious divorce under way. Judges almost always accept this request—we have not had any cases of judges' refusals. This has changed practices. It has not entirely resolved it, as some people do not care and remarry without the religious divorce. British Jews are very diverse, but we got the lawyers together, not the rabbis, and the lawyers could agree.[18]

At the same time, the rabbinical tribunals (the several British Beth Din) regularly engage in binding arbitration under the terms of the Arbitration Act, just as is (or can be) carried out by MAT in Nuneaton. Parties cannot appeal, although a civil court may intervene if there were procedural irregularities. They hear a range of civil disputes, including commercial disputes, but not in the domain of family law. In particular, they do not entertain requests regarding postdivorce payments. "Nor do they wish to do so," explained one of the key barristers who works with the Board of Deputies. "Sometimes they will mediate between divorcing couples but then not enter into matters which they consider should be resolved by civil family court." Often one party does not adhere to an award and the winning party goes to English courts, and the Arbitration Act receives a straightforward application.[19]

Does the application of the 2002 act to Jewish divorces have any implications for Islamic divorces? The question was raised in several discussions among lawyers and mosque officials that I attended, and the consensus was negative. Extending the 2002 law to Muslims would (if anything) allow men to slow down the civil divorce procedure by dragging their feet at the shariʿa council. But more important, it would be unnecessary for Muslim women, because they are getting civil divorces if they were married civilly, and a shariʿa council can award a divorce without the husband's consent—this is the key difference between the rabbinical and the shariʿa bodies.

A Test Case: When a Judge Invokes Shariʿa

There can, of course, be occasions when a judge may look into "shariʿa" or "Islamic law" in hearing a case, and this is another possible meaning of "recognition." The problem such a reference raises is how one would determine

Islamic law.[20] We have seen how shariʿa scholars debate such issues as the extent to which local practices might constitute shariʿa even without a textual basis, and how one combines the different textual sources of Islamic law. In doing this the council scholars echo debates occurring throughout the Muslim world, in the present and in the past.

Others might draw on a mixture of sources. As in the case examined below, a judge might ask for expert testimony on Islamic law, perhaps intending by his or her request to learn about Islamic jurisprudence, perhaps somewhat tempered by an account of contemporary practices in states with Islamic legal systems. For their part, ordinary Muslims might enter into a marriage or divorce with assumptions about Islam that are based on the laws and customs of a particular country. Furthermore, if they then seek an Islamic divorce through an Islamic Shariʿa Council in England, they might come to see their case through the lens of the procedures set down by that council. It is in the play of these three kinds of law, each with its own source of authority, that confusion may reign, but sometimes pragmatic creativity may find its justifications.

This variety of sources and understandings should indicate how complex a matter it is to speak of English courts "recognizing" Islamic law, as did the archbishop. If a judge seeks expertise, what is the object of his quest: Islamic legal theory, Islamic laws and customs in a particular country, or new English-shariʿa creations?

Case: *Uddin v. Choudhury*

Such are the issues to be found in a recent reported case in which a judge does appear to recognize the effects of a shariʿa judgment. The case, *Uddin v. Choudhury*, was decided in the Court of Appeal for England and Wales, Civil Division, at the Royal Courts of Justice, on October 21, 2009.[21] The appeal was from a judgment rendered in the Central London County Court on March 20 of the same year and concerned gifts that accompanied an Islamic marriage or nikah carried out in 2003 in London. The appellant, Mr. Uddin, was the father of the groom; the respondent, Ms. Choudhury, was the bride.

Certain facts were not disputed in the court proceedings. Both sets of parents had come to England from Bangladesh, and they had arranged the marriage in negotiations held between the two families. As usually is the case, both sides gave gifts to the others, to the bride and groom but also to relatives of each. These gifts included substantial amounts of gold jewelry. The marriage contract, the nikahnama, stated that the bride was due £15,000 in mahr, and that this had gone unpaid at the time of the nikah.

But the relationship did not work out. The original plan was to register the marriage legally sometime after the Islamic ceremony, but this was never done.

Nor, by admission of both parties, was the marriage consummated. The bride went to the Islamic Shariʿa Council in Leyton to ask that the nikah be dissolved. The husband agreed to this procedure on condition that his wife return the jewelry that had been given to her together with that portion of the mahr that had already been paid to her. She denied having received any mahr. In December 2004, the council dissolved the marriage; the council's records show that their decision contained no stipulations concerning jewelry or mahr.

But the husband's father pursued the matter in civil court. (He also initiated a civil suit against the Islamic Shariʿa Council for procedural irregularities; the suit was dismissed.) He claimed that the bride was obliged to return the gifts given her and to return additional items of jewelry worth £25,000, which he claimed she had taken from his and his son's home near London during a visit in October 2003, about two months after the marriage. The bride filed a counterclaim in the civil court. She said that she was due the £15,000 mahr that was promised in the marriage contract and payment of which came due upon dissolution of the marriage by the ISC. One should keep in mind that this was an Islamic marriage contract and that the couple had never been married (or divorced) in the eyes of English law; the case concerned obligations to pay, not the terms of a divorce settlement.

The judge appointed a single joint expert on the matter of shariʿa law (meaning that both parties accepted him as an expert). The judge asked the expert, the very barrister Faiz ul-Aqtab Siddiqi, whom we know from his leadership of Hijaz (chapter 9), to inform the court about the content of shariʿa law—not, we should note, to explain Islamic practices as carried out in Bangladesh or at the Islamic Shariʿa Council.[22] Siddiqi did so in a detailed brief, in which he made two major points. One was that unless stipulated in the contract, the gifts given at or around marriage were gifts pure and simple. Their possession was not contingent upon the success of the marriage and they did not have to be returned. They were not part of the mahr, whose payment is related to the marital status of the couple. The expert's second point was that the bride was due the mahr, to be paid in full, because the marriage had not been consummated and because this failure was not due to any refusal on her part. Although the brief was long, these were the two points that the judge took into consideration in making his decisions.

The judge found that the gifts were gifts and need not be returned, and thus found against the groom's father. He also ruled that the marriage contract was a valid contract and that the Islamic marriage ceremony had given it "legal effect." The court could and would enforce the contract. He thus found for the bride in her counterclaim and awarded her the £15,000 in mahr.

The groom's father, Mr. Uddin, sought to appeal, and asked the appellate court to grant him time to prepare his case. The wheels of justice turned rather quickly and the appellate judge's decision was issued in October 2009. The decision concerned the narrow question of whether Uddin could have more time to prepare his appeal but, in dismissing this petition, the appellate judge also affirmed the conclusions reached by the previous judge. He could not judge on the quality of testimony of the two sides, but he did hold that, first, the original judge had correctly understood the expert testimony on shariʿa law, against Uddin's several claims to the contrary, and, second, that the relevant matters of shariʿa law, on gifts and mahr, were so clear that "I do not think there is a real prospect of [arguments on] those points succeeding on appeal." The clarity came from framing these matters as having clear solutions in Islamic law, which, as presented by Siddiqi, looks just like English contract law.

This case generated some interest in the London legal community, as it is one of the few reported cases in recent years to concern the intersection of Islamic judgments and the English legal system. The judges assumed that there is something called "shariʿa law" that applies to all Muslims and that an expert can lay out in the form of a list of general rules. The expert's statements were taken as matters of fact, much as another expert might have testified about the content of German or French law in a contract case involving foreign law. But his testimony also evokes the way that in early modern times in, say, Morocco, a mufti would have been asked to restate the law. The court expert in the Uddin case, like the early modern mufti, provided a set of empirical statements about what Islamic law said on the particular topic at hand.

Thus, a number of important acts—giving jewelry to relatives, promising mahr to the wife, writing a marriage contract, dissolving a marriage—were taken as having a clear Islamic content and an English legal effect in the law of contracts. The gifts stay where they are, the mahr falls due, the Islamic contract has English legal force, and the Islamic marriage was validly dissolved. In this sense the civil judges recognized, not shariʿa, but contractual acts taken in an Islamic context.

Is a Mahr Obligation a Contract?

However, each of these acts of recognition merits some further analysis. Let us begin with the Islamic Shariʿa Council, the body whose dissolution of the marriage gave rise to these legal effects. ISC files show that they had dissolved the Islamic marriage, as the judges said.[23] They had treated it as a request for a khula, which indicates that the wife had initiated the divorce action, and that she thereby gave up her right to unpaid mahr and was required to return any mahr already given to her. In this case the scholars believed the wife's claim that the mahr had never been paid. (The husband claimed to the ISC that he had paid her the mahr; he changed his story in civil court.) The council ruled that she had no obligation to pay anything to him, but neither was the husband required to pay the promised mahr. The council's written judgment made no mention of any payments as conditions for the dissolution of the marriage. This absence of a ruling on mahr does not appear in the civil court account of what happened, and that is not surprising. The judge would not have seen the relevant council file, and even if he had, he would not have remarked on the *absence* of a stipulation for mahr payment. Instead, he heard the expert testimony, which said that mahr should be paid.

The logic of the khula decision by the ISC could be taken to support the claim made by Uddin (the husband's father) in the civil suit, summarized by the appellate judge, Lord Justice Mummery, in the following words: "the bride was not entitled to claim the *mehar* or dowry in circumstances where she had, of her own free will, walked out of the marriage. He says that in those circumstances the dowry should not be payable." This claim does correspond to the ISC practices in most cases. However, normally, if the ISC councillors are satisfied that a couple did not consummate their marriage and that such was the case for reasons *other than* the wife's refusal, they award the wife one-half the mahr due. In this case the ISC did not render a judgment about consummation because they were presented with conflicting claims about the facts of the matter. And because they did not issue a judgment about consummation, they did not award the wife any of the mahr. They treated the case as an ordinary khula case. As we have seen in earlier chapters, Islamic jurisprudence and ISC procedures link obligations to pay the mahr to the nature of the divorce.

But such a linkage was not recognized by the civil court, which treated the obligation to pay the mahr as a contractual matter, one that did not depend on the way in which the marriage was dissolved. As Lord Justice Mummery summarized, approvingly, the trial judge's findings (para. 7): "Next he decided that, as evidenced by the marriage certificate, there was a properly agreed dowry or *mehar*, and he found, on the basis of the evidence given by Mr. Saddiqui [*sic*], that that was a valid contract which, on the evidence he had heard, was enforceable by the court. There was no legal reason in the decided cases or in policy for refusing to enforce an agreement that the parties had made for the payment of the dowry. So he said that the counterclaim for the payment of that should succeed and there were no grounds for making deductions."

In other words, the relevant legal context for determining what sort of obligation the husband had regarding the mahr was that of English law ("decided cases or in policy"), and nothing in the law prevented considering the obligation to be a contract, enforceable by the court.[24]

What Did the Parties Think They Were Doing?

The judge doubtless decided the case against the background of one of the few reported English judgments concerning mahr, the 1965 case *Shahnaz v. Rizwan*.[25] In this case, a Muslim couple married in India with a marriage agreement that stipulated payment of mahr upon divorce. The couple divorced in England and the wife sued for the mahr as the enforcement of a contract. The court had to develop a position with respect to the argument raise by the husband's lawyers that it could not provide "ancillary relief" (a financial settlement) to "potentially polygamous marriages" (marriages contracted in a state where polygamy is allowed). The judge ruled that "under Mohammedan law such right to dower [mahr], once it had accrued as payable, was enforceable by civil action and was regarded as an assignable proprietary right" (par. 390).

This was a crucial move. The *Shahnaz* way of framing the case insulated the mahr agreement against two objections: that the marriage was potentially polygamous and thus could not be subject to English jurisdiction (according to laws of the time), and that the agreement was a kind of pre- or antenuptial contract. The judge found the right to the mahr "more closely to be compared with a right of property than a matrimonial right or obligation."

But if the mahr is a contractual obligation, then the judges would need to know the parties' understandings, including whether the parties intended the contract to be enforceable in law.[26] But what understandings would the parties have held? What would they have thought the material effects of dissolving an Islamic marriage to be? Above, we discussed three possible sources for such an understanding: the rules of Islamic jurisprudence, the procedures followed in the relevant Muslim-majority country, or the procedures followed in England's shariʿa councils.

The parties to *Uddin v. Choudhury*, who were of Bangladeshi background, might have brought to their marriage an understanding that any divorce initiated by the wife would be considered as a khula and thus, following Islamic jurisprudence, would require her to abandon her claim to mahr. Or they might have known of Bangladesh's Muslim Family Laws Ordinance and subsequent court decisions in that country holding that mahr contracts are enforceable as contracts regardless of the form taken by divorce proceedings.[27] Or, because the wife started Islamic divorce proceedings at the Islamic Shariʿa Council, she (at least) could be presumed to have agreed to abide by their procedures, which stipulate that she would not be paid mahr if she were granted a judicial dissolution.

Whichever set of rules was chosen as a point of reference, the result would be to embed the mahr contract in a set of shared understandings about Islamic marriage and divorce, whether these were derived from Islamic jurisprudence, state legal instruments, or the procedural rules followed by the ISC. Because English contract law places great weight on such understandings, especially when the contract is among relatives, they are germane to judicial interpretations of the contract in question, the agreement to pay mahr.[28] Asking about the parties' understandings would lead to examining the link between the rule of divorce and the rules for mahr repayment. But the judges in the *Uddin* case did not follow this logic. In effect they severed the link between the form of an Islamic divorce and the mahr obligations. Two reasons for doing so seem reasonable. First, the judge might have thought that making this link would bring the case onto the terrain of antenuptial agreement. English judges are not bound to enforce antenuptial agreements, although they may and sometimes do take them into account in a divorce settlement.[29] Second, the initial judge framed the questions put to the expert witness in terms of Islamic law as a species of foreign law rather than as the wife's and husband's understandings of Islam. This approach matches that taken by Muslim scholars who urge that Islamic law be freed of the cultural elements and local understandings that distort its true meaning. As Siddiqi told me in 2010, "Nikah is a contract and should be entered into through education and not based on cultural background, for example, on Pakistani or Indian ideas."

Taking Islamic law to be a set of contract-oriented rules, independent of social context, fits with English legal expectations that it be a kind of foreign law and with Siddiqi's own efforts to purify Islam of cultural backgrounds—and allows the judge to award the mahr without encountering the *Shahnaz* objection. But if in taking this approach the judge does not investigate the parties' understandings of their contracts, she or he risks ignoring the English as well as the Islamic approaches to contracts.[30]

Cases such as this appear rather seldom, for reasons explained to me by family lawyer Aina Khan: "There is very little case law on mahr contracts, clearly none saying they cannot be enforced as contracts. Look, there are three elements to a contract: offer, acceptance, and consideration, and you have all three, with the mahr as the consideration. Were there witnesses? Is there a written document? Then it can be enforced. It fits English civil contract law quite nicely. But there are almost no cases because people do not or cannot pay the fees, what, for one thousand pounds?"[31] She explained that the last case she had had like this was two and a half years previously. She gets inquiries every month, but people cannot or will not pay the fees, so they don't pursue it. They cannot get help from legal aid, because they want the case to be 80 percent certain, and these cannot be.

In addition (continued Khan), even though in a divorce proceeding mahr could be considered along with other assets and income, "it never is because the wife forgets there was mahr promised or paid. And in any case, it would just be offset by some other asset, so it does not really help here." Such was precisely the issue in the 2012 ISC case mentioned in chapter 5, where the couple disputed whether or not unpaid mahr had simply been lumped into the division of assets and liabilities in court. If the couple was not married, then the case for mahr would depend on claims of detrimental reliance, would go to Chancery not family court, and would be expensive, explained Khan—and furthermore "judges hate such cases" because of the difficulties of proof.

Are Gifts to Be Returned?

Uddin's original petition to the civil court concerned not the mahr but gifts of jewelry given pursuant to the marriage. The expert testimony declared them to be simple gifts, not to be returned. But that testimony was a restatement of Islamic shariʿa; it did not purport to describe the understandings and practices common in Bangladesh about marriage gifts. These understandings are complex and changing. In Bangladesh and elsewhere in South Asia, marriages include the exchange of gifts as well as payment of mahr. Both sides give gifts of jewelry and clothes, and, in particular, jewelry, and expensive items of jewelry are supposed to be handed down to children.

In Bangladesh the groom's side is increasingly likely to also demand a dowry from the bride, which could include requests that the bride purchase furniture for her husband's household, where she will live, and that her family buy jewelry to properly adorn her for the wedding. Though she wears the jewelry and it "theoretically" belongs to her, often the husband or his family will use it for subsequent marriages, so that, unlike the mahr, these gifts are not in all cases the bride's property.[32]

In practice, the disposition of these gifts depends on how the marriage turns out. If it lasts, they may be handed down to children. Moreover, families who receive gifts will be expected to reciprocate when gift-givers themselves marry off their children. But things are viewed differently if the marriage is of short duration, as was the case with the marriage in question in the Uddin litigation. As Khan explained it to me in 2010, "There is an unwritten code that if the bride walks out early (with no children) she hands back all that she received from the groom's side. This is even more the case if the marriage is not consummated; all is returned to both sides. In academic jargon, you could say that this is a 'constructive trust' and that the givers had 'detrimental reliance' on the marriage. This is a way for the English courts to recognize this unwritten contract."

Note that the logic of gifts and obligations invoked here is not one of Islamic law, nor is it written, and it is decidedly not the logic of a simple gift—if such ever exists. In this social logic, gifts create obligations to the givers as well as to the receivers. Uddin's argument that his son was due the gifts follows this logic. But the judges saw things through an entirely different lens. They said that unless the marriage contract said otherwise, the gifts were to be considered to be simple gifts that need not be returned.[33]

Now, there is an Islamic way of understanding the gifts that would support what the court said. It is one that distinguishes between a shariʿa that can be applied in any society, on the one hand, and the practices and expectations found in South Asia (or in another region), on the other, and that considers the latter to be outside the competence of a shariʿa-based decision. The issue is as follows: Do the social and legal expectations of people coming from a particular part of the world have a bearing on how scholars sitting on a multiethnic Islamic council in London decide cases? Or are these expectations rather matters of social expectations and practices, or ʿurf? The meta-issue is: Is ʿurf relevant to shariʿa? (Recall the similar issue raised in chapter 7 about the relevance of Pakistani or Saudi Arabian legal practices.)

This issue brings us back to the Islamic Shariʿa Council, where the tension of custom and shariʿa arises frequently. In a case they considered on February 24, 2010, each party asked to be compensated by the other for expenses and gifts. Khurram Bashir argued that the gold jewelry given to the wife must be returned, while Haitham al-Haddad did not see how jewelry was part of their discussion if it was not written down as mahr in the marriage contract. The discussions continued between the two scholars:

Khurram: All [gifts] must be returned, this goes to custom: all returned, "even a needle." When she claims her things, she should take her movables; immovables do not concern us. But gold always concerns the Shariʿa Council.

Haitham: How should we classify these gifts? Why should they be returned?

Khurram: The custom (ʿurf) is that the mahr is low but there is lots of gold. There was one wedding I celebrated of a doctor, and the gentleman asked me to write down one pound mahr; I was not happy: I asked, "Are you making a mockery of the wedding?" I asked if they were giving gold, and they were, quite a lot, and I said they should put that as mahr.

Haitham: Yes, but what does ʿurf do; does it consider this part of mahr?

Khurram: Yes.

Haitham: No, our rule is that [only that] which is written in the nikahnama, you should give it back, it is our rule.

Khurram: No, it is not our rule; we go with ʿurf.

In this discussion, which went on for some time thereafter, the issue was whether gold promised or given alongside an amount of money should be considered to be mahr and thus subject to the rules that apply to mahr in the case of a khula, or be considered outside the ken of the council entirely and thus not subject to a ruling. Khurram argued that the gold was mahr and that it would be better if people wrote it down as such, because often that which is explicitly mahr is laughably low. Often it is a nominal "thirty-two rupees," less than one British pound, a sum justified because at the time of Abu Hanifah, the founder of the Hanafi legal school predominant in Pakistan and Bangladesh, this was the equivalent of two dirhams, a sum referred to by the prophet Muhammad. Following this reasoning, that which is written in the contract as "mahr" is symbolic; the gift intended to provide the bride with bargaining power is the gold. Therefore, the gold should be considered as part of the mahr.

But Haitham countered that the council should only rule on the basis of the written contract. He argued that other gifts, like other property, were outside their self-imposed, jurisdictional limitations. In these cases, Haitham usually ends up agreeing with Khurram if he is convinced that in a particular case the gold was indeed part of the mahr. Often the wife writes it down as such in her application for a divorce, and in those cases these two councillors have no disagreement on this issue. But Haitham's starting point was that mahr is mahr and gifts are gifts, and gifts have nothing to do with the ISC's judgments. This also was the expert testimony to the civil court in the Uddin case, and as with Haitham's position, this argument reflects a view that seeks to place something called "shariʿa law" outside of any particular local set of social expectations.

If instead we turn to the ʿurf or customary practices, we would expect that when the marriage ended, the gifts would be returned, especially in the case of a short-lived marriage and a fortiori for a nonconsummated one. If the civil judges had wished to rule on the basis of shared contractual expectations, then they could have sided with Uddin and ordered the gifts returned. In either case, the judges' decision as rendered has little apparent base either in the understandings and practices of Bangladeshi Muslims or in the rules and procedures of the Islamic Shariʿa Council.

Conclusions

The Uddin case might look as if English judges had recognized shariʿa, but in fact what they did was to conceptualize the mahr agreement in terms of English contract law. True, in their view the mahr came due when the couple's Islamic divorce was decided by the Islamic Shariʿa Council. However, that action only had legal meaning insofar as it was already stipulated by contract as the event that would cause the contract to be enforced. It is clear from this analysis that an English civil court cannot base rulings on a simple statement of "Islamic shariʿa," because there is no single such set of rules and procedures—although one can easily find Islamic authorities who will say that their version of shariʿa has precisely this status. What the English courts can do is to analyze religious procedures—marriage, gift-giving, divorce—into those components that have legal relevance: promises, expectations, and actions. This does not have to be a one-way street, in that contracts, agreement, and intentions are places where shariʿa and English law can converge. But this is an art of finding overlaps in legal understandings, not applying shariʿa in English courts.

But if shariʿa and English law can get along in the tightly controlled domain of civil law, does this lead to accepting uses of shariʿa in the broader world of British society and politics? It depends, it turns out.

CHAPTER 11

When Can Shariʿa Be British?

IF, AS THEN ARCHBISHOP ROWAN WILLIAMS SAID IN 2008, BRITONS DRAW their values from their religious communities, it is not clear how many Britons think it a good idea for Muslims to do so. Britain has taken centuries to extend legal toleration to all. In the mid-seventeenth century, it extended it to dissenting Protestants and no further. Catholics were too loyal to the pope, as John Locke reminded the sovereign, and atheists could not be believed in court, for their oaths were meaningless to them. Catholics were allowed to stand for Parliament only in 1829, and Jews in 1858. The asymmetry between the Church of England and other religious communities has not entirely vanished, but Christians and Jews of various views, from very conservative to liberal, have pretty much been admitted to full cultural citizenship in Britain, as have atheists. The jury is still out on Muslims. How extensive is the cultural territory where shariʿa, in its broadest sense of the pathway Muslims should follow, can be accepted as British? Which institutions that instruct Muslims to follow that pathway cause a moral panic?

Banal Shariʿa

Some Islamic institutions deeply trouble at least some non-Muslims in Britain; others do so much less. Shariʿa councils are accused of threatening legal unity, oppressing women, and encouraging Islamic radicalism and domestic violence. But other institutions, despite the clear role of shariʿa, are relatively accepted. Why?

Mosques

The least controversial Islamic institution is the mosque, accepted as one more instance of a familiar English institution, the "church."

Recent outcries put this claim to the test. The loudest recent debate over a mosque project concerns a proposed mosque for Newham, close to the 2012 Olympics site in eastern London. As of 2015, the project remains controversial, not because it is a mosque but because of its size and because of its sponsor. It is routinely referred to as a "mega-mosque." If built as originally planned, it would be the largest religious structure in Britain, holding tens of thousands of worshippers. Some fear it would radically transform the neighborhood. Moreover, it was sponsored by the Tablighi Jamaʿat, the worldwide grassroots organization designed to call Muslims back to proper worship. Although sometimes charged with attracting Muslims who go on to be involved in jihad, it is perhaps more plausibly taxed with encouraging Muslims to create separate communities. For these reasons, even some Muslim organizations have opposed the project. A petition circulated among Muslims in Newham against the mosque received 2,500 signatures. Ghayasuddin Siddiqui, the cofounder of the Muslim Parliament, said, "We have too many mosques. I think it should not be built."[1]

But *not* challenged in these debates is the importance of worship and of mosques for British Muslims. Similarly, the many, persistent attacks on the East London Mosque (ELM) charge an illegitimate intertwining of religion and borough politics, and do not attack the mosque as an institution (see chapter 3). The ELM qua mosque has enjoyed the favor of the royal family and the country's legal establishment.

Other shariʿa-based practices are also seen as legitimate extensions of British institutions, among them halal food certification and shariʿa finance.

Halal Certification

Many in Britain seek food that is pure and healthy, defined in differing ways: made from organic produce or from happy animals, fitting vegan diets, having clear lines of provenance, or prepared according to religious dietary rules, as set out for Jews, Muslims, Sikhs, or Hindus. Jews set up organizations to regulate food preparation in the nineteenth century, beginning with the creation in 1804 of the London Board of Shechita.[2] Muslims have two major (and other minor) private halal certification services that inspect food and other products. The Halal Food Authority (HFA) was created in 1994 and works closely with major food producers and suppliers, from Kellogg's foods to British Airways. The Halal Monitoring Committee (HMC) was created in 2003, in response to complaints that the HFA was too lax in its determinations of what is permitted (halal) to Muslims.

Both services operate in national and European legal contexts, and, in particular, regarding the rules for animal slaughter. EU rules on hygiene and animal welfare have been transposed into the laws of the member states, assuring uniformity. These laws require the stunning of animals prior to slaughter but allow states to exempt religious slaughter, and Britain is one of those that does. Abattoirs would rather stun because doing so renders the animals immobile and saves time, and the government Food Standards Agency estimates that in 2011 more than 80 percent of the animals killed in the UK halal industry were stunned.[3] The HFA allows stunning—and this has been both a reason for its success with industry and for the challenges it has faced. Generally accepted Islamic rules stipulate that the animal remain alive until it is properly killed with a sharp knife blade and a pronouncement of the Basmalah. HFA finds that using an electric current that can be calibrated to the size of the animal meets this criterion.

If the HFA tends to operate with a lighter inspection touch, and to rely on a few widely accepted prohibitions and rules in its negotiations, the HMC can be seen more as a "bottom-up" network of butchers and producers, with a strong element of research and inquiry.[4] Shari'a scholarship plays a major role in shaping new HMC regulations. For example, one member of the Birmingham Central Mosque shari'a council, Sarfraz Mohammed (whom we met in chapter 8), had studied chemistry and fiqh, and plays an active role with the HMC. He explained the organization's origins and ways of reasoning to me:[5] "It was formed about ten years ago when there was widespread concern about non-halal meat that had been falsely labeled: BBC or Channel 4 ran one of their investigative programs on that. A few mosques in Leicester and London got together and formed the HMC just to certify the meat that was delivered to butcher shops in their localities, serving the Muslims who lived near those mosques. Then other butchers also started asking for certification; they saw an interest in doing so."

Notice how the impetus for creating the organization was one that is easily accessible to non-Muslims: to combat false advertising. But the HMC also created a niche for those Muslims who sought to be more scientific and more rigorous in terms of Islam. "Other questions started being asked," continued Sarfraz, "about which procedures were necessary for halal, questions about stunning, the mechanical blade, the tape recordings of the Basmalah, the use of CO_2.[6] The HMC takes the view that stunning is not allowed, to eliminate any doubt. Some chickens are weaker, and of one thousand, a few might die. In Islam there is an obligation to show that meat is halal, not to presume it." The HMC uses technology and strategy to assure customers that what they are getting is halal. "Inspectors enter their data on their phones with a GPS app that registers where they are, so if they just stay home and enter it we catch them—once we did, but in fact he had some problem so was texting the information from the abattoir to his wife, who entered it at home. We check the butcher shops four times a week, at random times, so they cannot say to themselves, 'Okay, it is after the Friday prayer so we know the HMC guy is going to come by.'"

Around 2008 the HMC began to study other products, where there had been a consumer demand for certification, such as cosmetics and beverages. They highlight their competence as investigative chemists: "For example, in an energy drink we found tyrosine that had been made from human hair and so was not halal. The producers and suppliers did not know of its origins.

They stopped shipping it then, and the producer changed the composition." These new forays require thinking about scriptural interpretation. Sarfraz explained that there were several ways of thinking about GMOs. "A verse says 'Don't change what God has made,' and that could be taken to mean that anything altered genetically is forbidden. But otherwise the issues that arise regard the content of what is inserted: if a tomato is altered, but not by using animal genes, then it could be acceptable. The general issue is transformation: bacteria provide a buffer between the pig in which it is grown and the vaccines given to humans. Bacteria in general are acceptable, because we know that at the time of the Prophet everyone ate yogurt, and that had live bacteria in it."

The HMC's efforts to achieve greater food purity come down to two things: using modern science to consistently apply juridical knowledge and rigorously inspecting producers and butchers to make sure they do not err in preserving the purity of the meat—for example, that halal products are not contaminated in the butcher shop. Given the premise—that Muslims should know whether what they eat fits scriptural commandments—the HMC appears as a highly rationalized endeavor. The premise itself is a form of truth in advertising: if you say it is halal, it better really be so.

And that is indeed how the British government views it. The government Food Standards Agency (FSA) enforces halal standards in that they fine food sellers who label food as halal without being able to back up their claims in some way. The relevant agency directive says that "officers are asked to consider action, where appropriate, against food business operators who sell and mis-describe *Halal* foods, in the same way as they would for any contravention of food law in food premises generally."[7] That there is a directive does not mean that the FSA has any means to tell what is halal from what is not: the only practical direction given in the circular is that if there is pork, the food is not halal! But once the government has taken on this task, they can be invited to do more, and this is the HMC's goal. They have urged the FSA to set precise standards. Sarfraz explained: "The issue for the FSA is misrepresentation. They should provide a limit, so, for example, 0.1 percent pork would not imply criminal intent because it could be because of animal grease used on a knife. They could establish a standard for pork content, above which the supplier would be held responsible and face penalties. Then we would as private bodies make rulings; perhaps it was animal grease on the blade, and would that contaminate the food?"

The HMC's logic is a secular one: how to assess fault. Its goal (and that of all halal certification) builds on state practices of assessing food purity, and benefits from the precedent of similar Jewish bodies. Their practices respond to the personal preferences of the individual consumer and admit of a plurality of answers and rules. As such they fit with British ideas about such bodies—in the same way that mosques fit into the institutional slot of "churches."

From time to time halal practices do raise controversy in Britain, largely on two issues that arise elsewhere in Europe as well. The first is animal welfare. Britain and the rest of Europe require stunning for reasons of animal welfare. Doesn't this mean that Muslims who do not stun are causing undesirable suffering in animals? Of course, the question is debatable: Is hanging chickens upside down and then dipping them into an electric bath for stunning really that wonderful? And in any case, most halal processing in Britain involves stunning.

The second objection involves accusations of stealth and deceit. When consumers learn, as they did in early 2014, that all New Zealand lamb is halal, and that Pizza Express serves halal meat, some object that they are being tricked into eating Muslim food, and the British National Party denounces "the horror and the barbarity of the alien practice," which is akin to "stoning to death and beheadings" and belongs to "another century and another place."[8] But as one commentator on the Pizza Express story recalled, "In the past four years, the UK media has broken the story to the British public at least a dozen times, warning about the widespread use of halal meat, yet somehow every new headline presents it as a new finding. In the latest Pizza Express episode, where the claim was that the chain was surreptitiously slipping halal chicken onto its menu, there was no secrecy at all: the chain's website clearly states it uses halal chicken. The 'secret' element, a popular angle in the halal story, serves to support the alarm that people are being hoodwinked by Muslims sneaking their way of life into the mainstream."[9]

The two issues can be best formulated as concerns for animal welfare and for transparency—and many, including Muslim and Jewish leaders and David Cameron, quickly called for better labeling of food products. Of course, these two issues can then become vehicles for some to denounce Islam. However, the efforts of Muslims to apply and seek state enforcement of dietary shariʿa clearly fit with mainstream British ideas about the rights of people to demand food purity.

Shariʿa Finance

The banality of shariʿa is still more striking regarding Islamic finance. We now move from mosques, abattoirs, and small offices in outer London, to the center of British policy and politics. In October 2013, David Cameron announced to the World Islamic Economic Forum in London that the Treasury was drawing up plans to issue a £200 million *sukuk*, a shariʿa-compatible bond. Doing so takes "pragmatism and political will," he said, noting that the City would now be a leader in Islamic finance around the world. "I want London to stand alongside Dubai as one of the great capitals of Islamic finance anywhere in the world."[10]

Well, Britain is also a leader in shariʿa councils. Both are institutions that seek to provide Muslims with shariʿa-compliant services that are not otherwise available. Why is one the cause for pride and state-led initiatives and the other for recriminations and a bill intended to curb their activity?

Money might be part of the answer. The government's glossy brochure on "UK Excellence in Islamic Finance," introduced by Cameron and by Baroness Sayeeda Hussain Warsi, showcases the dozens of mainstream investment, accounting, and law firms that are ready to help wealthy Muslims steer their money in a profitable and religiously proper way into UK coffers. It charts how Britain made the country safe for sukuk.[11] It shows how a key change occurred in 2003, when the Finance Act Stamp Duty Land Tax removed the double sales charge that Muslims faced if they made use of one shariʿa-friendly way of buying, say, a home by selling the home to a bank and then purchasing in installments at a higher price, the difference substituting for an interest payment (*murabaha*). Mainstream banks advertise their shariʿa-approved services. Lloyds vaunts the qualifications of the two Islamic scholars who guarantee the Islamic quality of their products.[12]

Shortly after Cameron's sukuk announcement, the *Guardian* explained why Britons might look with a friendly eye at shariʿa financing: "Some of the tenets of Islamic banking will appeal to anyone, Muslim or otherwise, who agrees with the underlying principles of equitable distribution for everyone, the ideals of fair trading, spending of wealth judiciously, and the well-being of the community as a whole. In the wake of the banking crisis, savers may also be drawn by Islamic banking's approach to investment: they can only invest in real assets, not financial instruments that are based on speculation."[13] Shariʿa bank offers look like other bank offers, with added concern for ethics and for investing in "real assets." The structure and techniques that characterize banks are the same with Islamic finance, and their offices, prospectuses, and lists of investment assets all look like those of other banks. They also must comply with general bank regulations.

As with halal certification enterprises, shariʿa-compliant finance continues and expands practices already familiar to Britons. It enlarges the range of instruments available to consumers as private matters, and its calls resemble secular appeals for consumers to invest in ethical companies. It champions transparency. It is also big business: in this field, the prime minister is shariʿa's biggest booster.

Schools and Religious Boundaries

If mosques, halal inspection, and shariʿa finance merely replicate institutions already at the heart of Britain, isn't the same true of Islamic schools? In terms of the legal and administrative framework, Islamic schools of different types simply slot into positions already occupied by Anglican schools, as well as by Catholic and Jewish schools.

Schools, of course, involve direct contact with children. Moreover, the recent proliferation of new kinds of schools has caused confusion and anxiety about who is responsible for schooling, and about what kinds of religious content are appropriate for which kinds of schools. Prayer with "Christian content" remains mandatory in all state-aided schools that are not "faith schools." Teaching Arabic in a school with nearly all Muslim students can be made to seem, in the right journalistic hands, like preparation for jihad. All this has yet to shake out, but in the meantime, it generates cloudiness and, sometimes, moral panic.

Background: Religion and Schooling in England

In May 2014, in the middle of controversies about Islamic schools in Birmingham, the archbishop of Canterbury, Justin Welby (successor to Rowan Williams), saw it necessary to defend faith schools, noting that they long predated state schools.[14] Indeed, until the 1902 Balfour Act, independent schools run by the Church of England taught most of those children who attended school. The 1902 act established local education authorities (LEAs) throughout England and Wales, gave them taxation powers, and placed church schools under their aegis. These voluntary schools were now funded by local taxpayers. The act was controversial in that the schools were owned and run mainly by the Church of England or by Catholics; Methodists, Baptists, and others had little interest in subsidizing these religions.[15]

Education debates since then have been shaped in part by tensions between the desire for independence by state-aided grammar schools, many centuries old, and the drive to open up the better secondary schools to all pupils. Multiple new funding schemes have been introduced, including the Academies Act 2010, one of the first bills introduced by David Cameron's government. Academies are run by nonprofit trusts and receive direct state aid (they are "maintained schools") and are free from local authority control. They are often compared, not very accurately, to US charter schools. They can diverge from the national curriculum in noncore subjects but are still inspected by Ofsted, the government's Office for Standards in Education, Children's Services and Skills, which inspects and regulates local services, including schools, children's centers, and skills providers.

As of April 2015, 4,583 of UK schools were academies, including the majority of Britain's secondary schools; and more than 400 were "free schools" that had never been under municipal control.[16] Some of these academies are called "faith schools" (not to be confused with "free schools"), which means that their charter explicitly recognizes a special place given to one religion at the school.

Pupils may be selected based on their religion. As a result of this multiplying of school types, a pupil may study at, say, a Church of England school, but depending on the school's legal status—the current four types in this continually shifting landscape seem to be controlled, aided, foundation, and academy—the religious aspects of school teaching and school life will differ.[17]

Muslim State-Aided Schools

The first state support for a Muslim school came in 1998, after many years of efforts by schools to receive funding, and it did so as part of an effort by New Labour to partner with churches in the field of education. Muslims came in on Anglicans' political coattails. The Islamia Primary School in Brent was granted a state grant in 1998, and was soon followed by the Al-Furqan Primary School in Birmingham. By 2007 seven Islamic schools received state aid, and by 2012 there were eleven state-aided Muslim schools (.05 percent of the state-aided total).[18] For comparison, in 2012 there were 4,598 Church of England schools and 2,010 Roman Catholic faith schools, all maintained by the state, plus thirty-eight Jewish schools. Independent (meaning nonstate-supported) Muslim schools exist in greater numbers and suffer from poor funding. Even independent schools must register with the state and meet certain requirements, including teaching a broad curriculum, and some have been closed for failing to do so. The Association of Muslim Schools lists fifty-four schools in the Midlands region, for example, only two of which receive state aid.[19]

Demand for Muslim state-supported or "maintained" schools came from parents concerned that their children be educated in a way consistent with Islamic values and that they do well on state examinations. Some of these schools do achieve results higher than the national average, and much higher than the results achieved by children from South Asian backgrounds in non-faith schools. For example, Bangladeshis in Tower Hamlets enjoy a growing number of such schools, and as a result their pupils, once the laggards on test day, now outscore whites on GCSE exams (taken at sixteen).[20]

Many state-supported schools are Muslim only in the sense that the vast majority of pupils are Muslims—for example, the Birmingham schools under scrutiny in 2014 for religious extremism were state-aided schools with no religious designation. And yet they are generally referred to as "Muslim schools" because the pupils are mostly Muslim and because there are Islamic aspects to at least the school ethos if not the curriculum. These schools seek ways to accommodate demands from pupils or parents for more Islamic content. One Birmingham state school brought in a speaker from the Sparkbrook mosque for assemblies, used Islamic materials as part of religious education, allowed students to organize for Friday prayer, allowed South Asian–style clothing (*sahwal kameez*) in school colors for girls, and allowed girls to opt out of swimming and to wear trousers for sport.[21] These demographic concentrations derive from British policy. Multiculturalism in Britain was part of official policy regarding schools more than for any other sector, and in the 1980s, efforts to ensure racial integration through busing were abandoned in favor of guarantees that ethnic groups could maintain their own linguistic and cultural identity. The result was many primary, middle, and upper schools with high concentrations of Asians.

In addition to the day schools are the many seminaries serving older students. Deobandis are particularly active in building seminaries, as well as primary and secondary schools. Eighty percent of British-trained imams were trained in Deobandi schools, as were many of the teachers in Muslim primary or secondary schools. In addition to the seminaries are the perhaps 1,600 madrasas, schools educating young men and women after hours or on weekends, which reached an estimated 200,000 Muslim children.[22]

"Muslim schools"—which, I emphasize, usually means schools with many Muslim pupils and some Islamic elements—have been the target of continued criticism. In 2005, Chief Inspector of Schools David Bell warned that such schools could weaken national cohesion. Ofsted's own report from that year found that 36 percent of Muslim schools needed to do better at promoting tolerance of other faiths—although they also found that 43 percent of Evangelical schools also had this problem.[23]

However, there are no clear guidelines for what is acceptable in an independent school. It enjoys a great deal of freedom, even when state-funded, to design its curricula and also its "paracurricular" activities, such as assemblies, prayers, holidays, and outings. May it discriminate? Well, it depends. By law, state-aided faith schools may discriminate against applicants not of the faith concerned. However, teachers must be hired regardless of faith. But the distinction is a matter of law rather than principles, as a nondiscrimination principle has already been violated by the rules for religion-specific admissions. At the very least, the matter is confusing. And this feature of school policy also engenders a lot of complaining by parents trying to get their children into Christian schools but unable to demonstrate their regular church attendance.[24]

A case in point is the Madani High School in Leicester (see chapter 3). In 2014 the school received attention for advertising for male teachers. The school withdrew the advertisement when the Department for Education pointed out that it was in conflict with British equality legislation. But this was after the school had split, in 2012, into separate girls' and boys' schools, and school heads believed, rightly or wrongly but reasonably, that hiring male teachers for the boys' school would be appropriate. (In 2013 the Ofsted report found that the school needed improvement but that the leadership was excellent.[25])

If controversies over mixing religion and politics often target London's Tower Hamlets, those about Islam in the schools often return to Birmingham. It was here that a moral panic erupted early in 2014.

The 2014 Birmingham "Trojan Horse" Controversy

In November 2013, the Birmingham City Council received a letter from an undisclosed source. The letter, quickly dubbed the "Trojan horse," purported to be a plan of attack sent from a Birmingham circle of Islamist plotters to counterparts in Bradford, advising them how to carry out a takeover of the local state schools by hijacking boards of governors in mainly Muslim areas and forcing out opposition.

Although commentators and officials agreed that the letter was a hoax, by February 2014 it was leaked to the media, and two high-profile politicians, Education Secretary Michael Gove and Home Secretary Theresa May, both contenders for Tory ascendancy, jumped on the letter to accuse each other of responsibility for the supposed instances of extremism it described. The accusations ricocheted around the dailies to the extent that Prime Minister Cameron took time away from the seventieth anniversary of D-Day landings in Normandy to berate them both for their overly evident desires to make political hay out of the "scandal."[26]

In June, Ofsted released a report on the controversy. The report singled out Park View Academy in Alum Rock, Birmingham, for criticism, mainly for not doing enough to educate pupils against extremism. Golden Hillock and Nansen Primary, the other two schools operated by the Park View Trust, were also downgraded.[27] In late 2013, Ofsted said that Golden Hillock "promotes students' spiritual, moral, social and cultural development well" and praised Park View Academy in that its pupils scored much higher on their GCSEs than their disadvantaged backgrounds predicted; Ofsted also mentioned that they had made "good progress with memorisation of the Qurʾan." Apparently, this was a good thing in 2013. The teachers "are consistent in their promotion of moderate and balanced views." Moreover, "the school has a strong link with local community police who are trained in preventing extremist ideology taking hold in schools." They noted that the school taught A-level courses in mathematics, biology, Urdu, and Arabic.[28]

Park View's academic results had not changed in 2014, but in the June 2014 report, the academy was downgraded to the lowest rating in leadership, as Ofsted inspections found evidence to support charges that the school was trying to remove secular teachers and make the school more Islamic. Among the charges were that Friday prayers were held, that Arabic was compulsory, and that the school organized a pilgrimage to Mecca.[29] Of course, at one time, prayers were obligatory in all English schools, only they were of the

Anglican sort. And one doubts that a visit to the Holy Land from a Church of England school—or perhaps even a Jewish one?—would raise outcries, or even eyebrows, although whether state funds were used could be a problem. And certainly teaching Latin—also the basis for an old faith—would not have raised the outcries that teaching Arabic did.

The upshot from the Birmingham uproar was that, if there was no conspiracy, some conservative Muslim leaders were indeed trying to make some schools more "Islamic." The incident also pointed to a breakdown in school governance, attributable in part to the Department of Education's pressure on schools to convert to academy status and the tendency to keep silent when Islam is involved.[30] But the matter showed that the boundaries between legitimate and illegitimate introduction of religious elements into a school were unclear. Some commentators suggested that if certain Birmingham schools just declared themselves "faith schools," then all would be fine, which suggested that the issue was more one of improper classification than encouraging extremism.

Nor is the problem just Islam, although it was convenient to present the matter as about Islamic extremism. As columnist Catherine Bennett observed in the *Guardian*, after recounting the criticisms of the Birmingham Muslim schools:

> It is difficult, for example, to conceive of a school more openly rejecting of Britain's predominantly secular culture than the Cardinal Vaughan comprehensive in Kensington, London, where 99.7% of the pupils are Catholic, the principal activity is "the apostolic mission of the Church" and "the teachings of Christ permeate all areas"—unless it is the Yesodey Hatorah Senior girls' school, a state-funded institution serving the Orthodox Jewish Charedi community in Stamford Hill in London. An Ofsted inspection in 2006 noted: "The Charedi community do not have access to television, the internet or other media. All members of the community aim to lead modest lives governed by the codes of Torah observance." It was marked grade one, "an outstandingly effective school."[31]

Furthermore, some of the issues cross faith lines. Evolution is reportedly dismissed in some Muslim and in some Evangelical schools.

The reactions raise the possibility that British Muslims who hold conservative views could be considered ineligible to serve on school committees—effectively relegating them to second-class citizenship. Education Secretary Gove said that state-supported school governors should be limited to those who hold "British values," which he defined as "democracy, the rule of law, individual liberty and mutual respect and tolerance of those with different faiths and beliefs." As stated, one could hardly object, but the Muslim Council of Britain warned that this would mean that conservative Muslims could be prevented from acting as governors.[32] That this worry has merit is supported by the 2014 survey cited in chapter 1: When asked to determine whether someone was “truly British,” 74 percent of British residents said you had to be born in Britain, and 24 percent said you needed to be Christian.[33]

Here we see the broader problem, namely, that Muslims, Jews, and other non-Christian religions may very well enjoy something close to formal equality with various forms of Christianity—the queen’s role as head of the Church of England notwithstanding—but they are not equally British, much less English.

Is Shariʿa Bad for Women?

Various grounds are sought for why Muslims still need to prove themselves. Often they concern the status of women. One small organization that has been highly active in framing public discussion of shariʿa councils in Britain, One Law for All, makes this argument: “We demand an end to all Shariʿa courts and religious tribunals on the basis that they work against and not for equality and human rights.”[34] Its most prominent spokeswomen are Iranian-born Maryam Namazie, who is also a spokeswoman for the Council of Ex-Muslims of Britain and is active in the Worker-Communist Party of Iran, and solicitor Charlotte Proudman, who has worked closely with Baroness Caroline Cox in her efforts to pass a bill limiting shariʿa councils.[35]

Multiculturalism, Shariʿa Councils, and the Taliban

One line of attack is that multiculturalism creates shariʿa and segregation, thereby promoting the denigration of women. Shariʿa councils are but one bit of evidence amassed to support this thesis. A striking representation of the argument was done in dance by the physical theater dance company DV8, which performed its composition *Can We Talk about This?* at London’s National Theatre in March 2012. For eighty minutes each evening, the dancers moved energetically while speaking texts culled from interviews. Juxtaposed were cruelties carried out by Muslims, at home or abroad, and weak-kneed responses by British leaders. Passing in review were the murder of Theo van Gogh, the Rushdie affair, honor killings, and forced marriages.

Among the many personages there were good guys: victims, oppressed Muslims or former Muslims, and the few courageous English people willing to speak up. And there were bad guys: weak English people, whose lily-livered natures were effectively dramatized by wishy-washy dance movements, but mainly Muslims: foul-mouthed, chanting, scary ones. This cartoonish representation of the current social world would be laughed off the page were it to be published in a reputable newspaper. And most of the content was very old news. But at the National Theatre, it met with enthusiastic applause.

The evening came with a large-format program that reproduced newspaper stories on many of the events covered in the performance. The director led off with a foreword in which he set out the play's political thesis: British multiculturalist policies, albeit well intentioned, had sanctioned gender inequality for Muslims, and had led well-meaning Britons to turn a blind eye to abuses committed by and often against Muslims. More concretely, "these same policies [had] also allowed 85 Shariʿa Councils to operate within Britain." The director then asked, "Why does Britain sanction a parallel quasi-legal system that doesn't offer Muslim women the same rights it confers on non-Muslim women?"[36] Opposite the foreword was a story from the *Daily Telegraph*, published at the time of the 2001 Bradford riots, vindicating Ray Honeyford for his 1985 warnings about the dangers of ethnic segregation in Bradford's schools, and a 2010 *Guardian* column by Keenan Malik headlined "Multiculturalism undermines diversity."

The linkages are clear: state multiculturalism leads to discrimination against Muslim women by "sanctioning" shariʿa councils—the number 85 is, as always, without foundation, but sounds scary—and creates a mind-set in which politicians are too frightened to confront real problems among Muslims at home and in South Asia. The problem with this thesis is that there is precious little evidence for it. So bare was the cupboard of British cases that the play cited as its main shameful instance of state multiculturalism the statement of a *German* woman judge who would not grant a divorce to a Muslim woman who complained of wife-beating, on grounds that Islam allowed it. Full stop of story in the play; in real life, the entire German legal and political establishment rose up as one to denounce the foolish judge. This inconvenient fact was, of course, not part of the play's narrative, and so what in real life was an instance of good sense prevailing was misleadingly used here to show how lily-livered the West had become.[37]

The BBC Exposé

One Law for All also argues that shariʿa councils promote domestic violence. On April 22, 2013, the BBC broadcast, under its Panorama format, an exposé on shariʿa councils centered on the Islamic Shariʿa Council in Leyton, London.[38] The program featured "undercover" reporting in the form of a woman pretending to be the victim of domestic violence speaking with the council's secretary general, Suhaib Hasan, and, in a separate session, with his wife at her home. It also aired interviews with women users of this and other shariʿa councils and with Suhaib. Baroness Cox is shown complaining of a "parallel legal system" in Britain. The two experts are Charlotte Proudman, introduced as a solicitor trying to help one of the women in Leeds (but who is the baroness's source of information on shariʿa councils), and Nazir Afzal, a Crown prosecution officer who condemns the advice given to women not to go to the police.[39]

In one scene, a couple appears before Suhaib. The filming seems to be open. They disagree over whether there was abuse and over whether the man was a good husband. Suhaib tells them to wait a month and then return. They only had a religious marriage. Reporter Jane Corbin comments: "another month; it's been a year already, and Leyton shariʿa council still isn't granting this woman a divorce . . . places like this control the lives of many Muslim women in Britain today." Suhaib then explains to Corbin that they are there to mediate and then give something the women cannot get elsewhere. He commented to me the following week that "in the first case in the Panorama program, they suggested we were forcing the wife back to a violent husband. In fact, they had been separated for a long time. I said that she would have to wait for one more month because we would take up her case one month later."[40]

Then the exposé goes undercover, with dramatic music. Suhaib meets the fictive client and says she should go to the police "if he starts hitting you, punching you, of course you have to report it to the police; that is not allowed," but also that "the police, that is the very, very last resort." Mrs. Hasan is approached for counseling and asks if the wife "tries to dress up and get ready" for her husband when he comes home from work. She also urges her to try "not the police but your in-laws," as "family life is going to break" if the police are called in. "The family is better," she stresses. When asked overtly later on, someone at the council (perhaps Suhaib) says that the police may have to be called but "that can be a step with irrevocable consequences."

So what did we hear? First, some excruciating questions from Mrs. Hasan about the wife's cooking and "did she have makeup?" Her daughter, Khola, later said that she was very angry with her mum at the old-fashioned way she talked with the undercover reporter about "making yourself pretty" and the like. She also said that the reporter had asked to meet with her mum, saying that she wanted to keep the marriage together. Such interviews with Mrs. Hasan are unusual. We also heard Suhaib, Mrs. Hasan, and perhaps others at the ISC say that if the husband was hitting the wife, she should call the police, but that otherwise it would be better to first try to involve family, and that calling the police would have "irrevocable consequences."

The Crown prosecutor, Nazir Afzal, saw these comments as meaning that the women "are deterred from seeking help and support." That does not seem to be a correct gloss on the recorded comments, which were: if you want to keep the marriage together, try family first, unless serious violence is involved, and in that case call the police. If the council's (and Khola's own) version of events is correct, the undercover reporter had prefaced the wife's requests to Suhaib and later to Mrs. Hasan by saying that she did not want a divorce and did not want to get her husband in trouble. Suhaib's comment: "The Crown Prosecution Service officer, he can say that people should go to the police, but he has no right to say we may not mediate; it is in the Qur'an that we do that, so let him discuss domestic violence, but it is not his place to tell me about Muslim personal law [he tapped his finger on the table to emphasize that; he was angry]."[41]

Issues of journalistic integrity and skillful editing aside, even the comments chosen by Corbin for inclusion in the program point to a certain cultural backwardness but do not support the accusations that the council condones violence, prevents women from seeking help against it, or intervenes in child custody matters—and nowhere in the case files and sessions I have studied have there been instances of what the council is accused of here.

Conservative Islam

The cultural content that makes the BBC program effective as an exposé are Mrs. Hasan's comments about what a wife should do. These expose a social conservatism and an acceptance of traditional gender roles. A similar critique of conservative practices is voiced by the author of an excellent study of Islamic social movements in Britain, Innes Bowen, in which she contrasts conservative Muslims' refusal to shake hands to the Aga Khan's cosmopolitanism in serving wine at table. She warns that "Deobandi Britain" increasingly looks like Afghanistan in its separation of men and women, and wonders if Tony Blair knew that "the rules enforced by law in Afghanistan were being adopted, voluntarily, in parts of Leicester, Dewsbury and Blackburn?" She concludes that "Illiberal Islam is thoroughly British these days."[42]

Counterposed throughout the BBC exposé and in other commentaries are two kinds of Muslims. Liberal or "moderate" Muslims fit in by adapting to English behavior and by embracing what are claimed to be modern British ideas about gender roles (freely mixing, equality)—regardless of whether non-Muslim British people in fact do behave in this way. Conservative Muslims, by contrast, don't shake hands, live by themselves in Leicester or Dewsbury, and might promote extremism. Shariʿa councils and Muslim schools have become the major objects of broad British fears about domestic Islam. Both seem to cross boundaries in a way that threatens the unity of Britain, or of England. The councils and schools are seen as perpetuating the segregation of Muslims from others, and in promoting conservative, or extremist, religious views. Moral boundaries are in question, at a time when many are unsure where the proper lines should be drawn separating religious matters from public matters, and how religious values ought to, if at all, shape public life.

CHAPTER 12

Internal Debates and Practical Convergences

IN CHAPTER 11 WE ENCOUNTERED BROAD BRITISH CONCERNS ABOUT MUSLIMS who promote conservative religious views. In March 2015, Home Secretary Theresa May conjoined disparate fears when she traced terrorism to Muslim extremists who "reject our values." Her examples of extremism included "the Trojan Horse plot to take over state schools in Birmingham"—recall that the Trojan horse letter was a hoax—religious schools, Tower Hamlets corruption, hate speakers invited to British universities, gender segregation, and the use of shariʿa law to discriminate against women.[1] She targeted shariʿa councils for investigation. In July, Prime Minister David Cameron echoed her speech, linking segregation, extremism, and shariʿa councils.[2]

British politicians and media generally frame these issues in similar ways, as a conflict between "British values" and "Islamic extremism." British values include democracy, toleration, and equality—praiseworthy ideals that nonetheless hardly sum up everyday life in a Britain where racism and gender discrimination are far from resolved. No one quotes racist e-mails or anti-Semitic jeers at soccer matches or wage inequality for women and men as examples of "British values." The values are aspirations, not descriptors of real life in Britain.

Fair enough, but when turning to "Islamic extremism," politicians search for the damning instance—what would be the counterpart to the racist e-mail. They create an assemblage of anecdotes: a homophobic phrase uttered at a mosque, Tower Hamlets cronyism involving the East London Mosque, gender-segregated seating at a university event, and jihadi recruiting. It is a mixed bag that groups conservative practices (often regarding gender), literalist views of scripture, and diatribes against evolution—all quite susceptible to criticism but neither unique to Islam nor against the law—with anti-Semitic attacks, "honor killings," and departures to fight in Syria. Rarely raised is the question of whether there could be a place in Britain for conservative Muslims. That question would be unpopular, as it would force one to also ask whether there is a place for other conservative people whose views are scripture-based and do not fit the liberal, British-values mold.

The real debate over Islam in Britain is taking place elsewhere, among Muslims. A flourishing of liberal cultural activists square off against their conservative opponents—less often meeting face-to-face than issuing competing appeals on the Internet or in meeting halls. The liberal British Muslim

TV—whose slogan is "Confidently Muslim, Comfortably British"—challenges conservative positions presented on the Islam Channel. The 2014 *Happy British Muslims* video was immediately countered by niqab-covered women admonishing Muslims not to sin.[3] Many other British Muslims are engaged in practical reasoning on issues of marriage, gender relations, work, economics, and science in a British social and knowledge context. They see it as important to reason in Islamic ways toward solutions that will work for Muslims in Britain. Indeed, we have seen shariʿa council scholars doing precisely this in their efforts to have their procedures converge with those of the civil courts and fit with the realities of British social and economic life. Conservative Muslims are engaged in adapting to Britain from Islamic starting points that also find acceptability in Deoband or Riyadh. Other Muslims, liberal or progressive, challenge those starting points but find Islamic scholarly antecedents in the traditions of al-Andalus or in Sufism.

Attending to these debates among Muslims not only avoids lumping together disparate elements into a notion of "Islamic extremism," it also gives us a finer-grained view of what the issues are. Even my use of "liberal" and "conservative" labels can misleadingly imply two coherent orientations, each based on some mixture of social habits and doctrinal conviction. It should surprise no one who has read this far that things are not this simple. Muslims (like everyone else) hold a wide range of views on any matter, many think in largely secular terms, and among those who might think of themselves as devout or practicing, there is a wide array of views and interpretations available to them. These internal debates provide a useful purchase on the range of responses by British Muslims to the challenges of adaptation.[4]

Here I draw on several disputes among Muslims that involve efforts to find "practical convergences," whereby different starting points can be retained and some harmonization of practices achieved. In the examples that follow, I trace the conditions under which convergence can succeed—in part by examining instances of stark failure. Practical convergence allows Muslims and others to preserve what they see as intrinsically valuable evaluative frameworks even as they inflect practices toward a common horizon. I contrast it with demands that Muslims renounce positions seen by others as incompatible with modern, liberal British values. Practical convergence can, I argue, offer a better way forward than demanding explicit agreement on contested social issues.

Liberal Marriage, Conservative Muslims

My main example involves an attempt to translate the terms of an Islamic marriage into a liberal framework. The distance across these frameworks may seem to be very small indeed: two distinct ways of formulating the "felicity conditions" for an Islamic marriage. The approach we have already examined seeks through slight "reasonable accommodations" to retain an evaluative framework that is more broadly acceptable to Muslims but adapts to British social conditions. It refrains from making those small steps explicit. The approach we will consider now explicitly resituates the basis for marriage in that liberal English framework, and outside the broader Islamic legal traditions.

Why would this issue be important? Accusations against Muslims of insufficient integration into Western societies often center on marriage: failure to register marriages, marrying children through coercion or before they reach an appropriate age, and divorcing without giving sufficient protection to wives. Individual rights are stacked up against the coercive force of a religious tradition. (We should recall that similar confrontations run through the recent history of Western societies: the impossibility of divorce within the Catholic Church, state law preventing no-fault divorce, second-class political and economic status for women, and bans on practices of contraception and abortion.)

In Islamic legal traditions and in English law, marriage is considered to be a contract between two freely choosing individuals—but not only that. Islamic ideas about the free consent of the parties can converge on, and nearly meet, liberal English ideas about marriage as a contract. But neither set of ideas tells the whole story. On the English side, minimal age and mandatory monogamy constrain choice, and the birth of children further constrains the parents' behavior. Divorce settlements must conform to ideas about fairness, and these ideas change with shifting societal ideas about responsibility and equality. Divorce usually requires a waiting period. On the Islamic side, the bride's guardian must consent to the marriage and, as we have seen, there are multiple ideas about how divorce can be accomplished. There are also varied and shifting ideas about child custody and a fair division of assets. In most Muslim-majority countries, these issues have been settled by statutes.

In Britain, efforts have been made to move both English and Islamic ideas closer to a liberal idea of marriage as a quasi-contractual union between two independent individuals ("quasi" because of the considerations of public interest mentioned above). It is easier to divorce today under English law than it was fifty years ago, and prenuptial contractual arrangements are gradually beginning to be entertained by courts. On the Islamic side, calls are routinely made for women to insist that the "delegated divorce" be included in their marriage contract, giving them the right to initiate a talaq.

One issue is registration of a religious marriage, or nikah, as a civil marriage. Most knowledgeable observers claim that marriages are less and less likely to be registered, although there are no firm data on the matter. We have already considered some of the reasons why a couple might have a nikah but not register the marriage. Some carry out the nikah so as to have sex or live together with the approval of their family, friends, and God, without yet having to commit to legal marriage. Some say that divorce is long and messy, so avoiding civil marriage is rational. In chapter 8 we encountered a case where the wife's parents, who were also the uncle and aunt of the husband, said they were very glad the couple had not registered the marriage because it was thereby easier to end.

But the case for Muslims to register their marriages is strong. Shariʿa council scholars usually agree on the importance of the legal safeguards it provides. A woman who was not legally married may appeal to a court for maintenance for her children, but if there are no children, she is not in a strong position to claim property or payments. Cohabitation carries few rights. As family law scholar Mavis Maclean put it, "there is no common-law marriage; there is a *myth* of common-law marriage." If the couple has a house, the husband is more likely to have put it in his name. In Birmingham, Amra Bone routinely asks women why they did not register, and most often they simply say that they did not get around to it.

The widely shared sense that inertia is probably the major cause of nonregistration—rather than domestic strategy or anti-British sentiment—has led many to wonder what steps could be taken to increase registration. One common suggestion is that more mosques apply for registrar status. In England, three religions—Church of England, Jews, and Quakers—have "celebrant status," meaning that a religious officer in good standing may perform a legal marriage regardless of where it is held—in a religious building, a community hall, or in a home.[5] (Church of England rules require that their vicars perform them in churches.) Becoming a religious officer in one of those three faiths automatically makes you eligible to perform marriages. For other faiths, the government registrar renders official a marriage performed at a registered place of worship; couples must go to the local marriage registrar and sign a form. However, the registrar may delegate his role to someone at a religious building that has been recognized as a place where legal marriages may be performed. After a trial period where a registry official comes to, say, a mosque, an officer of that mosque may become empowered to oversee the registration, acting as the registrar's deputy. Registration usually consists of the couple signing the government registry right after their religious ceremony. Such is routinely done at some mosques. The Birmingham Central Mosque, for example, does so, and their policy forbids mosque officers to perform nikah without registering the marriage immediately. The Leyton mosque also registers marriages.

Not all mosques wish to have this status of registrar. Two reasons are frequently mentioned. First, if a mosque registers a marriage, they thereby certify that the couple has the right to marry, that neither is already married, for example. The East London Mosque gave up its registrar status because of the legal burden of gathering this information. Second, most nikahs are not conducted in a mosque—I have heard estimates that 80 percent of marriages are conducted elsewhere, usually in the home. Would even fewer Muslims marry in a mosque if they knew that the marriage would automatically be civil as well as religious? Possibly so. Certainly the (relatively small but possibly growing) number of second, polygamous marriages could not be registered.

And yet expanding the availability of registering marriages, perhaps by extending "celebrant status" to Muslims and to members of other faiths, as does Scotland, could enhance women's legal rights within an Islamic religious context. Registration offers the possibility of a practical convergence onto a solution that retains Islamic frameworks and also improves women's property rights.

The Model Muslim Marriage Contract

Another proposal takes the opposite approach, by renouncing elements of Islamic marriage rules in favor of an explicitly liberal model of marriage. In August 2008, the Muslim Institute published a "model Muslim marriage contract" that claimed to improve women's rights while remaining within the rules of Islamic marriage.[6] The model contract was designed to "protect the rights of both parties to a nikah (non-registry marriage)." It requires detailed listing of any and all payments and gifts made pursuant to the marriage, to prevent the kind of confusion about mahr and gifts that we discussed in chapter 10. It also requires that, should the couple be unable to resolve differences through informal mediation, they go to a "reputable UK-based Shariʿah panel/body/council whose decision shall be morally binding on both parties." The contract was endorsed by a number of bodies, including the Muslim Law (Shariʿa) Council in West London, and a Muslim professionals' circle in West London, City Circle. Usama Hasan, Suhaib Hasan's son, was then director of City Circle and urged them to do so. "Perhaps I should not have done so," he said in light of the debates that were to follow.[7] The Muslim Council of Britain endorsed it (but later withdrew their endorsement).

At first glance the document seems to be a needed effort to get rights and responsibilities down on paper, reserving a role for the shariʿa councils. This last clause is not surprising, given that the author was the ISC scholar Mufti Barkatullah. And yet the ISC rejected it (as did a number of other bodies), largely over three issues: guardians, witnesses, and the talaq. In each case the issue was the contract's explicit departure from Islamic scripture.

First, although Islamic marriage requires the assent of a guardian, the contract states that "The parental or guardian's legal role finishes when children reach adulthood. Thereafter their role is optional and complementary." The clause explicitly erases the normative responsibility of a daughter to her father, and vice versa. Usama explains why his father rejected this clause but why he supported it: "The contract guarantees that a woman can choose her husband without her parents' permission and without the presence of a guardian (*wali*). My father has gone so far as to say that the local imam, for example, could serve as wali but there must be a wali, following a sound (*sahih*) hadith, recorded by Bukhari, that a woman cannot marry without a wali and that if she does so the marriage is invalid. But the Hanafis, unlike the other schools, never accepted the idea that a specific hadith trumps a general principle of the Qur'an, and in this case the general principle is that marriage involves free choice."

The second issue was witnesses, who must be Muslim men or twice the number of women. The contract allows men and women, Muslims and non-Muslims, to count equally as witnesses. "The purpose for requiring witnesses is that the marriage must be public," Usama explained, "hence hadiths about the beating of drums [to publicize the marriage]. Malikis do not insist on having witnesses as long as it is public. And Ibn Rushd argued that a non-Muslim may be a judge because it is a matter of technical knowledge."

Usama's sister, Khola, clarified where the issue lay: "The reaction was strong because these two issues [guardians and witnesses] are both in the Qur'an; my father said that this was as if you were giving up on the Qur'an."[8] It was the explicit abandoning of Qur'anic requirements in the name of free choice and gender equality that shocked the Islamic Shari'a Council scholars, even if in practice they stretched their rules in the direction of these new clauses.

A third issue regarded the husband's right to divorce. The contract says, "Neither party will end this contract unilaterally without recourse to arbitration/reconciliation by an independent Muslim professional body." This provision cancels a basic element of Islamic divorce law, namely, the right of the husband to unilaterally divorce his wife.

The Muslim marriage contract explicitly renounces Islamic rules and substitutes new rules that explicitly mirror English marriage rules, as if shari'a was not already perfect. As the Leyton council put it in their reply to the Muslim Institute, "Marriages have been taking place for centuries according to Shari'a guidelines and it is unacceptable to claim earlier generations were marrying according to a faulty system which we have now to put right. Nor is it feasible to posit our time as so drastically different to earlier times as needing a wholesale reform."[9]

The contract was a failure because it required Muslims to give up elements of their tradition. Often minorities are asked to explicitly renounce seemingly illiberal components of their tradition—demands that one sees less often made of Christians, for example, to publicly accept homosexual sex or abortion. Muslims, however, are screened for cultural acceptability in various countries, and are asked to abjure elements of Islam that are seen as keeping them on the wrong side of a particularly salient moral boundary. Dutch politicians demand that Muslims provide a clear answer on tolerance of gays; French Muslims are asked to sign a charter that makes explicit their loyalty to the Constitution; poll-takers across countries frequently ask Muslims to compare how important their religion and their country are to them, as if it were a zero-sum game. There are legitimate reasons for Muslims and others to refuse such acts of explicit renunciation of their own evaluative frameworks.

An alternative process of adaptation involves practical convergences of Islam with broad societal norms and expectations. These can involve pragmatic forms of reasoning from a socially desirable outcome back to an acceptable justification. Let me return to the Islamic Shariʿa Council to explore how this can work. One example has to do with the talaq. As we saw in chapter 4, a long-standing debate in Islam concerns a husband's pronouncement of three talaqs all at once, usually called the "triple talaq." Suhaib Hasan brought up this issue during one early conversation when I asked whether conflicts among legal schools ever arose on the council. He gave the "triple talaq" question as an example:[10]

> All four legal schools say that three talaqs at once count as three. But we start from the interest of the parties involved, and then because in the Prophet's time and thereafter the practice was to consider the three as only one, and because Ibn Taymiyyah supports this view, so we have a prestigious scholar to cite, we say it is only one, and there was no disagreement among us on that issue. The other shariʿa councils follow the Hanafi legal school and so consider the three talaqs together to count as three. I remember one case, where the woman was caught between us and her father, who wanted to follow the Hanafi school and so did not recognize her marriage to her husband after he had issued the triple talaq, even though we had given her a statement that it only counted as one. That was what led us to issue a fatwa on the matter; some of us urge that we only give a fatwa when someone comes to us with their individual case.

Now, in this case, Suhaib can say that they base their opinion on practices in the prophet Muhammad's time, but he first refers to the interests of the couple, which are that the marriage should not be unduly disrupted by an angry pronouncement. The case he then mentions, which gave rise to their fatwa, illustrates the point that the best interests of couples are served by interpreting the "triple talaq" as only one. Citing Ibn Taymiyyah (1263–1328) is practically useful, because no one sees him as soft on matters of fiqh, but this is a citation drawn on after their judgment has been made.

On other topics, the same scholars have sought solutions in Hanafi jurisprudence. For example, a Hanafi ruling makes it possible to argue that a civil marriage also constitutes an Islamic marriage, and this ruling makes life easier for Muslims who do not choose to have a separate nikah—and obviates the need to have a guardian present. As Suhaib justified this position, the civil marriage has the essential Islamic features built into it:

> There is an *ijab-kabul* [offer and acceptance] by both parties, and even if the amount of the dower is not set, it then automatically becomes the usual one for the economic status of the parents . . . The only problem that arises is that the consent of the guardian is not required at a civil marriage. The Ahl al-Hadith does require the explicit consent of the guardian. However, the Hanafi school says that if the couple elopes, the wife's guardian can invalidate the marriage only if the woman is marrying someone of lower status or the dower is too low. If he does not do this within a reasonable time, then the marriage is valid. Under that understanding, at a civil marriage, because the parents are there, the civil marriage is Islamically valid. We decided that we would follow the Hanafi school in this matter and recognize the civil marriage.[11]

In the civil marriage case, the scholars follow the Hanafi legal school, and yet in the triple talaq case, they follow Ibn Taymiyyah against the Hanafi and other legal schools, doing in practice something close to what the creators of the Muslim marriage contract had in mind. Suhaib's reasoning is pragmatic: choose a goal and then cite the appropriate justification. Here the goals are indicated by the social benefit of a cooling-off period for divorce, and that of recognizing a civil marriage as meeting the goals of Islam. Note that here we have a Salafi scholar arguing for a flexible, adaptive approach to thinking through Islamic marriage in Britain, and that labeling this reasoning as "conservative" tells us very little about motives, choice of sources, or social outcomes.

Most reforms of Islamic divorce law carried out by countries with Islamic legal systems have sought to preserve local Islamic understandings but to place conditions on their exercise: men have the right to divorce their wives, but only with a judge's permission; daughters need their fathers' consent to marry, but fathers cannot compel their daughters to marry. In this sense the ISC is doing something very much like what legal reformers have done in Indonesia, Morocco, and elsewhere, that is, preserve the space between religious authorities and legal authorities that allows for trading concepts across different registers, different understandings of law.[12]

Distinct Rationales, Practical Convergence

Scholars may justify their selection from the Islamic repertoire on socially pragmatic grounds: this interpretation will lead to the desired result, this other possible interpretation will not; so we choose the former. But at the same time, the council emphasizes that "the Sacred Law" does not itself change. They oppose those who would innovate in matters settled by revelation. In doing so, they seek to maintain their credibility with those Muslims in England and in Pakistan, or elsewhere, who attack this and other councils as illegitimate and as likely to water down shariʿa. The council thus finds itself publicly upholding a strict orthodoxy while simultaneously finding ways to draw from Islamic texts in such a way as to resolve practical difficulties.

This form of practical reasoning could expand the areas where English law is seen as having Islamic effects. As we have seen, both Suhaib Hasan at the London council and Amra Bone in Birmingham argue that if a husband does not contest a civil divorce, then the couple is also divorced in the eyes of God, what I called the theory of "couple's performativity" in chapter 6. Mufti Barkatullah would like civil courts to provide a form that would obviate the need to come to the shariʿa councils at all: "When they divorce in court they could tick a box where they agree to also be divorced Islamically. Then the husband would be giving the talaq, and they would not have to come to us; it would reduce our load. This would mean that the legal system recognizes that we have values, we are not just robots. Otherwise it is as if we are."

Apart from the above specific issues—allowing marriages without a wali, permitting non-Muslims to act as witnesses, and requiring that the husband declare grounds for talaq before issuing a certificate—the ISC practices (and those ideas and practices followed by many other Muslim figures) do converge on English legal and cultural ideas on four dimensions. First, both see marriage as an agreement between two parties, freely arrived at. Second, when a marriage is faltering, steps should be taken to mediate, either to preserve the marriage or to allow the parties to come to an agreement. Third, when a marriage fails, it should be ended, and both parties be supported in getting on with their lives, including giving the proof of religious divorce they may need—a principle already in English law through the 2002 Divorce (Religious Marriages) Act. Finally, agreements made at the time of marriage should be respected, and the reasonable expectations of the parties be the basis for a settlement—as is basic to contract law in English and Islamic law. As the comparative study of religion-based tribunals conducted by Gillian Douglas and her colleagues concludes, "For the Shariʿa Council, the focus is on determining whether the marriage is no longer workable, and there is a mandatory mediation stage prior to a ruling being given to see if the marriage can be saved. It could be said that the Shariʿa Council has a view of the process closest to the basis of current English divorce law as both focus on whether the marriage has 'irretrievably broken down.'"[13]

Convergence works best, I think, when each party can retain its own evaluative framework and find pathways for convergence: here those pathways include rethinking how one infers the intent of the husband and how one interprets the role of guardian or wali. A pluralism of frameworks can lead to convergence on the performative value of a single act, such as the husband's failure to contest a civil divorce—which can be seen in English law and in Islamic law as sufficient for a judge or council scholar to dissolve a marriage. Here is a case where discussions among Muslims have been inflected by broader frameworks of individual freedoms and rights: the most workable solution may be a practical convergence wherein scholars retain a normative reference to Islamic jurisprudence while guaranteeing those rights.[14]

Usama Hasan's Tribulations

But achieving this practical convergence is neither self-evident nor easy. We will stay with Suhaib Hasan's family to illustrate the travails associated with adapting Islamic thinking to a new context. I trace two efforts by Suhaib's son Usama to reconcile scripture with positions on two very distinct issues: men's treatment of their wives and the theory of evolution. One example is encouraging; the second is a clear failure. The examples also show us that the fault lines among Muslims do not come from a simple tension between liberal and conservative theologies but also involve socially conservative habits of thinking.

In many respects the Hasan lineage exhibits remarkable continuity. Suhaib's father, Abdul-Ghaffar Hasan (1913–2007), was an important scholar and teacher who taught in India and then moved to Pakistan at partition. He was best known for his knowledge of hadith. He was a leader in the Jamaat-e-Islami until 1957, when he split with the movement's leader, Abul Aʿla Maududi, over strategy. Hasan favored focusing on educating the masses; Maududi, although hardly against education, favored an electoral strategy. Hasan taught in Faislabad and Karachi until 1964, when the Islamic University of Medina hired him to replace the internationally recognized hadith scholar Muhammad Nasiruddin al-Albani, and to continue his Salafi line of scholarship and teaching.

According to Suhaib, his father's chain of knowledge in hadith (his *isnād*) reached back to al-Shawkani (1759–1834), a famous hadith scholar in Yemen, and to Bukhari (810–870), one of the preeminent collectors of hadith.[15] Abdul-Ghaffar Hasan's own father and grandfather had also been scholars of hadith: Suhaib has translated a 1905 work by his great grandfather that attacked the observance of the Prophet's birthday, the Mawlid, which has been a key topic of disagreement with Sufis. Usama was raised in a lineage of religious scholarship: "Both my parents were from Delhi, and their fathers and grandfathers were experts in hadith. My grandfather forbade the tele, and when he came to visit from there and I was seven, we had to hide the tele for the month while he was here."[16]

If Suhaib's father traveled and taught between Pakistan and Saudi Arabia, Suhaib himself journeyed farther afield: after Medina he went to Kenya and then to Britain, where he obtained a doctoral degree from the University of Birmingham in hadith studies. Suhaib's wife, mentioned in chapter 11, does a live call-in show on Iqra', with calls from women and men but mainly about women's concerns—"they are all polite and respectful," she told me. Their children have pursued diverse careers around the globe. Usama obtained degrees at Cambridge, King's, and Imperial in physics, mathematics, and electrical engineering, and is a fellow of the Royal Astronomical Society. Suhaib's daughter, Khola, has a master's in international and comparative law from SOAS (formally known as the School of Oriental and African Studies), University of London. One son is a pilot; another is a biomedical researcher in Portland; other children live in Kuala Lumpur and Kansas City. Some have married people from other backgrounds. Usama and Khola have continued their parents' work on Islam. Usama translated one of his grandfather's works.

Usama and Khola grew up as Salafi and, in contrast to stereotypes of Salafis as rigid, see their background as facilitating progressive and contextual thinking, as liberating them from the trap of traditionalist thinking. In a posting in which she complained about the narrow-mindedness of certain British self-styled Salafis, Khola writes:

> Salafi blood runs in my veins and is embedded in my psyche. I see the wisdom of its insistence on a close contact with the Qur'an and Sunnah. I know the importance of avoiding innovations and heresy in worship in order to keep the faith pure. I acknowledge the necessity of showing respect to 1,400 years of scholarship and intellectual thought. We cannot isolate the Qur'an from its historical context nor from the audience who were the first to hear it. It is precisely this Sunnah that tells us to separate the cultural context of Arabia from the mandatory rules on an Islamic life. Our faith has survived and prospered because generations of Muslims had the confidence and ability to interpret and adapt the framework of Scripture into their particular context. They looked beyond the superficial outward trappings of rules to the inner core of Islam, and they transmitted this beauty through the ages. But today I feel ashamed to call myself a salafi because of the arrogance, judgementalism, and lack of tolerance of these people.[17]

Usama followed closely in his father's footsteps at the same time that he pursued an elite education in the sciences. He studied Qur'an and hadith, and joined his father in the Salafi organization called JIMAS (Jamiat Ihyaa Minhaaj al-Sunnah [Movement of the Revival of the Prophet's Way]). JIMAS was founded in Britain in 1984. By the early 1990s it was led by Munawar Ali, known as Abu Muntasir, who came from Dhaka (Bangladesh). Usama said, "He read through literature here and decided to follow [the] Qur'an and Sunna only, and refused the legal schools. He came to the Leyton mosque, and my father was very happy that he came to that position on his own. For fifteen to twenty years the mosque was the base for JIMAS, and my father their senior sheikh."[18] As Usama remembered it, in the mid-1990s, the JIMAS leadership was composed of about fifteen people, including some converts, such as A. Green and A. Baker. Then, as it expanded, people branched off to form new movements. "Or they no longer had the time. We had weekly study circles then [*halaqa*]; I could not do that anymore [he was thirty-eight in 2010]. . . . Then Abu Muntasir went back to Leicester and led the Masjid al-Taqwa, a Salafi mosque, and did local work. Many people became more liberal. The hard-line Salafis formed Salafi Publications in Birmingham. There was a split over jihadi issues. The Birmingham people said that only a khalif could declare jihad. A number of us tasted a bit of jihad. I was in Afghanistan in December 1990. I was nineteen and still at Cambridge. A shell landed right near us from the Soviets. I got to shoot off guns: quite exciting, but we realized how close the shell came!"[19]

Daraba and Domestic Violence

By 2011, Usama positioned himself as "a post-Salafi, to start from Salafi tradition and work from it." He favors an approach through the *maqāsid ash-sharīʿa*, the overall objectives of God's revelations:

> It's the way everything must go; it is based on the fiqh of the Prophet's companions [the *sahabat*].[20] The Qur'an was taken by the Salafis to be a guide, not to be law. The caliph Umar suspended the penalties for theft, cutting off the hand, because the conditions were not appropriate, and Ibn Taymiyyah said better that the Tatar Muslims drink so they will not cause damage. The Qur'an's rules were a great progress over what was there before: women may serve as witnesses but count half as much as men, whereas before their word would not have been heard; they have one-half the inheritance of a male when before they had nothing. The verses on slavery are a good case: they lifted the status of slaves to human beings.[21]

Usama has tried to reframe the debate on gender and domestic violence. In keeping with his appeal to the maqāsid approach, he cites the Tunisian scholar Muhammad Al-Tahir Ibn Ashur (d. 1973):

> We need to change for gender equality especially. For example, the daraba verse: Ibn Ashur wrote that at the time the verse was given, a smack would have been accepted, including by the wife, but now the state is entitled to punish a husband who does that. Now, he was a traditionalist, although it is also true that he had to say certain things to keep the state happy. And the problem is that this implies abrogation of the verse; it is easier for the

Salafis than for the traditionalists to move toward accepting maqāsid because they are used to thinking in a rational way in the tradition.[22]

The verse in question is often called the "daraba verse" for its use of the verbal root *daraba*, usually translated as "to hit, beat." In chapter 9 we saw how the Hijaz speakers at a domestic violence meeting sought to play down the severity of what was meant by "to beat" and how they failed utterly to win over their listeners. Part of the verse (Q. 4:34) in question, as translated by Abdullah Yusuf Ali (the translation also used by Usama) is as follows:

> On whose part ye fear
> Disloyalty and ill-conduct,
> Admonish them (first),
> (Next), refuse to share their beds,
> (And last), beat them (lightly);
> But if they return to obedience,
> Seek not against them
> Means (of annoyance):
> For God is Most High,
> Great (above you all).

Usama's approach to this verse showcases his capacity to remain within a recognized Islamic jurisprudential framework and yet deliver a message that converges on mainstream English claims—not necessarily practice—about how men should treat their wives. Rather than arguing that the verb means something other than "to beat"—one apologetic move made by many contemporary Western Muslim writers—or declaring the verse to be superseded (the other Western move), Usama argues that reading from the Qur'an to the hadith shows a divine movement toward softening a man's treatment of his wife. The Prophet showed how to treat wives, and his is the example we should follow. In his writing, he cites other examples of this "gradualist" approach in the scriptures and by later jurists. Tellingly, although in keeping with his own intellectual lineage, Usama relies on the modern Salafi scholar al-Albani to argue that hadiths cited in support of wife-beating are weak in their transmission and those condemning it are sound.

This "post-Salafi" approach contrasts sharply with those adopted by other prominent British Muslims who have moved across different movements and positions as they have grown up, attended university, and moved into adulthood in Britain. Ed Hussain's (2009) story is the best-known: beginning in a Sufi family in Brick Lane, he joined a series of movements in school and university, ending with the separatist Hizb ut-Tahrir, until he developed what he considers liberal positions. Usama's trajectory is different because of the depth of his engagement in two streams of practice: a high-level education in science and mathematics and a deep engagement in the Islamic traditions. He remained active in the Leyton mosque until 2011, and served as sermon-giver in rotation with his father and Haitham al-Haddad. He also has taught at the Cambridge Muslim College, set up to teach Dar al-ʿUlum graduates (Dewsbury) about the real world: he taught science, astronomy, and global ethics in an eighteen-month diploma course.

In this case, Usama works to arrive at a set of practices from an Islamic argument grounded in Salafi scholarship. He does not start from a secular principle, but reasons within the tradition of Islamic jurisprudence, even if the result does not persuade everyone. It represents a convergence with Western ideas about violence that are now broadly accepted in England. But other efforts turn to danger, as with a dispute over evolution that led to a rift in the Leyton mosque, and death threats against Usama.

Darwin and Death Threats

During the time that Usama remained active at his mosque, he was publicly taking stands that were far from accepted by those in attendance. In a 2008 commentary in the *Guardian*, he argued that Muslims needed to accept evolution and that evolution was compatible with Islam.[23] As with the instance of the daraba verse, he based his argument on scripture.

Of the many who posted comments, the vast majority scoffed at the idea that religion should even be discussed together with science. But at the Leyton mosque (properly called the Masjid Tawhid), in January 2011 a visiting Saudi scholar answered a question by saying that Muslims could not pray behind someone who believed in evolution. Later that month, Usama was shouted down while giving a lecture to clarify his position; the debate came down to "did we descend from apes?"[24]

Immediately thereafter, Suhaib defended his son, giving a version of creation wherein "God breathed spirit into Adam," but that the creation of Adam from clay "took some evolutionary process." He drew the analogy to the gestation of Jesus, also created from breath, with the expression "Kun fayakūn" ("'Be!,' and it was"). But there, too, he said, there was a process in the womb. What happened, whether there was physical evolution, is a matter of interpretation, he said. He denounced the opinion that prayer behind Usama would not be valid.[25]

We can see Suhaib's effort as intended to sketch out a practical convergence: from far-apart starting points, these conservative Muslims and those accepting science could arrive at more than a simple modus vivendi, rather a consensus on the potential fit between evolution and divine creation. Similar convergences underpin the teaching of evolutionary biology in some, but far from all, conservative Christian and Muslim schools throughout the world.[26]

But the effort ran into strong opposition. A leaflet was distributed by "Islamic Awakening" that declared Usama an infidel. In February 2011 a group of the mosque's trustees ousted him from his role as imam. His father denounced this attempt as illegal. In March, Usama issued a partial retraction of his earlier statements, limited to saying that he did not believe that Adam and Eve had parents. He told me that he was trying to remain at the mosque to fight for a more open discussion of science. But by July he had been receiving death threats for several months and could no longer visit the mosque. He had stopped giving sermons and so had Haitham al-Haddad, "just to balance things off. One of these guys could put a knife in my side; five guys who were my friends issued these calls against me."[27] At that time I asked him about his position on evolution, and he replied, "I believe that the soul was progressively developed through evolutionary processes and that the outcome of those processes was Adam. . . . The position that humans have a special status within evolution is a cop-out for Muslims. Many are against evolution altogether."

That March I met with Suhaib at the ISC, and he brought up the dispute: "We had some trouble here . . . Usama has given talks about evolution and many have complained. I disagree with him, but he says, 'I am the scientist.'" He gave his version of the controversy: a scholar from Riyadh who knows Suhaib well had visited him at Leyton and then traveled to Birmingham, where someone asked him what he thought of people who believed the Darwinian theory. "Infidels" was the essence of his answer. There was a follow-up: "And what if you are praying behind someone who believes in Darwin; are your prayers valid?" He answered no, they were not. That claim led to the petition.

Suhaib continued the account:

> And then some people here in January 14 passed out pamphlets with this fatwa before prayer. About twenty people left the mosque, but the place was still packed. But now half the trustees want to throw Usama out of the mosque; they have done that. But we have the same number of people as do they, six, so they cannot do that. And the Charity Commission has ruled that he has to be able to explain his position. And now he has retracted the statements that Adam and Eve have parents. Because yes, perhaps there was evolution, that things found from 30,000 years ago do not exist today, and that does not mean that Adam had parents, because no one has found a link between a hominid just before Adam, and then Adam. They say that Adam's grave is in Sri Lanka and Eve's was found in Jeddah, but no one has found their parents' graves, right?

Here he paused and asked me, "What do you think?" I answered, waffling, "Yes, you can believe both." He continued, "So they should have taken Usama back, because he retracted the statement." He was very saddened by the events.

About a year later Usama and I talked again, and he explained that efforts at mediation were to involve Haitham al-Haddad and al-Dubayan (head of the London Central Mosque).[28] But by mid-2012 the mediation had stalled. In June the Charity Commission launched an inquiry into past associations of "terrorists" with the mosque, which because of the timing was treated by the press as "Mosque near Olympics site in 'terror link' investigation." Although Haitham's lectures were mentioned, links to Abu Qatada in 1998 and to Anwar al-Awlaki in 2003 (who at that time spoke widely in Britain and in the United States) were at the core of the criticism.[29] Neither the inquiry, nor threats to go to court, nor the work of a paid arbiter led to anything, and in the end, the Charity Commission, which has authority over the mosque, imposed a settlement by which no one directly involved in the dispute could be an officer of the mosque.[30] Usama had by then joined the Quilliam Foundation, an organization focused on combatting Islamic radicalism. This move cost him dearly in allegiance from other Muslims, some of whom have said to me that they see Quilliam's leaders as interested only in themselves.

Usama (and Suhaib) failed to convince the relatively conservative attendees of the Leyton mosque. In the meantime, Usama's sister, Khola, has adopted a less visible profile by writing a paper on the genetic dangers of cousin marriage and, after the Panorama broadcast (chapter 11), by taking up a new role at the mosque. Her effort is to try and translate the workings and ideas of the council in ways that can be easily understood by a wider public. Her cousin marriage book has been well received by government and academics but not by the community, who think she is "airing dirty linen" and that it is a minor problem. In Walthamstow the municipal council used it for a program in the schools. Khola sees herself as conservative in religious matters and indeed as a Salafi, for their focus on the scriptural texts. But she is unhappy with tendencies of Muslims to preserve unnecessary barriers to the wider society. "The shariʿa councils and burqas are perhaps symptomatic of something that worries me, that some Muslims are saying they don't want to be part of British society. With the hijab, it is different; if I go into a pub like this, I have done that in Ireland, and a few people glanced at me, 'Oh, she's different,' and then it was fine. But those who wear the burqa, it just cuts off communication."[31]

Usama and Khola do not stand for an entire generation of Muslims. The new generation of British Muslims is highly diverse, composed of people identifying as Salafi, Sufi, secular, academic, and working-class.[32] Usama, Khola, and many of the other younger British Muslims profiled here—Saba at the Birmingham council, the "sisters" working with Faiz ul-Aqtab Siddiqi in Nuneaton—are perhaps representative of a narrower band of young British Muslims. They all are trying to engage with shariʿa and with England, and at the same time with the anxieties of mediating between an older immigrant generation and the wider world of English society. Their goal is to carve out a workable place for Muslims, including conservative ones, in a British public sphere.

Beyond "Translation"

How do we characterize their efforts in the broader context of contemporary theory? The examples just discussed point toward substantive issues of gender equality in marriage and divorce, the authority of science, and, more generally, the respective claims made on citizens by religious conviction, state law, and the dominant terms of public debate in any one country.

The most influential attempts to arrive at broad normative positions on these issues grew out of studies of political deliberation in liberal democratic societies. Best identified with Jürgen Habermas but also influenced by the efforts of John Rawls to come to terms with pluralism, this work focuses on how, in the political arena, to construct equivalence relations between religious justifications ("God said so") and those presumed to be accessible to all ("it preserves life"). Habermas argues that when citizens bring religious reasons to public debates, they and others share a responsibility for translating those reasons into "generally accessible arguments."[33]

These positions are not antireligious. Habermas, in particular, affirms the importance of religious reasoning in the "informal public sphere," that is, outside the domain of political institutions, on two grounds. First, he makes the "functional" claim that religious arguments make valuable contributions to public discussions, especially concerning issues of meaning and identity. Second, he argues that one cannot pull out religious belief from the ways religious citizens form and justify their positions. Belief is not just "content" but a source of energy that "nurtures his or her entire life." The first ground means that nonbelieving citizens should, for their own interest, participate in the process of translating religious reasons into generally acceptable ones. The second ground means that nonbelieving citizens "must grasp their conflict with religious opinions as a *reasonably expected disagreement*."[34]

Habermas makes his argument with respect to justifications of the sort citizens might advance in debates over public policy: about abortion restrictions, or taxation, or foreign policy. It is relatively easy to imagine citizens arriving at these "translations," even if they have derived the same-sounding justification from different sources. Citizens might oppose abortion on grounds that one should not kill, but one might derive that position from Catholic teachings, from the Qur'an, or from a moral stand that has no explicitly religious derivation. Framing the problem as one of translation implies that the issue concerns propositions about the world that can be detached from distinct social and evaluative frameworks. It then appears as if the issue is neither epistemic nor social but one of pure form: by *p*, the Muslims mean *q*, and that is also what the Calvinists mean by *r*.

But the issues that arouse dispute and debate in Britain about Muslims are not of this order. They concern entire ways of organizing life, where gender relations, ways of dress, patterns of socializing, ideas about education and faith, artistic practices, and pronouncements about marriage and divorce coexist in varyingly weighted combinations—something more like a culture or a way of life than a cognitive stance. They concern how distinct orientations can coexist, whether the incommensurability that some perceive between them does not render one intolerable to the other—whether, for example, gender asymmetry renders conservative Islam unacceptable for some secularists, or unregulated sexuality makes secularism unacceptable to some Muslims.

These arguments take place in media of various kinds—in Habermas's terms, they have to do with the informal public sphere rather than the political arena. Often these diverse ways of speaking, anchored in local community practices and ways of life, become flattened onto a single evaluative grid when unearthed and "exposed" in media reportage.[35] The BBC Panorama exposé of the Leyton shariʿa council is a good example of this flattening. These arguments may bear on questions of policy—as in discussions about the right of schools to discriminate by gender or by faith. More commonly, anxieties about social and moral incommensurability and about practices deemed "un-British" motivate ministerial investigations or tabloid denunciations. Recall when Birmingham schools were criticized for a number of teaching practices that concerned Islam. Whether or not particular practices violated English law or school regulations was almost an afterthought. The scare-headlines, the credence in the "Trojan horse" letter, and the general moral panic that ensued were motivated by fears that Muslims were imposing a conservative Islamic agenda incompatible with British values.

At issue in these debates and fears is not rescuing the valuable cognitive or moral content from religious propositions for purposes of political deliberation, as Habermas says; it is assessing how far religious groups may deviate from a proclaimed British way of life when they take active part in the informal public sphere, in university discussions, school assemblies, or on shariʿa councils. When does "conservative" become "extreme," if the latter term has any fixable meaning at all?

Habermas also has views about the requirements for citizenship in Western countries. He requires three "epistemic stances," two of which seem to close off the debate rather early. One stance demands that everyone recognize the "institutionalized monopoly of modern scientific experts"; another concerns the "universalism of modern law and morality." For Habermas, these are among the "cognitive challenges of modernity" and the requirements for citizenship.[36] And yet these matters are far from settled, as citizens in many countries, and not only in Europe, ask: What are the rights to full cultural citizenship of people who accept neither of these stances?

Let me switch the lens and return to arguments internal to a religious tradition that can lead to convergence with a broadly held stance. Put in terms of this book, can and do Muslims derive broadly British, or what Habermas would call modern, stances from within the Islamic tradition? Note the resemblance, and yet also the gulf, between practical convergence and what Habermas posits when he says, "Only the participants and their religious organizations can resolve the question of whether a 'modernized' faith is still the 'true' faith."[37] Finding points of convergence across religious or secular orientations is quite different from positing a modernized version of each religion.

Working toward shared outcomes requires practices of derivation and justification, which are processes of reasoning, carried out in public ways. Focusing on these takes us away from the assumption that secular ways of thinking are rational and religious ones are only defectively so because they are grounded in revelation. Both ways of thinking can involve highly developed processes of inference and argumentation—and both have starting points that must be posited—the social contract, the moment of revelation. One could make a further argument to the effect that agreement on public reason in the political public forum is a kind of social compact, the converse of which is that citizens have the right to engage in restricted conversations in the informal public sphere.[38]

In political theory circles, an approach superficially similar to that proposed here is also referred to as "convergence." However, this "convergence interpretation" of public justification or public reason in political theory is different from what I speak of as practical convergence. The former is a loosening of the requirement in the "standard model" associated with Rawls concerning the need for consensus in the political domain, to allow for diverse views as to why a measure would be legitimate, as long as everyone agrees on this range of reasons as "reasonable," a key word for followers of Rawls. This sense of convergence concerns the range of public political debates that should be accepted by theorists as legitimate and thus capable of justifying the state's legal coercion.[39]

By contrast, "practical convergence" as used here refers to instances of reasoning toward a shared horizon from distinct starting points, studied as an empirical phenomenon. The main examples here have to do with substantive conceptions of gender equality and procedural conceptions of fairness. I would also argue that attesting to these processes of reasoning toward a shared horizon has a normative component, in that we can see them as positive instances of adaptation to a British context. An example from an Islamic-law country may help. Indonesian judicial rules and practices preserve the formal gender asymmetry in shariʿa that we have studied in earlier chapters of this book: for example, men have the power to divorce, whereas women must ask a judge to dissolve their marriage. But Indonesian legal rules and practices require that both men and women approach a court in order to divorce, and that they prove one or more of the same grounds for divorce. Thus, the formal asymmetry is preserved but substantively equal possibilities for divorce are achieved. The complete divorce picture is far from symmetric, in that postdivorce payments differ for men and women (as has been the case for most of recent Western history); the example is apposite but partial.

Our empirical findings concerning such arguments, their standing within the tradition, and their practical outcomes should have an impact on normative theory. If one can arrive at a shared set of practices from distinct and incommensurable starting points, then the rationale for demanding explicit translation weakens. Indeed, insisting on explicit propositional equivalency between starting statements and translated ones not only preformats the field of acceptable responses in a way that privileges some over others, it also hinders efforts to preserve distinct starting points. Universal, secular propositions no longer bear the trace of their derivation from scripture; they cannot. Such propositions thereby lose legitimacy for some practitioners of the tradition. This outcome is, I believe, deleterious for encouraging shared social lives, the sense that, in the specific terms of this study, one can be fully British and fully Muslim.

CHAPTER 13

Conclusions

THIS BOOK DESCRIBES A PROGRESSION, ITSELF ICONIC OF AN ARGUMENT. IT begins with the many ways in which British Muslims are concentrated: in their origins, their ethnic and doctrinal identifications, their British neighborhoods, and their institutions. These concentrations within British locations, ironically, support continued longings and travels outward: transnational gazes back to the authentic origins of a Sufi religious order in Pakistan, or to the cousins in Mirpur whose closeness and cooperation will require new cousin marriages, or to the Deobandi school in India whose century-old curriculum subtends claims to authenticity in new British surrounds. Concentrations in Britain facilitate collective and institutional nostalgias and conservatisms.

The idea that urban concentrations can have broad-scale social effects is of long date in urban sociology and geography; notable are reflections in the United States on what William Julius Wilson called "concentration effects" in inner cities, where the success of some in leaving the ghetto removed the very exemplars of economic stability that had made their aspirations possible.[1] The British Muslim concentration effects we have examined here are of a different sort. Concentration of people with similar pasts, old-country anchors, and theological tendencies makes it possible to draw rings around one's own group, and to build bridges back home without sensing a need to do so with those next door. Indeed, the strength of the multiple South Asian genealogies allows the hardening of oppositions within Leicester, or Bradford, or, on a different register, when Bangladeshi partisans of secular or Islamic politics compete in London's Tower Hamlets. Few incentives push people to construct new forms of justification when the old ones have a guaranteed audience, one that has been brought over from Gujarat or Lahore and is regularly replenished through transcontinental marriage.

But even if some Islamic public actors have seen little reason to move away from established modes of reasoning and practice, and the very welcoming soil of Britain has encouraged them to reproduce older forms, doing so in a new context has inevitably led to social transformations, all the more as the new contexts shift in response to these efforts. The East London Mosque developed its particular broad portfolio of services because its leaders sought to create and hold on to a position in a very particular socioecological niche, one defined by Bangladeshi politics, by local demands for social as well as religious services, and by the willingness of British parties and councils to work with religious associations. The diacritic defining of Barelvis versus Deobandis hardens and simplifies in the British climate, in which the long-established South Asian Sufi orders have a reduced capacity to bring together Muslims of a wide variety of backgrounds. In Leicester, or Bradford, Islamic diversity seems reduced to a conflict between two types of mosques—until one looks under the surface at the subtle continuation of crosscutting ties, such as Sufi genealogies among Deobandi school graduates.

The same point applies to the major institution studied here, the shariʿa councils. They are not replicas of anything existing today or yesterday in South Asia but an effort to create, on the basis of remembered social forms but in a new social context, mechanisms to respond to British Muslims' demands. Furthermore, the social contexts that infect these forms are multiple and recursive.

Thus, histories matter: different colonial policies, different immigration possibilities, and a less fractious South Asian Islamic landscape would likely have meant different British Islamic institutions today. And institutions matter: despite their doctrinal agreement, the rhythm and tone of hearings and discussions are quite different at the London and Birmingham shariʿa councils. In the one, we see judges moving along a court-like flowchart and debating among themselves about how best to interpret and apply shariʿa in England. In the other, we find women grounded in social work and medicine setting out to resolve problems, even if, as sidebars, doctrinal issues and differences emerge. Hijaz at Nuneaton showcases a completely different type of institution, whose marriage-dissolution activities are a sideline for building up a saintly dominion.

But we have also seen that individuals matter. Haitham al-Haddad strongly shapes the direction of debates at the Islamic Shariʿa Council; without his presence, the institution would—and may—take on a much more South Asian character in its legal and social references, and even in the language of deliberation. In Birmingham, Dr. Mohammad Naseem put a strongly idiosyncratic stamp on shariʿa council proceedings and judgments, and Amra Bone applied this approach and supplied a distinctive tone. And, above all, one can hardly imagine Hijaz without the barrister-cum-saint personality of Sheikh Faiz ul-Aqtab Siddiqi.

Implicit in this progression has been the contrast with other countries of Western Europe, particularly with France. The spatial concentrations characteristic of British Muslims contrast with the French experience in terms of the internal cohesiveness of the former, and the relative disarray of the latter. Immigrants to France faced formidable legal obstacles to creating local-level associations until 1981, and they did not settle in the sort of narrow-banded regional, ethnic, and religious patterns that we have seen for Britain. French Muslims from North Africa also enjoy broad-based agreement on a Maliki school and a relatively "objectives-oriented" approach. West African Sufi orders and Turkish mosques exist outside, and not in opposition to, the largely North African public sphere of French Islamic discourse.

British Muslims also enjoyed the greater receptivity of British lawmakers to religion-based institutional projects, whether schools, banks, or religious tribunals. French Muslims continue to face legal, social, and political impediments to constructing associations that might be construed as contesting secularity or creating religious enclaves. Furthermore, North Africans moving to France took with them ideas and habits about civil law forged in colonial experience and reinforced by postcolonial judicial reform, particularly in Tunisia, from where most major heads of French Islamic institutes originate. They assumed that marriage and divorce were public things, not contractual, and were matters for statutes and the judiciary. These ideas converged with French expectations, because they added up to a shared acknowledgment of the supremacy of state law. "In Tunisia when you are divorced, you are divorced, period," said one leading Islamic actor to me in Paris.[2] Little room here in French secularist terms or in North African Islamic ones for shariʿa councils.

So far, the particularity of British shariʿa councils seems to be due to the particularity of the broader British Islamic experience. But does this mean that these councils tell us nothing about a broader world of Islamic institutions and experiences? I think that the opposite is true: some of the basic features of Islamic jurisprudence become particularly salient in Britain because of the absence of state mechanisms to smooth over disputes and prevent foundational anxieties.[3]

If there is no state-mandated jurisprudence, then a wide variety of opinions can surface. The plurality of interpretation characteristic of shariʿa appears in the form of the seemingly never-ending debates among scholars to whom we listened in London and Birmingham. Even as they discussed particular cases, they were also discussing the relative importance of sources and methods. How far can scholars justify judgments on the basis of anything but the opinion of a legal school? What bearing should the customs and practices of Pakistan or Saudi Arabia, the objectives of shariʿa, or the intentions of God have on any particular case? On what basis does the state or a judge declare a law or a ruling to be Islamic? Here we have scholars ruling as judges in a world of states and laws, but outside the domain of any state that claims to be Islamic, and that has legislated answers to these questions.

But, of course, British Muslims do very much live in a state, and in a cultural climate, that challenges their suitability to be recognized as cultural citizens, as British, though perhaps never to be English. Shifting and undetermined are the terms of that challenge: Renounce shariʿa? Recast their Islam in a liberal form? Or develop multiple pathways—the root meaning of shariʿa—from the sources of Islam toward living together in an inclusive Britain?

Glossary

Ahl al-Hadith (People of the Hadith): scholars who follow Qur'an and hadith (as opposed to following one madhhab)

Ahl al-Sunnah wal-Jamaah (People of the Path and of the Community): a phrase sometimes used by Sufis or others to distinguish themselves from other Sunni orientations, particularly reformist groups such as Deobandis and Ahl al-Hadith

ʿālim (pl. *ʿulamāʾ*): scholar of Islam

Barelvi: a Sufi orientation or movement; the name derives from the scholar Ahmad Riza Khan Barelvi (1856–1921), from the town of Bareilly in Uttar Pradesh

biraderi: extended kin group in Pakistan or the diaspora

dar ul-qaza: nonstate tribunal (in South Asia)

Dar al-ʿUlum: a Deobandi school

Deoband: the school founded in 1867 in the north-central Indian town of Deoband, and others created in its mold

dharar: harm, damage

darurah (*darūra*): emergency, used to justify granting an exception to a rule

faskh: annulment or judicial dissolution of an Islamic marriage

fiqh: Islamic jurisprudence, the result of human interpretation of sacred texts

fiqh al-aqalliyāt: fiqh applicable to Muslims living as a minority in a state

fuqaha (*fuqahāʾ*): jurists

halal: permitted, lawful

ʿidda: waiting period between divorce and remarriage

ʿilla: God's reason (for a revelation)

Jamaat-e-Islami (JI): movement founded in 1941 by Abu Aʿla Maududi (1903–79) *khula* (*khulʿ*): divorce initiated by the wife and involving a payment from her to the husband; judicial dissolution

madhhab (pl. *madhāhib*): legal schools within Islam; the main Sunni schools are the Hanafi, Maliki, Shafiʿi, and Hanbali

mahr: marriage gift from groom to bride

maqāsid ash-sharīʿa: the overall objectives of God's revelations

maslaha: welfare

nikah: Islamic marriage

niyyah: intention

nushuz: disobedience

pir: spiritual guide, saint

qadi: Islamic judge

shariʿa (*sharīʿa, shariah*): moral or legal code, God's way or plan for humans

sheikh (shaykh): spiritual guide

Sunni: category including the majority of Muslims

Shiʾi: Muslim minority historically professing allegiance to descendants of ʿAli

Tablighi Jamaʿat: Islamic movement founded by Maulana Muhammad Ilyas (1885–1944), devoted to traveling and teaching

tafrīq: judicial divorce at the wife's request; in practice equivalent to faskh

talaq (*talāq*): divorce pronounced by the husband

talāq al-tafwīz: right to divorce delegated to the wife

tariqa: the Sufi path, a Sufi order

tasawwuf: Sufi practices of meditation and remembrance

ulama (*ʿulamāʾ*): scholars of Islam (pl. of *ʿālim*)

ʿurf: custom

wali: guardian, especially of a woman at nikah

Notes

Chapter 1
Why Shariʿa in Britain?

1. The 1997 report (Conway 1997) was followed in 2013 by a reassessment of the new post-2001 and post-2005 challenges (Alexander et al. 2013).

2. For a sweeping study of transformations in the meanings and uses of shariʿa, see Hallaq (2009), and for the diversity of contemporary shariʿa practices in the sense of legal practices, see Amanat and Griffel (2007).

3. Regarding regions, and in a more lighthearted way, it evokes the incoherence of how sports teams are constituted—an England and Wales cricket board, four British (and no United Kingdom) football associations, sometimes a football team for the Summer Olympics playing as "Great Britain," and uncertainty regarding rugby. And Scotland? Even the Scot most prominent in the 2014 effort to keep his natal land in the United Kingdom, Gordon Brown, called Britain "four nations in one state" (Gordon Brown, "Why Scotland should stick with Britain," *New York Times*, September 7, 2012, Sunday Review, 4). On this geographical theme, see Colley (2014).

4. "British attitudes harden towards immigrants," *Guardian*, June 17, 2014, http://www.theguardian.com/uk-news/2014/jun/17/immigration-british-attitudes-harden-benefits.

5. Locke (1983 [1685]) is the primary text for tolerating dissenting Protestants. See, among many other works, Colley (2009), Henriques (1961), and, on the broader topic of religious toleration in the West, Zagorin (2003).

6. The very well-informed and rightly praised (including by me) journalist Innes Bowen—no relation—sounds the alarm about conservative Islam in these terms. She warns that "Deobandi Britain" increasingly looks like Afghanistan in its separation of men and women, and wonders if Tony Blair knew that "the rules enforced by law in Afghanistan were being adopted, voluntarily, in parts of Leicester, Dewsbury and Blackburn?" She concludes that "Illiberal Islam is thoroughly British these days" ("British mosques aren't that moderate after all," *Spectator*, June 14, 2014, http://www.spectator.co.uk/features/9230671/who-runs-our-mosques/).

7. Wind-Cowie and Thomas Gregory (2011, 41).

8. Gallup Center for Muslim Studies (2009) and Pew Research Global Attitudes Project (2006).

9. See Bowen (2007, 2009).

10. See the contrast between Innes Bowen's (2014) findings for Britain and those by Ihsan Bagby (2012) for the United States.

11. On education and Islamic adaptations in France, see Bowen (2009); on piety and knowledge in France and Germany, see Jouilli (2015); and in France, see Fernando (2014).

12. In doing so, we also take account of patterns of integration in Britian, but do not reason directly from British political philosophy or national models to today's institutions. Among excellent studies of national models or philosophies, see Fetzer and Soper (2004) on church-state relations and Favell (2001) on citizenship. On the quite different approach to comparison favored here, in which the particular characteristics of institutions figure more prominently, see Bowen et al. (2014).

13. I will refer to particular literature in the course of the book, but as this paragraph suggests, the burgeoning literature on endogenous change within historical institutionalism, such as Mahoney and Thelen (2010), could benefit from the quite new ethnography of institutional adjustments and improvisations.

14. On fourteenth-century Morocco, see Powers (1994); for two quite different but very insightful views of Egyptian judges, scholars, and muftis, see Agrama (2012) and Dupret (2000). Compare how I examine uses of shariʿa in Indonesia in Bowen (2013).

Chapter 2
Transplanting Ties

1. The standard historical account of Muslim migration from South Asia to Britain is Ansari (2004), and see Gilliat-Ray (2010, 3–53) and the more ethnographic accounts by Esteves (2011), Gardner (1995, 35–64), Shaw (2000), and Werbner (1990).

2. See Bleich (2003) on race relations, with a useful contrast between Britain and France.

3. See Spencer (2007) on the Blair period.

4. On Iranian communities in Britain, see Spellman (2004); for an overall account of British Muslims, with special attention to the history and diversity of communities, see the excellent overview by Gilliat-Ray (2010).

5. By early 2015, attacks on Ahmadis had spread from Pakistan to Britain. See Jerome Taylor, "Hardliners call for deaths of Surrey Muslims," *Independent*, January 6, 2015, http://www.independent.co.uk/news/uk/home-news/hardliners-call-for-deaths-of-surrey-muslims-2112268.html.

6. The figures are taken from the Office of National Statistics (2011).

7. Communities and Local Government (2009, 25).

8. Shaw (2000, 27–30); see also Charsley (2013).

9. UK Office for National Statistics, 2011, Census data, https://docs.google.com/spreadsheet/ccc?key=0AonYZs4MzlZbdFY2LThicTlNSThHNHA5Q2hjUFRyanc#gid=9; Communities and Local Government, 2009.

10. Office for National Statistics, reported in "Where UK immigrants were born, 1951–2011," theguardian.com, December 17, 2013, http://www.theguardian.com/news/datablog/interactive/2013/dec/17/where-uk-immigrants-born-1951-2011-census-ons.

11. Shaw (2000, 14–34); Communities and Local Government (2009).

12. Shaw (2000, 16).

13. Lewis (2007, 46–53).

14. Eade and Garbin (2006, 182) and, more generally for this section, Gardner (1995, 35–43).

15. UK Office for National Statistics, Neighborhood Statistics, http://neighbourhood.statistics.gov.uk/dissemination/LeadTableView.do?adminCompAndTimeId=23808%

3A254&a=7&b=276743&c=London&d=13&r=1&e=13&f=21810&o=198&g=325264&i=1001x1003x1004x1005&l=1809&m=0&s=1428413502945&enc=1&nsjs=true&nsck=false&nssvg=false&nswid=1558.

16. Communities and Local Government (2008, 24).

17. UK Office for National Statistics, 2011 Census data, https://docs.google.com/spreadsheet/ccc?key=0AonYZs4MzlZbdFY2LThicTlNSThHNHA5Q2hjUFRyanc#gid=9; Communities and Local Government (2008).

18. Ibid.

19. On Bradford, see Lewis (2002, 2007) and Bolognani (2007); on segregation, including the quote from Lewis on language, see Goodhart (2011). A statistical analysis of segregation in Bradford (Greaves 2012) found a relatively high dissimilarity index (one measure of segregation) between Pakistani-majority schools and other schools; other analysts find that segregation is either stable or decreasing slightly (Simpson 2003); see Manchester University's analysis of 2011 census data as reported in Jessica Nightingale, "Bradford's population 'now mixing more,'" *Telegraph and Argus*, February 27, 2013, http://www.thetelegraphandargus.co.uk/news/10253190.Bradford_s_population__now_mixing_more/.

20. See Communities and Local Government (2009, 7) for the statistics cited here, and see Joly (1995) on Birmingham mosques and neighborhoods and Greaves (1996) on Sufi mosques. Joly's (1995, 29) characterization of the city is apt: "This population [of Muslim origin] is not homogeneous with regard to its national or ethnic origin, but the various groups have reconstituted dense networks and concomitant economic, social and religious activities, institutions and structures."

21. Office for National Statistics (2011).

22. Werbner (1990).

23. Ansari (2004, 179–81); Lewis (2007, 28).

24. See Poros (2011) for a detailed study of Gujarati migrants to London and New York.

25. See also the detailed analysis of Leicester residential patterns in Open Society Institute (2010), which makes the same argument for Leicester's Muslims more generally.

26. See Peach (2007); Finney and Simpson (2009).

27. Ansari (2004, 212); Goodhart (2011).

28. If Bradford exhibited the first tendency (Lewis 2002, 54–62), Birmingham is perhaps better characterized by the second (Joly 1995, 26–30).

29. The phrase is from Ansari (2004, 343), who provides a historical overview of these processes.

30. As several researchers have pointed out, neighborhood segregation in the UK, probably decreasing, is at a much lower level, however measured, than in the United States, and the term "ghetto" is surely misplaced. See Peach (1996, 2007) and Finney and Simpson (2009). Charsley (2013) emphasizes the multiple bases for identity claims and the dangers in attributing block-like characteristics to a "community." On this point more generally, see Brubaker (2004).

31. Pew Research Center (2011).

32. Peach (2006, 354); Shaw (2001); Ballard (1990, 230).

33. In Sheridan et al. (2013), the authors analyze the "Born in Bradford" study, conducted 2007–11, which found that 37 percent of the marriages of Pakistanis were with first cousins and conclude that "consanguinity was a major risk factor for

congenital anomaly, independent of deprivation, and accounted for almost a third of anomalies in babies of Pakistani origin."

34. See the discussion in Charlsey (2013, 7–12); she also notes the sharp rise in the number of Pakistani spouses granted residency in the UK after 2008.

35. On marriage patterns in the Punjab, see the series of studies by Roger Ballard (1990); the data on Oxford and UK comparisons are from Shaw (2001). For Bangladeshis, Katy Gardner (1995, 122) shows how decisions concerning migration to Britain by Sylhetis have been strongly shaped by processes of household formation and reproduction in Sylhet. A woman living in Sylhet might marry a man who resides in Britain, move into his family home in Sylhet, where she occupies the role of daughter-in-law, and may or may not eventually come to Britain.

36. Shaw (2001, 319); Werbner (1990, 347).

37. Shaw (2001, 324–25; 2006).

38. Shaw (2006).

39. See Shaw and Charsley (2006); Charsley (2013).

40. Shaw (2000, 154).

41. A June 4, 2013, discussion on the web forum Pakilinks, http://www.paklinks.com/gs/life-and-relationships/611520-british-pakistani-girls-marrying-pakistani-guys.html.

42. Reflecting back on his own arranged marriage to a close relative, the noted writer Ziauddin Sardar (2008, 171) writes, "How, I often wonder, could our family have been so prescient, so sure that our differences would provide the enduring strength of our marriage?"

43. In their by now somewhat dated study of marriages among Bradford Pakistanis and Tower Hamlets Bangladeshis, Samad and Eade (2003, 72–76) report a clear generational divide in attitudes toward transcontinental marriage, with older Pakistani and Bangladeshi men and women strongly in favor of such marriages and younger people more skeptical. But they also found that even the youngest married people they interviewed reported that parents decided for them: 57 percent of Pakistanis and 45 percent of Bangladeshis in the sixteen to thirty-four age-group said that their parents determined whom they would marry, without their having a say in the matter (see also Modood et al. 1997, 318).

44. Bolognani (2007).

45. From another point of view, the biraderis can be taxed with promoting parochial, caste-oriented, and backward views and loyalties; see the useful discussion in Lewis (2007, 46–56). My interest here is not in evaluating them but in tracing their conditions of existence.

CHAPTER 3
Islamic Topographies

1. For more on what is meant by "practical schemas," see Bowen et al. (2014).

2. See I. Bowen (2014, 26, 28, and passim) for the parallel Deobandi-heavy environment in Dewsbury, the UK headquarters of the Tablighi Jamaʿat, which is part of the Deobandi world of education. Innes Bowen's book offers a valuable but very different analysis of the many Islamic movements in Britain. On the Madani High

School initial admission's policy, see the 2007 BBC story, "Islamic School Criticised," http://www.bbc.co.uk/leicester/content/articles/2007/10/03/islamic_school_feature.shtml.

3. They belonged in particular to the Chishtiyyah order, but also to Naqshbandiyya, Qadiriyyah, and Suhrawardiyyah orders; see Bashir (2010) on the history of Deobandi Sufism.

4. Van der Veer (1994, 37–43). On the early social and political roles played by Indian Sufi shrines, see Eaton (1978); an excellent collection of articles on specific Indian shrines is Troll (1989). Gottschalk (2000) explores intertwining narratives of Hindu and Muslim pasts in a village context.

5. Much of this section is taken from Metcalf (1982), as reread through the lens of the more recent study of the colonial ʿulamaʾ by Zaman (2007, 17–59).

6. The curriculum was named for its author, Mullah Nizamuddin Sehalvi (d. 1748). In Britain it is used by both Deobandi and Sufi schools, with only minor differences. I have greatly benefited from discussions with Aamir Bashir about Deobandi pedagogy.

7. See Metcalf (1982, 46–86) on this transition in the role of the ʿulamaʾ.

8. On these developments in Uttar Pradesh, see Freitag (1988). For a sweeping view of postcolonial Indian Islam by a major Indian Muslim university figure, see Hasan (1997).

9. Zaman (2007, 25–27).

10. Then, as now, the teachers at Deobandi schools cite as important influences on their approach two scholars in particular: Ahmad Sirhindi (d. 1624) of the Mughal period, and Shah Wali Allah of Delhi (d. 1762), already mentioned, whose mid-nineteenth-century followers were to lead a revival movement across northern India. Both were scholars of tasawwuf as well as of the Hanafi madhhab. See Metcalf (1982) and Bashir (2010).

11. On the Deoband school and the "triangle" of pathways discussed here, see Metcalf (1982); for an analysis of the changing role of ʿulamaʾ in the Deobandi tradition in the twentieth century, see Zaman (2007); on the broader importance of language politics, see Cohn (1996).

12. As exemplified in the writings of Ashraf ʿAli Thanawi (Zaman 2008); see Werbner (2003, 2004) on these developments within transnational Sufi cults.

13. The Tablighi Jamaʿat, or "Society for Conveying the Faith," began in the 1920s when a Deobandi-trained ʿulamaʾ, Maulana Muhammad Ilyas Kandhlawi (1885–1944), urged followers to go out and remind Muslims of their religious obligations, but to refrain from entering into conflict and debates. In 1965 Muhammad Ilyas's great-nephew, Inʾam-ul-Hassan, became the third leader, or amir, and the movement expanded into Europe and North America. In addition, as traders or workers travel, they create a network among themselves. In particular, Gujaratis have spread the Tablighi message from South Asia to Britain through their work-related travel. On the movement, see especially Masud (2000), Sikand (2002), and the recent interviews in I. Bowen (2014).

14. See Reetz (2006) for an analysis of roles played in British Indian public discourse by members of the many maslaks; see Zaman (2012) for an important argument linking internal critique to public exchanges in South Asia and the Middle East.

15. Among the more prominent scholars making these arguments was Ashraf ʿAli Thanawi (d. 1943), in his 1931 publication *Al-Hila al-najiza liʾl-halilat al-ʿajiza*, cited in Zaman (2007, 29–31).

16. On the Bihishti Zewar, see Metcalf (1992); on Ashraf ʿAli Thanawi, see Zaman (2008).

17. Birt and Lewis (2011, 111), and their review of Deobandi movements in Britain more generally.

18. It may be that diasporas often produce more hardened lines of cleavage and conflict than exist in the origin country. When Dar al-ʿUlum graduate Sheikh Riyadh ul Haq had to leave his post as imam at Birmingham Central Mosque amid scandal over personal affairs, he settled in Leicester. But in September 2007, the *Times* carried a news item by Andrew Norfolk accusing Riyadh ul Haq of being the "home-grown cleric who loathes the British," based on quotes attacking Jews and urging Muslims to shun non-Muslims. Whatever the merits of Norfolk's piece, it emphasized the divides among Leicester's Muslim leaders.

19. See Ansari (2004, 354–55) on this mobilization, and Ansari (2004, 360–65) on the (largely unsuccessful) efforts to create national structures in this period.

20. City of Bradford Metropolitan District Council, http://www.bradford.gov.uk/bmdc/government_politics_and_public_administration/about_bradford_council.

21. Lewis (2002, 54–75); on Bradford, see also Lewis (2007), and the many studies of Bradford sponsored by the Joseph Rowntree Foundation available at http://www.jrf.org.uk/publications/browse/category/i#immigration.

22. The association is called the Jamiʿat-i Tabligh al-Islam, or Society for the Preaching of Islam, not to be confused with the completely different Tablighi Jamaʿat, http://www.jrf.org.uk/publications/browse/category/i#immigration; see Lewis (2002, 81–89).

23. On the Central Mosque, see chapter 8; on the Birmingham Ghamkol Sharif mosque and its ties to Pakistan, see Werbner (2003, 30–35, 149–51, 164–65) and Greaves (1996).

24. See Lewis (2002, 102–12) on the links among several institutions that make up a constellation around these schools, including the UK Islamic Mission and the Markfield Foundation.

25. I draw here mainly from Birt and Lewis (2011).

26. Ibid., 108–9.

27. See Peach (1996), who also reports that at the time of the 1991 census, 61 percent of people in Spitalfields ward self-identified as Bangladeshi, and one enumeration-level district within that ward reached 90 percent Bangladeshi. There are also concentrations of Bangladeshis in Oldham and Birmingham (Eade and Garbin 2006).

28. Unless otherwise noted, the following draws mainly from Eade and Garbin (2002, 2006) and from my own observations and interviews in Tower Hamlets in 2003, 2005, and 2013. See also Gest (2010, 71–125).

29. Eade and Garbin (2006, 184).

30. Although the mosque and centers are distinct buildings and perform distinct functions, they form one entity, and I often use "East London Mosque" to refer to the entire complex.

31. With partition and then the independence of Bangladeshi, the JI split into distinct organizations, now usually known (with slightly differing transcriptions) as Jamaat-i-Islami Pakistan, Jamaat-e-Islami Hindi, and Bangladesh Jamaat-e-Islami. On the distinctions, with a focus on the Indian organization, see Ahmad (2009). On the Pakistani JI in Britain, see I. Bowen (2014, 83–99).

32. Indeed, there is by now something of an established narrative genre of "how I became a radical and then found Moderation," the most illuminating of which is Husain (2009).
33. Interview with Abdul Qayum, East London Mosque, April 5, 2013.
34. Interview with Dilowar Hussein Khan, April 24, 2013.
35. For the first view, see Eade and Garbin (2006); for the second, complementary perspective, see Glynn (2002).
36. Andrew Gilligan runs stories to this effect; see, for example, "Lutfur Rahman's Muslim favouritism: The evidence," *Telegraph*, April 3, 2014, http://blogs.telegraph.co.uk/news/andrewgilligan/100266083/lutfur-rahmans-muslim-favouritism-the-evidence/, and, in response, Richard Seymour and Ashok Kumar, "The smear campaign against Lutfur Rahman is an insult to democracy," *Guardian*, May 30, 2014, http://www.theguardian.com/commentisfree/2014/may/30/lutfur-rahman-tower-hamlets-mayor-smear-campaign. On the Respect Party and the IFE, see Peace (2013).
37. Interview with director Mehboob Patel, Gardens of Peace Cemetery, Hainault, May 13, 2013.
38. On British national organizations, see Gilliat-Ray (2010, 108–12, 169–79); I. Bowen (2014, 90–94), and for a comparative view of national-level organizations across Europe, see Laurence (2012).

Chapter 4
Background to the Shariʿa Councils

1. From classic studies of kinship and marriage in Africa, to recognition of different notions of personhood and relationality in Melanesia and Asia, to anthropological and historical examinations of marriage and property in Europe, to studies of assisted reproduction, the study of marriage, kinship, and property has formed the backbone of comparative social anthropology. On the Church, see Goody (1983); for two recent perspectives of these topics in anthropology, see Peletz (1995) on kinship studies and Hirsch and Wardlow (2006) on marriage and romance.
2. On changing forms of marriage and divorce law in the West, see Glendon (1989; the quotation is from page 148).
3. For the following discussion of classical and Ottoman opinions and rulings, I draw from Tucker (2008, 84–132). A succinct analysis of family law on marriage and divorce can be found in Hallaq (2009, 271–86). On the debates in Egypt around family law reform, see Fawzy (2004), and an extensive study of family laws across Arab states is in Welchman (2007). I examine the Indonesian debates and changes in Bowen (2003).
4. The hadith is found in the collection by al-Bukhari: book 68, hadith 22 by one numbering scheme, and vol. 7, book 63, hadith 197 by another. There are many online collections, among them Sunnah.com, http://sunnah.com/bukhari/68/22.
5. On Lebanese courts, see Clarke (2012).
6. On these processes of recognition and rule, see Cohn (1996), Chatterjee (2010), and Galanter (1997); on the Shah Bano case, see Engineer (1987).
7. On Thanawi, see Zaman (2008). In Pakistan, where "Islamization" has largely resulted from the efforts of Western-trained scholars and officials, unofficial

tribunals have proved to be effective ways of regulating marital disputes (and of doing so with greater speed and lower costs), although more recently, Islamic divorces have been "fast-tracked" within the state legal system. On state Islamic tribunals in India and Pakistan, see Redding (2004) and Solanki (2011).

8. On the establishment of the Imarat-i Shariʿa Bihar, see Ghosh (1997), and on the wider array of contemporary councils, or Darul Qazas, see Hussain (2007), Redding (2010), and Lemons (2010). Hussain (2007, 78) says the Bihar Darul Qazas were functioning from 1917 on. The Shariat Application Act of 1937 provides a legal basis for their existence.

9. The JUH joined with the Congress Party in advocating a united India; see Ahmad (2009, 19–22).

10. On the Patna council, see Hussain (2007, 78, 86–91); for the study in Mumbai, see Solanki (2011, 278–81).

11. Nominally the Ahl al-Hadith are grouped together with others calling themselves Salafi, but in Britain (and elsewhere) some Salafi groups keep their distance; the attacks mentioned are featured regularly on the site http://www.salafitalk.net. The smaller the differences are, it seems, the bitterer and louder the attacks.

12. On ad-Darsh, see Wiegers (2011).

13. See al-Rasheed (2005, 171). The Islamic University at Medina and the Imam Muhammad ibn Saud Islamic University in Riyadh train a number of South Asian and British scholars. Their graduates who end up in Britain ally themselves with the Indian Ahl al-Hadith movement, whose scholars also refer to such scholars as Ibn Taymiyyah (d. 1328) and Shah Wali Allah in India (d. 1762).

14. Green Lane subsequently formed its own shariʿa council.

15. My description of the ISC reflects the situation during 2007–14. In April 2015, Haitham left the council. At about the same time, Suhaib Hasan's daughter, Khola, began to meet with clients. See my description of Khola's activities prior to 2015 in chapter 12.

16. See Birt (2005) and al-Rasheed (2005) on Saudi influence in Britain.

17. This and other details about the history of the ISC come from conversations with Suhaib Hasan on February 3, 2010, and April 29, 2013.

18. On the European Council, see Caeiro (2006).

19. See, for example, his article on musical instruments and other articles on the same website: http://www.islam21c.com/islamic-law/162-music-a-prohibited-and-fake-message-of-love-and-peace/. He was the focus of a July 14, 2014, Channel 4 interview concerning reports that he ignored women's accusations of domestic violence: "Does shariʿa allow a man to beat his wife?," with Fatima Manji, http://www.channel4.com/news/does-sharia-allow-a-man-to-beat-his-wife-video.

20. The organization Civitas claimed to have found "85 at least" shariʿa councils in Britain (MacEoin 2009, 69). They reach this number by counting correspondents as constituting separate tribunals. For example, they cite thirteen tribunals within the ISC network. These include Khurram Bashir's house and others in other cities. As we have seen, these are interview settings; the judgments are made in London. Civitas also includes in its count websites that offer fatwas as answers to submitted questions.

21. A report issued by Reading University (Bano 2012b) reported on telephone surveys done with twenty-two shariʿa councils, all but three operating under the

auspices of a mosque, and two of which were Shiʿa. The formal procedures were found to be nearly identical across all the councils, but the report gives little other information.

22. Shahid Raza traces his spiritual lineage through his sheikh, Moulana Syed Mukhtar Ashraf Jilani (1914–96) of Kichaucha, India, who belongs to the Ashrafia branch of the Chishti spiritual order.

23. Interview with Mufti [Abdul Qadir] Barkatullah, London, August 11, 2011.

24. Ibid.

25. Tas (2014).

Chapter 5
Improvising an Institution

1. This paragraph points toward large literatures in sociology and, to a lesser extent, in anthropology about ways to study institutions. "Improvising" brings to mind Goffman (1983) and his critique of overly organizational views of institutions within sociology. Meyer and Rowan (1977) provided a complementary and independent critique of what we might call "formalism" in the study of organizations, but, more importantly for our purposes, and for anthropology more generally, drew attention to the power of what they called "myths" about how a school, a hospital, or (we can extend their list) a shariʿa council ought to function in the standardizing of institutions across places. "Files" bring to mind very recent studies of documents (Latour 2010; Riles 2006) and bureaucracies (Gupta 2012; Hull 2012). For my own approach to institutions in a comparative vein, see Bowen et al. (2014).

2. Latour (2010); Latour's error is to take what he clearly shows to be the rather exceptional procedures of the French State Council to stand for what he calls Law; studying a *juge d'instruction* in a French trial would show processes closer to the science studied by Latour and other anthropologists and sociologists.

3. Among recent works that highlight this issue, Hirsch (1998) writing on Kenya and Terrio (2009) on French juvenile courts nicely juxtapose formal structures and social life; Comaroff and Roberts (1981) remains a touchstone in the field.

4. Hull (2012, 114–15).

5. A case might also begin when a woman contacts a scholar elsewhere in the UK, and in those cases, the initial letters might not make their way into the ISC files, and the initial document is the intake interview conducted by that "extramuros" scholar.

6. I only lightly edit these entries for clarity; ellipses indicate my omissions. I have drawn these first two letters from the ISC archives, taking care to redact them so as to avoid any identifying markers. Letters were sent to the ISC to be read and discussed by a number of scholars, in open sessions with visitors present. I did not tape-record live sessions with clients; my excerpts from sessions are based on written notes, made with the consent of the client. All excerpts from ISC formal deliberations are based on taped recordings, made openly and with the scholars' permission.

7. Forced marriage, though difficult to define and most notably to distinguish from arranged marriage, is one of the hot-button issues in recent British political debates; see a recent *Guardian* "datablog": Sophie Warnes, "How prevalent is forced marriage in the UK?," theguardian.com, July 22, 2014, http://www.theguardian.com/news/

datablog/2014/jul/22/how-prevalent-is-forced-marriage-in-the-uk. For a longer view, see Malik (2010, 73–78).

8. I base these claims on a sample taken from the ISC archives of eighty-five cases decided over the period 2007–10.

9. Sixty-four of the women are British citizens and thirty-five of the men; eighty-three of the women are UK residents, compared to fifty-four of the men.

10. Shaw and Charsley (2006). For these populations taken as a whole, but not for the women who petition for divorce at the ISC, spouses who travel to Britain to marry close kin are as likely to be women as men. It may be that transcontinental marriages with women from Pakistan are more likely to last than is the case for marriages with men from Pakistan, given that the common status asymmetries in the former case (gender roles, educational level, competence in English society) would be congruent, whereas in the latter case the wife would be more likely to have higher educational status and local social competence but to encounter expectations of female submissiveness from her Pakistani-born husband. These noncongruent asymmetries show up frequently in the divorce cases. An ongoing research project on "Marriage, Migration, and Integration" led by Katharine Charsley will doubtless expand our knowledge of these relationships of status and marriage, http://www.bristol.ac.uk/ethnicity/projects/mmi/.

11. Most women mention more than one problem in their marriage, and when there is a letter or interview in the file, a wide range of husband's faults are set out. For this simple tabulation, I chose the initial charge levied by the woman; we should remember that in many—if not most—cases, these charges were difficult to verify; the list relies entirely on the woman's claims.

12. Interview with Aina Khan, London, May 14, 2010.

13. This section comes from an interview with Atif Matin, July 14, 2010.

14. We can look at the files in a different way, starting not with decisions but with opening a file and then asking what became of each case. I compared the "input-output" relation for two samples ten years apart to see if the flow of procedures changed over time. The 1997 sample consists of 38 cases; the 2007 sample has 44 cases. For each sample, I started with a particular file and then examined every subsequent file, whether or not the process led to a decision. This process leaves us with two continuous periods of case filings. Several differences appear between the two samples. The 1997 sample includes 38 files out of a number sequence of 108 numbers, meaning that there were 70 numbers that dropped out of the sequence. These gaps occurred at a time when the files were not entered into a computer database, so it is difficult to ascertain the reasons for the gaps; perhaps a folder was opened in the case of simple inquiries to someone at the council. Of those 38 files, 19 led to decisions being made, 14 of which were the granting of a divorce; in the remaining 5 cases the scholars asked for additional information, which apparently was not provided. What of the remaining 38 files? Often they consist of two sheets of paper, a letter addressed to the council, and a letter from the ISC asking the petitioner to fill out the form. Evidently, in those cases the petitioners decided to go no further, for whatever reason. The 2007 sample includes 44 files out of 55 numbers, and of those 44 files, 34 led to decisions, of which 29 were divorce decrees. So once a file has been opened, it is more likely to lead to a decision in recent years than in the earlier period. Thirty-four of 44 cases begun in 2007 led to decisions, as compared with 19 of

38 cases in 1997. This difference suggests a marked improvement in the steps taken following the initial contact of the office, in record-keeping and follow-up.

15. I discuss this program in chapter 11.

16. As Ziba Mir-Hosseini (2001) showed in her study of a Tehran divorce court, much of what happens in court involves bargaining between the two parties, which never appears in files.

17. Please note that in the dialogue text, I use my initials (JRB) and mostly first names for the other speakers.

18. The delegated divorce clause gives the wife the right to effect a talaq if certain conditions are met. Most scholars and judges say that the judges must ascertain whether or not one of the conditions that trigger the talaq has indeed been met—so in practice, enforcing such a contract can be much like granting a khula. See Tucker (2008, 91–92) and Hallaq (2009, 283, 463).

CHAPTER 6
Unstable Performativity

1. The debate involved other philosophers as well and is well analyzed by Benjamin Lee (1997, 40–65). I draw from it the observation, emphasized by Lee, that "felicity" is not only subjective but also shifting. For an influential account of the broader issues of performativity, see Silverstein (1981).

2. I discuss this issue regarding the French recognition of Islamic state divorces in Morocco in detail in Bowen (2010, 157–78).

3. On the conceptual incompatibility of fiqh and the state, see Hallaq (2009, 357–70), and for an extended case analysis, see Dupret (2000).

4. The UK Foreign and Commonwealth Office will legalize religious divorce certificates. Pakistanis then take those to the Pakistani Consulate, which determines marital status for its citizens. See http://www.chamber-international.com/uploads/files/list-of-documents-fco-can-legalise.pdf.

5. Bokhari, interview, Birmingham, July 10, 2010.

6. Interview, Leyton, January 28, 2010. In his 2010 SOAS doctoral thesis, Haitham al-Haddad makes this point in the course of an analysis of the European Council on Fatwa and Research argument that Muslims living in non-Muslim lands should recognize the right of a non-Muslim judge to terminate their marriage because Muslims have accepted the laws governing the marriage contract when they marry. He argues (2010, 200–201) that they may have felt they needed to register their marriage for other reasons and so cannot be presumed to have given their consent.

7. *Exposing Shariʿa Council*, http://exposingshariacouncil.blogspot.com/. The blog is dated January 23, 2011, and does not appear to have attracted Google friends or blog members (although it did receive six Facebook likes). The blog rehearses the facts I describe about the case, making it a matter of public record.

8. Interview with Khurram Bashir, Birmingham, August 3, 2010. A similar two-stage theory was provided by Amra Bone of the Birmingham council described in chapter 8.

9. On these uncertainties in Islamic jurisprudence, see Hallaq (2009, 191–92, 283–86) and Tucker (2008, 95–100); I provide a simplified version as the ISC scholars

describe it. On the dar ul-qazas, see Redding (2010). But even in countries with positive legal systems that refer to Islam, statutes and jurisprudence coexist with older and sometimes quite divergent interpretations of fiqh, for example, when laws stipulate the divorce only occurs in a court and fiqh gives the husbands the right to effect a divorce with no such condition attached. The conflict there is between positive law and religious normativity, each with its own procedures for interpreting and applying texts; see Bowen (2003).

10. Interview with Maulana Shahid Raza, Wembley, May 2, 2013.

11. In her study of the Ealing council, Shah-Kazemi (2001, 37) confirms that the council considered the husband's refusal to pronounce the talaq to be grounds to declare faskh.

Chapter 7
Competing Justifications

1. Walzer (1983) and see also Boltanski and Thévenot (2006) and Lamont and Thévenot (2000). Walzer set out a line of thinking that continues to shape political theory, where it intersects a distinct line of work about the legitimacy of certain types of justification in public debates, an issue to which we will return in chapter 11 and that refers to Rawls (1999).

2. Looking at justifications provides a new way to read such classics in the ethnomethodological tradition of sociology as Cicourel (1987) and Garfinkel (1964), and to bring them together with such works in the anthropology of disputes as Comaroff and Roberts (1981).

3. For discussions of maslaha and its place in the broader field of Islamic legal reasoning, see Opwis (2007) and Zaman (2004); on current debates see Hallaq (2009, 504–14).

4. Haitham and the other scholars knew of and had approved my recording. I sat at the table with them and the recording device was in full view. On nushuz, see Hallaq (2009, 284–85).

5. Anthropological readers will recall Clifford Geertz's emphasis on haqq in his discussion of Islamic cultures of law, in Geertz (1983). The word can be translated as "truth" or as "right" and "reality." It is one of the names of God. It refers to the "right of God" in the sense of a public right; see Kamali (1993).

6. Khurram misstates the ages here.

7. Haitham's objections at this point remind me of those by the distinguished Syrian scholar Saʿid Ramadān al-Būtī regarding what he saw as simply adjusting shariʿa to Western realities; see Bowen (2010, 146–47) and Hallaq (2009, 511–14).

8. The discussion took place from here on in Arabic. I am indebted to LSE colleagues for help in translating and analyzing.

9. Haitham doubtless refers to the Permanent Committee for Islamic Research and Fatwas (al-Lajnah ad-Daimah lil-Buhuth al-ʿIlmiyyah wal-ifta), a committee of Islamic scholars that issues fatwas and prepares papers for the official Council of Senior Scholars.

10. The Hijri or Islamic year 1370 is about the Gregorian or Western year 1950 CE.

11. Al-Qaradawi has achieved recognition for his advocacy of the "middle way" (*wasatiyya*). Born in 1926 in Egypt, al-Qaradawi studied and taught at Al-Azhar

before moving to Qatar, where he created a faculty of shariʿa. Today he publishes his thoughts in books and (since 1997) on his website and through his contributions to the television station Al-Jazira; he also heads the committee responsible for the site Islam Online (IslamOnline.net). The idea of a fiqh for minorities may have originated in the mid-1990s with the Iraqi scholar Taha Jabir al-Alwani, who directs the School of Islamic and Social Sciences in Leesburg, Virginia, near Washington, DC, and whose book, *Towards a Fiqh for Minorities: Some Basic Reflections*, appeared in Arabic in 2000 and in English in 2003.

12. Al-Qaradawi (2002).

13. For recent discussions of the ideas of general interest and public good, see Opwis (2007) and Zaman (2004).

14. I discuss this trend at length in Bowen (2009).

15. For a discussion of these issues in the work of the Seljuk jurist Imam al-Haramayn al-Juwayni (d. 478/1085), see Rabb (2013).

16. See Bowen (2013).

17. On early modern Moroccan courts, see Powers (1994), and on these debates in contemporary circles, see Hallaq (2009), Opwis (2007), and Zaman (2012).

Chapter 8
When Women Rule in Birmingham

1. Interview with Dr. Mohammad Naseem, Birmingham, August 6, 2010.
2. Interview with Dr. Wageha Syeda, Birmingham, July 13, 2011.
3. Interview with Amra Bone, Birmingham, July 5, 2011.
4. For a recent discussion of debates in India about the triple talaq, see Rohe (2015, 292–308).
5. Jonathan Wynne-Jones, "Sharia: A law unto itself?," *Sunday Telegraph*, August 7, 2011.
6. Interview with Sarfraz Mohammed, Birmingham, April 23, 2013.

Chapter 9
Sufi Encompassments

1. I will use "Hijaz" to refer the entire complex of activities and the locale, and "MAT" for the narrower sphere of mediation and arbitration.
2. See Werbner's (2003) extensive analysis of the notion of "spiritual dominion" (*wilayat*) and more generally the idea of a regional Sufi cult, in Pakistan and in England. On Sufi graves and shrines in South Asia, see Kugle (2007, 47).
3. For more of the background, see Greaves (2000, 125–31).
4. Greaves (2000). In 2010, Judge Shahim Qureshi explained to me that most people still send bodies back to Pakistan for burial. "It's massive. Pakistani International Airways does not charge for the bodies because they get six to eight family members buying seats. They are used to getting calls from travel agents at the last moment asking for seats, and they usually have them." He shipped his own father's body back, as that had been his express wish.

5. Because I have come to know people who have approached Sheikh Siddiqi for advice through the intermediary of his staff, I do not have a scientific sampling of all those who make inquiries.

6. Sheikh Siddiqi himself, initially instructed in the Naqshbandiyya order, told me that he had studied for five years with a Qadiri sheikh in Medina, and obtained an *ijazah* from him, so that he could call on Qadiri leaders as well for inspiration.

7. The evening was also the occasion for the graduation ceremony for Hijaz students; the 2008 ceremony can be viewed at http://wn.com/official_suyuti_institute_video__Sheikh_zain_ul_aqtab_saddiqi__islam__hijaz_college__tassawwuf.

8. The mosque in The Hague was created in 1975 by Surinamese Muslims of Indian heritage who had moved to the Netherlands on Surinam's gaining independence. They were Barelvi Sufis, and some had a command of Urdu. The website for the Masjid Noeroel Islam (http://www.noeroelislam.com/) includes links to the websites for Hijaz and for the Siddiqis, father and son. Van Bommel (1992, 138) explains that at that time competing Surinamese organizations each identified with a well-known international spiritual leader.

9. See the excellent explanation of the act in Blackett (2009). A useful overview of changes thereafter affecting divorce is in Sanders (2014).

10. See the fuller discussion of this point in chapter 10. Recent changes in the use of the Arbitration Act for resolving financial disputes in divorce cases are also discussed there.

11. See MAT's website for their procedures and for references to the Arbitration Act of 1996, http://www.matribunal.com/. It is worth emphasizing that MAT does *not* arbitrate in matters of Islamic divorce.

12. Sheikh Zain ul-Aqtab Siddiqi and Maulana Arif, and others, teach a general course on Islam, covering history, tassawuf, and fiqh, among other subjects. Zain is listed as the founder of the Suyuti Institute on the site http://suyutiinstitute.com/index.html.

13. Interview with Arif Awan, April 4, 2013.

14. Interview with Siddiqi, Nuneaton, March 5, 2009.

15. Q. 2:231 on divorce; 4:34 on the practice in question: *idribu hunna*, from *daraba*. See the fuller discussion in chapter 12.

16. Interview with Siddiqi, Nuneaton, May 9, 2010.

17. Interview with Qamar Bhatti, Birmingham, July 11, 2011.

18. On Sufi Abdullah, see Greaves (2000, 118–25). Sufi Abdullah's own *pir*, Hazrat Shah (also known as Zindapir, "the living *pir*"), is from Kohat, on Pakistan's northwestern border (Werbner 2003).

19. He lived from 1077–1166 CE, a jurist and a Sufi, and was considered a saint by many Sufis.

20. See their site at http://www.haboard.com/board.html.

21. John Wood, "Halal chicken sold at KFC 'may not be "real halal",'" Food manufacture.co.uk, http://www.foodmanufacture.co.uk/Regulation/Halal-chicken-sold-at-KFC-may-not-be-real-halal. I suspect that Siddiqi's claim does reflect the tendency of many British imams to oppose the use of the mechanical blade.

22. And in part for that reason, in part because of the long-standing oppositions presented in chapter 3, the other shariʿa councils express skepticism regarding the Hijaz procedures. At Birmingham, for example, Saba Butt asked me, when I mentioned that I had been working with the council in Leyton and with the Nuneaton

people, "How did you find the Shariah council in Nuneaton? The people in Leyton, they are like us, they apply Qur'an and Hadith, but the others, they follow their own teachings." Interview, Birmingham, July 21, 2010.

Chapter 10
Shariʿa in English Law

1. Rowan Williams, "Civil and Religious Law in England: A Religious Perspective," lecture delivered February 7, 2008, at the Royal Courts of Justice, London, available at http://rowanwilliams.archbishopofcanterbury.org/, and in Griffith-Jones, ed. (2013, 20–33). See also commentaries by Robin Griffith-Jones and by Stephen Hockman in the same book. Lord Phillips, "Equality before the Law," speech delivered at the East London Muslim Centre, July 3, 2008, available at http://www.judiciary.gov.uk/media/speeches/2008/speech-lord-phillips-lcj-03072008.htm?wbc_purpose=Basic&WBCMODE=PresentationUnpublished.

2. MacEoin (2009, 2). Even serious think tanks confuse the shariʿa councils' work with binding arbitration, as when the US Council on Foreign Relations stated that "In late 2008, Britain officially allowed shariʿa tribunals governing marriage, divorce, and inheritance to make legally binding decisions if both parties agreed." The temporal reference is probably to Lord Phillips's speech; nothing legal had changed in this period. See the discussion below of what such a claim could mean in practice.

3. The first is the title of a story by Matthew Hickley, *Daily Mail* online, September 15, 2008, http://www.dailymail.co.uk/news/article-1055764/Islamic-sharia-courts-Britain-legally-binding.html; the second is the headline for a story by John Bingham, *Telegraph*, October 20, 2012, http://www.telegraph.co.uk/news/religion/9621319/Sharia-courts-as-consensual-as-rape-House-of-Lords-told.html. The second headline is (somewhat inaccurately) quoting Baroness Cox, sponsor of a bill aimed at regulating, possibly banning, shariʿa councils.

4. I owe this observation to Robin Griffith-Jones.

5. See the excellent explanation of the act by Blackett (2009).

6. Most notably the resolution of a mosque administration dispute in Waltham Forest in 2009, discussed in chapter 9; conversations with District Judge Shamim Qureshi, October 4, 2009, and see the 2010 report of the Charity Commission on the inquiry, http://forms.charitycommission.gov.uk/media/92113/charity_commission_annual_report_10_11.pdf. See also MAT's website for their procedures and for references to the Arbitration Act, http://www.matribunal.com/.

7. Lady Hale in *Radmacher v. Granatino* (2010) UKSC 42, para. 132.

8. August 13, 2010.

9. See Owen Bowcott, "Legal aid cuts have left family courts 'at breaking point,'" *Guardian*, July 29, 2014, http://www.theguardian.com/law/2014/jul/29/legal-aid-family-courts-breaking-point-lawyers.

10. In this section I draw heavily on explanations kindly offered by family lawyer and mediator Sarah Anticoni of the Charles Russell group, March 16, 2010.

11. A few disputed circumcision cases remain in the minds of judges as particularly difficult; see remarks by Judge Qureshi below and conversations with Sir Peter Singer, July 10, 2008, and again on May 28, 2014.

12. On this point, see the landmark case approving a prenuptial agreement (*Radmacher v. Gratino* [2010] UKSC 42), in which Chief Justice Phillips based the court's judgment on "respect for individual autonomy" (par. 78).
13. An early assessment of the arbitration initiative is by the barrister Rhys Taylor, "Family arbitration—A soft launch or a hard landing? Some provisional thoughts," Family Law Week, February 26, 2012, http://www.familylawweek.co.uk/site.aspx?i=ed96021. For the way things looked two years later, see Charlotte Sanders, "Arbitration in family cases—the way forward?" Family Law, February 28, 2014, http://www.familylaw.co.uk/news_and_comment/arbitration-in-family-cases-the-way-forward?#.VaV8GvmukkS.
14. The following comes from discussions and court observations with Judge Qureshi in Birmingham County Court over two days, May 24 and 25, 2010.
15. Interview with Sir Peter Singer, July 10, 2008.
16. John Bingham's headline for his story in the Sunday *Telegraph*, March 22, 2014, http://www.telegraph.co.uk/news/religion/10716844/Islamic-law-is-adopted-by-British-legal-chiefs.html.
17. Owen Bowcott, "Law Society withdraws guidance on sharia wills," *Guardian*, November 24, 2015, http://www.theguardian.com/law/2014/nov/24/law-society-withdraws-guidance-sharia-wills.
18. Interview with Eleanor Platt, February 1, 2010.
19. Interview with Jonathan Arkush, March 29, 2010.
20. In the United States, similar references have led to calls to "ban shariʿa" from courtrooms (Bowen 2012).
21. [2009] EWCA Civ 1205, official court transcript, http://www.bailii.org/ew/cases/EWCA/Civ/2009/1205.html. For a more complete analysis of the legal issues raised, see Bowen (2011b).
22. This request fits the standard English legal practice of seeking expert advice regarding anything other than English law, whether it be, say, German law or a religious legal system. I criticize this equation of Islamic law with foreign law below.
23. The following section is based on conversations with the council's chief clerk, Atif Matin, May 12, 2010, and on analysis of the relevant case file at the council.
24. The same position was argued by Ahmad Thomson, a solicitor who also advises the ISC, in a letter to the Charity Commission in 2006 in response to their queries about the ISC's procedures. These queries had been sparked by complaints by Uddin to his MP.
25. [1965] 1 QB 390. The two quotes are from paras. 390 and 401.
26. The difficulty of deciding whether a couple intends to be so bound was pointed out in *Balfour v. Balfour* (1919) 2 KB 571, where a husband's promise to pay his wife maintenance was considered not enforceable.
27. See Pearl and Menski (1998, 373–82); Sultana Kamal, "Dossier 4: Law for Muslim Women in Bangladesh," http://www.wluml.org/node/248.
28. For this point made in a non-mahr case, see *Khan v. Khan* (2007) EWCA Civ 399, para. 46. I thank Prakash Shah for pointing to the relevance of this case.
29. Amendments to the Matrimonial Causes Act 1973, at 24 (1d), allow them to do so but do not treat those agreements as contracts. The recent Supreme Court decision in *Radmacher v. Granatino* (2010) UKSC 42 introduces as *obiter* the view that such antenuptial agreements are legally enforceable contracts, subject to the scrutiny of the court for their fairness.

30. On this point I concur with Pascale Fournier (2010a, 78, 86) in her comparative study of mahr in Western courts.
31. Interview with Aina Khan, London, August 3, 2011.
32. Gardner (1995, 178–85); Huda (2006).
33. Perhaps I should emphasize at this point that my concern is not whether Uddin deserved to win the case but whether the judges correctly grasped the issues surrounding the marriage and its payments.

Chapter 11
When Can Shariʿa Be British?

1. Quoted on the website of the Center for Islamic Pluralism, http://www.islamicpluralism.org/556/international-director-al-alawi-on-london-tablighi-mega. On the controversy, see Pieri (2012) and I. Bowen (2014, 51–56).
2. London Board of Shechita, http://www.shechita.org/about-us/board-history/.
3. Food Standards Agency, Results of the 2011 FSA animal welfare survey in Great Britain, May 22, 2012, http://www.food.gov.uk/sites/default/files/multimedia/pdfs/board/fsa120508.pdf.
4. I draw here on Harvey (2010).
5. Interview with Sarfraz Mohammed, Birmingham, April 23, 2013.
6. These practices are all in use but are challenged by some jurists: for example, some say that the person wielding the blade must recite the Bismillah to the animal, but use of a mechanical blade and recorded recitations clearly speeds up the process.
7. FSA memo, reference ENF/E/10/038, September 29, 2010, in author's possession. See Harvey (2010) on halal certification agencies and Fischer (2011) on the lived experience of looking for halal in London.
8. See coverage in the *Guardian*, "Government steers clear of meat-labeling row," theguardian.com, May 8, 2014, http://www.theguardian.com/lifeandstyle/2014/may/08/government-steers-clear-meat-labelling-row, and, for the BNP's comments, http://www.bnp.org.uk/news/halal-%E2%80%94-tell-it-it.
9. Nesrine Malik, "The random Muslim scare story generator: Separating fact from fiction," *Guardian*, May 12, 2014, http://www.theguardian.com/world/2014/may/12/muslim-scare-stories-media-halal-sharia-niqab.
10. Nicolas Watt, "David Cameron to unveil plans for £200m Islamic bond," *Guardian*, October 28, 2013, including video of the PM's speech, http://www.theguardian.com/money/2013/oct/29/islamic-bond-david-cameron-treasury-plans.
11. "UK Excellence in Islamic Finance," https://www.gov.uk/government/uploads/system/uploads/attachment_data/file/367154/UKTI_UK_Excellence_in_Islamic_Finance_Reprint_2014_Spread.pdf.
12. "Strong Banking that Understands the Shariah Way," http://www.lloydsbank.com/assets/media/pdfs/islamic_account_welcome_pack.pdf.
13. Hilary Osborne, "Islamic finance—the lowdown on sharia-compliant money," theguardian.com, October 29, 2013, http://www.theguardian.com/money/2013/oct/29/islamic-finance-sharia-compliant-money-interest.
14. BBC News, "Archbishop of Canterbury defends faith schools," May 4, 2014, http://www.bbc.com/news/uk-27273053.
15. On the history of education in England, see Gillard (2011).

16. "Teach first," *Economist*, March 14, 2015, http://www.economist.com/news/britain/21646244-david-cameron-proposes-more-free-schools-struggles-co-ordinate-existing-ones-teach; "Open academies and academy projects in development," Gov.UK, https://www.gov.uk/government/publications/open-academies-and-academy-projects-in-development, figures as of March 15, 2015. In 2011, about one-third of all the schools in England receiving state aid were faith schools, two-thirds of those 7,000 faith schools were Church of England, and a bit less than one-third Roman Catholic, with small numbers of Jewish (42), Muslim (12), Sikh (3), and Hindu (1) schools (Oldfield et al. 2013). Sally Weale, "David Cameron announces 49 new free schools," *Guardian*, March 9, 2015, http://www.theguardian.com/education/2015/mar/09/david-cameron-faith-schools-academies. Between 2011 and 2013, 831 groups submitted applications to open free schools. Thirty-two of these came from Church of England groups, and 80 came from Muslim groups—but only 5 of the latter were approved. *Economist*, "Religious studies," April 26, 2014, http://www.economist.com/news/britain/21601251-giving-schools-more-autonomy-and-encouraging-religious-groups-run-them-will-produce.

17. See the explanation furnished by the Diocese of Chester, for example, http://www.chester.anglican.org/page_schools.asp?Page=42#.U9p5x2NLMkI.

18. "Maintained faith schools," Department for Education, Gov.UK, https://www.gov.uk/government/publications/maintained-faith-schools/maintained-faith-schools.

19. "Muslim schools," AMS.UK, http://ams-uk.org/muslim-schools/.

20. *Economist*, see note 16 in this chapter.

21. Joly (1995, 48).

22. Estimate from Birt and Lewis (2011, 116).

23. Rebecca Smithers, "Anger at Muslim schools attack," *Guardian*, January 18, 2005. Security concerns have been taken up by the broader Islamic education field. For example, the Association of Muslim Schools, whose member schools are mainly privately funded, shows the sort of concerns they encounter by their choice of FAQs: Do you promote gender equality; do you tolerate discrimination against non-Muslim teachers; do you allow schools that promote extremism—for all of which they give reassuring answers; http://ams-uk.org/muslim-schools/.

24. See, for example, the opinion piece and many commentators at Toby Young, "Sorry, campaigning mums—it's faith that makes faith schools work," *Spectator*, March 8, 2014, http://www.spectator.co.uk/life/status-anxiety/9152901/sorry-campaining-mums-its-faith-that-makes-faith-schools-work/.

25. The Leicester city report shows how local government actors evaluated the school's progress; see http://www.cabinet.leicester.gov.uk/documents/s46962/madani%20exec%20final%20report.pdf.

26. Richard Adams, "Trojan horse row: School at centre of allegations rated inadequate by Ofsted," theguardian.com, June 5, 2014, and "Is the Trojan horse row just a witch hunt triggered by a hoax?," *Guardian*, June 8, 2014.

27. BBC News, "Trojan Horse: 25 schools probed over alleged takeover plot," April 14, 2014.

28. Andrew Sparrow and Richard Adams, "'Trojan horse' row: Downing Street launches snap Ofsted visits," *Guardian*, June 9, 2014.

29. See, for example, Andrew Gilligan, "Government intervenes at school 'taken over' by Muslim radicals," *Telegraph*, May 4, 2014.

30. This latter concern surfaced later in 2014 when a long-standing sexual abuse ring was found to be operating in Rotherham and elsewhere in the north of England; most of the perpetrators were Pakistanis, and local police seem to have spent more effort on disproving victims' claims than in arresting perpetrators. Josh Halliday et al., "Rotherham: Police spent 'great deal of time' trying to disprove victim abuse," theguardian.com, August 28, 2014, http://www.theguardian.com/uk-news/2014/aug/28/rotherham-abuse-south-yorkshire-police-victims-john-mann-shaun-wright. Two major reports were commissioned on the Birmingham case. One, commissioned by Gove and supporting his alarms, was carried out by former counterterrorism chief Peter Clarke. See http://birminghamnewsroom.com/birmingham-city-council-response-to-ian-kershaw-review/. The second report, by independent education expert Ian Kershaw, found no evidence of a conspiracy to promote "an anti-British agenda, violent extremism or radicalization"; see Patrick Wintour, "Trojan Horse inquiry: 'A coordinated agenda to impose hardline Sunni Islam,'" theguardian.com, July 17, 2014, http://www.theguardian.com/uk-news/2014/jul/17/birmingham-schools-inquiry-hardline-sunni-islam-trojan-horse. Sarah Cassidy, "Trojan Horse report: Birmingham schools broke law with Islamic assemblies and banned sex education," *Independent*, July 18, 2014, http://www.independent.co.uk/news/education/education-news/trojan-horse-10-birmingham-schools-investigated-showed-elements-of-the-conspiracy-education-expert-finds-9615152.html.

31. Catherine Bennett, "Forget these 'Trojan horses'—the real issue is faith schools," *Observer*, June 7, 2014, http://www.theguardian.com/commentisfree/2014/jun/07/trojan-horse-infiltration-faith-schools-secular-education.

32. Richard Adams, "Governors of new academies and free schools told to abide by 'British values,', theguardian.com, June 19, 2014, http://www.theguardian.com/education/2014/jun/19/governors-academies-free-schools-british-values-michael-gove.

33. "British attitudes harden towards immigrants," theguardian.com, June 17, 2014, http://www.theguardian.com/uk-news/2014/jun/17/immigration-british-attitudes-harden-benefits.

34. One Law for All website, http://www.onelawforall.org.uk/about/.

35. The Arbitration and Mediation Services (Equality) Bill 2011 rests on claims that shariʿa councils constitute "a 'quasi-legal' system operating in parallel with our own which violates the principles of equality before the law and which is based on religiously sanctioned gender discrimination" (Proudman 2012, 9). The bill received its second reading in the House of Lords in October 2012, and in a reintroduced form received a new first reading in May 2013. Baroness Cox herself was responsible for bringing Geert Wilders to the UK in 2009, although the home secretary then banned him from entering the country; Haroon Siddique et al., "Far-right Dutch MP refused entry to UK," theguardian.com, February 12, 2009, http://www.theguardian.com/world/2009/feb/12/far-right-dutch-mp-ban-islam. Interested readers can continue to follow the bill's progress on an official timeline at http://services.parliament.uk/bills/2013-14/arbitrationandmediationequalityservices.html.

36. *Can We Talk about This?*, program, distributed at March 2012 performances, n.d., in author's possession.

37. The 2007 case involved Judge Christa Datz-Winter, who read the (in)famous *daraba* verse from the Qur'an in support of the idea that the wife and her husband came from a "Moroccan cultural environment in which it is not uncommon for a

man to exert a right of corporal punishment over his wife." After an outcry, including protests from Germany's Central Council of Muslims, she was removed from the case. Kate Connolly, "German judge invokes Qur'an to deny abused wife a divorce," *Guardian*, March 22, 2007, http://www.theguardian.com/world/2007/mar/23/germany.islam.

38. The program was produced by an independent organization, Blakeway Productions, for Panorama, and the reporter and producer was Jane Corbin, a respected senior reporter.

39. Excerpts can be found on the Gatestone Institute site at http://www.gatestoneinstitute.org/3682/uk-sharia-courts#; video can be found on YouTube at https://www.youtube.com/watch?v=4gZCFdHkd4A; the Islamic Shariʿa Council's response is at http://test.islamic-sharia.org/?page_id=131.

40. Interview with Suhaib Hasan, April 29, 2013.

41. Khola Hasan and Suhaib Hasan's comments were in a joint interview at Leyton, April 25, 2013.

42. Innes Bowen, "British mosques aren't that moderate after all," *Spectator*, June 14, 2014, http://www.spectator.co.uk/features/9230671/who-runs-our-mosques/. Innes Bowen is no relation, and I did provide a very positive blurb to her book, from which I draw in chapter 3.

Chapter 12
Internal Debates and Practical Convergences

1. "A Stronger Britain, Built on Our Values," March 23, 2015, https://www.gov.uk/government/speeches/a-stronger-britain-built-on-our-values.

2. "Extremism: PM Speech," July 20, 2015, https://www.gov.uk/government/speeches/extremism-pm-speech.

3. See www.britishmuslim.tv; www.islamchannel.tv; https://www.youtube.com/watch?v=gVDIXqILqSM (for HappyMuslims); https://www.youtube.com/watch?v=2bcwOJvpyJA (for the "official" Muslim response).

4. See the discussion of internal criticism in Nussbaum and Sen (1989).

5. Since 2010 Scotland has extended celebrant status to all faiths.

6. Available at http://www.muslimparliament.org.uk/Documentation/Muslim%20Marriage%20Contract.pdf. The Muslim Institute was created in 1972 by Pakistani British writers Kalim Siddiqi, Ziauddin Sardar, and others, as a think tank about the future of Muslim civilization. In 1992, Kalim Siddiqi also created the Muslim Parliament, which had the ambition of being a representative assembly but which also functioned as a space for discussion and publication; notably, it set out the principles by which Muslims could obey secular British authority. At Kalim Siddiqi's death in 1996, his associate (but no relation) Ghayasuddin Siddiqui became the leader of both bodies. During this time he and others moved from strong support for Saudi Arabia and then, in 1979, Iran, to positions more focused on rethinking Islam in a British context.

7. Usama Hasan, February 3, 2010.

8. Interview with Khola Hasan, January 25, 2010.

9. Quote is from a site that is no longer available; archived copy is in my possession.
10. Interview with Suhaib Hasan, Leyton, May 26, 2008.
11. Ibid., July 12, 2007.
12. Compare debates in India over a new model marriage contract, as discussed in Zaman (2004, 140–42).
13. Douglas et al. (2011, 45).
14. I develop this point with respect to the parallel developments in Indonesia in Bowen (2003).
15. Irtiza Hasan, "Suhaib Hasan on his father Abdal Ghaffar Hasan," posted on April 5, 2007, http://muslimmatters.org/2007/04/05/shaykh-suhaib-hasan-reminisces-on-his-fathers-life.
16. Interview with Usama Hasan, February 3, 2010.
17. Khola Hasan, "Debating the Niqab," Muslim Institute, http://www.muslim institute.org/blogs/front-featured/debating-niqab.
18. Interview with Usama Hasan, London, February 3, 2010.
19. Ibid., February 3, 2010.
20. Recall my observation in chapter 3 that, whereas this line of thinking plays a major role in public Islamic debates and arguments in France, it occupies a distinctly minority position in England vis-à-vis Deobandi Hanafi arguments.
21. Interview with Usama Hasan, July 6, 2011.
22. Ibid., February 3, 2010.
23. Usama Hasan, "Knowledge regained," theguardian.com, http://www.theguardian.com/commentisfree/2008/sep/11/religion.darwinbicentenary.
24. See the speech and the chaos at http://www.youtube.com/watch?v=TgR-xfJbQcQ.
25. Suhaib's speech is at http://www.youtube.com/watch?v=6CN-nBoazHI&x-yt-cl=71760083&x-yt-ts=1406138979. The well-known phrase "Kun fayakūn" indicates God's powers, and is found in the Qur'an, for example, at Q. 36:81–83, Surah Yasin, which is often used in connection with efforts at protection and power.
26. See Bowen (2010, 121–24) on a Muslim case, and for the conservative Christian Wheaton College, see http://www.wheaton.edu/Academics/Liberal-Arts/Faculty-Perspective-on-the-Natural-Sciences.
27. Interview with Usama Hasan, July 6, 2011.
28. Ibid., March 16, 2012.
29. *London Evening Standard*, June 8, 2012.
30. Usama Hasan, April 22, 2013.
31. Khola Hasan, ISC, Leyton, April 25, 2013.
32. See, for example, the interviews in Din (2006), Kabir (2010), and Mondal (2008).
33. Habermas (2006, 11). Rawls (1999) speaks more broadly of "comprehensive doctrines" rather than religion, and argues that liberal democratic societies operate on the basis of an "overlapping consensus" on a set of issues regarding politics and civic life. The range of debates, and hence the space in which such translations are necessary, is, for Habermas, much broader than Rawls's notion of "constitutional essentials"; Habermas (2006, 21n17) writes that "almost all controversial legal issues can be redefined such as to become issues of principle" and thus require these

cooperative acts of translation. Habermas's closest engagements with religion in its tensions with secularism (2010) suggest very little change in this view. Charles Taylor (2008) points out that Rawls's formulation avoids Habermas's problematic singling out of religious orientations as posing problems of translation. In Rawls's more capacious formulation, Marxism and Calvinism are both comprehensive doctrines whose justifications require translation.

34. The quotes are from Habermas (2006, 9, 10, 8, 15; the last has italics in the original).

35. Relevant here is the question posed by Povinelli (2001) about the social practices and forms of social power that are used to render commensurate disparate ethical and epistemological systems in liberal national societies. "Translation" may be one of the most broadly acceptable forms of this commensuration pressure.

36. Habermas (2006, 14).

37. Ibid., 19.

38. I find the strongest echoes of this view in Canadian debates about "reasonable accommodations," particularly as set out in the Bouchard-Taylor Report (Bouchard and Taylor 2008), but that report, and those discussions, are concerned with host society accommodations, as is Parekh's (2002) parallel discussion of immigrants to Britain. Closer to my own focus on debates among Muslims is March's (2009) analysis of Islamic openness to liberal citizenship, but his work is in the sphere of Islamic political theory rather than in that of debates about practical challenges. See also Massad's (2015) analysis of liberal critiques of Islam. Other than my own works on Indonesia and France already cited, and the many excellent anthropological studies of Islamic practical reasoning also cited here, I would direct readers interested in exploring the broader implications of recognizing religious convergences with secular law to, first, Charles Taylor's *A Secular Age* (2007) for the long view, and then to discussions of Catholic and Jewish accommodations to modern legal systems, such as in a recent work on religious and civil-legal domains in American family law (Nichols 2012).

39. See Vallier (2011) for an exposition and discussion of the convergence approach to public reason theory.

Chapter 13
Conclusions

1. The classic work is Wilson (1987); for an important comparative critique, see Wacquant (2007).

2. On the French experience in greater depth, see Bowen (2009).

3. On the manners by which colonial and postcolonial states flattened shariʿa into positive law, particularly in the family sphere, see Hallaq (2009, 443–73).

References

Abbas, Tahir. 2005. "Muslims in Birmingham, UK." Oxford: Centre on Migration, Policy and Society. http://www.compas.ox.ac.uk/fileadmin/files/Publications/Research_Resources/Urban/Birmingham_Background_Paper_0206.pdf.

Agrama, Hussein Ali. 2012. *Questioning Secularism: Islam, Sovereignty, and the Rule of Law in Modern Egypt.* Chicago: University of Chicago Press.

Ahmad, Irfan. 2009. *Islamism and Democracy in India: The Transformation of Jamaat-e-Islami.* Princeton: Princeton University Press.

Alexander, Claire, Victoria Redclift, and Ajmal Hussain. 2013. *The New Muslims.* London: Runnymede Trust.

Ali, N., V. S. Kalra, and S. Sayyid, eds. 2006. *A Postcolonial People: South Asians in Britain.* London: Hurst.

Amanat, Abbas, and Frank Griffel, eds. 2007. *Shari'a: Islamic Law in the Contemporary Context.* Stanford, CA: Stanford University Press.

An-Na'im, Abdullahi Ahmed. 2008. *Islam and the Secular State: Negotiating the Future of Shariʿa.* Cambridge: Harvard University Press.

Ansari, Humayun. 2004. *"The Infidel Within": Muslims in Britain since 1800.* London: Hurst.

Austin, J. L. 1975. *How to Do Things with Words.* 2nd ed. Cambridge: Harvard University Press.

Bader, Veit. 2007. "The Governance of Islam in Europe: The Perils of Modeling." *Journal of Ethnic and Migration Studies* 33 (6): 871–86.

Bagby, Ihsan. 2012. *The American Mosque, 2011.* Washington, DC: Council on American-Islamic Relations.

Ballard, Roger. 1990. "Migration and Kinship: The Differential Effect of Marriage Rules on the Processes of Punjabi Migration to Britain." In *South Asians Overseas: Contexts and Communities,* ed. C. Clarke, C. Peach, and S. Vertovec, 219–49. Cambridge: Cambridge University Press.

——. 2007. "Common Law and Common Sense: Juries, Justice and the Challenge of Ethnic Plurality." In *Law and Ethnic Plurality: Socio-Legal Perspectives,* ed. Prakash Shah, 69–105. Leiden: Martinus Nijhoff.

Bano, Samia. 2004. *Complexity, Difference and "Muslim Personal Law": Rethinking the Relationship between Shariah Councils and South Asian Muslim Women in Britain.* Unpublished doctoral dissertation. University of Warwick, Department of Law, Coventry, UK.

——. 2007. "Muslim Family Justice and Human Rights: The Experience of British Muslim Women." *Journal of Comparative Law* 1 (4): 1–29.

——. 2012a. *Muslim Women and Shari'ah Councils: Transcending the Boundaries of Community and Law.* London: Palgrave Macmillan.

——. 2012b. "An Exploratory Study of Shariah Councils in England with Respect to Family Law." Paper. University of Reading. https://www.reading.ac.uk/web/FILES

/law/An_exploratory_study_of_Shariah_councils_in_England_with_respect_to_family_law_.pdf.

Bashir, Aamir. 2010. *Shariʿat and Tariqat: A Study of the Deobandi Understanding and Practice of Tasawwuf.* MA dissertation, International Islamic University Malaysia.

Birt, Jonathan. 2005. "Wahhabism in the United Kingdom: Manifestations and Reactions." In *Transnational Connections and the Arab Gulf,* ed. Madawi Al-Rasheed, 168–84. Abingdon, UK: Routledge.

Birt, Jonathan, and Philip Lewis. 2011. "The Pattern of Islamic Reform in Britain: The Deobandis between Intra-Muslim Sectarianism and Engagement with Wider Society." In *Producing Islamic Knowledge: Transmission and Dissemination in Western Europe,* ed. Martin van Bruinessen and Stefano Allievi, 91–120. London: Routledge.

Blackett, Robert. December 2009. "The Status of Religious 'Courts' in English Law." In *Decisions, Decisions: Dispute Resolution & International Arbitration Newsletter,* 11–19.

Bleich, Erik. 2003. *Race Politics in Britain and France: Ideas and Policymaking since the 1960s.* Cambridge: Cambridge University Press.

Bolognani, Marta. 2007. "The Myth of Return: Dismissal, Survival or Revival? A Bradford Example of Transnationalism as a Political Instrument." *Journal of Ethnic and Migration Studies* 33 (1): 59–76.

Boltanski, Luc, and Laurent Thévenot. 2006. (Orig. French 1991) *On Justification: Economies of Worth.* Princeton: Princeton University Press.

Bouchard, Gérard, and Charles Taylor. 2008. *Building the Future: A Time for Reconciliation.* Quebec: Consultation Commission on Accommodation Practices Related to Cultural Differences.

Bowen, Innes. 2014. *Medina in Birmingham, Najaf in Brent: Inside British Islam.* London: Hurst.

Bowen, John R. 1989. "Salat in Indonesia: The Social Meanings of an Islamic Ritual." *Man* (n.s.) 24:299–318.

——. 2003. *Islam, Law and Equality in Indonesia: An Anthropology of Public Reasoning.* Cambridge: Cambridge University Press.

——. 2007. *Why the French Don't Like Headscarves: Islam, the State, and Public Space.* Princeton: Princeton University Press.

——. 2009. *Can Islam Be French? Pluralism and Pragmatism in a Secularist State.* Princeton: Princeton University Press.

——. 2010. "Muslims in the West: Europe." In *The New Cambridge History of Islam,* vol. 6, ed. Robert W. Hefner, 218–37. Cambridge: Cambridge University Press.

——. 2011a. "Islamic Adaptations to Western Europe and North America: The Importance of Contrastive Analyses." *American Behavioral Scientist* 55:1601–15.

——. 2011b. "How Could English Courts Recognize Shariah?" *St. Thomas Law Review* 7 (3): 411–35.

——. 2012. *Blaming Islam.* Cambridge: MIT Press.

——. 2013. "Contours of Sharia in Indonesia." In *Democracy & Islam in Indonesia,* ed. Mirjam Künkler and Alfred Stepan, 149–67. New York: Columbia University Press.

Bowen, John R., Christophe Bertossi, Jan Willem Duyvendak, and Mona Lena Krook, eds. 2014. *European States and Their Muslim Citizens: The Impact of Institutions on Perceptions and Boundaries.* Cambridge: Cambridge University Press.

Brubaker, Rogers. 2004. *Ethnicity without Groups.* Cambridge: Harvard University Press.

Caeiro, Alexandre. 2006. "The Social Construction of Shariʿa: Bank Interest, Home Purchase, and Islamic Norms in the West." *Die Welt des Islams* 44 (3): 351–75.

Carroll, Lucy. 1982. "Talaq-Tafwid and Stipulations in a Muslim Marriage Contract: Important Means of Protecting the Position of the South Asian Muslim Wife." *Modern Asian Studies* 16 (2): 277–309.

——. 1997. "Muslim Women and 'Islamic Divorce' in England." *Journal of Muslim Minority Affairs* 17 (1): 97–115.

Cesari, Jocelyne. 2004. *When Islam and Democracy Meet: Muslims in Europe and in the United States.* New York: Palgrave Macmillan.

Charsley, Katharine. 2006. "Risk and Ritual: The Protection of British Pakistani Women in Transnational Marriage." *Journal of Ethnic and Migration Studies* 32 (7): 1169–87.

——. 2013. *Transnational Pakistani Connections: Marrying "Back Home."* London: Routledge.

Chatterjee, Nandini. 2010. "English Law, Brahmo Marriage, and the Problem of Religious Difference: Civil Marriage Laws in Britain and India." *Comparative Studies in Society and History* 52 (3): 524–52.

Cicourel, Aaron V. 1987. "The Interpenetration of Communicative Contexts: Examples from Medical Encounters." *Social Psychology Quarterly* 50 (2): 217–26.

Clarke, Morgan. 2012. "The Judge as Tragic Hero: Judicial Ethics in Lebanon's Shariʿa Courts." *American Ethnologist* 39 (1): 106–21.

Cohn, Bernard S. 1996. *Colonialism and Its Forms of Knowledge: The British in India.* Princeton: Princeton University Press.

Colley, Linda. 2009. *Britons: Forging the Nation, 1707–1837.* 2nd ed. New Haven: Yale University Press.

——. 2014. *Acts of Union and Disunion.* London: Profile Books.

Comaroff, John L., and Simon Roberts. 1981. *Rules and Processes: The Cultural Logic of Dispute in an African Context.* Chicago: University of Chicago Press.

Communities and Local Government. 2008. *The Bangladeshi Muslim Community in England.* London: Department of Communities and Local Government.

——. 2009. *The Pakistani Muslim Community in England.* London: Department of Communities and Local Government.

Conway, Gordon. 1997. *Islamophobia: A Challenge for Us All.* London: Runnymede Trust.

Derrida, Jacques. 1988. *Limited Inc.* Evanston: Northwestern University Press.

Dewey, John. 1924. "Logical Method and the Law." *Cornell Law Quarterly* 10:17–27.

Din, Ikhlaq. 2006. *The New British: The Impact of Culture and Community on Young Pakistanis.* Aldershot (UK): Ashgate.

Douglas, Gillian, Norman Doe, Sophie Gilliat-Ray, Russell Sandberg, and Asma Khan. 2011. *Social Cohesion and Civil Law: Marriage, Divorce and Religious Courts.* Cardiff: Cardiff University.

Dupret, Baudouin. 2000. *Au Nom de Quel Droit.* Paris: Centre d'Études et de Documentation économique, juridique, et sociale.

Eade, John, and David Garbin. 2002. "Changing Narrative of Violence, Struggle and Resistance: Bangladeshis and the Competition for Resources in the Global City." *Oxford Development Studies* 30 (2): 137–49.

——. 2006. "Competing Visions of Identity and Space: Bangladeshi Muslims in Britain." *Contemporary South Asia* 15 (2): 181–93.

Eaton, Richard Maxwell. 1978. *Sufis of Bijapur, 1300–1700: Social Roles of Sufis in Medieval India.* Princeton: Princeton University Press.

Engineer, Asghar Ali. 1987. *The Shah Bano Controversy.* Stosius Inc. / Advent Books Division.

Esteves, Olivier. 2011. *De l'invisibilité à l'islamophobie: Les musulmans britanniques (1945–2010).* Paris: Presses de Sciences Po.

Favell, Adrian. 2001. *Philosophies of Integration: Immigration and the Idea of Citizenship in France and Britain.* 2nd ed. Houndmills, UK: Palgrave.

Fawzy, Essam. 2004. "Muslim Personal Status Law in Egypt: The Current Situation and Possibilities of Reform through Internal Initiatives." In *Women's Rights & Islamic Family Law*, ed. Lynn Welchman, 15–91. London: Zed Books.

Feldman, Noah. 2007. "Shari'a and Islamic Democracy in the Age of al-Jazeera." In *Shari'a: Islamic Law in the Contemporary Context*, ed. Abbas Amanat and Frank Griffel, 104–19. Stanford, CA: Stanford University Press.

Fernando, Mayanthi L. 2014. *The Republic Unsettled: Muslim French and the Contradictions of Secularism.* Durham, NC: Duke University Press.

Fetzer, Joel S., and J. Christopher Soper. 2004. *Muslims and the State in Britain, France, and Germany.* Cambridge: Cambridge University Press.

Finney, Nissa, and Ludi Simpson. 2009. *"Sleepwalking to Segregation"? Challenging Myths about Race and Migration.* Bristol, UK: Policy Press.

Fischer, Johan. 2011. *The Halal Frontier: Muslim Consumers in a Globalized Market.* New York: Palgrave Macmillan.

Fournier, Pascale. 2010a. "Flirting with God in Western Secular Courts: Mahr in the West." *International Journal of Law, Policy and the Family* 24 (1): 67–94.

———. 2010b. *Muslim Marriage in Western Courts: Lost in Transplantation.* Farnham, UK: Ashgate.

Freeland, Richard. 2000–2001. "The Islamic Institution of Mahr and American Law." *Gonz. J. Int'l L*, vol. 4. https://www.law.gonzaga.edu/files/GJIL-Vol4-Islamic Institution.pdf.

Freeland, Richard, and Martin Lau. 2008. "The Shari'a and English Law: Identity and Justice for British Muslims." In *The Islamic Marriage Contract: Case Studies in Islamic Family Law*, ed. Asifa Quraishi and Frank Vogel, 331–47. Cambridge: Harvard University Press.

Freitag, Sandra B. 1988. "Ambiguous Public Arenas and Coherent Political Practice: Kanpur Muslims, 1913–1931." In *Shari'at and Ambiguity in South Asian Islam*, ed. Katherine P. Ewing, 143–63. Berkeley: University of California Press.

Galanter, Marc. 1997. *Law and Society in Modern India*, 237–58. Oxford: Oxford University Press.

Gallup Center for Muslim Studies. 2009. "The Gallup Coexist Index 2009: A Global Study of Interfaith Relations." Washington, DC: Gallup Center for Muslim Studies. http://www.olir.it/areetematiche/pagine/documents/News_2150_Gallup2009.pdf.

Gardner, Katy. 1995. *Global Migrants, Local Lives: Travel and Transformation in Rural Bangladesh.* Oxford, UK: Oxford University Press.

———. 2002a. "Death of a Migrant: Transnational Death Ritual and Gender among British Sylhetis." *Global Networks* 2 (3): 191–204.

———. 2002b. *Age, Narrative and Migration: The Life Course and Life Histories of Bengali Elders in London.* Oxford: Berg, 2002.

Garfinkel, Harold. 1964. "Studies of the Routine Grounds of Everyday Activities." *Social Problems* 11 (3): 225–50.
Geaves, Ron R. 1996. "Cult, Charisma, Community: The Arrival of Sufi Pirs and Their Impact on Muslims in Britain." *Journal of Muslim Minority Affairs* 16 (2): 169–92.
——. 2000. *The Sufis of Britain: An Exploration of Muslim Identity.* Cardiff: Academic Press.
Geertz, Clifford. 1983. "Local Knowledge: Fact and Law in Comparative Perspective." In *Local Knowledge: Further Essays in Interpretive Anthropology*, by Clifford Geertz, 167–234. New York: Basic Books.
Gest, Justin. 2010. *Apart: Alienated and Engaged Muslims in the West.* London: Hurst.
Ghosh, Papiya. 1997. "*Muttahidah qaumiyat* in *aqalliat* Bihar: The Imarat i Shariah, 1921–1947." *Indian Economic Social History Review* 34 (1): 1–20.
Gillard, Derek. 2011. "Education in England: A Brief History." http://www.education england.org.uk/history/chapter03.html.
Gilliat-Ray, Sophie. 2010. *Muslims in Britain: An Introduction.* Cambridge: Cambridge University Press.
Glendon, Mary Ann. 1989. *The Transformation of Family Law: State, Law, and Family in the United States and Western Europe.* Chicago: University of Chicago Press.
Glynn, Sarah. 2002. "Bengali Muslims: The New East End Radicals?" *Ethnic and Racial Studies* 25 (6): 969–88.
——. 2014. *Class, Ethnicity and Religion in the Bengali East End: A Political History.* Manchester: Manchester University Press.
Goffman, Erving. 1983. "The Interaction Order." *American Sociological Review* 48:1–17.
Goodhart, David. July 2011. "A Tale of Three Cities." *Prospect.* http://www.prospect magazine.co.uk/features/bradford-burnley-oldham-riots-ten-years-on.
Goody, Jack. 1983. *The Development of the Family and Marriage in Europe.* Cambridge: Cambridge University Press.
Gottschalk, Peter. 2000. *Beyond Hindu and Muslim: Multiple Identity in Narratives from Village India.* Oxford: Oxford University Press.
Greaves, Ellen. 2012. "'Make Bradford British': The Parallel Lives of the Younger Generation." Centre for Market and Public Organisation: CMPO Viewpoint. http://cmpo.wordpress.com/2012/03/09/make-bradford-british-the-parallel-lives-of-the-younger-generation/.
Griffith-Jones, Robin. 2013. "Religious Rights and the Public Interest." In *Islam and English Law: Rights, Responsibilities and the Place of Shariʿa*, ed. Griffith-Jones, 188–204. Cambridge: Cambridge University Press.
——, ed. 2013. *Islam and English Law: Rights, Responsibilities and the Place of Shariʿa.* Cambridge: Cambridge University Press.
Gupta, Akhil. 2012. *Red Tape: Bureaucracy, Structural Violence, and Poverty in India.* Durham, NC: Duke University Press.
Habermas, Jürgen. 2006. "Religion in the Public Sphere." *European Journal of Philosophy* 14 (1): 1–25.
——. 2010. "An Awareness of What Is Missing." In *An Awareness of What Is Missing: Faith and Reason in a Post-Secular Age*, ed. Jürgen Habermas et al., 15–23. Cambridge, UK: Polity.
Haddad, Haitham al-. March 2010. *A Critical Analysis of Selected Aspects on Sunni Muslim Minority Fiqh, with Particular Reference to Contemporary Britain.* Doctoral

thesis, University of London, School of Oriental and African Studies (available at SOAS Special Collections).

Hallaq, Wael B. 2009. *Sharīʿa: Theory, Practice, Transformations.* Cambridge: Cambridge University Press.

Harvey, Ramon. 2010. "Certification of Halal Meat in the UK." Cambridge: HRH Prince Alwaleed Bin Talal Centre of Islamic Studies. http://www.cis.cam.ac.uk/assets/media/report_-_certification_of_halal_meat_in_the_uk.pdf.

Hasan, Mushirul. 1997. *Legacy of a Divided Nation: India's Muslims since Independence.* Delhi: Oxford University Press.

Hasan, Usama. 2011. "Have You Stopped Beating Your Wife? The Quran, Hadith and Domestic Violence." http://unity1.wordpress.com/2011/01/03/have-you-stopped-beating-your-wife-the-quran-hadith-and-domestic-violence/.

Hefner, Robert W., ed. 2004. *Remaking Muslim Politics: Pluralism, Contestation, Democratization.* Princeton: Princeton University Press.

Henriques, Ursula R. Q. 1961. *Religious Toleration in England, 1787–1833.* London: Routledge and Kegan Paul.

Herbert, Joanna. 2008. *Negotiating Boundaries in the City: Migration, Ethnicity, and Gender in Britain.* Aldershot, UK: Ashgate.

Hirsch, Jennifer S., and Holly Wardlow, eds. 2006. *Modern Loves: The Anthropology of Romantic Courtship and Companionate Marriage.* Ann Arbor: University of Michigan Press.

Hirsch, Susan F. 1998. *Pronouncing and Persevering: Gender and the Discourses of Disputing in an African Islamic Court.* Chicago: University of Chicago Press.

Huda, Shahnaz. 2006. "Dowry in Bangladesh: Compromising Women's Rights." *South Asia Research* 35:249–68.

Hull, Matthew S. 2012. *Government of Paper: The Materiality of Bureaucracy in Urban Pakistan.* Berkeley: University of California Press.

Husain, Ed. 2009. *The Islamist: Why I Became an Islamic Fundamentalist, What I Saw Inside, and Why I Left.* New York: Penguin.

Hussain, Sabiha. 2007. "Shariat Courts and Question of Women's Rights in India." *Pakistan Journal of Women's Studies: Alam-e-Niswan* 14 (2): 73–102.

Iqtidar, Humeira. 2011. "Secularizing Islamists? Jamaʿat-e-Islami and Jamaʿat-ud-Daʿwa in Urban Pakistan." Chicago: University of Chicago Press.

Jan, Najeeb A. 2010. *The Metacolonial State: Pakistan, the Deoband ʿUlama and the Biopolitics of Islam.* PhD dissertation, University of Michigan, Ann Arbor.

Johnson, Toni, and Lauren Vriens. 2013. "Islam: Governing under Sharia." Council on Foreign Relations. http://www.cfr.org/religion/islam-governing-under-sharia/p8034.

Joly, Danièle. 1995. *Britannia's Crescent: Making a Place for Muslims in British Society.* Aldershot, UK: Avebury.

———. 2001. *Blacks and Britannity.* Aldershot, UK: Ashgate.

Jones-Pauly, Christina. 2008. "Marriage Contracts of Muslims in the Diaspora: Problems in the Recognition of *Mahr* Contracts in German Law." In *The Islamic Marriage Contract: Case Studies in Islamic Family Law*, ed. Asifa Quraishi and Frank Vogel, 299–330. Cambridge: Harvard University Press.

Jouili, Jeanette S. 2015. *Pious Practice and Secular Constraints: Women in the Islamic Revival in Europe.* Stanford, CA: Stanford University Press.

Kabir, Nahid Afrose. 2010. *Young British Muslims: Identity, Culture, Politics and the Media.* Edinburgh: Edinburgh University Press.
Kamali, Mohammad H. 1993. "Fundamental Rights of the Individual: An Analysis of *Haqq* (Right) in Islamic Law." *American Journal of Islamic Social Sciences* 10 (3): 340–65.
Keshavjee, Mohamed. November 2008. "Alternative Dispute Resolution in a Diasporic Muslim Community in the United Kingdom." Doctoral thesis, Faculty of Law, University of London, School of Oriental and African Studies (Thesis 2991 in SOAS Archives).
Khan, Jemima. 2012. "The Marriage Business." *New Statesman.* March 15. http://www.newstatesman.com/society/2012/03/arranged-marriage-women-family?page=2.
Korteweg, Anna C., and Jennifer A. Selby, eds. 2012. *Debating Sharia: Islam, Gender Politics, and Family Law Arbitration.* Toronto: University of Toronto Press.
Kugle, Scott. 2007. *Sufis and Saints' Bodies: Mysticism, Corporeality, and Sacred Power in Islam.* Chapel Hill: University of North Carolina Press.
Lamont, Michèle, and Laurent Thévenot, eds. 2000. *Rethinking Comparative Cultural Sociology: Repertoires of Evaluation in France and the United States.* Cambridge: Cambridge University Press.
Latour, Bruno. 2010 [2002]. *The Making of Law: An Ethnography of the Conseil d'État.* Cambridge, UK: Polity.
Laurence, J. 2012. *The Emancipation of Europe's Muslims: The State's Role in Minority Integration.* Princeton: Princeton University Press.
Lee, Benjamin. 1997. *Talking Heads: Language, Metalanguage, and the Semiotics of Subjectivity.* Durham, NC: Duke University Press.
Lemons, Katherine. Fall 2010. "At the Margins of Law: Adjudicating Muslim Families in Contemporary Delhi." Doctoral thesis, University of California, Berkeley. http://escholarship.org/uc/item/6f66n4dn#page-1.
Leonard, Karen Isaksen. 2003. *Muslims in the United States: The State of Research.* New York: Russell Sage Foundation.
Lewis, Philip. 2002. *Islamic Britain: Religion, Politics and Identity among British Muslims.* 2nd ed. London: I. B. Tauris.
——. 2007. *Young, British and Muslim.* London: Continuum International.
Locke, John. 1983 (1685). *A Letter Concerning Toleration.* Ed. James H. Tully, trans. William Popple. Indianapolis: Hackett.
MacEoin, Denis. 2009. "Sharia Law or 'One Law for All?'" London: Civitas; Institute for the Study of Civil Society. http://www.civitas.org.uk/pdf/ShariaLawOrOneLawForAll.pdf.
Macfarlane, Julie. 2012. *Islamic Divorce in North America: A Shari'a Path in a Secular Society.* Oxford: Oxford University Press.
Mahmood, Saba. 2005. *Politics of Piety: The Islamic Revival and the Feminist Subject.* Princeton: Princeton University Press.
Mahoney, James, and Kathleen Thelen, eds. 2010. *Explaining Institutional Change: Ambiguity, Agency, and Power.* Cambridge: Cambridge University Press.
Malik, Maleiha. 2010. *Anti-Muslim Prejudice: Past and Present.* London: Routledge.
Mandaville, Peter. 2001. *Transnational Muslim Politics: Reimagining the Umma.* London: Routledge.
——. 2007. "Islamic Education in Britain: Approaches to Religious Knowledge in a Pluralistic Society." In *Schooling Islam: The Culture and Politics of Modern Muslim*

Education, ed. Robert W. Hefner and Muhammad Qasim Zaman, 224–42. Princeton: Princeton University Press.

March, Andrew F. 2009. *Islam and Liberal Citizenship: The Search for an Overlapping Consensus.* Oxford: Oxford University Press.

Massad, Joseph Andoni. 2015. *Islam in Liberalism.* Chicago: University of Chicago Press.

Masud, Muhammad Khalid. 1977. *Islamic Legal Philosophy: A Study of Abu Ishaq al-Shatibi's Life and Thought.* Islamabad: Islamic Research Institute.

——, ed. 2000. *Travelers in Faith: Studies of the Tablighi Jamaat as a Transnational Islamic Movement for Faith Renewal.* Leiden: Brill.

——. 2001. "Muslim Jurists' Quest for the Normative Basis of Shariʿa." Leiden: ISIM Occasional Papers.

Masud, Muhammad Khalid, Rudolph Peters, and David S. Powers, eds. 2006. *Dispensing Justice in Islam: Qadis and Their Judgments.* Leiden: Brill.

Maussen, Marcel. 2009. *Constructing Mosques: The Governance of Islam in France and the Netherlands.* Amsterdam: Amsterdam School for Social Science Research.

McLoughlin, Seán. 2005. "Mosques and the Public Space: Conflict and Cooperation in Bradford." *Journal of Ethnic and Migration Studies* 31 (6): 1045–66.

Menski, Werner. 2002. "Immigration and Multiculturalism in Britain: New Issues in Research and Policy." In *KIAPS: Bulletin of Asia-Pacific Studies*, Osaka, 12:43–66.

Metcalf, Barbara Daly. 1982. *Islamic Revival in British India: Deoband, 1860–1900.* Princeton: Princeton University Press.

——. 1992. *Perfecting Women: Maulana Ashraf ʿAli Thanawi's Bihishti Zewar.* Princeton: Princeton University Press.

Meyer, John W., and Brian Rowan. 1977. "Institutionalized Organizations: Formal Structure as Myth and Ceremony." *American Journal of Sociology*, 83:340–63.

Mir-Hosseini, Ziba. 1999. *Islam and Gender: The Religious Debate in Contemporary Iran.* Princeton: Princeton University Press.

——. 2001. *Marriage on Trial: A Study of Islamic Family Law.* Rev. ed. London: I. B. Tauris.

Modood, Tariq. 2005. *Multicultural Politics: Racism, Ethnicity, and Muslims in Britain.* Minneapolis: University of Minnesota Press.

Modood, Tariq, Richard Berthoud, Jane Lakey, and James Nazroo. 1997. *Ethnic Minorities in Britain: Diversity and Disadvantage.* London: Policy Studies Institute.

Mondal, Anshuman A. 2008. *Young British Muslim Voices.* Oxford: Greenwood.

Munir, Muhammad. 2014. "Judicial Law-Making: An Analysis of Case Law on Khulʿ in Pakistan." SSRN Working Papers. http://papers.ssrn.com/sol3/papers.cfm?abstract_id=2470734.

Naqshbandi, Mehmood. 2013. "UK Mosque Statistics." http://www.muslimsinbritain.org/. Nichols, Joel A. 2012. *Marriage and Divorce in a Multicultural Context: Multi-Tiered Marriage and the Boundaries of Civil Law and Religion.* Cambridge: Cambridge University Press.

Nielsen, Jørgen S., and Lisbet Christoffersen, eds. 2010. *Shariʿa as Discourse: Legal Traditions and the Encounter with Europe.* Farnham, UK: Ashgate.

Nussbaum, Martha C., and Amartya Sen. 1989. "Internal Criticism and the Indian Rationalist Tradition." In *Relativism: Interpretation and Confrontation*, ed. Michael Krausz, 299–325. Notre Dame, IN: University of Notre Dame Press.

Office for National Statistics. 2011. "What Does the 2011 Census Tell Us about Religion?" http://www.ons.gov.uk/ons/rel/census/2011-census/detailed-characteristics-for-local-authorities-in-england-and-wales/sty-religion.html.

Oldfield, Elizabeth, Liane Hartnett, and Emma Bailey. 2013. *More than an Educated Guess: Assessing the Evidence on Faith Schools.* London: Theos. http://www.theosthinktank.co.uk/files/files/More%20than%20an%20educated%20guess.pdf.

Open Society Institute. 2010. *Muslims in Leicester.* Budapest: Open Society Institute.

Opwis, Felicitas. 2007. "Islamic Law and Legal Change: The Concept of Maslaha in Classical and Contemporary Islamic Legal Theory." In *Shari'a: Islamic Law in the Contemporary Context*, ed. Abbas Amanat and Frank Griffel, 62–82. Stanford, CA: Stanford University Press.

Osanloo, Arzoo. 2008. *The Politics of Women's Rights in Iran.* Princeton: Princeton University Press.

Parekh, Bhiku. 2002. *Rethinking Multiculturalism.* Cambridge: Harvard University Press.

Peace, Timothy. 2013. "Muslims and Electoral Politics in Britain: The Case of the Respect Party." In *Muslim Political Participation in Europe*, ed. Jørgen S. Nielsen, 299–321. Edinburgh: Edinburgh University Press.

Peach, Ceri. 1996. "Does Britain Have Ghettos?" *Transactions of the Institute of British Geographers*, n.s. 21 (1): 216–35.

———. 2006. "Ethnicity and South Asian Religions in the London 2001 Census." *Transactions of the Institute of British Geographers*, n.s. 31 (3): 353–70.

———. 2007. "Sleepwalking into Ghettoisation? The British Debate over Segregation." In *Residential Segregation and the Integration of Immigrants: Britain, the Netherlands and Sweden*, ed. Karen Schönwälder, 7–40. Berlin: Wissenschaftszentrum Berlin für Sozialforschung, Discussion Paper Nr. SP IV 2007-602.

Pearl, David, and Werner F. Menski. 1998. *Muslim Family Law.* 3rd ed. London: Sweet & Maxwell.

Peletz, Michael G. 1995. "Kinship Studies in Late Twentieth-Century Anthropology." *Annual Review of Anthropology* 24:343–72.

Pew Research Center Forum on Religion and Public Life. 2011. "The Future of the Global Muslim Population, 2011." http://www.pewforum.org/2011/01/27/future-of-the-global-muslim-population-main-factors/#fertility.

Pew Research Global Attitudes Project. 2006. *The Great Divide: How Westerners and Muslims View Each Other.* Washington, DC: Pew Research Center. http://www.pewglobal.org/2006/06/22/the-great-divide-how-westerners-and-muslims-view-each-other/.

Phillips, Melanie. 2006. *Londonistan.* New York: Encounter Books.

Pieri, Zacharias. 2012. *Tablighi Jamaat.* London: Lapido Media.

Poros, Maritsa V. 2011. *Modern Migrations: Gujarati Indian Networks in New York and London.* Stanford, CA: Stanford University Press.

Povinelli, Elizabeth A. 2001. "Radical Worlds: The Anthropology of Incommensurability and Inconceivability." *Annual Review of Anthropology* 30:319–34.

Powers, David S. 1994. "Kadijustiz or Qadi-Justice? A Paternity Dispute from Fourteenth-Century Morocco." *Islamic Law and Society* 1:332–66.

Proudman, Charlotte Rachael. 2012. *Equal and Free? Evidence in Support of Baroness Cox's Arbitration and Mediation Services (Equality) Bill.* Document hosted by Equal and Free. http://www.secularism.org.uk/uploads/equal-and-free-16.pdf.

Qaradawi, Yusuf al-. 2002 [1990]. *Priorities of the Islamic Movement: The Coming Phase.* Swansea, UK: Awakening Publications.

Quraishi, Asifa, and Najeeba Syeed-Miller. 2004. "No Altars: A Survey of Islamic Family Law in the United States." In *Women's Rights & Islamic Family Law*, ed. Lynn Welchman, 177–229. London: Zed Books.

Rabb, Intisar A. 2013. "Islamic Legal Minimalism: Legal Maxims and Lawmaking When Jurists Disappear." In *Law and Tradition in Classical Islamic Thought: Studies in Honor of Professor Hossein Modarressi*, ed. Michael Cook, Najam Haider, Intisar Rabb, and Asma Sayeed, 145–66. New York: Palgrave.

Ramadan, Moussa. 2003. "Judicial Activism of the Shari'ah Appeals Court in Israel (1994–2001): Rise and Crisis." *Fordham International Law Journal* 27:254–98.

Rasheed, Madawi al-. 2005. "Saudi Religious Transnationalism in London." In *Transnational Connections and the Arab Gulf*, ed. Madawi al-Rasheed, 149–67. London: Routledge.

Rath, Jan, Rinus Penninx, Kees Groenendijk, and Astrid Meyer. 2001. *Western Europe and Its Islam.* Leiden: Brill.

Rawls, John. 1999. "The Idea of Public Reason Revisited." In *The Law of Peoples, with "The Idea of Public Reason Revisited,"* 129–80. Cambridge: Columbia University Press.

Redding, Jeffrey A. 2004. "Constitutionalizing Islam: Theory and Pakistan." *Virginia Journal of International Law* 44 (3): 760–827.

———. 2010. "Institutional v. Liberal Contexts for Contemporary Non-State, Muslim Civil Dispute Resolution Systems." *Journal of Islamic State Practices in International Law.* http://ssrn.com/abstract=1648945.

Reetz, Dietrich. 2006. *Islam in the Public Sphere: Religious Groups in India, 1900–1947.* New Delhi: Oxford University Press.

Rex, John, and Robert Moore. 1967. *Race, Community, and Conflict: A Study of Sparkbrook.* London: Oxford University Press.

Rex, John, and Sally Tomlinson. 1979. *Colonial Immigrants in a British City: A Class Analysis.* London: Routledge & Kegan Paul.

Riles, Annelise, ed. 2006. *Documents: Artifacts of Modern Knowledge.* Ann Arbor: University of Michigan Press.

Rohe, Mathias. 2015. *Islamic Law in Past and Present.* Leiden: Brill.

Rosen, Lawrence. 1989. *The Anthropology of Justice: Law as Culture in Islamic Society.* Cambridge: Cambridge University Press.

———. 2000. *The Justice of Islam.* Oxford: Oxford University Press.

Rosenblum, Nancy. 2000. *Membership and Morals.* Princeton: Princeton University Press.

Roy, Olivier. 2002. *L'Islam Mondialisé.* Paris: Seuil.

Saeed, Abdullah. 1996. *Islamic Banking and Interest: A Study of the Prohibition of Riba and Its Contemporary Interpretation.* Leiden: E. J. Brill.

Sageman, Marc. 2008. *Leaderless Jihad.* Philadelphia: University of Pennsylvania Press.

Saleh, Nabil A. 1986. *Unlawful Gain and Legitimate Profit in Islamic Law: Riba, Gharar and Islamic Banking.* Cambridge: Cambridge University Press.

Samad, Yunas, and John Eade. 2003. *Community Perceptions of Forced Marriage.* London: Foreign and Commonwealth Office.

Sardar, Ziauddin. 2008. *Balti Britain: A Journey through the British Asian Experience.* London: Granta.

Shachar, Ayelet. 2001. *Multicultural Jurisdictions: Cultural Differences and Women's Rights.* Cambridge: Cambridge University Press.

Shah, Prakash. 2007. "Rituals of Recognition: Ethnic Minority Marriages in British Legal Systems." In *Law and Ethnic Plurality: Socio-Legal Perspectives*, ed. Prakash Shah, 177–202. Leiden: Martinus Nijhoff.

Shah-Kazemi, Sonia Nurin. 2001. *Untying the Knot: Muslim Women, Divorce and the Shariah.* London: Nuffield Foundation.

Shaw, Alison. 2000. *Kinship and Continuity: Pakistani Families in Britain.* London: Routledge.

———. 2001. "Kinship, Cultural Preference and Immigration: Consanguineous Marriage among British Muslims." *Journal of the Royal Anthropological Institute* (n.s.) 7:315–34.

———. 2006. "The Arranged Transnational Cousin Marriages of British Pakistanis: Critique, Dissent and Cultural Continuity." *Contemporary South Asia* 15 (2): 209–20.

Shaw, Alison, and Katharine Charsley. 2006. "*Rishtas*: Adding Emotion to Strategy in Understanding British Pakistani Transnational Marriages." *Global Networks* 6 (4): 405–21.

Sheridan, Eamonn, John Wright, Neil Small, et al. 2013. "Risk Factors for Congenital Anomaly in a Multiethnic Birth Cohort: An Analysis of the Born in Bradford Study." *Lancet* 382, no. 9901:1350–59.

Sikand, Yoginder. 2002. *Origins and Development of the Tablighi-Jamaʿat (1920–2000): A Cross-Country Comparative Study.* Hyderabad: Sangam Books.

Silverstein, Michael. 1981. "Metaforces of Power in Traditional Oratory." Unpublished lecture, University of Chicago.

Simpson, Ludi. 2003. "Statistics of Racial Segregation: Measures, Evidence and Policy." Centre for Census and Survey Research, University of Manchester, Occasional Paper No. 24. *Urban Studies* 41 (3): 661–81.

Sniderman, Paul M., and Louk Hagendoorn. 2007. *When Ways of Life Collide.* Princeton: Princeton University Press.

Solanki, Gopika. 2011. *Adjudication in Religious Family Laws: Cultural Accommodation, Legal Pluralism, and Gender Equality in India.* Cambridge: Cambridge University Press.

Spellman, Kathryn. 2004. *Religion and Nation: Iranian Local and Transnational Networks in Britain.* New York: Berghahn Books.

Spencer, Sarah. 2007. "Immigration." In *Blair's Britain: 1997–2007*, ed. Anthony Seldon, 314–60. Cambridge: Cambridge University Press.

Stiles, Erin. 2009. *An Islamic Court in Context: An Ethnographic Study of Judicial Reasoning.* New York: Palgrave Macmillan.

Tas, Latif. 2014. *Legal Pluralism in Action: Dispute Resolution and the Kurdish Peace Committee.* Farnham, UK: Ashgate.

Taylor, Charles. 2007. *A Secular Age.* Cambridge: Harvard University Press.

———. 2008. "Secularism and Critique." Posted on the blog *The Immanent Frame.* http://blogs.ssrc.org/tif/2008/04/24/secularism-and-critique/.

Terrio, Susan J. 2009. *Judging Mohammed: Juvenile Delinquency, Immigration, and Exclusion at the Paris Palace of Justice.* Stanford, CA: Stanford University Press.

Troll, Christian W., ed. 1989. *Muslim Shrines in India.* Delhi: Oxford University Press.

Tucker, Judith E. 1998. *In the House of the Law: Gender and Islamic Law in Ottoman Syria and Palestine.* Berkeley: University of California Press.

———. 2008. *Women, Family, and Gender in Islamic Law.* Cambridge: Cambridge University Press.

Vallier, Kevin. 2011. "Convergence and Consensus in Public Reason." *Public Affairs Quarterly* 25 (4): 261–79.

Van Bommel, Abdulwahid. 1992. "The History of Muslim Umbrella Organizations." In *Islam in Dutch Society: Current Developments and Future Prospects*, ed. W.A.R. Shahid and P. S. van Koningsveld, 124–43. Kampen: Kok Pharos.

Van der Veer, Peter. 1994. *Religious Nationalism: Hindus and Muslims in India.* Berkeley: University of California Press.

Wacquant, Loïc. 2007. *Urban Outcasts: A Comparative Sociology of Advanced Marginality.* Cambridge, UK: Polity.

Walzer, Michael. 1983. *Spheres of Justice: A Defense of Pluralism and Equality.* New York: Basic Books.

Warner, Michael. 2002. "Publics and Counterpublics." *Public Culture* 14 (1): 49–90.

Weiss, Susan M., and Netty C. Gross-Horowitz. 2013. *Marriage and Divorce in the Jewish State: Israel's Civil War.* Waltham, MA: Brandeis University Press.

Welchmann, Lynn. 2007. *Women and Muslim Family Laws in Arab States: A Comparative Overview of Textual Development and Advocacy.* Amsterdam: Amsterdam University Press.

Werbner, Pnina. 1990. *The Migration Process: Capital, Gifts and Offerings among British Pakistanis.* New York: Berg.

———. 2002. *Imagined Diasporas among Manchester Muslims.* Oxford: James Curry.

———. 2003. *Pilgrims of Love: Anthropology of a Global Sufi Cult.* Indianapolis: Indiana University Press.

———. 2004. "Theorising Complex Diasporas: Purity and Hybridity in the South Asian Public Sphere in Britain." *Journal of Ethnic and Migration Studies* 30 (5): 895–911.

Wiegers, Gerard. 2011. "Dr. Sayyid Mutwalli ad-Darsh's *fatwas* for Muslims in Britain: The Voice of Official Islam?" In *Britain and the Muslim World: Historical Perspectives*, ed. Gerald MacLean, 178–91. Newcastle-upon-Tyne: Cambridge Scholars.

Williams, Rowan. 2008. "Civil and Religious Law in England: A Religious Perspective." Lecture delivered February 7, 2008, at the Royal Courts of Justice, London. http://people.bu.edu/joeld/sharia.pdf.

Wilson, William Julius. 1987. *The Truly Disadvantaged: The Inner City, the Underclass, and Public Policy.* Chicago: University of Chicago Press.

Wind-Cowie, Max, and Thomas Gregory. 2011. *A Place for Pride.* London: Demos.

Yates, Melissa. 2007. "Rawls and Habermas on Religion in the Public Sphere." *Philosophy & Social Criticism* 33 (7): 880–91.

Zagorin, Perez. 2003. *How the Idea of Religious Toleration Came to the West.* Princeton: Princeton University Press.

Zaman, Muhammad Qasim. 2004. "The ʿUlama of Contemporary Islam and Their Conception of the Common Good." In *Public Islam and the Common Good*, ed. Armando Salvatore and Dale F. Eickelman, 129–55. Leiden: Brill.

———. 2007. *The Ulama in Contemporary Islam: Custodians of Change.* Princeton: Princeton University Press.

———. 2008. *Ashraf ʿAli Thanawi: Islam in Modern South Asia.* London: Oneworld Publications.

———. 2012. *Modern Islamic Thought in a Radical Age: Religious Authority and Internal Criticism.* Cambridge: Cambridge University Press.

Index

PRINCETON STUDIES IN MUSLIM POLITICS

Diane Singerman, *Avenues of Participation: Family, Politics, and Networks in Urban Quarters of Cairo*
Tone Bringa, *Being Muslim the Bosnian Way: Identity and Community in a Central Bosnian Village*
Dale F. Eickelman and James Piscatori, *Muslim Politics*
Bruce B. Lawrence, *Shattering the Myth: Islam beyond Violence*
Ziba Mir-Hosseini, *Islam and Gender: The Religious Debate in Contemporary Iran*
Robert W. Hefner, *Civil Islam: Muslims and Democratization in Indonesia*
Muhammad Qasim Zaman, *The Ulama in Contemporary Islam: Custodians of Change*
Michael G. Peletz, *Islamic Modern: Religious Courts and Cultural Politics in Malaysia*
Oskar Verkaaik, *Migrants and Militants: Fun and Urban Violence in Pakistan*
Laetitia Bucaille, *Growing Up Palestinian: Israeli Occupation and the Intifada Generation*
Robert W. Hefner, ed., *Remaking Muslim Politics: Pluralism, Contestation, Democratization*
Lara Deeb, *An Enchanted Modern: Gender and Public Piety in Shiʿi Lebanon*
Roxanne L. Euben, *Journeys to the Other Shore: Muslim and Western Travelers in Search of Knowledge*
Robert W. Hefner and Muhammad Qasim Zaman, eds., *Schooling Islam: The Culture and Politics of Modern Muslim Education*
Loren D. Lybarger, *Identity and Religion in Palestine: The Struggle between Islamism and Secularism in the Occupied Territories*
Augustus Norton, *Hezbollah: A Short History*
Bruce K. Rutherford, *Egypt after Mubarak: Liberalism, Islam, and Democracy in the Arab World*
Emile Nakhleh, *A Necessary Engagement: Reinventing America's Relations with the Muslim World*
Roxanne L. Euben and Muhammad Qasim Zaman, eds., *Princeton Readings in Islamist Thought: Texts and Contexts from al-Banna to Bin Laden*
Irfan Ahmad, *Islamism and Democracy in India: The Transformation of Jamaat-e-Islami*
Kristen Ghodsee, *Muslim Lives in Eastern Europe: Gender, Ethnicity, and the Transformation of Islam in Postsocialist Bulgaria*
John R. Bowen, *Can Islam Be French? Pluralism and Pragmatism in a Secularist State*
Thomas Barfield, *Afghanistan: A Cultural and Political History*
Sara Roy, *Hamas and Civil Society in Gaza: Engaging the Islamist Social Sector*
Michael Laffan, *The Makings of Indonesian Islam: Orientalism and the Narration of a Sufi Past*

Jonathan Laurence, *The Emancipation of Europe's Muslims: The State's Role in Minority Integration*

Jenny White, *Muslim Nationalism and the New Turks*

Lara Deeb and Mona Harb, *Leisurely Islam: Negotiating Geography and Morality in Shiʿite South Beirut*

Esra Özyürek, *Being German, Becoming Muslim: Race, Religion, and Conversion in the New Europe*

Ellen McLarney, *Soft Force: Women in Egypt's Islamic Awakening*

Avi Max Spiegel, *Young Islam: The New Politics of Religion in Morocco and the Arab World*

Nadav Samin, *Of Sand or Soil: Genealogy and Tribal Belonging in Saudi Arabia*

Bernard Rougier, *The Sunni Tragedy in the Middle East: North Lebanon from al-Qaeda to ISIS*

Lihi Ben Shitrit, *Righteous Transgressions: Women's Activism on the Israeli and Palestinian Right*

John R. Bowen, *On British Islam: Religion, Law, and Everyday Practice in Shariʿa Councils*